Contents

Alphabetical Listing of Institutions by Country

Psychology Throughout the World

THE IUPsyS DIRECTORY:
MAJOR RESEARCH INSTITUTES AND
DEPARTMENTS OF PSYCHOLOGY

EDITOR'S PREFACE

Publication of *The IUPsyS Directory* continues a tradition of the International Union of Psychological Science (IUPsyS) of providing sources of information concerning psychology worldwide. Although this is the fifth directory, it is actually more like the first of a new series. The four preceding directories had a rather different database and scope as described fully in Mark R. Rosenzweig and Wayne H. Holtzman's article in this edition. As early as 1987, plans were begun for a fifth international directory of pyschologists, but members of the IUPSys Committee on Communication and Publications were concerned that the large and rapidly growing numbers of pyschologists were making such a directory unwieldy. We explored the possibility of publishing a directory that included only psychologists directly involved in research. However, it quickly became evident that this would not be an easy task. Some psychologists might have felt inappropriately omitted from such a directory. It was therefore decided to publish *The IUPsyS Directory: Major Research Institutes and Departments of Psychology*, in which the focus is on institutions. The directory is not limited to the countries in which the national organisation is a member of IUPsyS. Institutions from 147 countries are included.

We of course look forward to feedback on the usefulness and value of this new initiative. The directory aims to be an essential resource for any psychologist communicating with researchers in institutions anywhere in the world. We have attempted to identify and include all institutions where research in psychology is taking place, and to provide as much useful information as possible about each.

The directory is organized into two main sections:

The first includes the listing of institutions, country by country. Both the countries and the institutions are organized alphabetically. If a country is a member of the United Nations, it is the UN form of its name that has been used. Non-members of the UN have been named by the most identifiable form of the country's name. In many instances it has been difficult to decide exactly where an institution should be listed due to political changes within countries during the production of the directory. This has also led to difficulties in collecting and verifying information within those countries. We hope that the users of the directory will understand the complexity of arranging such geographically based information at a time of almost daily change.

The second part of the directory consists of short summaries about the organization of psychological research, teaching, and accreditation in individual countries. This section has been compiled from information supplied by the national psychological organizations within each country.

This directory was compiled by collecting addresses of institutions from a wide variety of sources. Members of the Executive Committee of IUPsyS helped to formulate these lists, checking that major institutions have been included and, when necessary, that inappropriate addresses were excluded. The institutions in these initial listings were then sent questionnaires requesting confirmation that they were appropriate for inclusion in the directory, and asking for additional information to aid communication such as telephone, fax and email numbers. Based on this information, some difficult decisions had to be made. For example, departments often include many independent research groups. As a rule (with a few exceptions), we provided only one entry per mailing address, thus listing only the general heading of the departments or institutions. In some cases, it was difficult to decide whether an entry really represented an institutional group where research is being carried out. As we adopted the explicit policy of avoiding inappropriate omissions, even at the risk of inappropriate entries, we have included a number of those institutions that fall into the difficult-to-decide category. Acknowledging these many questions, the IUPsyS and Lawrence Erlbaum Associates Ltd, publishers, have made every effort to ensure that the information contained in the directory is correct and complete, but take no responsibility for any errors or omissions in the text.

If your institution is not included in the directory, or the information is incomplete or incorrect, please complete the tear-out form at the back of the Directory and return it to the publishers Lawrence Erlbaum Associates Ltd. for inclusion or amendment in the next edition of the directory.

Finally, no publication of this kind comes into being without considerable dedication and effort. All our thanks go to the staff of Lawrence Erlbaum Associates Ltd who undertook the lion's share of the work. As Editor it is my privilege to emphasize the major contribution of the publisher. Our international research community has to acknowledge the great help we will all enjoy in our research communication and endeavours from such a publication.

Géry d'Ydewalle,
February 1, 1993

ABOUT THE IUPsyS

Mark R. Rosenzweig
University of California, Berkeley

Wayne H. Holtzman
University of Texas, Austin, USA

This Directory is an example of the many and varied publications and activities of the International Union of Psychological Science (IUPsyS). The present statement about the Union will describe briefly its activities, main characteristics, and structure; it will also recount some of the history of the Union. The Union has changed its name once and its acronym twice in the course of its history. For brevity and simplicity, we will usually refer to it as the Union or the IUPsyS at all stages of its history. The IUPsyS, as is the rule for international scientific unions, is an organization composed of 51 National Member organizations, not more than one National Member per country. Main activities of the Union, some of which will be described in more detail later, include: (a) sponsoring international congresses of psychology at regular intervals; (b) organizing and/or publishing a series of publications; (c) participating as a member organization in the International Council of Scientific Unions, which is the main international scientific body, and in the International Social Science Council, and cooperating with UNESCO; (d) fostering communication among its National Members and taking up questions and problems raised by them; (e) sponsoring and accomplishing a limited number of network activities and research projects considered to be of major interest for the purposes of the Union; and (f) conducting surveys of activities and resources of its National Members.

I. Organization and Administration of the Union
The legislative body and final authority of the Union is its Assembly, which meets every four years at the International Congress of Psychology. Each National Member, depending upon its category of membership in the Union, is entitled to send either one or two delegates to the Assembly. There is also the temporary category of Observer, without a vote in the Assembly. The administrative body of the Union is the Executive Committee, which usually meets once a year and whose members are in frequent communication. Further material about the administration of the Union will be found in its Statutes and Rules of Procedure, the current version of which is to appear in an issue of the *International Journal of Psychology* in 1993.

When the Union was established in 1951, there was discussion of the desirability of having a full-time executive officer, and the Statutes provided that "The central headquarters of the union shall be fixed by a decision of the Assembly". Nevertheless, the traditions of the preceding volunteer International Congress Committee were continued. No central headquarters were established and the Union did not have a legal venue; most of the records of the Union are kept wherever the Secretary-General is located, and the financial accounts are kept wherever the Treasurer is located. The volunteer nature of the administration has, in turn, limited the scope of activities of the Union. During the period 1988-1992 the importance of establishing a legal venue for the Union became apparent, and the Executive Committee prepared a recommendation to this effect for the 1992 Assembly. The Assembly then voted to establish a legal venue of the Union in Montréal. The mainly volunteer characteristics of the Union are largely determined by the small size of its financial resources. In 1991 the operating budget of the Union amounted to approximately $100,000. The income to cover these expenditures came from the following sources: dues of the National Members of the Union; funds received for special projects

The authors are former presidents of the International Union of Psychological Science. The first author is now the IUPsyS Chairman of the Standing Committee on Communication and Publications. The chapter is an abridged version of a paper which will appear in the *International Journal of Psychology* (1993).

from the International Social Science Council (ISSC) and from the International Council of Scientific Unions (ICSU); and interest on bank accounts and small amounts of royalties from publications.

Until 1984, the Statutes of IUPsyS provided for only one basic type of National Member: "Article 6. The members of the Union shall be national societies of scientific psychology, regularly established". When IUPsyS joined the International Council of Scientific Unions in 1982, the Executive Committee learned that all the other Unions in ICSU allow for an alternative form of National Membership: a national academy of sciences, national research council, or similar organization. Typically the national academy or national research council of a country does not participate directly in an international Union, but rather it sets up a National Committee for the discipline to exercise its membership. After having investigated the practices in some countries and after having discussed the question in detail, the Executive Committee recommended to the Assembly prior to the XXIII International Congress a revised Article 6 to permit membership by a national academy of sciences or similar organization; this was passed by the Assembly and appears in the current Statutes.

II. History of International Congresses and of the International Union of Psychological Science.
Almost from the very beginning of psychology as a modern science, international meetings of psychologists were organized to exchange ideas. There was discussion of the need for an international meeting of psychologists as early as 1881 (Kenna, 1969; Nuttin, 1992). The first such international congress was the International Congress of Physiological Psychology held in Paris in 1889, launched by the new Society of Physiological Psychology. Having established a pattern of regular congresses with an initial emphasis on physiological and experimental psychology, subsequent meetings were numbered serially and were referred to simply as the International Congress of Psychology. The two World Wars caused major gaps in the series. When the congresses resumed after the first World War, it was the intention to hold one every third year. The three-year cycle was disrupted by the Civil War in Spain and the second World War, only resuming again after 1948. Beginning in 1972, however, it was decided to change to a four-year cycle in order to coordinate activities with the International Association of Applied Psychology (IAAP). Since 1972 there has been a major international congress every two years, alternating between the International Congress of Psychology and the International Congress of Applied Psychology.

The Union does not itself organize the Congresses, but rather it delegates the organization to a national host committee. Typically at each Congress a few National Members offer their candidacies to be the host eight years in the future. Each candidate presents its plans and attractions to the Assembly which then makes its choice. If necessary, the Executive Committee may change the plan.

The International Union of Psychological Science was formally instituted at the XIII International Congress of Psychology at Stockholm, July 1951. The idea of forming an international organization of psychology with broader functions than merely arranging for a congress at regular intervals had already been formally discussed at the 1948 Congress in Edinburgh. During this same period, UNESCO was organized, and it offered the possibility of modest financial support to various international scientific unions. Accordingly, it was decided to establish an international union of psychological science with statutes similar to those of the unions already established for certain other sciences. Until then, a loosely organized group known as the International Congress Committee provided continuity from one congress to the next.

An ad hoc committee of leading psychologists drew up the original statutes for the new Union, and representatives of eleven charter member national psychological societies met to institute the Union at the Stockholm Congress in 1951. Nine other national societies were accepted as members shortly thereafter. The list of all the present National Members and the year in which each joined the Union is given in Table 1.

As will be seen in Table 1, the initial 20 National Members were largely from Western

TABLE 1
Years in which National Members were elected to IUPsyS

1951		1954		1976	
	Belgium*	1954	Yugoslavia	1976	Argentina
	Brazil	1957	Australia		Panama
	Canada		New Zealand	1979	Dominica
	Cuba		Poland	1980	China
	Denmark		Turkey	1984	Nicaragua
	Egypt		USSR	1988	Indonesia
	Fed. Rep. of	1962	South Africa		Nigeria
	Germany*		Venezuela	1992	Estonia
	Finland	1963	Czechoslovakia		Greece
	France*	1965	Philippines		Portugal
	Israel	1966	German Dem. Rep.		Singapore
	Italy*		Hungary		
	Japan*		India		
	Netherlands*		Mexico		
	Norway*	1969	Colombia		
	Spain		Iran		
	Sweden*	1972	Bulgaria		
	Switzerland*		Hong Kong		
	United Kingdom	1973	Korea		
	USA*	1974	Ireland		*Charter Members

Europe but also included Canada and the United States, Brazil, Cuba, Egypt, Uruguay, and Japan. The psychological society of Yugoslavia joined in 1954, followed by those of Poland and the USSR in 1957. Although the Egyptian society was represented at some of the first Congresses held under the auspices of the Union, it then stopped sending delegates, and its membership of the Union terminated in 1964; the Egyptian society rejoined in 1988. The society of the People's Republic of China joined in 1980. The National Members that have joined the Union recently come from the following countries: Nicaragua, elected in 1984; Zimbabwe, 1985; Indonesia, Nigeria, and Pakistan, 1988; Estonia, Greece, Portugal, and Singapore, 1992. The growth in number of National Members has been almost linear, with an average increase of almost one National Member per year. With further candidacies in various stages of processing, there is every sign that this growth will continue.

At the same time that the Union has been gaining National Members, the national societies of psychology have been gaining individual members. The numbers of individual members reported by National Members for 1970 and 1980 revealed an average growth of 90 percent over that decade; 18 of the 36 societies that already belonged to the Union in 1970 reported at least twice as many members by 1980, and only two societies reported losses (Rosenzweig, 1982). The decade 1980-1990 saw a further large increase in members of many of the national societies of psychology. As well as giving the memberships of the National Members, Rosenzweig (1982, 1984) also attempted to estimate the total numbers of psychologists in the countries represented in the Union and in the main regions of the world. The world total of psychologists for 1980 (using local definitions of psychologists) came to about quarter of a million. A similar estimate made for 1990 came to over half a million (Rosenzweig, 1992b, p.19).

Many psychologists familiar with the Union had long been accustomed to referring to it briefly as IUPS and may have been puzzled by the form IUPsyS that was adopted in 1982. Actually the Union was originally named The International Union of Scientific Psychology (IUSP), as is shown in the title pages of Congress proceedings in the Statutes published in *Acta Psychologica* in 1955, 1959, and 1961. The transition to The International Union of Psychological Science occurred in 1965. Most members of the Executive Committee preferred the change because they did not want to see an implication that some psychology is not scientific. French-speaking members, however, preferred to retain the distinction, so the original French version of the name remained unchanged

(Union Internationale de Psychologie Scientifique). The change of acronym to IUPsyS occurred in 1982 when the Union assumed membership in the International Council of Scientific Unions. A member of ICSU since 1955, the International Union of Physiological Sciences also used the acronym of IUPS. When psychology declared its candidacy for full membership in ICSU, one condition required for the election was that the psychological Union choose a different acronym from that already used in ICSU by the physiological Union. Various alternatives were considered, including changing the name of the Union back to the International Union of Scientific Psychology. Finally it was agreed to choose IUPsyS, and it is hoped that this has by now become familiar.

III. Publications of the IUPsyS

A continuing concern of the IUPsyS has been to assure the publication of the proceedings of its Congresses. Other publication activities have been added gradually in order to foster international communication in psychology.

The Rules of Procedure state "The reports of the International Congress shall be published in a uniform manner" (Section I,1.[d]). It has not always been possible to accomplish complete uniformity, but at least the proceedings have been published rather fully. In each case, publication is under the auspices of IUPsyS and is arranged by the host committee with the counsel of delegates of IUPsyS. Citations to the proceedings of the first 17 congresses are given by Kenna (1969). A few further remarks may help readers to locate some of the Congress publications, as well as providing some sidelights on the development of international psychology.

After the formation of the Union in 1951, the proceedings of the next four Congresses (XIV-XVII) were published as special numbers of the Acta Psychologica: European Journal of Psychology. Notices of the Union were also published in this journal from 1954 to the early 1960s, and beginning in 1956 the Secretary-General of the Union, Otto Klineberg, was listed as a member of the Editorial Board of the Journal. He continued to be listed as a member of the Editorial Board of Acta from 1960 through 1963 as President of the Union and then from 1964 through 1970 in a personal capacity. The proceedings of the XVIII Congress in Moscow in 1966 were published separately in several volumes in Moscow, and those of the XIX, XX, and XXI Congresses were also published locally by the host societies. For the XXII Congress in Leipzig, 10 of the 11 volumes of proceedings were published jointly by VEB Deutsche Verlag der Wissenschaften, Berlin, GDR, and North-Holland, the publishers of Acta Psychologica. The proceedings of the XXIII Congress in Acapulco and of the XXIV Congress in Sydney were published through North-Holland Publishing Company.

The publication of the proceedings of the XXV Congress in Brussels follows a different plan in the hope of securing a wider audience: Only the keynote addresses and state-of-the-art lectures are being published directly by the Congress Committee for the Union. Symposia are to be published in journals that are appropriate to the subject matter of each symposium to secure wider readership for these papers. The symposium publications are being arranged on the initiative of the symposium organizers, in some cases with the help of the Scientific Program Committee of the Congress. Two or three years after the Congress, citations to all the symposia will be published in the International Journal of Psychology.

By the 1960s it was felt that the Union should have its own journal publication, rather than relying on the hospitality of another journal to publish its news and notices. Under the succession of gifted and dedicated Editors, the Journal has steadily grown in size, scope and influence. Since 1991, the Journal has been published by Lawrence Erlbaum Associates Ltd., to whom inquiries about subscriptions or purchase of single numbers should be addressed. In the earlier years of the Journal there was an emphasis on cross-cultural psychology, but a broader scope was launched in 1979. Many issues of the Journal also include a second part, the International Platform for Psychologists. This section contains information on the IUPsyS and on activities of the National Members, and it includes an extensive listing of future international meetings and congresses. It also offers an opportunity to exchange news and opinions on psychology as an academic and applied profession and to discuss internationally significant psychological issues.

Occasional special numbers of the Journal are devoted to particular issues. Examples of such special issues are these: The Impact of Psychology on Third World Development (1984); Changing Concepts of Intelligence and Intellectual Functioning (1984); The Neo-Piagetian Theories of Cognitive Development: Toward an Integration (1987); Cross-Cultural Comparison of Psychological Data: Issues and Pitfalls (1989); Facial Asymmetry: Expression and Paralysis (1990); Social Values and Effective Organizations (1990); The Psychological Dimensions of Global Change (1991); and The Unity of Psychology (1992).

Four editions of the *International Directory of Psychologists* have been prepared by the Union. The first was produced in 1958 by the National Academy of Sciences - National Research Council of the United States. Its co-editors were Eugene H. Jacobson of the U.S. and H.C.J. Duijker of the Netherlands; Duijker was at that time Deputy Secretary-General of the Union. Only psychologists outside the United States were included in the International Directory because the American Psychological Association publishes a comprehensive directory of its large membership every few years. The first International Directory listed about 7,000 psychologists from 38 countries. It clearly filled a need, and almost immediately after its publication the editors planned a second edition to come out under the auspices of IUPsyS. For the second edition, which appeared in 1966, information was obtained for about 8,000 psychologists from 80 different countries. Eugene Jacobson served as Secretary-General of the Union from 1966 to 1972, and he launched plans for a much more ambitious third edition of the Directory. Unforseen delays intervened, however, and it was only in 1980 that IUPsyS published the third edition, edited by Eugene Jacobson and Gunther Reinert of the Federal Republic of Germany. The third edition listed about 17,000 psychologists from 100 countries. For the fourth edition, a new plan was devised to enlist the aid of the National Members to provide lists of psychologists. This led to a directory of about 30,000 names, published under the editorship of the Secretary-General of the Union, Kurt Pawlik (1985).

The Union does not have a publication program of its own, although sponsored projects often result in articles or books published elsewhere. A list of such publications prior to 1976 was presented by Holtzman (1976). Additional books, articles, and journals published under Union auspices from 1976 to 1984 were listed by Rosenzweig and Holtzman (1985). Further publications under the auspices of the Union include *The German Journal of Psychology, Concise Encyclopedia of Psychology* (Ed. Q. Jing, 1991; published in Chinese with Chinese, English, and Japanese indexes), and *International Psychological Science: Progress, Problems, and Prospects* (Ed. M.R. Rosenzweig, 1992a).

IV. Affiliations and Cooperation with Other International Scientific Organizations
A. Memberships in the International Social Science Council and in the International Council of Scientific Unions; Cooperation with UNESCO. The Union has been a member of the International Social Science Council (ISSC) since October 1952 when the ISSC was founded. The four other charter members of ISSC were also international associations representing a particular discipline—International Economic Association, International Committee of Comparative Law, International Political Science Association, and International Sociological Association. During the next twenty years, six additional international organizations joined the Council. Then, in 1972, the Council was transformed into a federation of eleven international associations. Since then, four new members have joined the Council, bringing the total number of regular member associations to fifteen. As an active participant in ISCC programs, the IUPsyS receives from the ISSC an annual financial subvention. Originally this came from a grant from UNESCO, but now the ISSC finances the subvention from several sources, including UNESCO.

Shortly after the Union was established, the Executive Committee decided to seek membership for it in the International Council of Scientific Unions (ICSU). The Council is the apex of international scientific bodies. It has, as members, international scientific unions as well as certain national organizations such as national academies of science, national research councils, or similar bodies. The ICSU takes up major scientific questions of international importance and helps to set international scientific policies. For more information about the ICSU, see Baker (1982) and the ICSU Year Books.

In 1951, when the Union was established, the ICSU had ten scientific unions as members, mainly from the physical and biological sciences. The initial inquiry of IUPsyS in the early 1950s was rebuffed with the reply that the time was not appropriate for its candidacy for membership in the ICSU. In the late 1970s it was suggested that an associate membership in the ICSU might be an appropriate initial step. Accordingly, the Union applied for associate membership, with the proviso that such membership would in no way be considered as a barrier to full membership at a later date, and IUPsyS became an Associate Member of ICSU in 1980. The Union's campaign for full membership in ICSU was renewed, and support was gained from several international scientific unions already in ICSU and from several National Members. IUPsyS President Friedhart Klix was asked to make a presentation before the Admissions Committee of ICSU in September, 1982, and later that month the Assembly of ICSU elected IUPsyS as the twentieth international scientific union to be a full member.

As of 1984, the IUPsyS began to participate in the Assembly of ICSU, and it subsequently joined some of the ICSU special projects and committees. The IUPsyS also introduced a project on man-machine systems into the ICSU agenda. It is hoped that through the agency of ICSU, psychologists will be able to play a larger role in bringing psychological expertise to bear on problems of international importance and that the IUPsyS will be able to collaborate more closely with other international unions on topics of mutual concern.

The IUPsyS has given active support to the International Geosphere-Biosphere Program (IGBP) of the ICSU and to a related program, the Human Dimensions of Global Environmental Change (HDGEC) developing under the ISSC. In the original descriptions of the IGBP, stress was placed on human activities that are causing climatological changes and changes in the earth's surface, and on the necessity of modifying human activities to prevent or reduce adverse changes in the geosphere-biosphere. As the program developed, however, by far the largest activities have concerned climatology, oceanography, and studies of the earth's surface, with only a small role for the behavioural and social sciences. The ISSC therefore set up the complementary HDGEC program in which the IUPsyS is a charter member and in which it is playing an active role.

At present, the only international scientific unions that belong both to the ISSC and the ICSU are the International Geographical Union (IGU) and the IUPsyS. The IGU and the IUPsyS thus serve as a bridge between the international organizations of the natural sciences and of the behavioral and social sciences.

After the Union was organized with impetus from UNESCO, for several years it received a modest annual subvention from UNESCO through the ISSC, and the present ISSC subvention to the IUPsyS continues to be supported in part by a grant from UNESCO. In recent years, the Union's ties with UNESCO have become stronger. For example, the Union has received grants from UNESCO for several projects that helped to further UNESCO programs, and it has prepared expert reports at the request of UNESCO.

B. Organizations Affiliated with the IUPsyS. In early meetings of the Executive Committee shortly after formation of the International Union of Scientific Psychology, there was considerable discussion of how the newly formed Union could best relate to other international associations in psychology. As the Union had national associations as members rather than individual psychologists, it was decided in 1955 that certain international associations should be represented at the Assembly as observers. Initially referred to as "associated organizations", the new statutes adopted in the 1960s referred to them as "affiliates", a term that still stands today within the IUPsyS statutes.

Currently, there are nine affiliates of IUPsyS: the International Association of Applied Psychology (IAAP), the Sociedad Interamericana de Psicologia (SIP), the Association de Psychologie Scientifique de Langue Franaise (APSLF), the International Council of Psychologists (ICP), the European Association of Experimental Social Psychology

(EAESP), the International Association for Cross-Cultural Psychology (IACCP), the International Society for Comparative Psychology (ISCP), the International Society for the Study of Behavioral Development (ISSBD), and the European Association of Personality Psychology (EAPP). Being an affiliate member of IUPsyS does not involve any special privileges, obligations, or status in any real sense of the word. Therefore, affiliates pay no dues. Four criteria are employed by the Assembly in reviewing petitions from international organizations requesting affiliation with IUPsyS: (1) the association should be regional or global in its geographic coverage, comprised of psychologists from two or more nations; (2) the members of the society must be individuals rather than institutions or organizations; (3) the purposes of the society must be essentially psychological and scientific in nature; and (4) the majority of members in the society must be psychologists. In addition, two other factors are considered: (1) the size, significance, and scope of activities undertaken by the society; and (2) the history and probable future stability of the society.

V. Fostering Communication with and among the National Members of the IUPsyS
Psychological organizations can often benefit by learning about each other's activities, plans, and problems, so the Union fosters such exchanges. Some of the main ways are noted briefly here.

The Union secretariat sends regular communications to its National Member organizations, including an annual report of Union activities. In return, it has recently begun to request that each of its National Members send an annual or biennial report of its activities to the Secretary-General of the Union. Before each quadrennial meeting of the Assembly, convened at an International Congress of Psychology, the Secretary-General sends out the preliminary agenda, prepared with the aid of the Executive Committee, and requests National Member organizations to submit additional agenda items. The Assembly meetings provide a major occasion for exchange of information and points of view. Midway between successive regular Assembly meetings, the Union holds a minor, non-voting Assembly meeting during the Congress of the IAAP. The formal and informal Assembly meetings offer opportunities to raise and discuss questions of interest and concern to the international community of psychological scientists. Such questions are also taken up in statements and articles in the International Platform section of the *International Journal of Psychology*. Each National Member of the IUPsyS is encouraged to designate a correspondent to the International Platform section, and individual psychologists also contribute to this forum.

The IUPsyS also sponsors some regional meetings, symposia, and advanced training workshops. One such symposium took up "Development of indigenous psychology" in 1992 at the fourth Asian Regional IACCP Congress in Katmandu. Also in 1992 the Union organized a five-day advanced level training workshop on "Psychosocial dimensions of global environmental conditions and change" in Kuala Lumpur, Malaysia, with representatives from eight Southeast Asian countries. Such meetings help to break down the barriers to communication among psychologists from developing countries, a problem about which many of them complain.

At the initiative of the IUPsyS, and in cooperation with the IACCP, Advanced Training Seminars, to follow immediately after the XXC International Congress of Psychology in Brussels, were organized for psychologists from developing countries. The expertise for these Seminars was volunteered by host psychologists, and the costs of travel and housing for the participants from developing countries were paid by grants from UNESCO, IUPsyS, some of the national psychological organizations, and other sources. The seminars provided reviews of advanced methods and recent theoretical developments within particular areas of psychology, with explicit attention to the relevance of existing psychological knowledge to non-Western contexts. Timing the Seminars immediately after the International Congress made it possible for most of the participants in the Seminar to attend the Congress, thus offering further benefits to the participants and increasing the representativity of the Congress.

VI. Projects under the IUPsyS Committee on Research
The Union sponsors several research activities and special projects. Several networks organized symposia at the occasion of the XXV International Congress of Psychology in Brussels (1992).

The International Network of Human Development and Child Research Centers has continued its active participation in the UNESCO Initiative Program in the field of human development, which concentrates on community-school projects for the psychological development of the young child and the family in developing countries. The Network has continued to enlarge its Directory of Human Development Research Centers with the aid of its established network of research scientists in behavioral development. Fruitful cooperation with the International Society for the Study of Behavioral Development (ISSBD), an affiliate of the IUPsyS, was continued in this and other projects of the Union's Network Program. Noteworthy is the recent UNESCO publication of the *International Directory on the Young Child and the Family Environment*, which contains information on about 670 institutions in 116 countries.

The International Network of Psychology-based Man-Computer Interaction Research (MACINTER) continued the project on testing models of human-computer interaction. A MACINTER workshop on "Cognitive modelling and psychological experiments on human-computer interaction", was held in conjunction with the World Congress on Human-Computer Interaction, 1991, Germany; it permitted exchanges on first results in comparison of models. The MACINTER group was invited to organize workshops at the European Conference on Cognitive Ergonomics in Hungary, 1992, and at the Work Display Unit International Conference in Berlin, 1992. A symposium was organized for the 1992 International Congress of Psychology on human-computer interaction (Wandke & Klix, 1992). Because of the increased workload in editing the *MACINTER News*, it is planned to combine it with the newsletter of the European Association of Cognitive Ergonomics.

The International Network of Research Centers in Cognitive Science, Artificial Intelligence, and Neuroscience continued its listing of research centers in the first part of 1991, but as this work proceeded, it became obvious that most centers and departments of psychology claim to have research under way in some or all of these areas. Analysis of the results of this survey suggested that the network should be reorganized to deal with taxonomy and classification in psychology and in particular in cognitive psychology. The Executive Committee approved this change and asked the Network Coordinator to prepare a work program.

The International Network Project on the Psychology of Global Change (formerly the International Network of Research Centers in Behavioral Ecology/Environmental Psychology) continued work in liaison with the activities of the International Geosphere-Biosphere Program (IGBP) of ICSU and the ISSC program on Human Dimensions of Global Environmental Change (HDGEC). The revised and enlarged contributions to the 1990 symposium in Kyoto on "The psychological dimensions of global change" were published as a special issue of the *International Journal of Psychology* of 1991. In October 1991 members of the Network participated in the first conference of the newly established ISSC-HDGEC Working Group on "Perception and awareness of global environmental change" in Barcelona. With support from ISSC, the Network organized and convened a first Regional Training Seminar in Psychology of Global Change, held in Malaysia in March, 1992.

The International Network of Centers of Research in Psychology in Developing Countries has continued to enlarge its directory of researchers and institutions engaged in psychological research in developing countries, and a new edition should appear soon. The Network was co-convenor of the Regional Training Seminar held in Malaysia in 1992, mentioned in the paragraph above. The efforts of the Network helped importantly in the organization of the Nepalese Psychological Association in 1991. The Network supported a symposium on "Indigenous psychology" at the 4th Regional Congress of the International Association for Cross-Cultural Psychology held in Katmandu, Nepal, January 1992, in conjunction with a special meeting of the Network.

The International Research Project on Psychological Issues of Communication continued its worldwide activities on scientific exchange through electronic mail on topics of jointly mediated activity in the areas of learning, cognition, and development. The combined plenary/subgroup network structure of the email exchange system was further developed, allowing for effective communications among more than 250 active partners around the world. Members of this project have concentrated on broadening email contacts between Russia and the countries of Eastern Europe and the rest of the world. A public access node was opened by Dr Belyaeva's group at the Vega Laboratory in Moscow. Using the method of participant observation, members carefully documented and analyzed the dynamics of growth in the use of this system.

The Psychology and Health Network continued to focus on issues of preventive behavioral medicine and health training, with special attention to problems of health psychology training in developing countries. The former coordinator of the Network published a chapter on health psychology in a book published under the auspices of the IUPsyS (Holtzman, 1992). Publication of the Network's HEALTHNET Newsletter continues successfully.

VII. International Surveys Conducted Under the Auspices of the IUPsyS
Two surveys have been conducted in recent years under the auspices of the IUPsyS. The first gathered information about training in psychology; it was conducted by Mary C. Nixon for the IUPsyS standing Committee on Development of Psychology as a Science and as a Profession. The Committee organized a symposium on this survey and related topics at the XXV International Congress of Psychology in Brussels (Azuma, 1992).

The second recent IUPsyS survey gathered information about resources for psychological research around the world: human resources, financial resources, and the status and recognition accorded to psychological science. This survey was conducted in 1991, and responses were obtained from organizations or individuals in 38 of the 48 countries with member organizations in the Union at that time. The results of the survey are presented and discussed in Rosenzweig (1992b). These surveys present information about psychology that is not only of interest to many psychologists around the world but may also assist planning by both national and international organizations. Where the surveys reveal major gaps in current knowledge, this may stimulate further attempts to gather basic information.

References
Azuma, H. (1992). IUPsyS symposium on "Development of psychology as a science and as a profession". *International Journal of Psychology, 27*: 3-4, 652.
Baker, F.W.G. (1982). *The International Council of Scientific Unions: A Brief Survey*. Paris: International Council of Scientific Unions.
Holtzman, W.H. (1976). The XXVth anniversary of the International Union of Psychological Science. *International Journal of Psychology, 11*, 3-18.
Holtzman, W.H. (1992). Health Psychology. In M.R. Rosenzweig (Ed.). *International psychological science: Progress, problems, and prospects* (pp.199-226). Washington, D.C.: American Psychological Association.
Kenna, J.C. (1969). International Congress of Psychology. *Bulletin of the British Psychological Association, 22*, Supplement, 44-48.
Nuttin, J.R. (1992). Les premiers congrès internationaux de psychologie. In M. Richelle, & H. Carpintero (Eds.). Contributions to the history of the international congresses of psychology. *Revista de Historia de la Psychologia Monographs* (pp.7-74).
Pawlik, K. (Ed.) (1985). *International directory of psychologists*. Amsterdam: North-Holland.
Rosenzweig, M.R. (1982). Trends in development and status of psychology: An international perspective. *International Journal of Psychology, 17*, 117-140.
Rosenzweig, M.R. (1984). U.S. psychology and world psychology. *American Psychologist, 39*, 877-884.
Rosenzweig, M.R. (Ed.). (1992a). *International psychological science: Progress, problems and prospects*. Washington, D.C.: American Psychological Association.

Rosenzweig, M.R. (1992b). Resources for psychological science around the world. In M.R. Rosenzweig (Ed.) *International psychological science: Progress, problems, and prospects* (pp.17-74). Washington, D.C.: American Psychological Association.

Rosenzweig, M.R. & Holtzman, W.H. (1985). The International Union of Psychological Science. In K. Pawlik (Ed.). *International directory of psychologists* (pp.3-15). Amsterdam: North-Holland. (An abridged version appeared in the *International Journal of Psychology*, 1986, *20*, 753-764.)

Wandke, H. & Klix, F. (1992). [Symposium on human-computer interaction]. *International Journal of Psychology, 27*: 3-4, 648-649.

PRESIDENT'S INTRODUCTION

At the time of writing, 35 years have passed since the publication of the first edition of the *International Directory of Pyschologists* in 1958. These 35 years mark a phase of rapid growth and development of psychological science, across all fields of research and areas of specialization; in academic research and professional practice, in the teaching of psychological methods and knowledge at all educational levels, and in the development of psychology as a science of behavior bringing together biological and social perspectives, covering normal and abnormal behavior and encompassing both pure and applied research (as expressed in Article 1 of the Statutes of the International Union of Psychological Science). In this development, international cooperation and exchange have become a growing necessity and opportunity, both in the interest of promoting psychology (as a science and as a profession), and in bringing psychology to bear in response to the social challenges and demands of our time. Here the *International Directory of Psychologists*, published under the auspices of the International Union of Psychological Science (IUPsyS), has become an important source for cross-national reference. Following publication of the first edition, a second edition of the directory was published in 1966, a third in 1980, and a fourth edition in 1985.

In this series, the present fifth edition marks a turning point in directory design, also borne out by a change of title; from a directory of individual psychologists to: *The IUPSyS Directory: Major Research Institutes and Departments of Psychology*. The change has become necessary because of the exponential increase in the number of psychologists to be considered in a new edition - rendering such a task impracticable in more than one respect. We trust this new format will also make the directory more useful as a quick-access ready-to-use reference guide in international psychological science. In addition to institutional entries, national descriptions of psychology throughout the world are provided for a large number of countries containing useful summary information on the situation and development of psychology at a national level. Readers seeking to contact individual psychologists are advised to do so through the institution at which this psychologist is known to be working or, lacking such information, through the respective national society/association of psychology. An introductory chapter by M.R. Rosenzweig and W.H. Holtzman presents updated information on the International Union of Psychological Science, its history, structure, and major activities.

The IUPsyS is grateful to Géry d'Ydewalle, who agreed to serve as Editor of this new edition of the directory, and to Michael Forster, Rohays Perry and their staff at Lawrence Erlbaum Associates Ltd. for accomplishing this publishing task and for making this volume available at a price level which, hopefully, will facilitate its world-wide circulation. May this new directory serve its purpose and contribute to the development of international cooperation and exchange in psychological science!

Kurt Pawlik   Hamburg
President of the IUPsyS   January 1993

AFGHANISTAN

Kabul Univ. (Pohantoon)
Jamal Mina
Kabul
Psychology, Dept. of

Nangarhar, Bayazid Roshan Univ.
Jalalabad
Nangarhar
Psychology, Dept. of

ALBANIA

Tiranë, Enver Hoxha Univ.
Tiranë
Psychology, Dept. of

ALGERIA

Alger Univ.
2 rue Didouche Mourad
Alger
Sciences Sociales Psych., Inst. des

Oran University
Es Senia
Oran
Psychology & Science of Education, Inst. of
Dept. Head: Marouf Ahmed
Phone: (213) (6) 38 70 75

ARGENTINA

Aconcagua, Univ. del
Catamarca 147
5500 Mendoza
Psychology, Dept. of

Argentina de la Empresa, Univ.
Libertad 1340
1016 Buenos Aires
Psychology, Dept. of

Belgrano, Univ. de
Federico Lacroze 1959
1426 Buenos Aires
Psychology, Inst. of

Buenos Aires, Univ. de
Calle Viamonte 430/444
1053 Buenos Aires
Psychology, Fac. of

Buenos Aires, Univ. Nac. del Centro de la Provincia de
Gral Pinto 399
7000 Tandil
Psychology, Dept. of

Caece, Univ. de
Avda de Mayo 1396
1085 Buenos Aires
Psychology, Dept. of

Catamarca, Univ. Nac. de
San Martin 821
4700 Catamarca
Psychology, Dept. of

Child Neuropsychology Centre
No. 4. 080 Nazca Ave
Postal Code No. 1419
Fed. Capital
CENI
Dept. Head: Roberto Mario Paterno
Phone: (54) (1) 572 9738

Comahue, Univ. Nac. del
Buenos Aires 1400
Neuquén
Psychology, Dept. of

Concepción del Uruguay, Univ. de
8 de Junio 522
3260 Concepción del Uruguay
Entre Ríos
Psychology, Dept. of

Córdoba, Univ. Nac. de
Trejo 323
5000 Córdoba
Psychology, Dept. of

Cuyo, Univ. Cat. de
Casilla de Correo 2
Suc. 4
5400 San Juan
Psychology, Dept. of

Cuyo, Univ. Nac. de
Centro Universitario
Parque San Martín
5500 Mendoza
Psychology, Dept. of

Entre Rios, Univ. Nac. de
Galarza 617
3260 Concepción del Uruguay
Entre Rios
Psychology, Dept. of

John F Kennedy, Univ. Argentina
Calle Bartolomé Mitre 1411
1037 Buenos Aires
Psychology, Dept. of

Jujuy, Univ. Nac. de
Bolivia 2335
4600 San Salvador de Jujuy
Psychology, Dept. of

La Plata, Univ. Cat. de la
Calle 13 No. 1227
1900 La Plata
Psychology, Dept. of

La Rioja, Univ.
Provincial de
Avda Ortiz de Ocampo 1700
5300 La Rioja
Psychology, Dept. of

Litoral, Univ. Nac. del
Boulevard Pellegrin 2750
3000 Santa Fé
Psychology, Dept. of

Lomas de Zamora, Univ.
Nac. de
CC 95
1832 Lomas de Zamora
Pca de Buenos Aires
Psychology, Dept. of

Lujáan, Univ. Nac. de
CC 221
6700 Luján
Buenos Aiires
Psychology, Dept. of

Mar del Plata, Univ.
Nac. de
Juan Bautista Alberdi
2695
7600 Mar del Plata
Pca de Buenos Aires
Psychology, Dept. of

Mendoza, Univ. de
Avda Boulogne-sur-Mer
665
5500 Mendoza
Psychology, Dept. of

Misiones, Univ. Nac. de
Avda Corrientes 2565
3300 Posadas
Misiones
Psychology, Dept. of

Museo Social Argentino,
Univ. del
Av. Corrientes 1723
1042 Buenos Aires
Psychology, Dept. of

Nordeste, Univ. Nac. del
25 de Mayo 868
3400 Corrientes
Psychology, Dept. of

Norte Santo Tomás de
Aquino, Univ. de
9 de Julio 165, CC 32
4000 San Miguel de
Tucumán
Psychology, Dept. of

Pampa, Univ. Nac. de la
9 de Julio 149
6300 Santa Rosa
La Pampa
Psychology, Dept. of

Patagonia San Juan
Bosco, Univ. Nac. de la
CC 786
Correo Central 9000
Comodoro Rivadavia
Chubut
Psychology, Dept. of

Río Cuarto, Univ. Nac.
de
Ruta Nac. 36 Km 601
5800 Río Cuarto
Córdoba
Psychology, Dept. of

Rosario, Univ. Nac. de
Córdoba 1814
2000 Rosario
Psychology, Dept. of

Salta, Univ. Cat. de
Ciudad Univ.
Campo Castañares
Casilla 18
4400 Salta
Psychology, Dept. of

Salta, Univ. Nac. de
Buenos Aires 177
4400 Salta
Psychology, Dept. of

Salvador, Univ. del
Rodríguez Peña 640
1020 Buenos Aires
Psychopedagogy, Fac. of

San Jan, Univ. Nac. de
Avda Ignacio de la Roza
391(E)
6#, 5400 San Juan

San Luis, Univ. Nac. de
Lavalle 1189
5700 San Luis
Psychology, Dept. of

Santa Fé, Univ. Cat. de
Echagüe 7151
3000 Santa Fé
Psychology, Dept. of

Santa Maria de los
Buenos Aires, Univ.
Cat. Argentina
Juncal 1912
1116 Buenos Aires

Santiago del Estero,
Univ. Nac. de
Avda Belgrano (S) 1912
4200 Santiago del Estero
Psychology, Dept. of

Santiago del Estero,
Univ. Cat. de
Campus Universitario
Alsina Prolongación
4200 Santiago del Estero

Sur, Univ. Nac. del
Avda Colón 80
8000 Bahía Blanca
Psychology, Dept. of

Tecnológica Nac., Univ.
de
Sarmiento 440
6# piso
1347 Buenos Aires
Psychology, Dept. of

Tucumán, Univ. Nac. de
Ayacucho 491
4000 San Miguel de
Tucumán
Psychology, Dept. of

ARMENIA

**Yerevan State
University**
Ul. Mravyana 1
Yerevan, 375049
Psychology, Dept. of

AUSTRALIA

**1st Psychological
Research Unit**
NBH 3-44
Northbourne House
Turner, ACT 2601
*Dept. Head: Lieut. Col. R.
C. Furry*
Phone: (61) (6) 266 5722
Fax: (61) (6) 266 5137

**Adelaide Childrens'
Hospital**
North Adelaide
SA 5006
Psychiatry Dept.

Adelaide, Univ. of
POB 498
Adelaide, SA 5001
*Psychology Dept.
Other Depts: Psychiatry;
Education
Dept. Head: Christopher
J. Cooper*
Phone: (61) (8) 228 5229
Fax: (61) (8) 224 0464
Telex: AA89141 UNIVAD

Alcoa of Australia
POB 161
Kwinana
WA 6167
Training & Admin. Dept.

Austin Hospital
Studley Rd
Heidelberg
Victoria 3084
*Clinical Psychology Dept.
Dept. Head: Dr Jeannette
Milgrom*
Phone: (61) (3) 450 5187
Fax: (61) (3) 459 3380

Australian Cath. Univ.
40 Edward St.
North Sydney
NSW 2060
*Psychology Dept.
Other Depts: Sociology*

**Australian Council for
Educational Research**
9 Frederick St.
Hawthorn
Victoria 3122

**Australian Dept. of
Health**
POB 100
Woden, ACT 2606

**Australian Graduate
School of Management**
Univ. of New South Wales
POB 1
Kensington
NSW 2033
*Dept. Head: Prof. Boris
Kabanoff*
Phone: (61) (2) 931 9267
Fax: (61) (2) 662 7621
Email: boris@
agsm.unsw.oz.au

Australian Inst. of Sport
POB 176
Belconnen
ACT 2616
Dept. Head: Jeffrey Bond
Phone: (61) (6) 252
1236/252 1557
Fax: (61) (6) 1603

**Australian National
Univ.**
POB 4
Canberra, ACT 2601
*Psychology Dept.
Other Depts: Sociology;
Social Psychiatry Res.
Unit*

**Baillie Henderson
Hospital**
Hogg St.
Toowoomba
Queensland 4350

Ballarat Univ. College
POB 663
Ballarat
Victoria 3353
*Life Sciences Fac.,
Psychology Dept.
Other Depts: Business &
Information
Management; Arts,
Education & Humanities
Dept. Head: Raymond K.
Watson*
Phone: (61) (53) 339612
Fax: (61) (53) 339205
Email: psy@ buc.edu.au

Bethesda Hospital
30 Erin St.
Richmond
Victoria 3121
*Dept. Head: Dr Jennie
Ponsford*
Phone: (61) (3) 420 5239
Fax: (61) (3) 427 9856

Blamey Barracks
Milpo
Kapooka
NSW 2661
Psychology Unit

Bloomfield Hospital
Orange, NSW 2800
Psychology Dept.

Bond Univ.
Gold Coast
Queensland 4429
Humanities & Social
Services
Other Depts: Information
& Computing Sciences;
Business

Bouvery Family
Therapy Centre
35 Poplar Rd
Parkville
Victoria 3052

Bundaberg Base
Hospital
POB 34
Bundaberg
Queensland 4670
Dept. Head: Dr Marsh
May
Phone: (61) (71) 521
222
Fax: (61) (71) 531 779

Cairnmillar Inst.
993 Burke Rd
Camberwell
Victoria 3124
Other Depts: Australian
Foundation of
Aftermath Reactions
Dept. Head: Dr Francis
MacNab
Phone: (61) (3) 813
3400
Fax: (61) (3) 882 9764

Calvary Hospital ACT
Inc.
POB 254
Jamison Centre
Canberra
ACT 2614
Psychology, Dept. of
Dept. Head: Alan Jones
Phone: (61) (6) 201 6080
Fax: (61) (6) 201 6210

Canberra, Univ. of
POB 1
Belconnen
ACT 2616
Centre for Sports Studies
Other Depts:
Administrative Studies
Dept. Head: Dr John B.
Gross
Phone: (61) (6) 2012009

Canberra, Univ. of
POB 2
Belconnen
ACT 2616
Centre for Applied
Psychology
Dept. Head: Dr Linda
Hort
Phone: (61) (6) 2012653

Catholic Family Welfare
POB 364
Moonah
Tasmania 7009
Dept. Head: Sister
Philippa Chapman
Phone: (61) (2) 781660
Fax: (61) (2) 781005

Central Queensland,
Univ. College of
Rockhampton Mail
Centre
Queensland 4702
Social Sciences Fac.
Other Depts: Health
Science; Education

Charles Sturt Univ.
Murray Campus
POB 789
Albury, NSW 2640

Charles Sturt Univ.
Mitchell Campus
Panorama Ave
Bathurst
NSW 2795

Charles Sturt Univ.
Private Bag 99
Bathurst
NSW 2795
Social Science Dept.
Other Depts: Teacher
Education

Charles Sturt Univ. -
Riverina
POB 588
Wagga Wagga
NSW 2650
Dept. Head: Dr Tony
Linford
Phone: (69) 222249
Fax: (69) 22792
Email: casey@
zac.riv.csu.edu.au

Chisholm Inst. of
Technology
Monash Univ.
900 Dandenong Rd
Caulfield East
Victoria 3145
Applied Psychology Dept.
Other Depts: Community
Service School of
Business

Community
Development, Dept. of
Giles House
POB 2681
Alice springs
NT 5750

Community Health
Centre
284 Peele St.
Tamworth
NSW 2340

Community Health
Centre
cnr. Stewart Ave / Parry
St.
Hamilton, NSW 2303

**Community Service
Centre**
POB 52
Inala
Queensland 4077

**Community Welfare
Centre**
55 Duncraig Rd
Applecross, WA 6153
*Child Care & Assessment
Dept.*

**Community Welfare
Service**
55 Swanston St.
Melbourne
Victoria 3000
Program Development

**Corio Counselling
Centre**
Manifold St.
Geelong west
Victoria 3218
Special Services

**Corrective Services
Dept.**
POB 31
Sydney, NSW 2001

**Counselling Guidance
& Clinical Services**
273 High St.
Preston
Victoria 3072

**Counselling &
Guidance Centre**
52 Ovens St.
Wangaratta
Victoria 3677

CSIRO
Kintore Ave
Adelaide
SA 5000
Human Nutrition, Divn. of

CSIRO
POB 56, Highsett
Victoria 3190
Building Research Divn.

**Cumberland College of
Health Sciences**
POB 170
Lidcombe
NSW 2141
*Behavioural Science
Dept.*

**Curtin Univ. of
Technology**
POB U1987
Perth
WA 6001
*School of Psychology
Other Depts: Health
Sciences Divn.;
Education; Social
Sciences Fac.
Dept. Head: Prof. Denis
Glencross*
Phone: (61) (9) 351
7867
Fax: (61) (9) 351 2464
Email: glencross-dj@
cc.curtin.edu.au

**Dandenong Student
Services**
186 Foster St.
Dandenong
Victoria 3175

Darling Downs Inst.
Post Office
Darling Heights
Toowoomba
Queensland 4350
*Student Services Dept.
Other Depts: Behavioural
Science
Dept. Head: Kath
Ellerman*
Phone: (61) (76) 31 2389
Fax: (61) (76) 31 2880

Deakin Univ.
221 Burwood Highway
Burwood
Victoria 3125
*Special Education &
Disability Studies
Other Depts: Intellectual
Disability
Dept. Head: Prof. Simon
H. Haskell*
Phone: (61) (3) 805 3480
Fax: (61) (3) 805 3526

Deakin Univ.
Burwood Campus
221 Burwood Highway
Burwood, Victoria 3125
*Disability Studies Dept.
Dept. Head: Dr Joseph
Graffam*
Phone: (61) (613) 805
3191
Fax: (61) (613) 805 3594

Deakin Univ.
Geelong, Victoria 3217
*Psychology, Dept. of
Dept. Head: Prof. Boris
Crassini*
Phone: (61) (52) 271410
Fax: (61) (52) 272021

Deakin Univ.
Rusden Campus
662 Blackburn
Clayton North
Victoria 3168
*Dept. Head: Prof. Marita
McCabe*
Phone: (61) (3) 542 7271
Fax: (61) (3) 542 7229

Deakin Univ.
Toorak Campus
336 Glenferrie Rd
Malvern
Victoria 3144
Phone: (61) (3) 823 5282
Fax: (61) (3) 822 4980

Defence-Navy, Dept. of
POB 706
Darlinghurst, NSW 2010
Psychology Section EAA
Dept. Head: James
Tennent
Phone: (61) (2) 359 2670
Fax: (61) (2) 359 2681

DEIR
239-41 Bourke St.
Melbourne, Victoria 3000
Occ. Psychology Section

Directorate of
Psychology-Army
CP4-6-11 Campbell Park
Canberra, ACT 2600
Dept. Head: Col. W. H. Hall
Phone: (61) (6) 266 3897
Fax: (61) (6) 266 2789

Early Child
Development, Inst. of
4 Madden Grove
Kew, Victoria 3101

East Sub Child
Guidance Centre
Birrell St.
Waverley, NSW 2024

East Sydney
Technology College
Forbes St.
Darlinghurst, NSW 2010
Counselling Unit
Dept. Head: Peter Ellis
Phone: (61) (2) 3398614
Fax: (61) (2) 3398614

Edith Cowan Univ.
Joondalup, WA 6027
Psychology, Dept. of
Dept. Head: Prof. Noel
Howieson
Phone: (61) (9) 405
5555
Fax: (61) (9) 300 1257

Edith Cowan Univ.
Pearson St.
Churchlands, WA 6018
Arts & Applied Sciences
School

Education & The Arts,
Dept. of
233b Charles St.
Launceston
Tasmania 7250
Guidance Services
Dept. Head: Philip
Doyle
Phone: (61) (3) 362406
Fax: (61) (3) 317882

Educational
Assessment &
Parental Guidance
Centre
Johnston St.
Peppermint Give
WA 6011

Family Court
Counselling
4th Floor, Temple Court
75-85 Elizabeth St.
Sydney, NSW 2000

Family Studies,
Inst. of
Lewis House
766 Elizabeth St.
Melbourne
Victoria 3000

Flinders Univ. of South
Australia
POB 2100
Adelaide, SA 5001
School of Psychology
Other Depts: Community
Medicine
Dept. Head: Prof. N. T.
Feather / Prof. N. Bond
Phone: (61) (8) 201 2192
Fax: (61) (8) 2566

Flying Training
School 1
RAAF Base Williams
Point Cook, Victoria 3029
Senior Psychologist
Dept. Head: D. Seychell
Phone: (61) (3) 368 1439
Fax: (61) (3) 368 1234

Gladesville Hospital
Victoria Rd
Gladesville, NSW 2111
Psychology Dept.
Dept. Head: Judith
Spragg
Phone: (61) (2) 816 0222
Fax: (61) (2) 816 0221

Gold Coast Univ.
College of Griffith Univ.
Nathan
Queensland 4111
Nursing & Health
Sciences Divn.
Other Depts: Education
& the Arts

Graylands Hospital
Graylands
WA 6010
Psychology Dept.
Dept. Head: Robin
Christophers
Phone: (61) (9) 347 6730
Fax: (61) (9) 385 2701

Griffith Univ.
Mt Gravatt Campus
Nathan
Queensland 4111
School of Cognition &
Learning, Fac. of
Education
Other Depts: Health &
Behavioural Science
Dept. Head: Prof. John
Bain
Phone: (61) (7) 875 5635
Fax: (61) (7) 875 5910

Guidance & Special Education Branch
POB 1500,
Cairns
Queensland 4870

Guidance & Special Education Unit
24 Gordon St.
Bowen
Queensland 4805

Guidance Services
Floor 14
Education Centre
31 Flinders St.
Adelaide, SA 5001

Hastings District Hospital
Morton St.
Port Macquarie
NSW 2444
Dept. Head: Michael A. Burke
Phone: (61) (65) 833944
Fax: (61) (65) 849531

Hillcrest Hospital
Univ. of Adelaide
POB 202
Adelaide, SA 5001
Dept. Head: Donald Sandford
Phone: (61) (8) 2669211
Fax: (61) (8) 2614092

Intellectual Disability Services
Western Regional Office
POB 224
Footscray, Victoria 3011
Other Depts: CSV Head Office, 115 Victoria Parade, Fitzroy, Victoria 3065
Dept. Head: Ian Pollerd
Phone: (61) (3) 689 7455
Fax: (61) (3) 687 6226

Intellectual Disability Services
POB 760
Geelong
Victoria 3220
Behaviour Intervention Support Team, Otways Region
Dept. Head: Susan Moore
Phone: (61) (52) 264540
Fax: (61) (52) 264550

James Cook Univ.
Townsville
Queensland 4811
Psychology & Sociology, Dept. of
Other Depts: Education; Behavioural Science
Dept. Head: J. Michael Innes
Phone: (61) (77) 814182
Fax: (61) (77) 795435

Kororoit Community Mental Health Service
POB 472
1 Andrea St.
St Albans
Victoria 3021
Dept. Head: Dr Peter Cook
Phone: (61) (3) 364 1888
Fax: (61) (3) 367 3517

La Trobe Univ.
Bundoora
Victoria 3083
Psychology, Dept. of
Other Depts: Genetics; Education; Sociology; Counselling Service
Dept. Head: Dr Geoff Cumming
Phone: (61) (3) 479 2935
Fax: (61) (3) 478 0603

Launceston General Hospital
Launceston
Tasmania 7250
Psychiatry, Dept. of
Dept. Head: Bill McIntosh
Phone: (61) (3) 327745
Fax: (61) (3) 327773
Telex: 7745

Lidcombe Hospital
Joseph St.
Lidcombe, NSW 2141
Dept. Head: Dr Skye McDonald
Phone: (61) (2) 646 8310
Fax: (61) (2) 646 5978

Lincoln School of Health Sciences
La Trobe Univ.
Bundoora, Victoria 3083
Behavioural Health Sciences Dept.
Dept. Head: Heather Gardner
Phone: (61) (3) 479 1750
Fax: (61) (3) 479 1783

Macquarie Univ.
North Ryde, NSW 2113
Behavioural Science, School of
Other Depts: Education
Dept. Head: Prof. George Couney
Phone: (61) (2) 8058067
Fax: (61) (2) 8058062

Marianist College
McMahon's Rd
Frankston
Victoria 3199

Maroubra Community Health Centre
1130 Garden St.
Maroubra Junction
NSW 2035

Marriage Education
POB 675E GPO
Melbourne
Victoria 3001

**Marriage Guidance
Council S. A. Inc.**
55 Hutt St.
Adelaide, SA 5000
*Dept. Head: Graham J.
Wilks*
Phone: (61) (8) 223 4566
Fax: (61) (8) 232 2898

Mayday Hills Hospital
Residence 7
Beechworth
Victoria 3747

Mazenod College
Kernot Ave
Mulgrave, Victoria 3170

McAuley College
243 Gladstone Rd
Dutton Park
Queensland 4102

Melbourne, Univ. of
4 Madden Grove
Kew
Victoria 3101
*Early Childhood Studies,
School of
Dept. Head: Prof. G.
Parmenter*
Phone: (61) (3) 854 3333
Fax: (61) (3) 860 3348

Melbourne, Univ. of
Parkville
Victoria 3052
*Educational Psychology
& Special Education,
Dept. of
Dept. Head: Assoc. Prof.
Graham Clunies-Ross*
Phone: (61) (3) 344 4949
Fax: (61) (3) 349 1915

Melbourne, Univ. of
Parkville
Melbourne, Victoria 3052
*Psychology Dept &
School of Behavioural
Science
Other Depts: Higher
Education Centre;
Student Counselling;
Community Medicine*
Phone: (61) (3) 344 6377
Fax: (61) (3) 347 6618

**Mental Health
Commission**
Hampden Rd
Hobart, Tasmania 7000

Mental Health Research
35-37 Poplar Rd
Melbourne, Victoria 3052

**Mental Retardation
Divn.**
POB 502, Sth. Melbourne
Victoria 3205

Monash Univ.
Clayton, Victoria 3168
*Psychology Dept.
Other Depts: Education;
Counselling Service
Dept. Head: Prof. R. H.
Day*
Phone: (61) (3) 565 3968
Fax: (61) (3) 565 3948
Telex: 32691AA
Email: roz@
monul.cc.monash.oz

Monash Univ.
Switchback Rd
Churchill, Victoria 3842
*Psychology Section,
School of Social Sciences
Dept. Head: Dr
Christopher O. Fraser*
Phone: (61) (51) 226339
Fax: (61) (51) 226359

**Mornington Student
Services**
64 Tanti Ave
Mornington, Victoria 3931

Murdoch Univ.
Murdoch, WA 6150
*Psychology Dept.
Other Depts: Education;
Social Sciences*

New England, Univ. of
Armidale
NSW 2351
*Psychology Dept.
Other Depts: Education;
Behavioural Studies
Centre
Dept. Head: Prof. William
Noble*
Phone: (61) (67) 732527
Fax: (61) (67) 729816
Email: wnoble@
metz.une.03.au

**New South Wales, Univ.
of**
POB 1, Kensington
NSW 2033
*Psychology, School of
Other Depts: Education;
Australian Graduate
School of Management;
Social Work; Student
Counselling
Dept. Head: Prof.
Barbara Gillam*
Phone: (61) (2) 697
3041/3034
Fax: (61) (2) 662 6279

**New South Wales, Univ.
of**
Prince of Wales Hospital
High St.
Randwick
NSW 2031
*Tumbatin Clinic
Psychiatric Unit*

Newcastle, Univ. of (NSW)
Callaghan, NSW 2308
Special Education Centre
Dept. Head: Dr Philip J.
Foreman
Phone: (61) (49) 216275
Fax: (61) (49) 216939

Newcastle Univ.
Shortland
Newcastle
NSW 2308
Psychology Dept.
Other Depts: Medicine
Dept. Head: Prof. D. C.
Finlay
Phone: (61) (49) 215935
Fax: (61) (49) 216902
Email: psdcf@
cc.newcastleedu.au

Northern Territory Univ.
POB 40146
Casuarina, NT 0811
Humanities & Social
Science Dept.

Nursery School Teachers College
146 Burren St.
Newtown, NSW 2042

Oakleigh Student Service
3 Chester St.
Oakleigh
Victoria 3166

Oakrise
Child & Adolescent
Service
Kelham St.
Launceston
Tasmania 7250
Dept. Head: Dr M. David
McGeorge
Phone: (61) (3) 322867

Oblate Education Centre
37 Woniora Rd, POB 70
Hurstville, NSW 2220

Office of Corrections
20 Albert Rd
South Melbourne
Victoria 3206
Psychological Services
Dept. Head: Irene Haas
Phone: (61) (3) 698 6630
Fax: (61) (3) 698 6643

Officer Cadet School
Milpo
Portsea, Victoria 3944
Student Counsellor

Orange Community Health Centre
POB 993
Orange, NSW 2800

Orano Children's Home
87 Elgar Rd
Burwood
Victoria 3125

Parramatta Child Health Centre
48 George St.
Parramatta, NSW 2150

Phillip Inst. of Technology
Plenty Rd
Bundoora
Victoria 3083
Business School

Prince Charles Hospital
Rode Rd
Chermside
Queensland 4032
Winston Noble Unit
Dept. Head: Lee Beames
Phone: (61) (7) 350 8111
Fax: (61) (7) 350 8614

Prince Henry Hospital
POB 233
Matraville
NSW 2036
Psychiatry, Divn. of
Dept. Head: Jillian Ball
Phone: (61) (2) 694 5601
Fax: (61) (2) 311 3670

Prince Henry's Hospital
St Kilda Rd
Melbourne
Victoria 3004
Monash Psy. Med. Dept.

Princess Alexandra Hospital
Ipswich Rd
Woollongabba
Queensland 4102
Psychology, Dept. of
Dept. Head: Maureen
Field
Phone: (61) (7) 240 2885
Fax: (61) (7) 240 2100

Psychiatric Opd Repat. Hospital
Concord
NSW 2139

Psychiatric Research Unit
Northbourne House
NBH 3-26
Canberra, ACT 2601

Queen Elizabeth Hospital
Adelaide Univ.
Woodville Rd
Wooodville, SA 5011
Psychiatry Dept.

Queensland Deaf Society
c/o 34 Davidson St.
Newmarket
Queensland 4051

Queensland, Univ. of
Brisbane
Queensland 4072
Psychology, Dept. of
Other Depts: Education;
Social Work; Student
Counselling; Speech &
Hearing; Schonell
Research Centre
Dept. Head: Prof. David
Siddle
Phone: (61) (7) 365 6230
Fax: (61) (7) 365 4466
Email: davids@
psych.psy.uq.oz.au

Queensland Univ. of
Technology
POB 284, Zillmere
Queensland 4034
School of Social Science
Dept. Head: Prof. Gisela
Kaplan
Phone: (61) (7) 864 4610
Fax: (61) (7) 864 4995
Email:
Kaplan@qut.edu.au

RAAF Psychology
Service
288 Edward St., Brisbane
Queensland 4000

Repat. General Hospital
Univ. of Sydney
Concord, NSW 2139

Repat. General Hospital
Univ. of Western
Australia
Monash Ave
Hollywood, WA 6009
Psychiatry, Dept. of

Repat. Hospital
Univ. of Melbourne
Banksia St.
Heidelberg, Victoria 3081
Psychology Dept.

RMIT
124 La Trobe St.
Melbourne
Victoria 3000
Administrative Studies
Dept.
Other Depts: Humanities
& Social Sciences

Rockhampton Base
Hospital
Canning St.
Rockhampton
Queensland 4700
Psychology Dept.
Dept. Head: Paul
Loganathan
Phone: (61) (79) 316376
Fax: (61) (79) 221040

Rockingham District
Office
POB 1
Rockingham
WA 6168
District Guidance
Officer

Rosemount Hospital
Cartwright St.
Windsor
Queensland 4030
Psychology Dept.

Royal Children's
Hospital
Univ. of Melbourne
Parkville, Victoria 3052
Psychiatry &
Behavioural Science
Dept.

Royal Melbourne
Hospital
Univ. of Melbourne
Clinical Science Building
Melbourne
Victoria 3050
Psychiatry Dept.

Royal Park Psychiatric
Hospital
Univ. of Melbourne
Private Bag No. 3
Parkville, Victoria 3052
Dept. Head: Jane
Edwards
Phone: (61) (3) 389 2222
Fax: (61) (3) 388 0302

Royal Prince Alfred
Hospital
Univ. of Sydney
Camperdown
NSW 2050
Psychiatry, Dept. of

Royal Rehabilitation
Centre, Sydney
POB 6
Ryde, NSW 2112
Psychology Dept.
Dept. Head: Gillian Fox
Phone: (61) (2) 807 1144
Fax: (61) (2) 809 6071

Royal South Sydney
Hospital
Univ. of New South Wales
Joynton Ave.
Zetland, NSW 2017
Psychology Dept.
Dept. Head: Agnes
Rappaport
Phone: (61) (2) 697 8133
Fax: (61) (2) 697 8105

Rozelle Hospital
Univ. of Sydney, POB 1
Rozelle, NSW 2039

Selby Centre
Selby St.
Shenton park, WA 6008
Neurosciences Unit
Dept. Head: Dr Linda
Hayward
Phone: (61) (9) 3820856
Fax: (61) (9) 3820817

SO2 Development
HQ Trg Cmd
POB 39, Darlinghurst
NSW 2010
Psychology Dept.

**Social Biology
Resources Centre**
139 Bouverie St.
Carlton, Victoria 3053

SOPSYCHS-HQTC
VB-D-314
Victoria Barracks
Melbourne
Victoria 3004

**South Australia, Univ.
of**
108 Kermode St.
North Adelaide
SA 5006
Kindergarten Dept.

**South Australia, Univ.
of**
Murray Park Campus
POB 2471
Adelaide
SA 5001
Psychology Dept.

**South Australia, Univ.
of**
North Terrace
Adelaide
SA 5000
*Psychology, School of
Dept. Head: Dr Jacques
C. Metzer*
Phone: (61) (8) 302 2211
Fax: (61) (8) 302 2213

**South Australia, Univ.
of**
Salisbury Campus
Smith Rd
Salisbury East
SA 5109

South Australia, Univ. of
Underdale Campus
Holbrooks Rd
Underdale, SA 5032
*Early & Middle
Childhood, Dept. of*

**Southern Queensland,
Univ. of**
Toowoomba, 4350
*Applied Psychology Dept.
Dept. Head: Dr G Tehan*
Phone: (61) (76) 312 100
Fax: (61) (76) 361 762
Telex: AA 40010
Email: tehan@
zeus.wsq.edu.au

Spastic Centre
POB 164
Brookvale, NSW 2100
Rehabilitation Dept.

St Columba College
Nedlands
WA 6009
*Family Counselling
Service*

State College of Victoria
POB 179
Coburg, Victoria 3058

Stockton Hospital
Fullerton Rd
Stockton, NSW 2295
Psychology Dept.

Sturt CAE
Sturt Rd
Bedford Park, SA 5042
*Health Science & Educ.
Fac.*

**Sunshine Hospital &
Health Centre**
176-90 Furlong Rd
St Albans, Victoria 3021
Child Psychiatry Unit

Sutherland Hospital
Univ. of New South
Wales
POB 21
Caringbah, NSW 2229

**Swinburne Univ. of
Technology**
POB 218
Hawthorn
Victoria 3122
*Psychology Dept.
Other Depts:
Mathematics Dept.;
Student Health & W. U.
Dept. Head: Prof. Ken
Heskin*
Phone: (61) (3) 819 8203
Fax: (61) (3) 818 3647
Email: ken heskin@
buster.xx.swin.oz.au

**Sydney College of the
Arts**
POB 226
Glebe
NSW 2037

Sydney, Univ. of
Sydney
NSW 2006
*Psychology Dept.
Other Depts: Counselling
Service; Education;
Behavioural Sciences
Dept. Head: Prof. Helen
C. Beh*
Phone: (61) (2) 692 2609
Fax: (61) (2) 692 2603
Email: helen@
psychvax.psych.su.oz

**Sydney Univ. of
Technology**
POB 123
Broadway
NSW 2007
*Human. & Social Science
School*

**Tasmania at Hobart,
Univ. of**
POB 252C
Hobart
Tasmania 7001
Psychology, Dept. of
Other Depts: Education;
  Counselling Service;
  Teacher Education Divn.
Dept. Head: Dr Iain
  Montgomery
Phone: (61) (2) 202237
Fax: (61) (2) 202883
Email: iain@ psychnet.
  psychol.utas.edu.au

Tasmania CAE
POB 1214
Launceston
Tasmania 7250
Teacher Education Divn.

**Thomas Walker
Hospital**
Concord West
NSW 2138
*Rivendell Adolescent
  Unit*

Travancore Clinic
50 Flemington Rd
Flemington
Victoria3031

Trinity College
Riversdale Drive
Perth
WA 6000

**Tweed Heads & District
Hospital**
Florence St.
Tweed Heads
NSW 2485
Psychology Dept.
Dept. Head: Christine
  Salisbury
Phone: (61) (75) 360540
Fax: (61) (75) 360 510

Victoria Post
21 Coppin Grove
Hawthorn, Victoria 3121
Secondary Education

**Victoria, State College
of**
221 Burwood Highway
Burwood, Victoria 3125

**Victoria, State College
of**
Hastings Rd
Frankston, Victoria 3199

**Victoria Univ. of
Technology**
RMIT Campus
POB 2476
Melbourne
Victoria 3000

**Victoria Univ. of
Technology**
Footscray Campus
POB 63
Footscray, Victoria 3011

**Victoria Univ. of
Technology**
POB 12233
A'Beckett St.
Victoria 3000
*Applied Social Science &
  Communications*
*Other Depts: Health
  Sciences; General
  Studies*

**Victoria Univ. of
Technology**
Western Inst. Campus
POB 315
St Albans, Victoria 3021

**Vocational Guidance
Bureau**
159 Auburn St.
Goulburn, NSW 2580

**Warrington Park Y & C
Services**
Great Western Highway
St Mary's, NSW 2760

Watkins Medical Centre
225 Wickham Terrace
Brisbane
Queensland 4000

**Western Australia, Univ.
of**
Nedlands, WA 6009
Psychology, Dept. of
*Other Depts: Education
  Dept.; Human
  Movement & Rec.
  Studies; Counselling
  Services*
Dept. Head: Dr Chris
  Pratt
Phone: (61) (9) 380 3247
Fax: (61) (9) 380 1006
Telex: AA92992
Email: chris@
  psy.uwa.oz.au

Western Sydney, Univ. of
POB 1000
St Mary's, NSW 2760
*Nursing & Community
  Studies (Hawkesbury)*
*Other Depts: Community
  & Welfare Studies
  (Macarthur); Education
  & Language Studies
  (Macarthur); Education;
  Humanities & Applied
  Social Sciences (Nepean)*

Westmead Hospital
Westmead, NSW 2145
*Clinical Psychology, Dept.
  of*
Dept. Head: Prof. Stephen
  Touyz
Phone: (61) (2) 633 6686
Fax: (61) (2) 893 9062
Telex: AA120298

Woden Valley Hospital
Yamba Drive
Woden, ACT 2606
Psychology 11
Dept. Head: Dr M.
Consuelo
Barreda-Hanson
Phone: (61) (6) 244 2045
Fax: (61) (6) 285 3127

Wollongong, Univ. of
POB 1144
Wollongong, NSW 2500
Psychology Dept.
Other Depts: Counselling
Service

Wolston Park Hospital
Univ. of Queensland
Wacol
Queensland 4076
Psychology Service
Dept. Head: Michael Free
Phone: (61) (7) 271 8489
Fax: (61) (7) 271 4008

Workcover Authority of
NSW
Locked Bag 10
Clarence St.
Sydney
NSW 2001
Dept. Head: Dr Richard
Teo
Phone: (61) (2) 370 5123
Fax: (61) (2) 370 6104

AUSTRIA

Bundesinst. f.
Gehörlosenbildung
Maygasse 25
1130 Wien

Graz, Univ.
Auenbruggerplatz 2
8036 Graz
Medizinsche Psychologie,
Inst. f.

Graz, Univ.
Glacisstrasse 23
8010 Graz
Psychologie, Inst. f.

Graz, Univ.
Hans-Sachs-Gasse 3/2
8010 Graz
Other Depts: Inst. f.
Erziehungswissen-
schaften, Abt. f. Päd.
Psychologie
Dept. Head: Prof. Dr L.
Blöschl
Phone: (43) (316) 380
2550

Graz, Univ.
Schubertstrasse 6a
8010 Graz
Abt. f. Klinische
Psychologie

Graz, Univ.
Univ. platz 2
A-8010 Graz
Psychologie, Inst. f.
Dept. Head: Prof. Dr
Gerold Mikula
Phone: (43) (316) 380
5110
Fax: (43) (316) 382130
Email: mikula@
edvz.uni-graz.ada.at

Heilpädagogische
Station
Krottendorferstrasse 60
8052 Graz

Innsbruck Univ.
Peter Mayr-strasse 1a
6020 Innsbruck
Psychologie, Inst. f.

Innsbruck Univ.
Sillgasse 8/1
A-6020 Innsbruck
Past. Psychologisches Abt.

Johannes Kepler Univ.
Linz
A-4045 Linz/Auhof
Dept. Head: Prof.
Hermann
Brandstatter
Phone: (43) (732) 2468
Fax: (43) (732) 2468
Telex: 22323
Email: aearn@ k220270

Johannnes Kepler Univ.
Linz
A-4040 Linz/Auhof
Inst. f. Päd. und
Psychologie, Abt. f. Päd.
Psychologie und
Bildungswissenschaft
Dept. Head: Prof. Dr Karl
H. Seifert
Phone: (43) (732) 2468
Fax: (43) (732) 2468

Klagenfurt Univ.
Univ. sstrasse 67
9202 Klagenfurt
Psychologie, Inst. f.

Kuratorium f.
Verkehrssicherheit
Zweigstelle Salzburg
Südtiroler Platz 3
5021 Salzburg

Kuratorium f.
Verkehrssicherheit
Annichstrasse 24
6020 Innsbruck

Landesarbeitsamt
Berufsberatung
Siebenstädterstrasse
23
A-5020 Salzburg

Landesnervenklinik
Salzburg
Ignaz-Harrerstrasse
5020 Salzburg

Linz Univ.
A-4040 Linz Auhof
Päd. Psychologisches
Inst.

Magistrat Graz
Tummelplatz 9/I
8010 Graz
Psychologische
Beratungstelle

Medizinsche
Psychologie, Inst. f.
Univ. Wien
Lazarettgasse 14
1090 Wien
Medizin. Fak.

Medizinsche
Psychologie u.
Psychotherapie,
Inst. f.
Auenburgerplatz 22
8010 Graz

Neurologische Univ.
klinik
Währinger Gürtel 18-20,
6A
1090 Wien
Neuropsychology Dept.
Dept. Head: Prof. Dr
Rudolf Quatember
Phone: (43) (222) 40400
Fax: (43) (222) 40400

Neurologisches
Krankenhaus
Rosenhügel
Riedelgasse 5
1130 Wien
Kinderabteilung

Neuropsychiatrie des
Kinder u.
Jugendalters,
Uni-Klinik f.
Wöhringergürtel 74-6
1090 Wien

Pädagogische Akad.
Georgiengasse 85
8020 Graz

Pädagogische Akad. d.
Bundes
Kaplanhofstrasse 40
4020 Linz

Pädagogische Akad. d.
Diözese
Salesianumweg 3
4020 Linz
Dept. Head: Dr Siegfried
Wlasaty
Phone: (43) (732) 772666
Fax: (43) (732) 772666

Psychiatrisches
Krankenhaus
Baumgartner Höhe 1
1140 Wien

Psychologie, Inst. f.
Liebiggasse 5
1010 Wien
Dept. Head: Prof. Dr
Giselher Guttmann
Phone: (43) (222) 40103
Fax: (43) (222) 402 7900
Email: a6213daj@
awiuni11.bitnet

Psychologie, Inst. f.
Liebiggasse 5
A1010 Wien
Developmental
Psychology, Dept. of
Dept. Head: Prof. Brigitta
Rollett
Phone: (43) (222) 40103

Psychologie, Inst. f.
Liebiggasse 5
A1010 Wien
Methodology, Dept. of
Dept. Head: Prof.
Gerhard Fischer
Phone: (43) (222) 40103

Psychologischer Dienst
Schottenring 24
A1010 Wien

Psychotherapeutische
Ambulanz d. Wiener
Gebietskranken-
kasse
Mariahilfstrasse 85-7
1060 Wien

Rehabilitationszentrum
f. Herz- u. Kreislaufer-
krankungen
7431 Bad Tatzmanns-
dorf

Rehabilitationszentrum-
Meidling
Kundratstrasse 37
1120 Wien
Psychologische Station

Rheumaklinik
Oberammergau
Hubertusstrasse 40
8103 Oberammergau

Salzburg, Univ. of
Akademiestrasse 22
5020 Salzburg
Psychologie, Inst. f.
Dept. Head: Prof. Dr
Wolfgang Klimesch
Phone: (43) (662) 8044
Fax: (43) (662) 8044

Salzburg, Univ. of
Ignaz-Harrer-Strasse 79
A-5020 Salzburg
Forensic Psychiatry
Inst.
Dept. Head: Prof.
Bernhard Mitterauer
Phone: (43) (662) 8044
3850
Fax: (43) (662) 8044 3860
Email: mitter@
edv2.uni-salzburg.ada.at

Schulpsycholog.
Beratungstelle f.
berufsbildende m/h
Schulen
Strozzigasse 2/4
1080 Wien

Schulversuche und
Schulentwicklung,
Zentrum f.
Hans Sachs-Gasse 14/III
A-8010 Graz
*Abt. II / Päd. Psychol. Inst.
Dept. Head: Dr Günther
Grogger*
Phone: (43) (316) 8287 330
Fax: (43) (316) 8287 336

Sozialarbeit, Akad. f.
Freytaggasse 32, 1210
Wien

Technische Univ. Wien
Thersianumgasse 27
1130 Wien

Wien, Univ.
Kinderspitalgasse 15
1095 Wien
Umwelthygiene, Inst. f.

Zentrum f. Amb. Rehab.
d. PV-Ang.
Wehlistrasse 127
1020 Wien

AZERBAIJAN

Baku State University
Ul. Patrisa Lumumba 23
Baku
370073 Azerbaidzhan
Psychology, Dept. of

BAHRAIN

Arabian Gulf Univ.
POB 26671, Manama
Psychology, Dept. of

**Arts, Science &
Education, Univ. Coll.
of**
POB 1082
Psychology Dept.

Bahrain, Univ. of
POB 32038, Isa Town
Psychology, Dept. of

BANGLADESH

Chittagong, Univ. of
University Post Office
Chittagong
Psychology, Dept. of

Dhaka, Univ. of
Ramna
Dhaka -1000
Psychology, Dept. of
Dept. Head: Prof. M.
Anisur Rahman

Jahangirnagar Univ.
Savar, Dhaka
Psychology, Dept. of

Rajshahi, Univ. of
Rajshahi
Psychology, Dept. of
Dept. Head: Dr
Mozammel Huq
Phone: (880) (721) PB X
6041 9/425

BELARUS

Gomel State Univ.
Sovetskaya ul. 104
Gomel
246699
Psychology, Dept. of

Grodno State Univ.
Ul. Ozheshko 22
Grodno, 230023

Lenin State Univ.
Leninskii prospekt 4
Minsk 220080

BELGIUM

**Antwerpen, Univ.
Ziekenhuis**
Wilrijkstraat 10
B 2650 Edegem
Clinical Psychology Dept.
Dept. Head: Chris Schotte
Phone: (32) (3) 829 11 11
Fax: (32) (3) 829 05 20

BCTP
Meir 21, bus 12
2000 Antwerpen
Psychology Dept.
Dept. Head: Herman
Verbraecken
Phone: (32) (3) 232 39 49
Fax: (32) (3) 226 10 95

**Bruxelles, Centre de
Guidance Ville de**
rue Ste Catherine 11
1000 Bruxelles

Bruxelles, Univ. Libre de
Ave. Fr. Roosevelt 50
1050 Bruxelles
Sciences Psychologiques
et Pedagogiques, Fac. de
Dept. Head: Prof. Alex
Lefebvre
Phone: (32) (3) 650 32 68
Fax: (32) (3) 650 31 36

Bruxelles, Univ. Libre de
Route de Lennik 808
1070 Bruxelles
Ecole de Santé Publique

Bruxelles, Vrije Univ.
Pleinlaan 2
1050 Bruxelles
Psychology &
Educational Sciences
Dept. Head: Prof. H.
Slooee
Phone: (32) (2) 641 25 17

**Centre d'Enseignement
et de Traîtement
Différenciés**
Ave. Albert Dumont 40
1200 Bruxelles

CRS
Bruynstroot
B-1120 Bruxelles (NoH)
Psychological Research
Section
Dept. Head: N Wauters
Phone: (32) (2) 268 0050
Fax: (32) (2) 268 0050

**Etudes Psychologiques,
Les - Centre de
Recherches**
rue Edith Cavell 21
1180 Bruxelles
Centre Petite Enfance et
Famille
Other Depts: Centre pour
Adolescents
Dept. Head: Jacqueline
Danze
Phone: (32) (2) 343 63 92

Leuven, Univ. of
A. Z. Gasthuisberg
Herestraat
3000 Leuven
Neuro- en
Psychofysiologie, Lab.
voor

Leuven, Univ. of
Tiensestraat 102
B-3000
Leuven
Psychology, Dept. of
Dept. Head: Prof. Eddy
Van Aveemaet
Phone: (32) (16) 28 56
11
Fax: (32) (16) 28 60 00

Liège, Univ. de l'Etat à
Sart Tilman B18
4000 Liège
Psychologie, Institut de

Limburgs Univ.
Centrum
Univ. Campus
3590 Diepenbeek
Health Psychology
Section
Dept. Head: Prof. Jan
Vinck
Phone: (32) (11) 22 99 61
Fax: (32) (11) 22 32 84
Email: 39948@ luc.b

Louvain, Univ. Cat.
de
Voie de Roman Pays 20
1348 Louvain-la-Neuve
Psychologie et des
Sciences de l'Education,
Fac. de
Dept. Head:
Jacques-Philippe
Leyens
Phone: (32) (10) 47 43 69
Fax: (32) (10) 47 48 34
Email: -responsable@
psp.ucl.ac.be

Louvain, Univ. Cat.
de
Cliniques St. Luc
Ave. Hippocrate 10
1200 Bruxelles
Neurologie Dept.

Mons, Univ. de l'Etat à
Faculté des Sciences
Psycho-pédagogiques
Place du Parc 22
7000 Mons
Orthopédagogie, Dépt. d'
Dept. Head: Magerotte
Ghislain
Phone: (32) (65) 37 31 77
Fax: (32) (65) 37 30 54
Telex: 57764 ue mons b
Email: pmagerot@
bmsuem11.bitnet

Psychiatrisch Univ.
Centrum St. Jozef
Leuvensesteenweg 517
3070 Kortenberg
Clinical Psychology Dept.

Rijksuniv. Gent
H. Dunantlaan 2
9000 Gent
Fac. van de
Psychologische en
Pedagogische
Wetenschappen

Vrije Univ. Brussel
Pleinlaan 2
Gebouw. C
1050 Brussel
Genetische Psychologie,
Dienst voor
Other Depts: Centrum
voor Organisatie en
Comsumptier-
psychologie

William Lennox, Centre
Neurologique
6 Allée de Clerlande
1340 Ottignies
Neuropsychology, Dept.
of
Dept. Head: Prof. Th. de
Barsy
Phone: (32) (10) 43 02 11
Fax: (32) (10) 41 19 72

BENIN

Benin, Univ. Nat. du
Abomey-Calavi
BP 526
Cotonou
Psychology, Dept. of

BOLIVIA

Beni, Mariscal José
Ballivián, Univ.
Técnica del
Casilla de Correo 38
Trinidad
Beni
Psychology, Dept, of

Boliviana, Univ. Cat.
CP 4805
La Paz
Psychology, Dept, of

Gabriel Renée Moreno,
Univ. Autónoma
CP 702
Sta. Cruz de la Sierra
Psychology, Dept, of

Juan Misael Saracho,
Univ. Autónoma
CP 51
Tarija
Psychology, Dept, of
Dept. Head: Lic. Oscar
Acha Espinoza
Phone: (591) 23825

Oruro, Univ. Técnica de
CC 49
Avda 6 de Octubre
Oruro
Psychology, Dept, of

San Andres, Univ.
Mayor de
Casilla 6042
La Paz
Psychology, Dept, of

**San Francisco Xavier
de Chuquisaca, Univ.
Mayor, Real y
Pontificia**
Apdo 212, Sucre
Psychology, Dept, of

**San Simon, Univ. Mayor
de**
Casilla 992
Cochabamba
Psychology, Dept, of

Siglo XX, Univ. Nac. de
CP 27
Llallagua
Psychology, Dept, of

**Tomas Frías, Univ.
Autónoma**
Casilla 36, Petosí
Psychology, Dept, of

BOSNIA AND
HERZEGOVINA

**Banja Luci,
Univ.'D.P.Stari' u**
78000 Banja Luka
Trg Palih Boraca 2/II
Psychology, Dept. of

**Mostaru, Univ. 'D.
Bijedic' u**
88000 Mostar
Trg '14 Februar' b.b.
Psychology, Dept. of

Sarajevo, Univ. u
71000 Sarajevo
Obala vojvode Stepe 7/II
Post Fah 186
Psychology, Dept. of

Tuzli, Univ. u
75000 Tuzla
M. Fizovia-Fiska 6
Bosnia-Herzegovina
Psychology, Dept. of

BRAZIL

Acre, Univ. Fed. do
CP 500, Campus
Universitario
BP 364, Km 04
69900 Rio Branco
Acre
Psychology, Dept. of

Alagoas, Univ. Fed. de
Campus A. C. Simöes
BR/101 norte, Km 14
Cidade Universitária
570810 Maceió AL
Psychology, Dept. of

Amazonas, Univ. do
Av. Getúlio Vargas 381
Centro
69013 Manaus AM
Psychology, Dept. of

Bahia, Univ. Fed. da
Rua Augusto Viana s/n
Canela
40000 Salvador, BA
Psychology, Dept. of

**Blumenau, Univ.
Regional de**
Rua Antônio da Veiga 140
CP 7e
89010 Blumenau, SC
Psychology, Dept. of

Brasília, Univ. de
CP 15-2951
70910 Brasília
DF
Psychology, Inst. of

Bra⌐ Cubas, Univ. de
Rua Fra. Rodgrigues
Filho 1233
CP 511
08730 Mogi das Cruzes
SP
Psychology, Dept. of

**Campinas, Pont. Univ.
Cat. de**
CP 317
Rua Marechal Deodoro
1099
13100 Campinas
SP
Psychology, Dept. of

**Campinas, Univ.
Estadual de**
Cidade Univ. 'Zeferino
Vaz'
CP 1170
13081 Campinas
SP
*Psychology & Psychiatry,
Dept. of*
*Dept. Head: Prof. Dr.
Dorgival Caetano*
Phone: (55) (192) 39 4819
Fax: (55) (192) 39 4717

Caxias do Sul, Univ. de
CP 1352
Rua Fr. Getúlio Vargas
1130
95070 Caxias do Sul
RS
Psychology, Dept. of
*Dept. Head: Maria de
Lourdes Skrebski*
Phone: (55) (54) 222 4133
Fax: (55) (54) 222 8223
Telex: 543734

Ceara, Univ. Estadual do
Campus do Itaperí
Av. Paranjana 1700
60715 Fortaleza
CE
Psychology, Dept. of

Ceara, Univ. Fed. do
Av. da Univ. 2853
CP 1000
60000 Fortaleza
CE
Psychology, Dept. of

**Espirito Santo, Univ.
Fed. do**
Av. Fernando Ferrari
Goiabeiras
29000 Vitória
ES
Psychology, Dept. of

**Feira de Santana, Univ.
Est. de**
BR 116, Km 3
Campus Universitário
44030 Feira de Santana
Bahia
Psychology, Dept. of

**Fluminense, Univ. Fed.
de**
CP 1050
Rua Miguel de Frias 9
Icaraí
24220 Niterói, RJ
Psychology, Dept. of

Fortaleza, Univ. de
CP 1258
Av. Washington Soares
1321
Edson Queiroz Block
60810 Fortaleza, CE
Psychology, Dept. of

Gama Filho, Univ. de
Rua Manoel Vitorino
625
Piedade 20740
Rio de Janeiro
RJ
Psychology, Dept. of

**Getulio Vargas
Fundacio**
Praia de Botafogo 190
Sala 1108
Botafogo
22250 Rio de Janeiro
*Superior de Estudos e
Pesquisas Psicossociais,
Inst.*

Goiás, Univ. Cat. de
Av. Universitária
CP 86
74000 Goiânia, GO
Psychology, Dept. of

Goiás, Univ. Fed. de
CP 131
Campus Samambaia
Km 7
74000 Goiânia, GO
Psychology, Dept. of

**Hospital da Univ. Fed.
de Sta. Maria**
Campus Universitário
Sta. Maria, RS

Ijuí, Univ. de
CP 560,Rua São
Francisco 501
Bairro St. Geraldo
98700 Ijuí
Rio Grande de Sul
Psychology, Dept. of

Itaúna, Univ. de
Rua Capitão, Vicente 10
CP 100
35680 Itaúna, MG
Psychology, Dept. of

**Juiz de Fora, Univ. Fed.
de**
Rua Benjamin Constant
790
CP 656
36100 Juiz de Fora
MG
Psychology, Dept. of

**Julio de Mesquita
Filho, Univ. Estadual
Paulista**
Praça da Sé 108
Centro
01001 São Paulo
SP
Psychology, Dept. of

**Londrina, Univ.
Estadual de**
CP 6001
Celso Garcia Cid/PR
445-Km 370
Campus Universitário
86051 Londrina, PR
Psychology, Dept. of

Maranhao, Univ. Fed. do
Largo dos Amores 351
65020 São Luís, MA
Psychology, Dept. of

**Maringá, Fund. Univ.
Est. de**
Av. Colombo 3690
CP 331
87020 Maringá
Psychology, Dept. of

**Mato Grosso, Fund.
Univ. Fed. de**
CP 649
Cidade Univ.
Campo Grande, MT
Psychology, Dept. of

**Mato Grosso, Univ. Fed.
de**
Av. Fernando Corrês s/n
78000 Cuiabá, MT
Psychology, Dept. of

**Minas Gerais, Pont.
Univ. Cat. de**
Av. Dom Jose Gaspar 500
CP 2686
30550 Belo Horizonte
MG
Psychology, Dept. of

**Minas Gerais, Univ.
Fed. de**
Cidade Universitária
Pampulha, CP 1621
31270 Belo Horizonte,
MG
Psychology, Dept. of

Mogi das Cruzes, Univ. de
CP 411
Cândido Xavier de
  Almeida Souza 200
08780 Mogi das Cruzes
SP
Psychology, Dept. of

Ouro Preto, Univ. Fed. de
Rua Diogo de Vasconcelos
122
35400 Ouro Preto, MG
Psychology, Dept. of

Pará, Univ. Fed. do
Av. Augusto Corrêa
s/n Campus Universitário
Bairro do Guamá
66060 Belém, PA
Psychology, Dept. of

Paraíba, Univ. Fed. de
Campus Universitário
58059 João Pessoa, PB
Psychology, Dept. of

Paraná, Pont. Univ. Cat. do
Rua Imac. Conceição 1150
Prado Velho
CP 670
80210 Curitiba, PR
Psychology, Dept. of

Paraná, Univ. Fed. do
Rua 15 de Novembro 1299
CP 441
80001 Curitiba
PR
Psychology, Dept. of

Passo Fundo, Univ. de
Bairro São José
CP 567
99050 Passo Fundo
RS
Psychology, Dept. of

Pelotas, Univ. Cat. de
Rua Félix da Cunha 412
CP 402
96010 Pelotas
RS
Psychology, Dept. of

Pelotas, Univ. Fed. de
Campus Universitário
96159 Pelotas
RS
Psychology, Dept. of

Pernambuco, Fund. de Ensino Superior, Univ. de Pernambuco
Av. Agamenon
  Magalhães
s/n
Santo Amaro
50040 Recife
PE
Psychology, Dept. of

Pernambuco, Univ. Cat. de
Rua do Príncipe 526
Boa Vista
50058 Recife
PE
Psychology, Dept. of

Pernambuco, Univ. Fed. de
Av. Prof. Moraes Rego
Cidade Universitária
50739 Recife
PE
Psychology, Dept. of

Pernambuco, Univ. Fed. Rural de
CP 2071
Rua D. Manoel de
  Medeiros s/n
Dois Irmãos
50000 Recife
PE
Psychology, Dept. of

Petrópolis, Univ. Cat. de
Rua Benjamin Constant
213
Centro, CP 90944
25621 Petrópolis, RJ
Psychology, Dept. of

Piauí, Univ. Fed. do
Cidade Universitária
Bairro Ininga
64000 Teresina, PI
Psychology, Dept. of

Piracicaba, Univ. Metodista de
Rua Rangel Pestana 762
CP 68
13400 Piracicaba, SP
Psychology, Dept. of

Ponta Grossa, Univ. Estadual de
Praça Santos Andrade s/n
CP 992-993
84100 Ponta Grossa, PR
Psychology, Dept. of

Rio de Janeiro, Univ. do Estado do
Rua São Fr. Xavier 524
Maracanã
20550 Rio de Janeiro
RJ
Psychology, Dept. of

Rio de Janeiro, Univ. Fed. do
Av. Brig. Trompowski s/n
21941 Rio de Janeiro
RJ
Psychology, Dept. of

Rio de Janeiro, Univ. Fed. Rural do
Km 47
Rodovia Rio São Paulo
23851 Seropédica
Rio de Janeiro
Psychology, Dept. of

**Rio de Janeiro, Pont.
Univ. Cat. do**
Rua Marquês de São
 Vicente 225
Gávea
22453 Rio de Janeiro, RJ
Psychology, Dept. of

**Rio dos Sinos, Univ. do
Vale do**
Av. Unisinos 950
CP 275
93020 São Leopoldo, RS
Psychology, Dept. of

**Rio Grande do Norte,
Univ. Fed. do**
Cidade Universitária
s/n
Lagoa Nova
59000 Natal, RN
Psychology, Dept. of

**Rio Grande do Norte,
Univ. Reg. do**
Cidade Universitária
CP 70
59600 Mossoró, RN
Psychology, Dept. of

**Rio Grande do Sul,
Pont. Univ. Cat. do**
Av. Ipiranga 6681
CP 1429
90620 Porto Alegre, RS
Psychology, Dept. of

**Rio Grande do Sul,
Univ. Fed. do**
Av. Paulo Gama 110
90049 Porto Alegre, RS
Psychology, Dept. of

**Rio Grande, Fund. Univ.
do**
Rua Eng. Alfredo Huch 475
CP 474, 96200 Rio Grande
RS
Psychology, Dept. of

**Rondonia, Fund. Univ.
Fed. de**
Av. Presidente Dutra 2965
78900 Porto Velho, RO
Psychology, Dept. of

**Sagrado Coração, Univ.
do**
Rua Irm Arminda 10-50
CP 511
17001 Bauru, SP
Psychology, Dept. of

São Carlos, Univ. Fed. de
Rodovia Washington Luiz
Km 235, CP 676
13560 São Carlos, SP
Psychology, Dept. of
*Dept. Head: Dr Celso
 Goyos*
Phone: (55) (162) 748361
Fax: (55) (162) 712081
Telex: 162369 SCUF-BR

São Francisco, Univ. e
Av. Senador Lacerda
 Franco, 458
CEP: 13. 250
ITABA, São Paulo
*Centro Clínico de
 Psicologia*
Phone: (55) (11) 435 1104

São Francisco, Univ. de
Rua Alexandre Rodrigues
 Barbosa
45 - ITATIBA, São Paulo
Psychology, Dept. of
*Dept. Head: Konrad
 Lindmeier*
Phone: (55) (11) 435 1262
Fax: (55) (11)435 1933

**São Paulo, Pont. Univ.
Cat. de**
Rua Monte Alegre 984
Perdizes
05014 São Paulo, SP
Psychology, Fac. of

**São Paulo, Univ. de &
FFCL de S. André**
Caixa Postal 11. 454
São Paulo, SP
Psychology, Inst. of

São Paulo, Univ. de
CP 8191
05508 São Paulo, SP
Psychology, Inst. of

Salvador, Univ. Cat. do
Praça 2 de Julho 7
40000 Salvador, BA
Psychology, Dept. of

Sergipe, Univ. Fed. de
Cidade Universitária
Rosa Elze
49100 São Cristóvão, SE
Psychology, Dept. of

**Sta. Catarina, Univ.
Fed. de**
Cidade Universitária
CP 476
88045 Trindade
Florianópolis, SC
Psychology, Dept. of
*Dept. Head: Rafael
 Raffaelli*
Phone: (55) (482) 31 9402
Fax: (55) (482) 31 9572
Email: psi1rrl@ brufsc

**Sta. Catarina, Univ. do
Est. de**
Cidade Universitária
Av. Madre Benvenuta 499
CP D-34, Itacorubi
88000 Florianópolis, SC
Psychology, Dept. of

**Sta. Cecília dos
Bandeirantes, Univ. de**
Rua Luiz de Camões 64
Encruzilhada, CP 1213
11015 Santos, SP
Psychology, Dept. of

Sta. Maria, Univ. Fed. de
Rua Mal. Floriano
  Peixoto, 1750
97. 060 Sta. Maria
RS
Psychology, Inst. of
Dept. Head: Prof.
  Alberto Manuel
  Quintana
Phone: (55) 221 8987
Fax: (55) 221 6959
Telex: 230 UFSM

Taubaté, Univ. de
Av Tiradentes 500
12030 Taubaté
SP
Psychology, Dept. of
Dept. Head: Prof. Helena
  Maria Cursino de
  Moura Hirye
Phone: (55) (122)
  327555
Fax: (55) (122) 327660

Uberlândia, Univ. Fed. de
Av. Engenheiro Diniz 1178
CP 593
38400 Uberlândia
MG
Psychology, Dept. of

Viçosa, Univ. Fed. de
Av. P. H. Rolfa s/n
36570 Viçosa MG
Psychology, Dept. of

BULGARIA

Plovdisvski Univ. 'Paisij Hilendarski'
4000 Plovdiv
Car Asen 24
Psychology, Dept. of

Sofiiski Univ. 'Kliment Ohridsky'
1504 Sofia, Ruski 15
Philosophy, Fac. of

Veliko Tarnovski Univ. 'Kiril i Metodii'
Veliko Tarnovo
T. Tarnovski 1
Psychology, Dept. of

BURKINA FASO

Ouagadougou, Univ. de
BP 7021
Ouagadougou
Psychology, Dept. of
Dept. Head: Maxime
  Koudougou Kabre
Phone: (226) 307813
Fax: (226) 307242
Telex: 55270BF uniovaga

BURUNDI

Burundi, Univ. du
BP 1550
Bujumbura
Psychology, Department of

CAMEROON

Douala, Centre Univ. de
BP 2701
Douala
Psychology, Dept. of

Dschang, Centre Univ. de
POB 96
Dschang
Psychology, Dept. of

Ngaoundéré, Centre Univ. de
BP 454
Ngaoundéré
Psychology, Dept. of

Yaoundé, Univ. de
BP 337
Yaoundé
Psychology, Dept. of

CANADA

Acadia Univ.
Wolfville
Nova Scotia
B0P 1X0
Psychology, Dept. of
Dept. Head: Dr Myles
Genest
Phone: (1) (902) 542
2201
Fax: (1) (902) 542 3323

Addiction Research Foundation
33 Russell St.
Toronto
Ontario
M5S 2S1
Dept. Head: Dr Helen M.
Annis
Phone: (1) (416) 595
6022
Fax: (1) (416) 595 5017

C

Alberta Children's Hospital
1820 Richmond Rd. S.W.
Calgary
Alberta
T2T 5C7
Behavioural Research
Unit
Dept. Head: Dr Bonnie J.
Kaplan
Phone: (1) (403) 229
7365
Fax: (1) (403) 229 7221

Alberta Hospital
POB 307
Edmonton
Alberta
T5J 2J7
Psychology, Dept. of
Dept. Head: Dr Charles
N. Banner
Phone: (1) (403) 472
5392
Fax: (1) (403) 472 5291

Alberta Hospital
POB 1000
Ponoka
Alberta
T0C 2H
Psychology, Dept. of

Alberta Research Council
POB 8330, Postal Station
F
Edmonton
Alberta
T6H 5X2
Phone: (1) (403) 450
5111

Alberta Univ. Hospital
8440-112 St.
Edmonton
Alberta
T6G 2B7
Clinical Psychology, Dept.
of
Dept. Head: J. G. Eustace
Phone: (1) (403) 492 6896
Fax: (1) (403) 492 0316

Alberta, Univ. of
6-123D Education North
Bldg.
Edmonton
Alberta
T6G 2G5
Developmental
Disabilities Centre
Other Depts: Educational
Psychology; Nursing;
Theoretical Psychology
Dept. Head: Dr J. P. Das
Phone: (1) (403) 492 4505
Fax: (1) (403) 492 1318
Email: useroops@
ualtamts.bitnet
Email: useroops@
mts.ucs.ualta.ca.internet

Alberta, Univ. of
Bio Sciences Bldg.
Edmonton
Alberta
T6G 2E9
Psychology, Dept. of
Dept. Head: Eugene C.
Lechelt
Phone: (1) (403) 492 5216
Fax: (1) (403) 492 1768

Algoma Univ. College
Sault Ste-Marie
Ontario
P6A 2G
Dept. Head: Dr Linda
Sorensen
Phone: (1) (705) 949 2301
Fax: (1) (705) 949 6583

Allen Memorial Inst.
1025 Pine Ave. West
Montréal
Québec, H3A 1A1
Psychology, Dept. of
Dept. Head: Ian F.
  Bradley
Phone: (1) (514) 842 1231
Fax: (1) (514) 843 1644

Applied Behaviour
Analysis Program
Southwestern Regional
  Centre
R. R. # 1, Blenheim
Ontario N0P 1A0
Clinical Dept.
Dept. Head: Dr F. J.
  Barrera
Phone: (1) (519) 676 5431
Fax: (1) (519) 676 5836
Email: MCSS Network
  (Ontario) Barrera@
  fsrc.1a

Applied Research
Consulting House
2021 Cliff Rd.
Mississauga, Ontario
L5A 3N7

Arbutus Society for
Children
2400 Arbutus Rd.
Victoria
British Columbia
V8N 1V7
Psychology, Dept. of
Dept. Head: Dr Michael
  Joschko
Phone: (1) (604) 721 6797
Fax: (1) (604) 721 6837

Atlantic Child
Guidance Centre
Garden Park
1464 Tower Rd.
Halifax
Nova Scotia B3H 4L4

Beechgrove Children's
Centre
POB 777
Kingston
Ontario
K7L 5H1
Dept. Head: Dr Leonard
  Harris
Phone: (1) (613) 549 5600
Fax: (1) (613) 549 3635

Behaviour Science
Research & Education
Divn.
Surrey Place Centre
2 Surrey Place
Toronto
Ontario M5S 2C2
Dept. Head: Maurice A.
  Feldman
Phone: (1) (416) 925 5141
Fax: (1) (416) 923 8476

Bell Canada
620 Belmont, F. 11
Montréal
Québec
H3B 2M3
HQ Management
  Sciences

Bishop's Univ.
Lennoxville
Québec
J1M 1Z
Psychology, Dept. of

Brandon Univ.
270 18th St.
Brandon
Manitoba
R7A 6A9
Psychology, Dept. of
Dept. Head: Dr B.
  Corenblum
Phone: (1) (204) 727 9677
Fax: (1) (204) 726 4573
Email: bubarry@
  ccm.umanitoba.ca

British Columbia, Univ.
of
2075 Wesbrook Place
Vancouver
British Columbia
V6T 1W5
Psychology, Dept. of
Other Depts: Education
Dept. Head: Prof.
  Richard C. Tees
Phone: (1) (604) 822 3245
Fax: (1) (604) 822 6923
Email: richard-tees@
  mtsg.ubc.ca

British Columbia, Univ.
of
Vancouver
British Columbia
V6T 2A1
Psychology, Divn. of
Dept. Head: Peter D.
  McLean
Phone: (1) (604) 822 7333
Fax: (1) (604) 822 7756

British Columbia, Univ.
of
Vancouver
British Columbia
V6T 1Z5
Educ. Psychology &
  Special Educ. Dept.
Dept. Head: Dr Patricia
  Arlin
Phone: (1) (604) 822 8229
Fax: (1) (604) 822 3302

Brock Univ.
St Catharines
Ontario, L2S 3A1
Psychology, Dept. of
Other Depts: Child
  Studies; Education
Dept. Head: Linda
  Rose-Krasnor
Phone: (1) (416) 688
  5550
Fax: (1) (416) 688 6922

**Calgary District
Hospital Group**
2210-2nd St. S. W.
Calgary
Alberta
T2S 1S6
Psychology, Dept. of
Dept. Head: William G.
  McElheran
Phone: (1) (403) 541 2125
Fax: (1) (403) 541 2595

**Calgary General
Hospital**
841 Centre Ave. East
Calgary
Alberta
T2E 0A1
Psychology, Dept. of
Other Depts: Forensic
  Services G-1

Calgary, Univ. of
2500 Univ. Dr. N. W.
Calgary
Alberta
T2N 1N4
Psychology, Dept. of
Other Depts: Medicine;
  Student Counselling
  Services; Social Welfare;
  Educational Psychology
Dept. Head: Dr Donald
  W. Kline
Phone: (1) (403) 220 5561
Fax: (1) (403) 282 8249

**Camp Hill Medical
Centre**
1763 Robie St.
Halifax
Nova Scotia
B3H 2G2
Psychology Dept.
Dept. Head: Dr
  Christopher D. Bilsbury
Phone: (1) (902) 420
  2509
Fax: (1) (902) 420 2684

**Canadian Mem.
Chiropractice
College**
1900 Bayview
Toronto
Ontario
M4G 3E6
Dept. Head: Gregory
  Hamovitch
Phone: (1) (416) 482 2340
Fax: (1) (416) 482 9745

**Cape Breton, Univ.
College of**
Sydney
Nova Scotia
B1P 6L2
Psychology, Dept. of
Dept. Head: Dr Gary
  Collier
Phone: (1) (902) 539
  5300
Fax: (1) (902) 562 0119

**Cariboo, Univ. College
of the**
POB 3010
Kamloops
British Columbia
V2C 5N3
Dept. Head: Dr Danalee
  Goldthwaite
Phone: (1) (604) 828
  5512
Fax: (1) (604) 371 5510
Email: dgoldthwaite@
  cariboo.bc.ca

Carleton Univ.
Ottawa
Ontario
K1S 5B6
Psychology, Dept. of
Dept. Head: Bill Jones
Phone: (1) (613) 788
  2600
Fax: (1) (613) 788 3667
Email: bill-jones@
  carleton.ca

**Centracare Saint John
Inc.**
POB 3220
Stn. B, St John
New Brunswick, E2M
  4H7
Psychology Dept.
Other Depts: Research
  Dept: Dr Sonja Ziganaw
Dept. Head: James K.
  Horgan
Phone: (1) (506) 635 7550
Fax: (1) (506) 635 7550

**Centre de Dev.
Corrective**
1300 Montée St-François
Laval, Québec, H7C 1S5
Psychologie, Service de

**Centre de
Réadaptation**
Lethbridge
7005 Ouest de
  Maisonneuve
Montréal, Québec, H4B 1T

**Centre Hospitalier
Douglas**
6875 Lasalle Blvd
Verdun
Québec, H4H 1R3
Geriatric & Medical
  Services
Other Depts: Eating
  Disorder Unit
Dept. Head: Dr Erika J.
  Gutbrodt
Phone: (1) (514) 761 6131

**Centre Hospitalier Juif
Sir Mortimer B. Davies**
4333 Côte Ste-Catherine
Montréal
Québec, H3T 1E4
Psychology Divn.
Dept. Head: Dr Nathan
  Greenberg
Phone: (1) (514) 340 8210

**Centre Hospitalier
Louis-H. Lafontaine**
7401 rue Hochelaga
Montréal
Québec, H1N 3M5
*Dept. Head: Germain
    Lavoie*
Phone: (1) (514) 251 4000
Fax: (1) (514) 251 0533

Charlottetown Centre
Charlottetown
Prince Edward Island
C1A 4Z1
*Early Childhood Ed.,
    Dept. of*

**Chedoke-McMaster
Hospitals**
POB 2000
Hamilton
Ontario
L8N 3Z
*Dept. Head: H. I. J. van
    der Spuy*
Phone: (1) (416) 521 2100
Fax: (1) (416) 521 7938

Child's Place, The
2611 Labelle St.
Windsor
Ontario
N9A 4G4

**Children's Hospital of
Eastern Ontario**
401 Smyth Rd.
Ottawa
Ontario
K1H 8L1
*Other Depts: Cardiology;
    Genetics; Neonatology;
    Neurology;
    Orthopaedics; Social
    Work
Dept. Head: John T.
    Goodman*
Phone: (1) (613) 737 2492
Fax: (1) (613) 738 3216

**Chisholm Educational
Centre**
235 Bowman St.
Hamilton
Ontario, L8S 2T

**Clarke Inst. of
Psychiatry**
250 College St.
Toronto
Ontario, M5T 1R8
*Cognitive Behaviour
    Therapy Unit
Other Depts: Gender
    Identity Clinic;
    Psychology
Dept. Head: Zindel V.
    Segal*
Phone: (1) (416) 979 2221
Fax: (1) (416) 979 0170

**Clarke Inst. of
Psychiatry**
950 Yonge St.
8th Floor
Toronto
Ontario, M4W 2J4
Family Court Clinic

Clinical Inst.
33 Russell St.
Toronto
Ontario, M5S 2S1
*Addiction Research
    Foundation*

Concordia Univ.
1455 de Maisonneuve
    Blvd. West
Montréal
Québec, H3G 1M8
*Psychology, Dept. of
Other Depts: Human
    Dev., Ctr for Research;
    Education
Dept. Head: Norman
    Segalowitz*
Phone: (1) (514) 848 2211
Fax: (1) (514) 848 3494

Dalhousie Univ.
Halifax
Nova Scotia
B3H 4J1
*Psychology, Dept. of
Other Depts: Counselling
    & Psychiatric Serv.
Dept. Head: Dr Richard
    E. Brown*
Phone: (1) (902) 494
    3417
Fax: (1) (902) 494 6585
Email: cgraham@
    adm.dal.ca

Dawson College
535 Viger St.
Montréal
Québec
H2L 2P3

**Dellcrest Children's
Centre**
1645 Sheppard Ave.
    West
Downsview
Ontario
M3M 2X4

Douglas Hospital
4485 Bannantyne Ave.
Verdun
Québec
H4G 1E2

**Dr Everett Chalmers
Hospital**
POB 9000
Fredericton
New Brunswick
E3B 5N5
Psychology Dept.

**Earlscourt Child &
Family Centre**
46 St Clair Gardens
Toronto
Ontario
M6E 3V4

**Environmental
Medicine, Inst. of**
POB 2000
Downsview
Ontario M3M 3B9
Defence & Civil

Foothills Hospital
1403 - 29th St. N. W.
Calgary
Alberta T2N 2T9
Psychology, Dept. of
Other Depts:
Neuropsychology
Dept. Head: Dr Barry D.
Bultz
Phone: (1) (403) 670 1340
Fax: (1) (403) 670 2525

**G. F. Strong
Rehabilitation Centre**
4255 Laurel St.
Vancouver
British Columbia V5Z
2G9

Glendon College
2275 Bayview Ave.
Toronto
Ontario M4N 3M6
Psychology, Dept. of

Glenrose Hospital
10230-111th Ave.
Edmonton
Alberta T5G 0B7
Psychology Dept.
Dept. Head: Sharon Kelly
Phone: (1) (403) 471 7969
Fax: (1) (403) 471 7976

Guelph, Univ. of
Guelph
Ontario N1G 2W1
Psychology Dept.
Dept. Head: Dr Michael
L. Matthews
Phone: (1) (519) 824 4120
Fax: (1) (519 837 8629

**Hamilton Psychiatric
Hospital**
POB 585
Hamilton
Ontario L8N 3K7
Psychology, Dept. of
Dept. Head: Dr Louisa B.
Gembora
Phone: (1) (416) 388 2511
Fax: (1) (416) 385 0702

Health Sciences Centre
St John's
Newfoundland
A1B 3V6
Dept. Head: Olga J. Heath
Phone: (1) (709) 737 7378

**Hospital for Sick
Children**
555 Univ. Ave.
Toronto
Ontario M5G 1X8
Psychology, Dept. of
Dept. Head: Dr Brian
Shaw
Phone: (1) (416) 598 6787
Fax: (1) (416) 598 7505

**Izaak Walton Killam
Hospital**
5850 Univ. Ave.
Halifax
Nova Scotia
B3J 3G9
Psychology, Dept. of
Dept. Head: Dr G. Wayne
MacDonald
Phone: (1) (902) 428 8454
Fax: (1) (902) 428 8826
Email: byrne@ ac.dal.ca

Jewish General Hospital
4333 Côte Ste. Catherine
Montréal
Québec
H3T 1E4
Community Psychiatry
Inst.

Jewish General Hospital
5750 Côte des Neiges
Montréal
Québec
H3T 1E2
Herzl Family Practice

**Joseph Brandt
Memorial Hospital**
1230 North Shore Blvd
Burlington
Ontario
L7R 4C4
Psychiatry, Dept. of

Kingston Penitentiary
POB 22
Kingston
Ontario
K7L 4V7
Psychology Dept.
Phone: (1) (613) 545 8460
Fax: (1) (613) 545 3617

Lakehead Univ.
Thunder Bay
Ontario
P7B 5E1
Dept. Head: Dr Ken
Rotenburg
Phone: (1) (807) 343 8441
Fax: (1) (807) 343 8023

Laurentian Univ.
Ramsay Lake Rd.
Sudbury
Ontario
P3E 2G6
Psychology, Dept. of

Laval Univ.
Sainte Foy
Québec
G1K 7P4
Psychology, School of
Dept. Head: Richard
Cloutier
Phone: (1) (418) 656 5383
Fax: (1) (418) 656 3646

Lethbridge, Univ. of
Lethbridge
Alberta
T1K 3M4
Psychology, Dept. of
Other Depts: Education

London Board of
Education
165 Elmwood Ave.
London
Ontario
N6A 4T5
Dept. Head: Dr George
Phills
Phone: (1) (519) 452 2106
Fax: (1) (519) 455 7648

London Psychiatric
Hospital
POB 2532
London
Ontario
Psychology, Dept. of

Luther Univ. College
Regina
Saskatchewan
S4S 0A2
Psychology, Dept. of
Dept. Head: Paul M.
Antrobus
Phone: (1) (306) 585
5037
Fax: (1) (306) 585 5267

Manitoba, Univ. of
770 Bannatyne Ave.
Winnipeg
Manitoba
R3E 0W3
Psychiatry Dept.,
Behavioural Science
Section
Dept. Head: John L.
Arnett
Phone: (1) (204) 787
3876
Fax: (1) (204) 787 4879

Manitoba, Univ. of
Winnipeg
Manitoba R3T 2N2
Psychology, Dept. of
Dept. Head: Dr Bruce
Tefft
Phone: (1) (204) 474 9338
Fax: (1) (204) 269 3599
Telex: (7) 587721

McGill-Montréal
Children's Hospital
3640 de la Montagne
Montréal
Québec H3G 2A8
Learning Centre

McGill Univ.
1205 Dr Penfield Ave.
Montréal
Québec H3A 1B1
Psychology, Dept. of
Dept. Head: Dr Anthony
Marley
Phone: (1) (514) 398
6100
Fax: (1) (514) 398 4896
Email: anne@
psych.mcgill.ca

McGill Univ.
3700 McTavish St.
Montréal
Québec H3A 1Y2
Educational Psychology
Phone: (1) (514) 398 4240

McMaster Univ.
1280 Main St. West
Hamilton
Ontario L8S 4K1
Psychology Dept.
Dept. Head: Dr Harvey P.
Weingarten
Phone: (1) (416) 525
9140
Fax: (1) (416) 529 6225
Email: psych@
mcmaster.ca

McMaster Univ.
Hamilton
Ontario
L8N 3Z5
Clinical Epidem., Dept. of
Dept. Head: Dr George
Browman
Phone: (1) (416) 525
9140
Fax: (1) (416) 577 0017
Email: townsen@
mcmail.mcmaster.ca

McMaster Univ.
Hamilton
Ontario
L8N 3Z5
Psychiatry, Dept. of
Dept. Head: Dr Edward
Kingstone
Phone: (1) (416) 521
2100
Fax: (1) (416) 521 5083

Mental Health Centre
Oak Ridge Divn.
Penetanguishen
Ontario
L0K 1P0

Mental Health Services
367 Sunset Drive
St Thomas
Ontario
N5P 3V9
Adolescent & Childrens
Comm.

Metropolitan Toronto
Forensic Service
1001 Queen St. W.
Toronto
Ontario
M6J 1H4
Dept. Head: David
Nussbaum
Phone: (1) (416) 535
8501
Fax: (1) (416) 583 4327

Michener Center
POB 5002
Red Deer
Alberta
T4H 5Y5
Psychology, Dept. of

Missisauga Hospital
100 Queensway West
Mississauga
Ontario L5B 1B8
Psychology, Dept. of
Phone: (1) (416) 848 7387
Fax: (1) (416) 848 7140

Moncton, Univ. de
Edifice Taillon
Moncton
New Brunswick
E1A 3E9
Psychologie, Dept. de
Dept. Head: Dr Terez
Retfalvi
Phone: (1) (506) 858 4203
Fax: (1) (506) 858 4585

Montréal Children's
Hospital
2300 Tupper St.
Montréal
Québec H3H 1P3
Psychology, Dept. of
Dept. Head: Dr Philip R.
Zelazo
Phone: (1) (514) 934 4400
Fax: (1) (514) 934 4337

Montréal Inst. for
Human Development
4665 Draper Ave.
Montréal
Québec H4A 2P5

Montréal Neurological
Inst.
3801 University St.
Montréal
Québec
H3A 2B4

Montréal, Univ. de
CP 6128
Montréal OC
H3C 3U7
Physiologie, Dept. de
Dept. Head: Dr Luc
Granger
Phone: (1) (514) 343 6503
Fax: (1) (514) 343 2285

Mount Allison Univ.
Sackville
New Brunswick E0A 3C0
Psychology, Dept. of

Mount St Vincent Univ.
166 Bedford Highway
Halifax
Nova Scotia B3M 2J6
Psychology, Dept. of
Dept. Head: Dr Ann
Krane
Phone: (1) (902) 443 4450
Fax: (1) (902) 445 3960
Email: kranea@
ash.msvu.ca

Network North/Réseau
Nord
66 Elm St.
Suite 200
Sudbury
Ontario P3C 1R8
Psychology, Dept. of
Dept. Head: Dr Joseph
Persi
Phone: (1) (705) 671 7301
Fax: (1) (705) 675 7049

New Brunswick, Univ. of
Bag Service #45444
Fredericton
New Brunswick
E3B 6E4
Psychology, Dept. of
Dept. Head: Catherine
Ann Cameron
Phone: (1) (506) 453 4707
Fax: (1) (506) 453 4505

New Brunswick, Univ. of
POB 5050
St John
New Brunswick
E2L 4L5
Psychology, Dept. of
Dept. Head: A. E. Wilson
Phone: (1) (506) 648 5640
Fax: (1) (506) 648 5528

New Caledonia, College
of
3330 22nd Ave.
Prince George
British Columbia
V2N 1P8
Psychology, Dept. of

Newfoundland,
Memorial Univ. of
St John's
Newfoundland
A1B 3XG
Psychology, Dept. of
Other Depts: Counselling
Centre; Health Studies;
Psychiatry
Dept. Head: Dr Abraham
S. Ross
Phone: (1) (709) 737 8495
Fax: (1) (709) 737 4000
Email: abraham@
kean.ucs.mun.ca

North York General
Hospital
4001 Leslie
Willowdale
Ontario
M2K 1E1
Psychology Dept.
Other Depts: Child
Development &
Counselling Service
Dept. Head: Walter D.
Hambley
Phone: (1) (416) 756
6676
Fax: (1) (416) 756 6384

Ontario Inst. for Studies in Education
252 Bloor St. W.
Toronto
Ontario M5S 1V6
Applied Psychology, Dept. of
Dept. Head: Dr Mary Alice Guttman
Phone: (1) (416) 923 6641
Fax: (1) (416) 926 4725
Telex: 06217720

Oshawa General Hospital
24 Alma St.
Oshawa
Ontario L1G 2B9
Alexandra Clinic
Dept. Head: Dr Michael Paguin
Phone: (1) (416) 433 4345
Fax: (1) (416) 433 4338

Ottawa General Hospital
501 Smyth Rd.
Ottawa
Ontario K1H 8L6
Clinical Psychophysiology Lab.

Ottawa, Univ. of
145 Jean-Jacques Lussier
Ottowa
Ontario K1N 6N5
Psychology, School of
Dept. Head: Pierre Baron
Phone: (1) (613) 564 3363
Fax: (1) (613) 564 9569
Email: ncarter@ acadvm1.uottowa.ca

Oxford County Board of Education
POB 636
Woodstock
Ontario N4S 7Z8
Psychology Dept.

Peel Memorial Hospital
20 Lynch St.
Brampton
Ontario
L6W 2Z8
Psychology, Dept. of

Personnel Psychology Centre
Room A1760, West Tower
300 Laurier Ave. W.
Ottawa,
Ontario, K1A 0M7
Dept. Head: Ken Grant
Phone: (1) (613) 996 7481
Fax: (1) (613) 992 9694

Philippe Pinel Inst.
10905 Blvd Henri Bourassa Est.
Montréal
Québec
H1C 1H1
Dept. Head: Marie-France Dionne
Phone: (1) (514) 648 8461
Fax: (1) (514) 494 4406

Prince Edward Island Univ.
Charlottetown
Prince Edward Island
C1A 4P3
Psychology, Dept. of
Dept. Head: Dr Philip Smith
Phone: (1) (902) 566 0563
Fax: (1) (902) 566 0420
Email: smithp@ upei.ca

PsychHealth Centre
771 Bannatyne Ave
Winnipeg, Manitoba
Clinical Health Psychology, Dept. of
Dept. Head: Dr John L. Arnett
Phone: (1) (204) 787 3876
Fax: (1) (204) 787 4879

Québec à Hull, Univ. du
P. B. 1250, Stn B, Hull
Québec, J8X 3X7
l'éducation, Dépt. de
Dept. Head: Steen Esbensen
Phone: (1) (819) 595 4415
Fax: (1) (819) 595 4459

Québec à Hull, Univ. du
P. B. 1250, Stn B, Hull
Québec, J8X 3X7
Human Sciences, Dept. of
Dept. Head: Monique Massé
Phone: (1) (819) 595 2216
Fax: (1) (819) 595 2216

Québec à Montréal, Univ. du
Montréal
Québec H3C 1P3
Psychologie, Dept. de
Dept. Head: Robert J. Vallerand
Phone: (1) (514) 987 4826
Fax: (1) (514) 987 7953

Québec à Trois Rivières, Univ. du
Trois-Rivières
Québec, G9A 5H
Psychology Dept.
Other Depts:
Neuropsychology;
Education

Queen's Univ.
Kingston
Ontario, K7L 3N6
Psychology, Dept. of
Other Depts: Education;
Psychiatry; Business, School of
Dept. Head: Dr Rudolf Kalin
Phone: (1) (613) 545 6005
Fax: (1) (613) 545 2499
Email: kalinr@ qucdn

Queensway-Careton Hospital
3045 Baseline Rd.
Ottawa
Ontario, K2H 8P4
Psychology, Dept. of

Red Deer Regional Hospital Ctr
3942-50 A Ave.
Red Deer
Alberta, T4N 4E7
Psychiatry, Dept. of

Regina, Univ. of
Regina
Saskatchewan
S4S 0A2
Psychology, Dept. of
Dept. Head: Dr Cannie Stark-Adamec
Phone: (1) (306) 585 4221
Fax: (1) (306) 585 4780

Regional Psychiatric Centre
POB 3000, Abbotsford
British Columbia
V2S 4P4

Rehabilitation Centre, The
505 Smyth Rd.
Ottawa
Ontario K1H 8M2
Psychology, Dept. of
Dept. Head: J. L. D'Eon
Phone: (1) (613) 739 5317
Fax: (1) (613) 737 7056

Rideau Correctional & Treatment Centre
Merrickville
Ontario K0G 1N0
Psychology Dept.
Dept. Head: Dr Hugh Marquis
Phone: (1) (613) 269 4771
Fax: (1) (613) 269 3583

Rideau Regional Centre
POB 2000
Smiths Falls
Ontario K7A 4J7
Psychology Dept.
Dept. Head: William R. Barnes
Phone: (1) (613) 284 0123
Fax: (1) (613) 283 3463

Rosemont, College de
6400 16th Ave.
Montréal
Québec H1X 2S
Psychology, Dept. of
Dept. Head: Pierre Jacques
Phone: (1) (514) 376 1620
Fax: (1) (514) 376 3211

Rotman Research Inst.
3560 Bathurst St
North York
Ontario M6A 2E1

Royal Ottawa Hospital
1145 Carling Ave.
Ottawa
Ontario K1N 7Z4
Psychology, Dept. of
Dept. Head: H. Bruce Ferguson
Phone: (1) (613) 722 6521
Fax: (1) (613) 722 5048

Royal Victoria Hospital
687 Pine Ave. West
Montréal
Québec H3A 1A1
Psychology Dept.

Ryerson Polytechnic Inst.
Toronto
Ontario M5B 1E8
Psychology, Dept. of
Dept. Head: John D. Roth
Phone: (1) (416) 979 5000

Saskatchewan, Univ. of
Saskatoon
Saskatchewan
K7N 0W0
Psychology Dept.
Other Depts: Educational Psychology; Nursing
Dept. Head: Jim Cheesman
Phone: (1) (306) 966 6666
Fax: (1) (306) 966 6630
Email: cheesman@
    sask.usask.ca

Scarborough College
Univ. of Toronto
West Hill
Ontario
M1C 1A4
Psychology Group, Life Sciences Divn.
Dept. Head: John M. Kennedy
Phone: (1) (416) 287 7400
Fax: (1) (416) 287 7642

Selkirk Mental Centre
Selkirk
Manitoba
R1A 2B5
Psychology, Dept. of
Dept. Head: Jay W. Brolund
Phone: (1) (204) 482 3810
Fax: (1) (204) 785 8936

Shaughnessy Hospital
4500 Oak St.
Vancouver
British Columbia
V6H 3N1
Psychology Divn.
Other Depts: Psychiatry

Sherbrooke, Univ. de
Sherbrooke
Québec
J1J 2P
Psychologie, Dépt. de

Simon Fraser Univ.
Burnaby
British Columbia
V5A 1S6
Psychology Dept.
  Research Group
Other Depts:
  Criminology; Univ.
  Counselling Serv.
Dept. Head: Dr A. Roger
  Blackman
Phone: (1) (604) 291 3354
Fax: (1) (604) 291 3427
Email: psyche@
  server.psyc.sfu.ca

Sir M.B. Davis-Jewish
General Hospital
3755 Côte St Catherine
Rd
Montréal
Quebec H3T-1E@

St Clare's Mercy
Hospital
St John's
Newfoundland, A1C 2H5
Psychology, Dept. of
Dept. Head: Heili
  Strawbridge
Phone: (1) (709) 778 3399
Fax: (1) (709) 738 0080

St Francis Xavier Univ.
POB 100, Antigonish
Nova Scotia
B2G 1C0
Psychology, Dept. of

St Joseph's Hospital
268 Grosvenor St.
London
Ontario
N6A 2M2
Psychology, Dept. of
Dept. Head: W. G. Newby
Phone: (1) (519) 646
  6100
Fax: (1) (519) 646 6148

St Joseph's Hospital
301 James St. S.
Hamilton
Ontario L8N 1Y4
Psychology Dept.
Other Depts: Behavioural
  Medicine Unit
Phone: (1) (416) 521 6035
Fax: (1) (416) 521 6066

St Mary's Univ.
Halifax
Nova Scotia B3H 3C3
Psychology, Dept. of
Dept. Head: Darryl Bruce
Phone: (1) (902) 420 5846
Fax: (1) (902) 420 5261
Email: dbruce@
  husky1.stmarys.ca

St Thomas Psychiatric
Hospital
POB 2004, St Thomas
Ontario, N5P 3V9
Dept. Head: Dr A. B.
  Scheid
Phone: (1) (631) 8510
Fax: (1) (633) 0852

St Thomas Univ.
Fredericton
New Brunswick E3B 5G3
Psychology, Dept. of

Sunnybrook Medical
Centre
2075 Bayview Ave.
Toronto
Ontario, M4N 3M5
Psychology, Dept. of

Surrey Place Centre
2 Surrey Place
Toronto
Ontario M5S 2C2
Dept. Head: Maurice A.
  Feldman
Phone: (1) (416) 92 5141
Fax: (1) (416) 923 8476

Thistletown Regional
Centre
51 Panorama Court
Rexdale
Ontario M9V 4L8

Toronto East General
Hospital
825 Coxwell Ave.
5th Floor, Toronto
Ontario, M4C 3E7
Psychology, Dept. of

Toronto General
Hospital
8 Eaton N-238, Toronto
Ontario M4J 2Z5
Psychology Dept.

Toronto Hospital
College Wing - 2 Room
  332
200 Elizabeth St.
Toronto
Ontario M5G 2CA
Psychology, Dept. of
Dept. Head: Brian F. Shaw
Phone: (1) (416) 340 3319
Fax: (1) (416) 340 4739
Email: thpsy.uucd

Toronto, Univ. of
100 St George St
Toronto
Ontario M5S 1A1
Psychology, Dept. of
Dept. Head: A. M. Wall
Phone: (1) (416) 978 3406

Toronto, Univ. of
45 Walmer Rd., Toronto
Ontario M5R 2X3
Inst. of Child Study
Dept. Head: Dr Carl M.
  Corter
Phone: (1) (416) 978 3455
Fax: (1) (416) 978 6485
Email: ccorter@
  ics.utoronto.ca

Toronto, Univ. of
455 Spadina Ave.
Toronto
Ontario, M5S 2G3
Studies of Aging Centre
Dept. Head: Victor W.
  Marshall
Phone: (1) (416) 978 7910
Fax: (1) (416) 978 4771
Email: carnet@vm.
  utcs.utoronto.ca.bitnet

Toronto, Univ. of
Erindale College
Missisauga
Ontario L5L 1C6
Research in Human
  Development Centre

Toronto, Univ. of
McMurrich Bldg.
Toronto
Ontario M5S 1A8
Behavioural Science,
  Dept. of
Dept. Head: Harvey A.
  Skinner
Phone: (1) (416) 978 8606
Fax: (1) (416) 978 2087

Traffic Injury Research
Foundation
171 Nepean St.
Nepean
Ontario
K2P 0B4
Dept. Head: Herbert M.
  Simpson
Phone: (1) (613) 238 5235
Fax: (1) (613) 238 5292

Transportation
Development Centre
Place de l'Aviation
1000 Sherbrooke W.,
  Suite 2421
Montréal
Québec
H3A 2R3

Trent Univ.
Peterborough
Ontario
K9J 7B8
Psychology, Dept. of
Dept. Head: Peter Watson
Phone: (1) (705) 748 1535
Fax: (1) (705) 748 1580
Email: psychology@
  trentu.ca

Trinity Western Univ.
7600 Glover Rad
Langley
British Columbia
V3A 6H4
Psychology, Dept. of

Univ. Hospital
London
Ontario
N6A 5A5
Psychological Services
Dept.
Dept. Head: Dr Margaret
  T. Hearn
Phone: (1) (519) 663 3461
Fax: (1) (519) 663 3743

Univ. Hospital
Saskatoon
Saskatchewan
S7N 0X0
Psychology Divn.
Dept. Head: Dr Larry
  Shepel
Phone: (1) (306) 966 2341
Fax: (1) (306) 966 2340

Vancouver General
Hospital
855 West 12th Ave.
Vancouver
British Columbia
V5Z 1M9
Psychology, Dept. of
Dept. Head: James P.
  Schmidt
Phone: (1) (604) 875 4824

Victoria General
Hospital
Halifax
Nova Scotia
B3H 2Y9
Psychology, Dept. of
Dept. Head: Dr Murray
  Schwartz
Phone: (1) (902) 428
  2196
Fax: (1) (902) 428 2148
Email: schwartz@
  ac.dal.ca

Victoria, Univ. of
Victoria
British Columbia
V8W 3P5
Psychology, Dept. of
Dept. Head: David F.
  Hultsch
Phone: (1) (604) 721
  7525
Fax: (1) (604) 721 8929
Email: psycbit@
  uvvm.uvic.ca

Waterford Hospital
Waterford Bridge Rd.
St John's
Newfoundland
A1E 4J8
Psychology Dept.
Dept. Head: Dr Hassan
  Khalili
Phone: (1) (709) 364
  0485
Fax: (1) (709) 364 0804

Waterloo, Univ. of
Waterloo
Ontario N2L 3G1
Psychology, Dept. of
Other Depts: Health
  Studies
Dept. Head: T. Gary
  Waller
Phone: (1) (519) 885 1211
Fax: (1) (519) 746 8631

Wellesley Hospital
160 Wellesley St. E.
Toronto
Ontario
M4Y 1J3
Dept. Head: Dr Lorne A.
Switzman
Phone: (1) (416) 926 4909
Fax: (1) (416) 926 4874

Western Ontario, Univ.
of
Althouse College
London
Ontario
N6G 1G7
Educ. Psychology, Dept. of
Dept. Head: Carol
Crealock
Phone: (1) (519) 661 2088
Fax: (1) (519) 661 3833
Telex: 0647134
Email: crealock@ uwo.ca

Western Ontario, Univ.
of
London
Ontario
N6A 5C2
Psychology, Dept. of
Other Depts: Addiction
Research Foundation
Dept. Head: William A.
Roberts
Phone: (1) (519) 661
2067
Fax: (1) (519) 661 3961
Email: dawn@
psych.uwo.ca

Weyburn Mental Health
Centre
POB 1056
Weyburn SK
S4H 2L4
Dept. Head: P. Alexander
Bowser
Phone: (1) (306) 848 2800
Fax: (1) (306) 848 2835

Whitby Psychiatric
Hospital
Whitby
Ontario L1N 5S9
Psychology, Dept. of

Wilfrid Laurier Univ.
Waterloo
Ontario
N2L 3C5
Psychology, Dept. of
Dept. Head: Dr Keith
Horton
Phone: (1) (519) 884
1970
Fax: (1) (519) 886 9351
Email: khorton1@
mach1.wlu.ca

Windsor, Univ. of
401 Sunset Ave.
Windsor
Ontario
N9B 3P4
Psychology, Dept. of
Dept. Head: R. Robert Orr
Phone: (1) (519) 253
4232
Fax: (1) (519) 973 7050

Winnipeg, Univ. of
515 Portage Ave.
Winnipeg
Manitoba
R3B 2E9
Psychology, Dept. of
Dept. Head: G. R. Norton
Phone: (1) (204) 786
9130
Fax: (1) (204) 786 1824
Email: norton@
uwpg02.bitnet

Worker's Rehabilitation
Centre
POB 3067
Stn B, St John
New Brunswick E2M
4X7

York Univ.
296 BSB
4700 Keele St.
North York
Ontario M3J 1P3
Psychology Dept.
Other Depts:
Administration Studies
Dept. Head: Dr David W.
Reid
Phone: (1) (416) 736 5116
Fax: (1) (416) 736 5814
Email: apestabi@ um2

CENTRAL AFRICAN
REPUBLIC

Bangui, Univ. de
BP 1450
Bangui
Psychology, Dept. of

CHAD

Tchad, Univ. du
BP 1117
Ave Mobutu
N'Djamena
Psychology, Dept. of

CHILE

Adolfo Ibañez, Univ. de
Balmaceda 1625
Recreo, Viña del Mar
Psychology, Dept. of

Antofagasta, Univ. de
Avda Angamos 601
Casilla 170
Antofagasta
Psychology, Dept. of

Arturo Prat, Univ.
Campus Playa Brava
Avda 11 de Septiembre
2120
Iquique
Psychology, Dept. of

Atacama, Univ. de
Casilla 240
Copiapó
Psychology, Dept. of

Bíobío, Univ. de
Avda Collao 1202
Casilla 5-C, Concepción
Psychology, Dept. of

Central, Univ.
Casilla 6D
San Bernardo
Psychology, Dept. of

Central, Univ.
Carlos Silva V No. 9783
La Reina, Santiago
School of Psychology
Research
Dept. Head: Emilio
Moyano Díaz
Phone: (56) (2) 2733461
Fax: (56) (2) 2735203

Chile, Pontificia Univ.
Cat. de
Casilla
114-D, Santiago
Psychology, Dept. of

Chile, Univ. Austral de
Casilla 567
Valdivia
Psychology, Dept. of

Chile, Univ. de
Avda Bernardo O'Higgins
1058
Casilla 10-D, Santiago
Psychology, Dept. of

Ciencas de la
Educación, Univ. de
Playa Ancha de
Prat 659
Casilla 34-V
Valparaíso
Psychology, Dept. of

Ciencias de la
Educación, Univ.
Metropolitana de
Casilla 147
Correo Central
Santiago
Psychology, Dept. of

Concepción, Univ. de
Casilla 20-C
Concepción
Psychology, Dept. of

Diego Portales,
Univ.
Avda Ejército 260
Santiago
Psychology, Dept. of

Federico Santa Maria,
Univ. Técnica
Avda España 1680
Casilla 110V
Valparaíso
Psychology, Dept. of

Frontera, Univ. de la
Avda Francisco Salazar
01145
Casilla 54-D
Temuco
Psychology, Dept. of

Gabriela Mistral,
Univ.
Avda Ricardo Lyon 1177
Santiago
Psychology, Dept. of

Magallanes, Univ. de
Casilla 113-D
Punta Arenas
Psychology, Dept. of

Norte, Univ. Cat. del
Avda Angamos 0610
Casilla 1280
Antofagasta
Psychology, Dept. of

Santiago de Chile, Univ.
de
Alameda Libertador
Bernardo O'Higgins
3363
Casilla 442
Correo 2
Santiago
Psychology, Dept. of

Serena, Univ. de la
Avda Raúul Bitrán N.
sln.
La Serena
Psychology, Dept. of

Talca, Univ. de
2 Norte 685
Casilla 721
Talca
Psychology, Dept. of

Tarapacá, Univ. de
Gen. Velasquez 1775
Casilla 7-D
Arica
Psychology, Dept. of

Valparaíso, Univ. de
Casilla 123-V
Valparaíso
Psychology, Dept. of

Valparaíso, Univ. Cat. de
Avda Brasil 2950
Casillo 4059
Valparaíso
Psychology, Dept. of

CHINA

Beijing Medical College
Beijing 100083
Psychiatry Dept.

Beijing Normal College
Beijing 100037
Inst. of Educational
Sciences

Beijing Normal Univ.
Beijing 100875
Psychology Dept.
Other Depts:
Developmental
Psychology

Central China Normal Univ.
Wuchang
Hubei 430070
Education Dept.

Chinese Academy of Sciences
POB 1603
Beijing 100012
Psychology, Inst. of
Dept. Head: Prof.
QichengJing
Phone: (86) (1) 256
6099

Chinese Academy of Social Sciences
Beijing 100732
Inst. of Philosophy

East China Normal Univ.
Shanghai 200062
Psychology Dept.
Other Depts: Psychology,
Research Inst. of
Dept. Head: Zhi-liang
Yang
Phone: (86) (21) 2577577
Fax: (86) (21) 2576217
Telex: 33328 ECNU CN

Hangzhou Univ.
Hangzhou
Zhejiang 310028
Psychology Dept.
Dept. Head: Prof.
Zu-Xiang Zhu
Phone: (86) (571)
871224
Fax: (86) (571) 870107

Harbin Normal Univ.
Harbin Heilongjiang
150080
Educational Sciences,
Dept. of
Dept. Head: Wu Wan-
Sen
Phone: (86) (451) 64579
Fax: (86) (451) 65382

Hunan Normal Univ.
Changsha
Hunan 410081
Education, Dept. of
Dept. Head: Guang-Hui
Tu
Phone: (86) (731)
83131-512

Jining Mental Hospital
Jining
Shandong 272151
Dept. Head: Chen Wei
Phone: (86) (573)
301433

Kunming Normal College
2 Kunshi Rd.
Kunming 650031
Yunnan
Educational Sciences,
Inst. of
Dept. Head: Prof. Zhang
Shi-Fu
Phone: (86) (871)
52522
Telex: Suzhou 5868

Mental Health Inst. of Zhejiang Province
Hangzhou
Zhejiang 311122
Dept. Head: Zhang
Tong-Yan
Phone: (86) (571) 5292-3
Fax: (86) (571) 23760
Telex: 33328 ECNU CN

Nanjing Normal Univ.
Nanjing 210024
Education Dept.
Dept. Head: Prof. Zhen
Yu Wang
Phone: (86) (25) 303666
Fax: (86) (25) 307448

Peking Univ.
Beijing 100871
Psychology, Dept. of
Dept. Head: Zhu Ying
Phone: (86) (1) 256 1166
Fax: (86) (1) 256 4095
Telex: 22239 PKUNI CN

Second Affiliated Hospital, The
Changsha, Hunan 410011
Psychiatry Dept.
Dept. Head: Xiao Yang Dai
Phone: (86) (731) 550269

Suzhou Univ.
Suzhou, Jiangsu
Education Science Dept.
Dept. Head: Zhu Yongxin
Phone: (86) (512) 223614
Fax: (86) (512) 771918
Telex: Suzhou 5868

Tianjin Normal Univ.
Tianjin 300073
Education Sciences Dept.
Dept. Head: Shan Deli
Phone: (86) (22) 00164
Fax: (86) (22) 318489

COLOMBIA

Administración Pública, Escuela Superior de
Apdo Aéreo 29745
Apdo Nac. 2085
Diagonal 40
No. 46A-37
Bogotá
Psychology Dept.

Administración y finanzas y Tecnologías, Univ. Escuela de
Apdo Aéreo 3300
Avda Las Vegas
Carrera 49 No. 7-50
Medellín, Antioquia

Antioquia, Univ. de
Apdo Aéreo 1226
Santafé de Bogatá
Medellín
Antioquia
Psychology, Fac. of
Dept. Head: Dr Leonor
  Ma. Restrepo
Phone: (57) (4) 233 0599
Fax: (57) (4) 263 8282

Atlántico, Univ. de
Carrero 43
No. 50-53 Apdo Aéreo
  1890
Barranquilla, Atlántico
Psychology Dept.

Bogotá, Jorge Tadeo Lozano Fund. Univ. de
Apdo Aéreo 34185
Calle 23 No. 4-47
Bogotá
Psychology Dept.

Bolivariana - Seccional Bucaramanga
Calle 33 # 21-28
Bucaramanga,
Norte de Santander
Psychology, Fac. of
Dept. Head: Dr Cristina
  Higuera de Escalante
Phone: (57) (76) 425 598

Bolivariana, Univ. Pontificia
Apdo Aéreo 1178
Calle 52 No. 40-88
Medellín, Antioquia
Psychology Dept.

Bucaramanga, Univ. Autónoma de
Calle 48
No. 39-234
Apdo Aéreo 1642
Bucaramanga
Psychology Dept.

Caldas, Univ. de
Apdo Aéreo 275
Manizales
Caldas
Psychology Dept.

Cartagena, Univ. de
Apdo Aéreo 1382
Cartagena
Bolívar
Psychology Dept.

Católica de Colombia, Univ.
Cra 15 # 47-31 (via a
  Pance)
Apdo Aéreo 029832
Santafé de Bogatá
Psychology, Fac. of
Dept. Head: Dr Carlos
  Vargas
Phone: (57) (1) 269 8348

Cauca, Univ. del
Apdo Nac. 113
Calle 5 No 4-70
Popayán
Cauca
Psychology Dept.
Dept. Head: Olga Velasco
  de Herrera
Phone: (57) (928)
  231066
Fax: (57) (928) 244851

Colombia, Univ. Externado de
Calle 12
1-17 Este
Bogotá
Psychology Dept.

Colombia, Univ. la Gran
Carrera 6 No. 13-40
Apdo Aéreo 7909
Bogotá
Psychology Dept.

Colombia, Univ. Libre de
Carrera 6 No. 8-06
Bogotá
Psychology Dept.

Colombia, Univ. Ped. y Tecnológia de
Apdo Aéreo 1094 y 1234
Carretera Central del
  Norte
Tunja
Boyacá
Psychology Dept.

Colombia, Univ. Incca de
Apdo Aéreo 14817
Bogotá
Psychology Dept.

Colombia, Univ. Nac. de
Santafé de Bogatá, D. C.
Psychology, Dept. of
Dept. Head: Dr Cristina
  Torrado
Phone: (57) (1) 244 0859

Colombiano de Estudios Superiores de Incolda, Inst
Apdo Aéreo 25608
(Unicentro)
Cali
Psychology Dept.

Córdoba, Univ. de
Apdo Aéreo 354
Carretera a Cereté
Km 5, Montería, Córdoba
Psychology Dept.

Diego Luis Córdoba,
Univ. Tecnológica del
Chocó
Carrera 2A No. 24-22
Quibdó, Chocó
Psychology Dept.

Francisco José de
Caldas, Univ.
Distrital
Carrera 8 No 40-78
Bogotá
Psychology Dept.

Fundación Univ.
Central
Carrera 5A No. 21-38
Bogotá
Psychology Dept.

Guajira, Univ. de la
Apdo Aéreo 172
Riohacha
Psychology Dept.

INCCA de Colombia,
Univ.
Cra. 13 # 24-15
Santafé de Bogotá
*Psychology, Progamme
of*
*Dept. Head: Dr Rosa
Suarez Prieto*
Phone: (57) (1) 241 3361
Fax: (57) (1) 282 4932

Javeriana, Pontificia
Univ.
Carrera 7a #40-62
Apdo Aéreo 56710
Santafé de Bogotá
D. C.
Psychology, Fac. of
*Dept. Head: Arnoldo
Aristizábal Hoyos*
Phone: (57) (1) 245 8076
Fax: (57) (1) 288 2335
Email: ujaveria@
andescol

Javeriana - Seccional
Cali, Pontificia
Univ.
Calle 18 # 121-30 (via a
Pance)
Apdo Aéreo 26230
Cali, Valle
Psychology, Dept. of
*Dept. Head: Dr Leonor
Maria Sandoval*
Phone: (57) (23) 393
041

Konrad Lorenz,
Fundación Univ.
Calle 77 # 11-63
Santafé de Bogatá
D. C.
Psychology, Fac. of
*Dept. Head: Dr Patricia
Valbuena Posada*
Phone: (57) (1) 212
8395

Latinoamericana, Univ.
Autónoma
Carrera 55 No. 49-51
Apdo Aéreo 3455
Medellín
Psychology Dept.

Los Andes, Univ. de
Carrera 1A No. 18A-70
Apdo Aéreo 4976
Bogotá
Psychology, Dept. of
*Dept. Head: Dr Hernán
Escobedo*
Phone: (57) (1) 283
9942
Fax: (57) (1) 284 1890

Los Llanos Orientales,
Univ. Tecnológica
de
Apdo Aéreo 2621
Villavicencio
Meta
Psychology Dept.

Magdalena, Univ.
Tecnológia del
Apdo Aéreo 731
Santa Marta
Psychology Dept.

Manizales, Corp. Univ.
Apdo Aéreo 357
Carrera 23 No. 60-63
Manizales
Psychology Dept.

Manizales, Fundación
Univ. de
Cra. 9a. # 19-03
Apdo Aeréo 868
Manizales, Caldas
Psychology, Fac. of
*Dept. Head: Dr Luis
González López*
Phone: (57) (68) 841
450

Medellín, Univ. de
Apdo Aéreo 1983
Carrera 87 No. 38-65
Belén Los Alpes
Medellín
Antioquia
Psychology Dept.

Metropolitana para la
Educación Superior,
Corporación
Cra. 42 Este# 75-B-109
Baranquilla
Atlántico
*Psychology, Programme
of*
*Dept. Head: Dr Luis
Chamartin*
Phone: (57) (58) 353
757

Nariño, Univ. de
Carrera 22 No. 18-109
Pasto
Nariño
Psychology Dept.

Norte, Univ. del
Apdo Aéreo 1569
51820 Barranquilla
Atlántico
Psychology, Dept. of
Other Depts: Costa
Atlántica Project
Dept. Head: Dr José
Amar y Amar
Phone: (57) (58) 345 364
Fax: (57) (58) 350 722

Omega (Pacientes
Terminales), Fundación
Cra. 30 No. 89-79
Santafé de Bogotá
D. C
Dept. Head: Dr Isa
Fonnegra do Jaramillo
Phone: (57) (1) 236 5004

Pamplona, Univ. de
Apdo Aéreo 1046
Carrera No. 4-38
Pamplona
Santander del Norte
Psychology, Dept. of
Phone: (57) (978) 682750
Fax: (57) (978) 680581

Paula Santander, Univ.
Francisco de
Avda Gran Colombia
Barrio Colsag
Apdo Aéreo 1055
Cúcuta
Norte de Santander
Psychology Dept.

Pedagógica Nac., Univ. de
Apdo Aéreo 75144
Calle 73
No. 11-73
Bogotá
Psychology Dept.
Dept. Head: Rafael Avila
Penagos
Phone: (57) (1) 2486837
Fax: (57) (1) 2111293

Pereira, Univ. Libre,
Seccional de
Apdo Aéreo 1330
Calle 40 No. 7-30, Pereira
Psychology Dept.

Psychology &
Gerontology, Centre of
Calle 62 No. 3-58
Apdo Aéro 52366
Santafé de Bogotá, D. C
Dept. Head: Dr Elisa
Dulcey-Ruiz
Phone: (57) (1) 210 1715

Quindío, Univ. del
Calle 12 Norte Avda
Bolívar
Apdo Aéreo 460
Armenia, Quindío
Psychology Dept.

Risaralda, Univ. Cat.
Pop. del
Calle 20 No. 3-65
Apdo Aéreo 2435, Pereira
Psychology Dept.

Salle, Univ. de la
Carrera 2, No. 10-70
Apdo Aéreo 28638
Bogotá
Psychology Dept.

San Buenaventura,
Univ. de
Calle 73, No. 10-45
Apdo Aéreo 75010,
Bogotá
Psychology Dept.

San Buenaventura,
Univ. de
Apdo Aéreo 7370
Medellín, Antioquia
Psychology Dept.
Dept. Head: Dr German
Alonso Bautista Romero
Phone: (57) (4) 231 460

Santander, Univ.
Industrial de
Apdo Aéreo 678
Bucaramanga
Santander del Sur
Psychology Dept.

Sto Tomás, Univ.
Carrera 9A, No. 51-23
Apdo Aéreo 52519
Bogotá 2
D. C.
Psychology, Fac. of
Dept. Head: Dr Javier
Giraldo Jaramillo
Phone: (57) (1) 249 5490

Sucre, Univ. de
Apdo Aéreo 406
Calle 1
No. 22-58
Sincelejo
Sucre
Psychology Dept.

Surcolombiana, Univ.
Avda Pastrana Borrero
con Carrera 1A
Neiva
Huila
Psychology Dept.

Tolima, Univ. del
Apdo Aéreo No. 546
Santa Helena
Ibagué
Tolima
Psychology Dept.

Valle, Univ. del
Ciudad Univ.
Meléndez
Apdo Nac. 439, Cali
Vale del Cauca
Psychology Dept.
Dept. Head: Prof.
Miralba Correa
Phone: (57) (23) 3393 041
Fax: (57) (23) 392 311

CONGO

Marien-Ngouabi, Univ.
BP 69
Brazzaville
Psychology, Dept. of

COSTA RICA

Centro America, Univ. Aut. de
Apdo 7637
San José 1000

Costa Rica, Univ. de
Ciudad Univ. 'Rodrigo Facio'
San Pedro de Montes de Oca
San José
Psychology, School of
Other Depts:
  Psychological Research:
  Marco Fourvier Facio
Dept. Head: Ignacio
  Dobles Oropeza
Phone: (506) 531265
Fax: (506) 243706

Estatal a Distancia, Univ.
Apdo 474
2050 S. Pedro de Montes de Oca
San José
Psychology, Dept. of

Nacional, Univ.
Apdo 86-3000
Heredia
Psychology, Dept. of

CÔTE D'IVOIRE

Côte d'Ivoire, Univ. Nat. de
01 BP V34
Abidjan 01
Psychology, Dept. of

CROATIA

Mariboru, Univ. v
62000 Maribor
Krekova Ulica 2
Psychology, Department of

Rijeci, Sveuciliste 'V. Bakaric'
51000 Rijeka
Trg Rijecke Rezolucije 7/1
Psychology, Dept. of

Splitu, Sveucilite u
58000 Split
Livanjska 5/1
Psychology, Dept. of

Zagreb, Univ. of
Salajeva 3
41000 Zagreb
Psychology, Dept. of
Dept. Head: Prof.
  Vladimir Kolesaric
Phone: (38) (41) 620187
Fax: (38) (41) 513834

CUBA

Camagüey, Univ. de
Carretera de Circunvalación
Km. 5 1/2
Camagüey 74650
Psychology, Dept. of

Centro Univ. "Hnos. Saiz"
Vicerrectoría Docente
Martí 270 esq. 27 de Noviembre
Pinar Del Río 20100
Psychology, Dept. of
Dept. Head: Dr Angel
  Notario de la Torre
Phone: (53) 2325
Fax: (53) (582) 5813
Telex: (53) (582) 103
Email: tinored.cui@ gc.org

Habana, Univ. de la
Calle San Rafael #1168, esq.
Mazon Plaza
Ciudad Havana
CP 10400
Psychology, Dept. of
Dept. Head: Albertina
  Mitjans Martinez
Phone: (53) (7) 32 2757
Telex: (53) (7) 32 1272

Las Villas, Univ. Central de
Carretera de Camajuaní
Km 5 1/2
Santa Clara
Ville Clara
C. P. 54830
Psychology, Dept. of
Dept. Head: Dr. Luis
  Felipe Herrera Jiménez
Phone: (53) (7) 81 363

Oriente, Univ. de
Avda Patricio Lumumba s/n
Santiago de Cuba
Psychology, Dept. of
Other Depts: Ciencias
  Sociales y Humanísticas
Dept. Head: María del
  Pilar Soteras del Toro
Phone: (53) 32004
Fax: (53) 32689
Telex: 061345 Univtecu

CZECH REPUBLIC

Centrum Poradensko - Psychologickych Služ ieb
Sovietskych Hrdinov P. P. 101
089 01 Svidník
Dept. Head: Dr Zoltán
  Šafran
Phone: (42) (937) 22 507

Charles Univ.
Hradcanské námestí 5
118 42 Praha 1
Psychology, Dept. of
Dept. Head: Sona
Hermochová
Phone: (42) (2) 536332

Detská psychiat.
ambulance
V úvalu 84
151 12 Praha 5
Fak. nemocnice

Fak. nemocnice 2
Sermírská 5
169 00 Praha 6

Fak. rízení Vysoké školy
ekonomické
nám. A. Zápotockého 4
130 00 Praha

FFUK
Katedra
Celetna 20, 11000 Praha 1

Foniatrická ambulance
ORL kliniky Fak.
nemocnice
I. P. Pavlova
775 00 Olomouc

Inst. hygieny a
epidemiologie
Srobárova 48
100 42 Praha 10

Inst. pro dalí
vzdeláváni lékaru a
farmaceuti v Praze
Kabinet psychologie ILF
Vídenská 800-G 2
146 29 Praha 4

J.E., Univ.
Jihlavská 100
657 15 Brno
Psychiatrická klinika

Krajská ped-psy.
poradna
Norberta Fryda 21
370 01 Ceské
Budejovice

Krajská ped-psy.
poradna
Polská 1543
708 00 Ostrava 4

Krajská ped-psy.
poradna
Prokopova 30
303 86 Plzen

Masarykova Univ. Brno
FF
Psychologicky ústav
Arne Nováka 1
660 88 Brno
Dept. Head: Prof.
Vladimír Smékal
Phone: (42) (5) 750 050
Fax: (42) (5) 753 050

Metra Blansko
Kybeova 53
678 23 Blansko

Okresní manzelská a
predmanzelská
poradna
CSA 12
360 01 Karlovy Vary

Okresní manzelská a
predmanzelská
poradna
755 01 Vsetín

Okresní ped-psy.
poradna
470 01 Ceská Lípa

Okresní ped-psy.
poradna
Chelického 555
386 01 Strakonice 1

Okresní ped-psy.
poradna
Krnov
K mustku 5, 794 00 Krnov

Okresní ped-psy.
poradna
Václavkova ul. 8
ZS
293 01 Mladá Boleslav

Okresní ped-psy.
poradna
ZS U Dervenych domku
695 00 Hodonín

OPPP
Komenského 8
467 52 Jablonec nad
Nisou
Pedagogicko-
psychologická

Ostravsko-karvinské
doly
nám. Ríjnov revoluce 6
728 30 Ostrava 1

Pedagog. fak. Ceské
Budejovice
Branišovská 25
370 05 Ceské Budejovice

Pedagog. fak. UK
M. D. Rettigové 4
110 00 Praha 1

Pedagog. fak. UP
Univerzitní nám 1
771 41 Olomouc

Pedagog.-psychol.
poradna
Mírové nám. 1466
POB 117
397 01 Písek
Dept. Head: Dr Sylva
Hönigová
Phone: (42) (362) 3387

**Pedagog.-psychol.
poradna mesta Brno**
Zachova 1
602 00 Brno

Pedagog. ústav Jana A.
Komenského CSAV
Máchova 7
120 00 Praha 1
*Dept. Head: Dr Isabella
Pavelková*
Phone: (42) (2) 25 40 94
Fax: (42) (2) 25 44 30

**Poradna pro rodinu,
manželství a
mezilidské vztahy
MUP**
Spytihnevova 6,
NVP Spytihvevova 6
128 00 Praha 2
*Dept. Head: Dr Petr
Šmolka*
Phone: (42) (2) 43 88 33

**Psychiatrická
ambulancia
OUNZ**
356 79 Sokolov

**Psychiatrická klinika
fak. nemocnice**
I. P. Pavlova 12
775 00 Olomouc

**Psychiatrická klinika
FNsP Brno-
Bohunice**
Jihlavská 102
657 15 Brno

**Psychiatrická
lécebna**
Ustavní 91
181 00 Praha 8
*Dept. Head: Dr. Peter
Weiss*
Phone: (42) (2) 857
4349
Fax: (42) (2) 855 9754

**Psychiatrická
polikliniky
OUNZ**
537 27 Chrudim

**Psychologicky ústav
CSAV**
Husova 4
110 00 Praha 1
*Dept. Head: Dr Pavel
Rícan*
Phone: (42) (2) 231
4436

**Ústav racionalizace
rízení a práce**
Smetanova 49
656 01 Brno

**Ústav rozvoje vysokych
kol CSR**
Jindriská 29
110 00 Praha 1

**Ústav silnini a mestské
dopravy**
Vehrdova 4
118 00 Praha 1

**Ústav sociální pée pro
mládez**
Ceské Budejovice
tr. Míru 88
370 00 Ceské Budejovice

**Ustrední ústav
zelezniního
zdravotnictví**
Italská 37
120 00 Praha 2

**Vyskumny ústav práce
a sociálních vecí**
Palackého ná)m 4
120 00 Praha 2
*Dept. Head: Dr Jirí
Šandera*
Phone: (42) 29 86 98
Fax: (42) 29 77 31

**Vyskumny ústav
psychiatricky**
181 03 Praha 8, Bohnice

DENMARK

Aalborg, Univ. of
Langagervej 6
9220
Aalborg Ost

Aarhus
Kommunehospital
DK-8000
Aarhus C
Neurosurgery Dept.

Aarhus Univ.
Asylvej 4
DK-8240
Risskov
Psychology, Inst. of
Other Depts: Alcohol and
Drug Research
Dept. Head: Knud-Erik
Sabroe
Phone: (45) (86) 17 55
11
Fax: (45) (86) 175973

Copenhagen, Univ.
of
Njalsgade 88
DK-2300
Copenhagen S
Psychological Lab.
Dept. Head: Aksel
Mortensen
Phone: (45) 31 54 22 11
Fax: (45) 32 96 31 38
Email: mortensen@
vax.psl.ku.dk

Copenhagen, Univ. of
Njalsgade 90
DK-2300
Copenhagen S
Clinical Psychology, Inst.
of
Dept. Head: Judy
Gammelgaard
Phone: (45) 31 54 22 11
Fax: (45) 32 96 31 38

Copenhagen, Univ. of
Sankt Peders
Straede 19
DK-1453 Copenhagen K
Criminal Science Inst.

County Hospital
Service of Funen
Odense Univ.
Hospital
Kloevervaenget 18
DK-5000 C

Danish Inst. for
Education Research
Hermodsgade 28
DK-2200 Copenhagen N

Environmental &
OccupationalG
Medicine, Inst. of
Universitetsparken
Building 180
DK-8000
Aarhus C

Gentofte Hospital
DK-2900 Hellerup
Neuromedical Dept. 621

Odense Sygehus
DK-5000 Odense C
Occupational Medicine
Clinic

Psychiatric Hospital
Skovagervej 2
DK-8240 Risskov
Clinical Psychology
Dept. Head: Peter Elsass
Phone: (45) (86) 177777
Fax: (45) (86) 175977

Psychiatric Hospital
Skovagervej 2
DK-8240 Risskov
Psychogerontology,
Centre of
Dept. Head: Pia
Fromholt
Phone: (45) (86) 177777
Fax: (45) (86) 175977

Psychoneuro-
endocrinology
Research,
International Centre
of
Asylvej 4
DK-8240
Risskov
Other Depts:
Qualitative Method
Development;
Thriving and Crisis
Studies
Dept. Head: Helmuth
Nyborg
Phone: (45) (86) 17 55
11
Fax: (45) (86) 17 59 73

Rigshospitalet
9, Blegdamsvej
DK-2100
Copenhagen Ø
Clinical Psychological
Section
Other Depts: Medical
Psychology
Dept. Head: Prof. Alice
Theilgaard
Phone: (45) 35 45 61 81
Fax: (45) 35 45 62 60

Roskilde Univ.
POB 260
Marbjergvej 35
DK-4000
Roskilde
Educational Psychology,
Dept. of

Royal Danish School of
Education Studies
Emdrupvej 101
DK-2400 Copenhagen NV
*Education & Psychology
Dept.*
*Dept. Head: Mads
Hermansen*
Phone: (45) 39 69 66 33
Fax: (45) 39 66 00 81

System Evaluation,
Centre of
Finlandsgade 26
*Dept. Head: Benedikte
Madsen*
Phone: (45) (86) 102160

Technological Inst.
Gregersensvej
DK-2360 Taastrup
Copenhagen

Technical Univ. of
Denmark
Building 301
DK-2800 Lyngby
*Working Environment,
Dept. of*
*Dept. Head: Per Langaa
Jensen*
Phone: (45) 45 93 66 88
Fax: (45) 45 93 66 20

DOMINICA

Este, Univ. Central
del
Av. de Circunvalación
San Pedro de
Macorís
Mental Health, Dept. of
*Dept. Head: Ana Amelia
Feliu de Tavárez*
Phone: (809) 529 3562
Fax: (809) 529 5146

Eugenio María de
Hostos, Univ.
Apdo Postal 2694
Santo Domingo

Interamericana Univ.
Apdo Postal 20687
Santo Domingo

Madre y Maestra, Pont.
Univ. Cat.
Autopista Duarte
Santiago de los Caballeros
Psychology, Dept. of

Nordestana, Univ.
Apdo 239
San Francisco de
Macorís
Psychology, Dept. of

Pedro Henríquez
Urena, Univ.
Nacional
Apdo 1423
Santo Domingo
Psychology, Dept. of

Santo Domingo, Univ.
Aut. de
Ciudad Universitari
Apdo 1355
Santo Domingo
Psychology, Dept. of

Santiago, Univ.
Tecnológica de
Apdo 685
Santiago
Psychology, Dept. of

EQUADOR

Cuenca, Univ. Cat. de
POB 19A
Cuenca
Psychology, Dept. of

Cuenca, Univ. de
Avda 12 de Abril
Sector 16
Apdo 168
Cuenca
Psychology, Dept. of

Ecuador, Pont. Univ.
Cat. del
Avda 12 de Octubre
1076 y Carrión
Apdo 2184, Quito
Psychology, Dept. of

Ecuador, Univ. Central
del
Avda América y A. Pérez
Guerrero
Apdo 3291, Quito
Psychology, Dept. of

Esmeraldas, Univ.
Técnica de
Avda Nuevo Horizonte
Apdo 179, Esmeraldas
Psychology, Dept. of

Guayaquil, Univ. de
Casilla 471, Guayaquil
Psychology, Dept. of

Loja, Univ. Nac. de
Casilla Letra 'S'
Calle B
Valdivieso RocafuerteLoja
Psychology, Dept. of

Loja, Univ. Técnica
Particular de
Apdo 608
Loja
Psychology, Dept. of

Machala, Univ. Técnica
de
Casilla 466
Machala
Psychology, Dept. of

Manabi, Univ. Técnica
de
Apdo 82
Portoviejo

Santiago de Guayaquil,
Univ. Cat. de
Casilla 4671, Guayaquil
Psychology, Dept. of

EGYPT

Ains-Shams Univ.
Abbasya, Cairo
Psychology, Dept. of
Dept. Head: Prof. Faraq
A. Taha

Ains-Shams Univ.
Abbassya
Cairo
Childhood Studies,
Higher Inst. for
Dept. Head: Prof. Qadri
M. Hefni

Ains-Shams Univ.
Heliopolis
Cairo
Educational Psychology,
Dept. of
Other Depts: Mental
Health
Dept. Head: Prof. Fouad
A-L. H. Abou-Hatab
Phone: (20) (2) 258 1243

Ains-Shams Univ.
Fac. of Girls
Al-Marghany
Heliopolis
Cairo
Psychology, Dept. of
Dept. Head: Prof. Amina
M. Kazim

Al-Azhar Univ.
Nasr City
Cairo
Educational Psychology,
Dept. of
Other Depts:
Handicapped Children
Studies, Centre of;
Humanities for Girls;
Psychology
Dept. Head: Prof. Farouk
M. Sadek

Al-Mansoura Univ.
Univ. Post Office 35516
Al-Mansoura
Educational Psychology,
Dept. of
Dept. Head: Prof. Salah
A. Mourad

Alexandria Univ.
22 El-Geish Ave.
Al-Shatbi, Alexandria
Psychology, Dept. of
Dept. Head: Prof. Ahmed
Abel-Khalik

American Univ. in Cairo
POB 2511
113 Sharia Kasr El-Aini
11511 Cairo
Soc-Anthro-Psychology,
Dept. of
Dept. Head: Dr Kent
Weeks
Phone: (20) (2) 357 6763
Fax: (20) (2) 355 7565
Telex: 92224 AUCAI UN
Email: sbright@ auc.eg

Asuit Univ.
Asuit
Psychology, Dept. of
Dept. Head: Prof. Sabra
M. Ali

Cairo Univ.
Orman, Giza, Cairo
Psychological Research,
Centre of
Dept. Head: Prof.
Abul-Halim Mahmoud
El-Sayed

Educational Research
& Development, Nat.
Centre of
Cairo
Dept. Head: Prof. Izzat
Abul-Mawgoud

El-Menia Univ.
El-Menia
Psychology, Dept. of
Dept. Head: Prof. Hamid
El-Abd

Examination &
Educational
Evaluation, Nat.
Centre of
Ministry of Education
Falaky St.
Cairo
Dept. Head: Prof. Fouad
A-L. H. Abou-Hatab
Phone: (20) (2) 354
4347

Helwan Univ.
25 Al-Mansour
Mohammed
Zamalek
Cairo
Educational Psychology,
Dept. of
Dept. Head: Prof. Amal
A. M. Sadek
Phone: (20) (2) 340 6844

Helwan Univ.
96 Ahmed Ouraby
St.
Mohandissen
Cairo
Psychology, Dept. of

Mansoura Univ.
Univ. Post Office 35516
Mansoura

Menoufia Univ.
Shebeen
El-Koam
Psychology, Dept. of

Social & Criminological
Research, Nat. Centre
of
Ibn-Khaldoun Square
Embaba
Giza
Dept. Head: Prof. Nahid
Saleh

Sohag Univ.
Sohag
Psychology, Dept. of
Dept. Head: Prof.
Hassanin M. El-Kamel

Suez Canal Univ.
El-Shikh Zayed
Ismailia
Psychology, Dept. of
Dept. Head: Prof. Nabil
El-Zahhar

Tanta Univ.
Tanta
Psychology, Dept. of
Dept. Head: Prof.
Abdel-Wahab Kamel

Zagazig Univ.
Zagazig
Psychology, Dept. of
Dept. Head: Prof. M. A.
Dousoukis

EL SALVADOR

Centroamericana Jos
Univ. de
Apdo (01) 168
San Salvador
Psychology Dept.

El Salvador, Univ. de
Final 25
Apdo Postal 1383
San Salvador
Psychology Dept.

El Salvador, Univ. Nac.
de
7 Avenida Sur No. 722
San Salvador
Psychology Dept.

ESTONIA

Tallinn Pedagogical
Univ.
Narva Maantee 25
EE-0102 Tallinn
Psychology, Dept. of
Dept. Head: Voldemar
Kolga
Phone: (7) 142 424 950
Fax: (7) 142 425 933

Tallinn Pedagogical
Univ.
Narva Maantee 25
EE-0102 Tallinn
Environmental
Psychology Research
Unit
Dept. Head: Toomas Niit
Phone: (7) 0142 426 586
Fax: (7) 0142 425 339
Email: tniit@
tpedi.ew.su

Tallinn Technical Univ.
200108 Tallinn
Ehitajate tee 5
Psychology, Dept. of

Tartu, Univ. of
Tiigi 78-328
EE-2400 Tartu
Psychology, Dept. of
Dept. Head: Prof. Peeter
Tulviste
Phone: (7) 01434 30063
Fax: (7) 01434 35440
Email: jyr1@ tartu.ew.su

Tartu, Univ. of
Tiigi 78-331
EE-2400 Tartu
Psychometrics, Lab. of
Dept. Head: Avo Luuk
Phone: (7) 01434 30825
Fax: (7) 01434 35440
Email: jyr1@
tartu.ew.su

ETHIOPIA

Addis Ababa Univ.
POB 1176
Addis Ababa
Psychology, Dept. of

Asmara, Univ. of
POB 1220
Asmara
Eritrea
Psychology, Dept. of
Dept. Head: Prof. Rezene
H. Mariam
Phone: (251) (4) 113600
Telex: 42091

FIJI

South Pacific Univ.
POB 1168
SUVA
Fiji
Education, School of

FINLAND

Åbo Akademí Univ.
Domkyrkotorget 3
SF-20500 Turku
Psychology, Dept. of
Dept. Head: Prof. Pekka
Niemi
Phone: (358) (21) 654
406
Fax: (358) (21) 654 833
Email: bblomqvist@
finabo.abo.fi

**Helsingin
Yliopisto/Helsingfors
Univ.**
Fabianinkatu 28
SF-00100 Helsinki
Psychology, Dept. of
Dept. Head: Liisa
Keltikangas-Järvinen
Phone: (358) (0) 191
3246
Fax: (358) (0) 191 3379
Email: keltikangas@
cc.helsinki.fi

Helsinki, Univ. of
Fabianinkatu 28 A
Social Psychology, Dept.
of
Dept. Head: Prof. Rauni
Myllyniemi
Phone: (358) (0) 191
3272
Fax: (358) (0) 191 2973
Telex: 124690 unih sf
Email:
rauni.myllyniemi@
helsinki.fi

F

Helsinki, Univ. of
Ritarikatu 5
SF-00170 Helsinki
Psychology, Dept. of
Dept. Head: Prof. Göte
Nyman
Phone: (358) (0) 191
1911
Fax: (358) (0) 191 3443
Email: gnyman@
cc.helsinki.Fi

Helsinki, Univ. of
Ritarikatu 5
SF-00170 Helsinki
General Psychology
Divn.
Dept. Head: Prof. Risto
Näätänen
Phone: (358) (0) 191 3446
Fax: (358) (0) 191 3443
Telex: 124690 unih sf

**Helsinki Univ. Central
Hospital**
Lapinlahdentie
00180 Helsinki
Dept. Head: Olavi
Lindfors
Phone: (358) (0) 69501
Fax: (358) (0) 6950313

**Helsinki Univ. of
Technology**
Otakaari 4 A
SF-02150 Espoo
Industrial Psychology,
Lab. of
Dept. Head: Prof. Veikko
Teikari
Phone: (358) (0) 451 3650
Fax: (358) (0) 451 3665

Joensuu, Univ. of
POB 111
80101 Joensuu
Psychology, Dept. of
Dept. Head: Prof.
Yrjö-Paavo Häyrynen
Phone: (358) (73) 1514264
Fax: (358) (73) 151 4533
Telex: 46183 joy sf
Email: hayrynen@
joyl.joensuu.fi

Jyväskylä, Univ. of
POB 35
SF-40100 Jyväskylä,
Psychology, Dept. of
Dept. Head: Heikki
Lyytinen
Phone: (358) (41) 602863
Fax: (358) (41) 602841
Email: hlyytinen@
finsyu.bitnet

Kuopio Univ. Hospital
SF 70210 Kuopio
Psychiatry, Dept. of
Dept. Head: Prof.
Johannes Lehtonen
Phone: (358) (71) 172956
Fax: (358) (71) 172966

Lapland, Univ. of
96101 Rovaniemi
Social Sciences
Dept. Head: Prof. Kyöshi
Urponen
Phone: (358) (60) 324621
Fax: (358) (60) 324699

**Occupational Health,
Inst. of**
SF-00250 Helsinki
Psychology, Dept. of
Dept. Head: Prof. Raija
Kalimo
Phone: (358) (0) 47 471
Fax: (358) (0) 414 634
Email: rkal@
occuphealth.fi

**Social Insurance Inst.,
The**
Höyläämötie 1
POB 78
SF-00381 Helsinki
*Research & Development
Centre*
Dept. Head: Esko Kalimo
Phone: (358) (90) 565
3057
Fax: (358) (90) 434 3500

Tampere, Univ. of
POB 607
Kalevantie 4
33101 Tampere
Psychology, Dept. of
*Dept. Head: Matti
Syvänen*
Phone: (358) (31) 156
111
Fax: (358) (31) 157 345
Telex: 22263 tayk sf
Email: pskako@
kicio.vta.fi

Tampere, Univ. of
Yliopistonkatu 38
PL 607
33101 Tampere
*Sociology & Social
Psychology, Dept. of*
*Dept. Head: Prof.
Veronica
Stolte-Heiskanen*
Phone: (358) (31) 156
111
Fax: (358) (31) 156080

Turku, Univ. of
Arwidssoninkatu 1
SF 20500 Turku 50
Psychology Dept.
*Dept. Head: Prof. Kirsti
Lagerspetz*
Phone: (358) (21) 63351
Fax: (358) (21) 6335060
Email: pyysalo@
sara.utu.fi

FRANCE

**AFPA, Centre
Psychotechnique**
12 ave de Crimée
35100 Rennes

**AFPA, Centre
Psychotechnique**
5 rue de la République
94005 Saint Maneé

**Aix-Marseille CNRS,
Univ. de**
B.P. 71
13277 Marseille

**Aix-Marseille, Univ. d'
(Aix-Marseille 2)**
70 route Léon
Lachamp
13288 Marseille
Cedex 09
Psychologie
Other Depts: Santé
*Dept. Head: Christian
Ducreux*
Phone: (33) 91 26 90 00

Aix-Marseille, Univ. d'
Le Pharo
blvd Charles Livon
13007 Marseille
CTMC

**Blaise Pascal, Univ. de
(Clermont-Ferrand
2)**
34 ave Carnot
63006 Clermont-
Ferrand
Cedex
*Psychologie Sociale
Lab.*
*Other Depts: Enfant;
Travail*
*Dept. Head: Jean-Marc
Monteil*
Phone: (33) 73 40 63 63

Bordeaux 2, Univ. de
Domaine Univ.
Esplanade des Antilles
33405 Talence
Psychologie, Lab. de
*Other Depts: Emploi;
Enfant; Langage;
Processus d'Acquisition;
Psychologie; Santé*
*Dept. Head: Mme
Marilou
Bruchon-Schweitzer*
Phone: (33) 56 84 50 50

Bordeaux 2, Univ. de
Domaine Univ.
Esplanade des Antilles
33405 Talence
Psychologie Génétique
*Dept. Head: Alain
Laflaquiere*
Phone: (33) 56 84 50 50

Bordeaux 2, Univ. de
Domaine Univ.
Esplanade des Antilles
33405 Talence
*Centre de Recherche de
Sociologie et
Psychologie de
l'Education et de la
Formation*
*Dept. Head: Pierre
Clanche*
Phone: (33) 56 84 50 50

**Bourgogne, Univ. de
(Dijon)**
Faculté de Lettres
36 rue Chabot-Charny
21000 Dijon
*Psychologie Clinique et
Psycho-pathologie*
*Other Depts: Processus
Cognitifs; Processus
d'Acquisition*
*Dept. Head: Bernard
Gibello*
Phone: (33) 80 39 57 29

Bourgogne, Univ. de (Dijon)
2 blvd Gabriel
21000 Dijon
Psychologie, Dépt. de
Dept. Head: Jean Emile
Gombert
Phone: (33) 80 39 57 01
Fax: (33) 80 39 57 67
Email: gombert@ frccub11

Caen, Univ. de
Esplanade de la Paix
14032 Caen. Cedex
Psychologie Sociale,
Centre d'Etude de
Other Depts:
Communication;
Education; Enfant;
Langage; Psychologie
(Processus Cognitifs)
Dept. Head: C. Chabrol
Phone: (33) 31 45 55 00

Caen, Univ. de
Esplanade de la Paix
14032 Caen. Cedex
Psychologie Génétique,
Lab. de
Dept. Head: Jean
Drevillon
Phone: (33) 31 45 55 00

Campus de Beaulieu
35042 Rennes
Ethologie, Lab d'

Catholique de l'Ouest, Univ.
3 Place Andre Leroy
B.P. 808
49005 Angers. Cedex
Recherches Operatoires
en Psychologie et
Sciences Sociales Lab.
Other Depts: Psychologie
Sociale; Emploi
Dept. Head: Guy Minguet
Phone: (33) 41 81 66 00

Centre d'Etude de l'Expression - CMME
Clinique des Maladies
Mentales et de
l'Encephale
100 rue de la Santé
75014 Paris
Psychologie; Psychiatrie;
Art
Dept. Head: C. Wiart
Phone: (33) (1) 45 89 21
51

Centre Hospitalier
79021 Niort
Psychothérapique de
Goise, Ctr.

Centre Hospitalier Spécialisé
rue Paul Lintier
53100 Mayenne

Centre Hospitalier Spécialisé
38120 Saint Egrève

Centre Hospitalier Univ.
38700 La Tronche
Grenoble

Charles de Gaulle, Univ. de (Lille 3)
Pont de Bois
B.P. 149
59653 Villeneuve d'Ascq
Cedex
Activités Cognitives et
Linguistiques, Lab. de
Other Depts: Enfant;
Environnement;
Langage; Processus
d'Acquisition;
Psychologie Sociale;
Psycho-pathologie;
Dept. Head: Pierre
Leconte
Phone: (33) 20 91 92 02

Charles de Gaulle, Univ. de (Lille 3)
Pont de Bois
B.P. 149
59653 Villeneuve
d'Ascq
Cedex
Centres de Recherches de
Psychologie
Dept. Head: Regis
Verquerre
Phone: (33) 20 91 92 02

Claude Bernard, Univ. de (Lyon 1)
Hôpital Spécialisé du
Vinatier
95 blvd Pinel
69677 Bron Cedex
Psychiatrie Clinique et
Biologique
Other Depts:
Psycho-pathologie;
Psychotherapie;
Psychosomatique;
Alcoolisme
Dept. Head: Michel
Marie-Cardine
Phone: (33) 72 35 86 11

Claude Bernard, Univ. de (Lyon 1)
Hôpital Neurologie
59 blvd Pinel
69003 Lyon
Psychologie Medicalé,
Lab. de
Dept. Head: Jean Guyotat
Phone: (33) 72 35 72 35

Clermont 2, Univ. de
34 ave Carnot
63037 Clermont-Ferrand
Psychologie Sociale de la
Cognition, Lab. de
Phone: (33) 73 40 64 63
Fax: (33) 73 40 64 31
Email: psycle@
frmop11.bitnet

CNRS (URA 315)
41 rue Gay Lussac
75005 Paris
*Psychobiologié du
Développement
Other Depts: Psychologie
(Processus d'Acquisition)
Dept. Head: Jean-Pierre
Lecanuet*
Phone: (33) (16) 1 44 10
78 83
Fax: (33) (16) 1 43 26 88
16
Email: upbe@ frors31

Cochin, Hôpital
Pavillon Ollier
Centre des grands brûlés
27 rue du Faubourg St
Jacques
75014 Paris

**Conservatoire Nat. des
Arts et Metiers (CNAM)**
41 rue Gay Lussac
75005 Paris
*Recherche de l'Inst. Nat.
d'Etude du Travail et
d'Orientation
Professionnelle, Service
de - INETOP
Other Depts: Psychologie
(Processus
d'Acquisition); Travail
(Orientation
Professionnelle)
Dept. Head: Michel
Huteau*
Phone: (33) (1) 43 29 12
23

**CRAM, Ctr.
Psychotechnique**
14 place St Etienne
31000 Toulouse

CRAM Prévention
14 rue Seyboth
67010 Strasbourg

Dijon, Univ. de
2 blvd Gabriel
21000 Dijon
*Psychologie, Section de
Dept. Head: Michel
Fayol*
Phone: (33) 80 39 57 44
Fax: (33) 80 39 57 67

EHESS
10 rue Monsieur le
Prince
75006 Paris
*Groupe d'études et
recherches sur la
science*

**Etudes bioclimatiques,
Ctr. du**
21 rue Becquerel
67087 Strasbourg

**Européen de
Psychothérapie, Inst.**
á "L'Arbre Vert"
12 rue St Julien le
Pauvre
75005 Paris
Phone: (33) 46 34 51 56

**Foyer d'orientation
éducative**
136 rue de Paris
94220 Charenton le
Pont

**Franche-Comte, Univ.
de (Besançon)**
30 rue Megevand
25030 Besançon
Cedex
*Formation et de
Recherche
Psychopédagogiques,
Ctr. de
Other Depts:
Enseignement
Dept. Head: Charles Bried*
Phone: (33) 81 66 54 40

**Franche-Comte, Univ.
de (Besançon)**
30 rue Megevand
25030 Besançon
Cedex
*Lab. de Psychologie
Expérimentale et
Cognitive
Dept. Head: Mme Annie
Vinter*
Phone: (33) 81 66 66 66

**François Rabelais,
Univ. de (Tours)**
3 rue des Tanneurs
37041 Tours
Cedex
*Psychologie
Expérimentale, Lab.
de
Dept. Head: Daniel
Alaphilippe*
Phone: (33) 47 36 65
56
Fax: (33) 47 36 64 10

**François Rabelais,
Univ. de (Tours)**
3 rue des Tanneurs
37041 Tours
Cedex
*Recherche sur la
Première Enfance,
Equipe de
Dept. Head: Mme
Geneviève Boulanger*
Phone: (33) 47 36 66
00

**François Rabelais,
Univ. de (Tours)**
3 rue des Tanneurs
37041 Tours
Cedex
*Psychologie Sociale, Lab.
de
Dept. Head: Claude
Tapia*
Phone: (33) 47 36 66 00

François Rabelais, Univ. de
3 rue des Tanneurs
37041 Tours
Section Psychologie
Dept. Head: Roger
Fontaine
Phone: (33) 47 36 65 56
Fax: (33) 47 36 66 72

Geriatrie, Ctr. de
2 rue Auguste Renoir
72700 Allonnes

Gestalt-Thérapie, Inst. Français de
8 rue Paul-Louis
LandeGiner de Los Rios
33000 Bordeaux
Dept. Head: Jean-Marie
Robine
Phone: (33) 56 92 01 69
Fax: (33) 56 91 80 15

Grenoble 1, Univ. Scientifique, Technologique et Médicale
Hôpital Sud
38130 Echirolles
Psychologie Médicale Lab.
Other Depts: Psychologie
Clinique; Psychiatrie;
Criminologie
Dept. Head: Jacques
Boucharlat
Phone: (33) 76 09 80 50

Grenoble 2, Univ. de Sciences Sociales
Bâtiment Sciences de
l'Homme et de la Société
B.P. 47 X
38040 Grenoble Cedex
Psychologie Clinique et
Pathologique, Lab. de
Dept. Head: Gérard
Poussin
Phone: (33) 76 82 54 00

Grenoble 2, Univ. de Sciences Sociales
Bâtiment Sciences de
l'Homme et de la
Société
B.P. 47 X
38040 Grenoble Cedex
Psychologie Sociale, Lab.
de
Dept. Head: Jean-Léon
Beauvois
Phone: (33) 76 82 54 00

Grenoble 2, Univ. de Sciences Sociales
Bâtiment Sciences de
l'Homme et de la
Société
B.P. 47 X
38040 Grenoble Cedex
Psychologie
Expérimentale, Lab. de -
LPE
Dept. Head: Guy
Tiberghien
Phone: (33) 76 82 54 00

Guidance Infantile, Ctr. de
10 rue Saint-Léon
31000 Toulouse

Haute Bretagne, Univ. de
4 Place Saint Melaine
35000 Rennes
Psychologie de
l'Education, Lab. de
Other Depts:
Criminologie; Enfant;
Environnement;
Famille; Gérontologie;
Handicapés; Sport;
Santé; Travail
Dept. Head: Prof. Michel
Deleau
Phone: (33) 99 63 27 27
Fax: (33) 99 63 57 58
Email: sabatier@ uhb.fr

Haute Bretagne, Univ. de
Campus de Villejean
6 ave Gaston Berger
35043 Rennes. Cedex
Lab. Armoricain Univ.
d'Etudes et de
Recherches
Psycho-Sociales
Dept. Head: François le
Poltier
Phone: (33) 99 33 52 52

Haute Bretagne, Univ. de
Campus de Villejean
6 ave Gaston Berger
35043 Rennes Cedex
Cliniques
Psychologiques, Lab.
de
Dept. Head: Loick
Villerbu
Phone: (33) 99 33 52 52

Haute Bretagne, Univ. de
Campus de Villejean
6 ave Gaston Berger
35043 Rennes Cedex
Psychologie de l'Enfant,
Lab. de
Dept. Head: Mme
Myriam Pradet
Phone: (33) 99 33 51 43
Fax: (33) 99 33 51 75

Haute Bretagne, Univ. de
Campus de Villejean
6 ave Gaston Berger
35043 Rennes
UER Psychologie
Sociale
Dept. Head: Jacques
Degouys
Phone: (33) 99 33 51
43
Fax: (33) 99 33 51 75

Hautes Etudes en Sciences Sociales (EHESS), Ecole des
54 blvd Raspail
75270 Paris, Cedex 06
Psychologie Sociale, Lab. de
Other Depts: Santé; Environnement; Psychologie (Processus Cognitifs); Enfant
Dept. Head: Serge Moscovici
Phone: (33) (1) 49 54 25 25

Hautes Etudes en Sciences Sociales (EHESS), Ecole des
54 blvd Raspail
75270 Paris, Cedex 06
Etude des Processus Cognitifs et du Langage, Centre d'
Dept. Head: Michel Imbert
Phone: (33) (1) 49 54 20 70
Fax: (33) (1) 45 44 93 11
Email: upec14@ frors31.bitnet

Hautes Etudes en Sciences Sociales (EHESS), Ecoles des
54 blvd Raspail
75270 Paris, Cedex 06
Sciences Cognitives et Psycholinguistiques, Lab. de
Dept. Head: Jacques Mehler
Phone: (33) (1) 49 54 20 00

Henri Rousselle, Hôpital de
1 rue Cabanis
75014 Paris
Psychologie, Lab. de

Hervé de Guebriant, Ctr.
CMB Mescoat
29220 Landerneau

IDERIC - Inst. d'Etudes et de Recherches Interethniques et Interculturelles
Bât. A
63 blvd de la Madeleine
06000 Nice
Phone: (33) 93 44 82 44
Fax: (33) 93 97 20 42

Information et d'Orientation, Centre d'
14 rue du Commandant Brasseur
93600 Aulnay

INRIA - Nat. Research Inst. on Computer Science & Automation
Domaine de Voluceau
B.P. 105
78153 Le Chesnay Cedex
Ergonomics Psychology Project
Dept. Head: Dominique Louis Scapin
Phone: (33) (1) 39 63 55 07
Fax: (33) (1) 39 63 53 30
Telex: 697 033F
Email: scap@ archie.inria.fr

INSERM U94
16, ave Doyen Lépine
69500 Bron
Dept. Head: Dr Jean Decety
Phone: (33) 78 54 65 78

Jour pour enfants, Hôpital de
4 blvd A. Blanqui
75013 Paris
Fondation de Rothschild

LERS
31 Av. P. V. Couturier
Paris
Neuropharmacology Dept.

Lettres et Sciences Humaines, Fac. des
98 blvd Edouard Herriot
B.P. 369
06007 Nice

Lettres et Sciences Humaines, Fac. des
30 rue Megevand
25030
Besançon

Lille (FLSH), Univ. Cat. de
60 BD Vauban
BP 109
F-59016 Lille
Cedex
Psychologie, Dépt. de
Dept. Head: Claude Lukasiewicz
Phone: (33) 20 57 43 04
Fax: (33) 20 42 07 91

Louis Pasteur, Univ. (Strasbourg 1)
12 rue Goethe
67000 Strasbourg
Recherche sur les Dimensions Sociales et Incidences Subjectives du Langage, Lab. de
Other Depts: Enfant; Jeunesse; Processus Cognitifs; Psychanalyse; Psychologie; Psychopathologie; Sociologie;
Dept. Head: Mme Andrée Tabouret-Keller
Phone: (33) 88 35 82 00

Louis Pasteur, Univ. (Strasbourg 1)
12 rue Goethe
67000 Strasbourg
Psychologie Clinique, Génétique et Sociale, Lab. de - LPCGS
Dept. Head: Mme Edith Lecourt
Phone: (33) 88 35 82 00

Lumière, Univ. de (Lyon 2)
5 ave Pierre Mendes-France
CP 11
69676 Bron Cedex
Recherches Cliniques sur les Formations Intermdiares, Ctr. de
Dept. Head: René Kaes
Phone: (33) 78 77 23 23

Lumière, Univ. de (Lyon 2)
5 ave Pierre Mendes-France
CP 11
69676 Bron Cedex
Psychologie Sociale, Lab. de
Dept. Head: Bruno du Pouget
Phone: (33) 78 77 23 23

Lumière, Univ. de (Lyon 2)
5 ave Pierre Mendes-France
CP 11
69676 Bron Cedex
Psychologie Génétique et Cognitive de Terrain, Lab. de
Dept. Head: Jean-Marie Dolle
Phone: (33) 78 77 23 23

Lumière, Univ. de (Lyon 2)
5 ave Pierre Mendes-France
CP 11
69676 Bron Cedex
Psychologie Expérimentale, Lab. de
Dept. Head: Michel Defayolle
Phone: (33) 78 77 23 23

Lumière, Univ. de (Lyon 2)
5 ave Pierre Mendes-France
CP 11
69676 Bron Cedex
Etudes et d'Analyse de la Cognition et des Modèles, Lab. de - LEACM
Dept. Head: Robert Martin
Phone: (33) 78 77 23 23

Lumière, Univ. de (Lyon 2)
5 ave Pierre Mendes-France
CP 11
69676 Bron Cedex
Psychologie Clinique, Lab. de
Dept. Head: Jean Guillaumin
Phone: (33) 78 77 23 23

Luminy, Fac. des sciences de
Case 901
13288 Marseille Cedex
Sciences Humaines, Dépt. de

Maison de cure méd. de C. Celton
37 blvd Gambetta
92130 Issy les Moulineux

Maison des Sciences de l'Homme (MSH)
54 blvd Raspail
75270 Paris
Paris Cedex 06
Psychologie Sociale, Lab. Européen de - LEPS
Phone: (33) (1) 49 54 20 00

Maison des Sciences de l'Homme (MSH)
54 blvd Raspail
75270 Paris
Paris
Cedex 06
Psychologie du Travail et des Organisations, Réseau Européen de - ENOP
Phone: (33) (1) 49 54 22 48

Maladies Mentales, Clinique des
100 rue de la Santé
75014 Paris

Médicine Préventive, Ctr. de
2 ave du Doyen J. Parisot
54500 Vandoeuvre les Nancy

Metz, Univ. de
Ile du Saulcy
57045 Metz Cedex 1
Recherches en Sciences Sociales, Ctr. de
Other Depts: Psychologie Sociale; Travail
Dept. Head:
Gustave-Nicolas Fischer
Phone: (33) 87 30 40 12

Montpellier 1, Univ. de
700 ave du Pic Saint Loup
34000 Montpellier
Recherche en Sciences et Techniques des Activités Physiques et Sportives, Lab. de
Other Depts: Sociologie; Psychologie; Education; Sport
Dept. Head: Prof. Marc Durand
Phone: (33) 67 54 45 25
Fax: (33) 67 04 22 17

Nancy 2, Univ. de
23 blvd Albert 1er
54015 Nancy Cedex
Psychologie Génétique, Lab. de
Other Depts: Psychologie; Enfant; Handicapés
Dept. Head: Paul Dickes
Phone: (33) 83 96 16 14

Nanterre, Univ. de (Paris X)
200 ave de la République
92001 Nanterre Cedex
Education et Formation, Lab. de - LEF
Other Depts: Formation Permanente; Psychanalyse; Psychologie; Psychologie Clinique; Psychopathologie; Sociologie; Travail
Dept. Head: Mme Monique Linard
Phone: (33) (1) 40 97 72 00

Nanterre, Univ. de (Paris X)
200 ave de la République
92001 Nanterre Cedex
Recherches sur les Remaniements Psychiques, Ctr. de
Dept. Head: Jean-Michel Petot
Phone: (33) (1) 40 97 72 00

Nanterre, Univ. de (Paris X)
200 ave de la République
92001 Nanterre Cedex
Psychologie Expérimentale et Différentielle, Lab. de
Dept. Head: Mme Anne Lancry
Phone: (33) (1) 40 97 72 00

Nanterres, Univ. de (Paris X)
200 ave de la République
92001 Nanterre Cedex
Équipe representations sociales et processus idéologiques
Dept. Head: Jean-Pierre Deconchy
Phone: (33) (1) 40 97 78 11
Fax: (33) (1) 40 97 71 58
Email: meyer@ u-paris10.fr

Nantes, Univ. de
Chemin de la Sensive du Tertre
B.P. 1025
44036 Nantes Cedex 01
Psychologie, Lab. de
Other Depts: Psychologie Clinique; Psychologie Sociale; Psychanalyse
Dept. Head: Luc Ricordeau
Phone: (33) 40 74 74 01

Neurophysiologie, Lab. de
place Eugène Bataillon
34060 Montpellier

Neuropsychologie de la Sénescence Normale et Pathologique
2 rue d'Alésia
75104 Paris
Neuropsychology Dept.
Other Depts: Cerebral ageing; Alzheimer's Disease
Dept. Head: François Boller
Phone: (33) (1) 45 81 44 21
Fax: (33) (1) 45 89 68 48
Email: unit324@ frccrm51

Nice, Univ. de
28 Parc Valrose
06034 Nice
Psychology, Deot. of

Paris 7, Univ. de
13 rue Santeuil
75005 Paris
Recherche en Psychosomatique, Unité de
Dept. Head: Mahmoud Sami-Ali
Phone: (33) (1) 45 87 41 17

Paris 7, Univ. de
13 rue Santeuil
75005 Paris
Psychologie Clinique, Lab. de
Other Depts: Psychologie; Psychologie Sociale; Psychopathologie (Biologie); Psychophysiologie; Sociologie
Dept. Head: Mme Claude Revault D'Allonnes
Phone: (33) (1) 45 87 41 17

Paris 7, Univ. de
Centre Censier
13 rue Santeuil
75005 Paris
*Recherche sur
l'Adolescence*
*Dept. Head: Philippe
Gutton*
Phone: (33) (1) 45 87 41
17

**Paris 8, CNRS Univ.
de**
2 rue de la Liberté
93526 Saint Denis
Cedex 2
Psychologie Cognitif
*Dept. Head:
Jean-François Richard*
Phone: (33) (1) 49 40 64
89
Fax: (33) (1) 49 40 67 54
Email: upsc001@
frors31.earn

**Paris 8, CNRS Univ.
de**
2 rue de la Liberté
93526 Saint-Denis Cedex
2
*UFR de Psychologie,
Pratiques Cliniques et
Sociales*
Phone: (33) 49 40 64 71
Fax: (33) 49 40 67 54

**Paris-Dauphine, Univ.
de (Paris 9)**
Place du Maréchal de
Lattre de Tassigny
75775 Paris Cedex 16
*Changement Social, Lab.
de - LCS*
*Other Depts: Psychologie
Sociale; Sociologie*
*Dept. Head: Vincent de
Gaulejac*
Phone: (33) (1) 45 05 14
10

**Paris-Nord, Univ. de
(Paris 13)**
ave Jean-Baptiste
Clément
93430 Villetaneuse
*Psychologie Clinique
Sociale et
Développementale, Lab.
de*
*Other Depts: Famille;
Psychologie Sociale;
Psychopathologie*
*Dept. Head: Maurice
Dayan*
Phone: (33) (1) 49 40 30
00

**Paris-Nord, Univ. de
(Paris 13)**
ave Jean-Baptiste
Clément
93430 Villetaneuse
Jeu et le Jouet, Lab. de
Dept. Head: Jean Perrot
Phone: (33) (1) 49 40 30
00

Pasteur, Hôpital
30 ave de la Voie Romaine
B.P. 69 06002 Nice
Cedex
*Psychiatrie et Psychologie
Médicale*
Dept. Head: Guy Darcourt
Phone: (33) 92 03 77 51
Fax: (33) 93 53 32 88

**Paul Sabatier, Univ. de
(Toulouse 3)**
Hôpital la Grave
Place Lange
31052 Toulouse Cedex
*Psychiatrie et Psychologie
Médicale, Lab. de*
*Other Depts: Psychiatrie;
Psychologie Clinique;
Toxicomanie*
Dept. Head: Pierre Moron
Phone: (33) 61 42 61 19

**Paul Valéry, Univ. de
(Montpellier 3)**
B.P. 5043
Route de Mende
34032 Montpellier
Cedex 1
Psychologie Cognitif
*Other Depts:
Communication;
Education;
Gérontologie;
Processus
d'Acquisition;
Psychanalyse;
Psychologie Sociale;
Psychopathologie;
Santé; Sport*
*Dept. Head: Prof. J. F.
Chatillon*
Phone: (33) 67 79 15 97
Fax: (33) 67 14 23 95

**Paul Valéry, Univ. de
(Montpellier 3)**
B.P. 5043
Route de Mende
34032 Montpellier
Cedex 1
*Etudes et de Recherches
en
Psychotemporalités,
Centre d'*
*Dept. Head: Jean-Marc
Ramos*
Phone: (33) 67 14 20 00

**Paul Valéry, Univ. de
(Montpellier 3)**
B.P. 5043
Route de Mende
34032 Montpellier
Cedex 1
*Psychologie
Sociale et du Travail,
Lab. de*
*Dept. Head: Claude
Louche*
Phone: (33) 67 14 20 00

**Paul Valéry, Univ. de
(Montpellier 3)**
B.P. 5043
Route de Mende
34032 Montpellier
Cedex 1
*Psychologie de l'Enfant
et de l'Adolescent,
Lab. de*
*Dept. Head: Henri
Lehalle*
Phone: (33) 67 14 21 98

**Paul Valéry, Univ. de
(Montpellier 3)**
B.P. 5043
Route de Mende
34032 Montpellier
Cedex 1
*Psychologie Clinique,
Lab. de*
*Dept. Head: Jacques
Birouste*
Phone: (33) 67 14 20
00

**Paul Valéry, Univ. de
(Montpellier 3)**
B.P. 5043
Route de Mende
34032 Montpellier
Cedex 1
*Recherche en
Psychopathologie
Clinique, Equipe de*
*Dept. Head:
Bruere-Dawson*
Phone: (33) 67 14 21
52

Pédiatrie I
Maison de la Mère et
l'enfant
Quai Moncousu
44100 Nantes
*Dept. Head: Dr.
Michael
Sanchez-Cardenas*
Phone: (33) 40 08 34 83

**Picardie, Univ. de
(Amiens)**
Campus Univ.
rue Solomon Mahlangu
80025 Amiens Cedex
*Etudes et Recherches
Pluridisciplinaires en
Psychologie - CERPP*
*Other Depts: Psychologie
Clinique;
Psychopathologie;
Psychologie Sociale*
*Dept. Head:
Paul-Laurent Assoun*
Phone: (33) 22 95 06 15

Poitiers, Univ. de
ave du Recteur Pineau, 95
96022 Poitiers
Psychologie du Langage
Dept. Head: Eric Espéret
Phone: (33) 49 45 32 45
Fax: (33) 49 45 33 01
Email: psylan@ frupts51

Poitiers, Univ. de
ave du Recteur Pineau, 95
96022 Poitiers
Psychologie, Dépt. de
*Dept. Head: Dr Catherine
Tourette*
Phone: (33) 49 45 32 45
Fax: (33) 49 45 33 01

**Pratique des Hautes
Etudes, Ecole**
EPHE IIIe Section
28 rue Serpente
75006 Paris
*Psychologie Cognitive de
la Communication*
*Other Depts: Psychologie
Expérimentale
(Processus
d'Acquisition, Lecture)*
*Dept. Head:
Marie-France Ehrlich*
Phone: (33) (1) 40 51 98 53
Fax: (33) (1) 40 51 70 85

**Pratique des Hautes
Etudes, Ecole**
EPHI IIIe Section
41 rue Gay Lussac
75005 Paris
*Psychobiologie
Différentielle*
*Other Depts:
Psychologie
Expérimentale*
*Dept. Head: Etienne
Mullet*
Phone: (33) (1) 43 29 12
23

**Preé-Orientation,
Ctr.**
32 blvd Jean Casse St
Barthélémy
13014 Marseille

**Provence St-Jerôme,
Univ. de**
13397 Marseille 13
*Psycho-physiologie, Lab.
de*

**Provence, Univ. de
(Aix-Marseille 1)**
29 ave Robert
Schuman
13621 Aix-en-Provence
Cedex 1
*Psychologie Cognitive ,
Centre de Recherche
en*
*Other Depts:
Environnement:
Psychologie (Processus
Cognitifs, Processus
d'Aquisition, Analyse
d'Evaluation);
Santé*
*Dept. Head: Prof.
Jean-Paul Caverni*
Phone: (33) 42 20 60 96
Fax: (33) 42 20 59 05
Email: crepco@
frmop11.bitnet

Provence, Univ. de
29 ave Robert Schuman
13621 Aix-en-Provence
Psychologie Sociale, Lab.
Dept. Head: Jean-Claude
Abric
Phone: (33) 42 59 99 30

Psychologie de
l'apprentissage, Lab.
de
rue des Géraniums
13014 Marseille

Psychologie de l'Enfant,
Lab. de
Ecole Jules Ferry
1 rue des Chailliers
92000 Nanterre
Dept. Head: Matty Chiva

Psychologie du Travail,
Ctr. de
Passage du Commerce
blvd René Levasseur
72000 Le Mans

Psychologie du Travail
PTT, Ctr
302 rue Garibaldi, Lyons

Psychologie Génétique,
Lab. de
46 rue Saint-Jacques
75005 Paris

Psychologie, Inst. de
12 rue Goethe
67000 Strasbourg
Section clinique
Dept. Head: Michele
Grosclaude
Phone: (33) 88 35 82 03
Fax: (33) 88 35 84 49

Psychologie
Pathologique, Lab. de
18 rue de la Sorbonne
75005 Paris

Psychologie Prévention
des Accidents
28 rue de Rouen
21000 Dijon

Psychologie Sociale,
Lab. de
18 rue de la Sorbonne
75005 Paris

Psychologues
Praticiens, Ecole
21 rue d'Assas
75270 Paris
Cedex 06
Dept. Head: Jean-Pierre
Chartier
Phone: (33) (1) 45 48 17
75
Fax: (33) (1) 42 22 71 45

Psychosociologiques,
Ctr. d'Etudes
37 ave Gambetta
74000 Annecy

Psychotechnique, Ctr.
de
3 rue d'Espagne
B.P. 2201
35022 Rennes

Psychotechnique
Régional, Ctr.
64 rue Lamartine
63000 Clermont-Ferrand

Psychothérapique, Ctr.
59880 Saint Saulve

Purpan, CHU
place du D. Baylac
31052 Toulouse
Cedex
Neuro-psychologie, Dept.
de
Dept. Head: Dr. M. Puel
Phone: (33) 61 49 89 26
Fax: (33) 61 49 95 24

Réadaptation Service,
Inst. Nat. de
14 rue du Val d'Osne
94410 Saint Maurice
Dept. Head: Dr Gagnard

Recherche
Pédagogique, Inst.
Nat. de
DP 3
91 ave Ledru-Rollin
75011 Paris

Reims, Univ. de,
Champagne-Ardenne
57 rue Pierre Taittinger
51096 Reims
Cedex
Psychologie Appliquée,
Lab. de
Other Depts: Lab. de
Psychologie Cognitive
Dept. Head: Prof. Michèle
Carlier
Phone: (33) 26 05 36 48
Fax: (33) 26 05 36 46

René Descartes, Univ.
de (Paris 5)
28 rue Serpente
75270 Paris
Cedex 06
Psychologie Différentielle,
Lab. de
Other Depts: Antillais;
Education;
Gérontologie;
Migrations (Minorites);
Psychiatrie; Psychologie
(Processus Cognitifs);
Psychologie Sociale;
Psychopathologie; Santé;
Dept. Head: Jacques
Lautrey
Phone: (33) (1) 40 51 98
60
Fax: (33) (1) 40 51 70 85
Email: upec010@
frors31.bitnet

René Descartes, Univ.
de (Paris 5)
28 rue Serpente
75270 Paris Cedex 06
Psychologie
Expérimentale
Dept. Head: Claude
Bonnet
Phone: (33) (1) 40 51 98 54

René Descartes, Univ.
de (Paris 5)
28 rue Serpente
75270 Paris Cedex 06
Recherches en
Psychologie Projective,
Groupe de
Dept. Head: Mlle Nina de
Traubenberg
Phone: (33) (1) 40 51 98
98

René Descartes, Univ.
de (Paris 5)
45 rue des Saints Pères
75270 Paris Cedex 06
Centre Charles Richet de
Recherches et d'études
des Dysfonctions de
l'Adaptation
Dept. Head: François
Raveau
Phone: (33) (1) 42 86 20
98

René Descartes, Univ.
de (Paris 5)
46 rue Saint Jacques
75005 Paris Cedex 06
Psychologie du
Développement et de
l'Education de l'Enfant
Dept. Head: Prof. Janine
Beaudichon
Phone: (33) (1) 40 46 29
95
Fax: (33) (1) 40 46 29 93
Email: ulpg0008@
frors31.bitnet

René Descartes, Univ.
de (Paris 5)
Chu Sainte Anne
100 rue de la Santé
75014 Paris
Psychologie Médicale,
Lab. de
Dept. Head: Bertrand
Samuel-Lajeunesse
Phone: (33) (1) 45 65 80 00

René Descartes, Univ.
de (Paris 5)
Hôpital Necker-Enfant
Malades
149 rue de Sèvres
75743 Paris Cedex 15
Psychiatrie Adulte
Dept. Head: Yves Pelicier
Phone: (33) (1) 42 73 87 42

Rennes 2, Univ. de
4 place Saint-Melaine
35000 Rennes
Psychologie de
l'Education, Lab. de
Dept. Head: Prof. Michel
Deleau
Phone: (33) 99 63 27 77
Fax: (33) 99 63 57 58
Email: deleau@ uhb.fr

Rouen, Univ. de
Place Emile Blondel
B.P. 118
76134 Mont Saint-Aignan
Cedex
Etude des Processus de
Décision, Lab. d'
Other Depts:
Communication
(Processus Cognitifs);
Enfant; Langage;
Psychologie
Expérimentale
(Ergonomie); Sociologie
Dept. Head: Michel
Moscato
Phone: (33) 35 14 60 00

Rouen, Univ. de
rue Lavoisier
B.P. 108
76134 Mont Saint-Aignan
Cedex
Psychologie, Lab. de
Dept. Head: Prof. Claude
Lemoine
Phone: (33) 35 14 61 15
Fax: (33) 35 14 61 04

Rouen, Univ. de
rue Lavoisier
B.P. 108
76134 Mont Saint-
Aignan
Cedex
Groupe de Sciences de
l'Education
Dept. Head: Jean-Claude
Forquin
Phone: (33) 35 14 61 08

Rouen, Univ. de
rue Lavoisier
B.P. 108
76134 Mont Saint-
Aignan
Cedex
Lab. Psychologie des
Régulations
individuelles et Sociales
Dept. Head: Prof. Claude
Lemoine
Phone: (33) 35 14 61 15
Fax: (33) 35 14 61 04

Saint-Charles, Centre
Univ.
162 rue Saint-Charles
75740 Paris
Cedex 15
Psychologie de l'Art, de la
Culture et de
l'Environnement, Lab. de
Dept. Head: Michel
Imberty
Phone: (33) (1) 45 54 97
24

Saint-Marguerite, Hôpital
13008 Marseille
Centre Inter-Régional de Recherches en Psychopathologie Clinique
Other Depts: Psycho-pathologie; Psychanalyse
Dept. Head: Yves Poinso
Phone: (33) 91 83 50 82

Saint Pierre Le Tampon, Hôpital Int. de
B.P. 350
97448 St Pierre
Pédopsychiatrie, Service de

Saint-Vincent de Paul, Hôpital3
74 ave Denfert-Rochereau
75014 Paris
Psychiatrie Infantile, Unité de
Dept. Head: Bernard Golse
Phone: (33) (1) 40 48 81 84
Fax: (33) (1) 40 48 83 20

Salpétrière, Hôpital de
CNRS URA654 - LENA
47 blvd Hôpital
75651 Paris
Cedex 13
Psychophysiologie Cognitive
Other Depts: Maladies syst. nerveux; Neuro-psychologie
Dept. Head: Bernard Renault
Phone: (33) (1) 45 70 23 59
Fax: (33) (1) 44 24 39 54
Email: martiner@ frciti51

Savoie, Univ. de (Chambery)
Domaine Univ. de Jacob-Bellecombette
B.P. 1104
73011 Chambery
Cedex
Centre de Recherches et d'Applications Psychologiques et Sociologiques
Other Depts: Psychologie Sociale; Psychopathologie; Enfant; Mythologie
Dept. Head: Charles Amourous
Phone: (33) 79 75 85 85

Sciences de Luminy CASE 901, Fac des
13288 Marseille
Sciences Humaines, Dépt. de

Secteur Psychologie
5 rue Géo Chavez
75020 Paris
Cedex

SNCF
3 blvd Wilson
67000 Strasbourg
Psychologie Appliquée, Ctr. de

Sport et de l'Education Physique (INSEP), Inst. Nat. du
11 ave du Tremblay
75012 Paris
Psychologie, Lab. de
Other Depts: Sport; Psychologie (Performance)
Dept. Head: Guy Missoum
Phone: (33) (1) 43 74 11 21
Fax: (33) (1) 43 74 54 11

Toulouse le Mirail, Univ. de (Toulouse 2)
5 allée Antonio Machado
31058 Toulouse Cedex
UFR de Psychologie
Other Depts: Formation Permanente; Handicapés; Psychologie Clinique; Psychologie Expérimentale; Psychologie Sociale; Psychopathologie
Dept. Head: Prof. H. Sztulman
Phone: (33) 61 50 48 15
Fax: (33) 50 42 09

Toulouse le Mirail, Univ. de (Toulouse 2)
5 allée Antonio Machado
31058 Toulouse Cedex
Centre d'études et de recherches sur les processus psychologiques
Dept. Head: Henri Sztulman
Phone: (33) 61 50 47 50
Fax: (33) 61 50 49 50

Toulouse le Mirail, Univ. de (Toulouse 2)
5 allée Antonio Machado
31058 Toulouse Cedex
Neuropsycholinguistique - Jacques Lordat, Lab. de
Dept. Head: Jean-Luc Nespoulous
Phone: (33) 61 50 42 50

Toulouse le Mirail, Univ. de (Toulouse 2)
5 allée Antonio Machado
31058 Toulouse
Cedex
La Découverte Freudienne
Dept. Head: Michel Lapeyre
Phone: (33) 61 50 42 50

**Toulouse le Mirail,
Univ. de (Toulouse 2)**
5 allée Antonio
Machado
31058 Toulouse
Cedex
*Etude des Processus
Mentaux et Cognitifs
dans le Travail et
l'Education, Groupe d'
Dept. Head: Gérard
Lamouroux*
Phone: (33) 61 50 42 50

**Toulouse le Mirail,
Univ. de (Toulouse 2)**
5 allée Antonio
Machado
31058 Toulouse
Cedex
*Personnalisation et
Changements Sociaux
Dept. Head: J. Larrue &
J. M. Cellier*
Phone: (33) 61 50 48 21
Fax: (33) 61 50 49 50
Email: cellier@
frcict&1.bitnet

**Toulouse le Mirail,
Univ. de (Toulouse 2)**
5 allée Antonio
Machado
31058 Toulouse
Cedex
*Recherche en Education
et Didactique, Equipe
Univ. de
Dept. Head: Jacques
Fijalkow*
Phone: (33) 61 50 42 50

Tours, Univ. de
3 rue des Tanneurs
37041 Tours

**Travail et Psy.
Appliquée**
18 rue Gaston de
Caillavet
75015 Paris
Psychologie Dept.

**Tribunal de Grande
Instance**
B.P. 1030
67070 Strasbourg
Comité de probation

**UER des Sci. Sociales et
Psycho.**
Bât. E
Esplanade des Antilles
33405 Talence

**UER Inst. de
Psychologie**
28 rue Serpente
75006 Paris

**UER Psychologie et Sci.
Sociales**
ave de l'Univ.
69500 Bron

**UER Sci. du comp. et de
l'educ.**
rue Lavoisier
76130 Mont St Aignan

**Val de Grâce,
Hôpital du**
74 blvd de Port Royal
75230 Paris
*Neurology &
Neuropsychology, Dept.
of
Dept. Head: Dr Daniel
Béquet*
Phone: (33) 40 51 41 00
Fax: (33) 46 33 07 90

**Vincennes à
Saint-Denis, Univ. de
(Paris 8)**
2 rue de la Liberté
93526 Saint-Denis
Cedex 02
*Psychologie Cognitive du
Traitement de
l'Information Symbolique
Other Depts:
Communication;
Langage; Linguistique;
Psychologie (Processus
d'Aquisition); Psychologie
Sociale; Psychologie
(Relations
Interculturelles)
Dept. Head:
Jean-François Richard*
Phone: (33) (1) 49 40 67 89

**Vincennes à
Saint-Denis, Univ. de
(Paris 8)**
2 rue de la Liberté
93526 Saint-Denis
Cedex 02
*Recherche sur l'Humour
et le Comique, Equipe
Interdisciplinaire de*
Phone: (33) (1) 49 40 67
89

**Vincennes à
Saint-Denis, Univ. de
(Paris 8)**
2 rue de la Liberté
93526 Saint-Denis
Cedex 02
*Psychologie
Anthropologique
Interculturelle
Dept. Head: Geneviève
Vermes*
Phone: (33) (1) 49 40 67 89

GEORGIA

**Abkhazian AM Gorkii
State Univ.**
Ul. Tsereteli 9
Sukhumi
384900 Abkhazskaya
Psychology, Dept. of

**Tbilisi, I.
Dzhavakhiladze Univ.**
Pr. Chavchavadze 1
Tbilisi
380028
Psychology, Dept. of

Technical Univ.
Ul. Kostava 63
Tbilisi
380075
Psychology, Dept. of

GERMANY, FEDERAL REPUBLIC OF

**Akademie d.
Wissenschaften**
1086 Berlin
Kurstrasse 33
*Kybernetik / Info.
prozesse, Inst.*

**Allgemeine
Krankenhaus
Ochsenzoll**
Langenhorner Chaussee
560
2000 Hamburg 65

**Angewandte Psych.,
Inst. f.**
Markt 14
2300 Kiel 1

**Anstalten der Inneren
Mission**
Lindenstrasse 14
2720 Rotenburg

G

**Arbeitsmedizin,
Zentralinstitut**
1134 Berlin
Nöldnerstrasse 40/42

**Arbeitsphysiologie,
Inst. f.**
Ardeystrasse 67
4600 Dortmund
*Work Psychology, Dept.
of
Other Depts: Ergonomics;
Physiology
Dept. Head: Herbert
Heuer*
Phone: (49) (231) 1084
302
Fax: (49) (231) 1084 340
Email: heuer@arb-phys.
uni-dortmund.de

Augsburg Univ.
Alter Postweg 120
8900 Augsburg
*Lehrstul Psychologie,
Phil. Fak. 1*

Augsburg Univ.
Memmingerstrasse 14
8900 Augsburg
Lehrstuhl f. Psychologie I

Bamberg Univ.
Markusplatz 3
8600 Bamberg
*Lehrstuhl Psychologie II
Dept. Head: Prof. Dr.
Dietrich Dörner*
Phone: (49) (951) 863 589
Fax: (49) (951) 601 511
Email: gordes@ppp.
uni-bamberg.dbp.de

Bamberg Univ.
Postfach 1549
8600 Bamberg
*Psychophysiologie, Abt.
Dept. Head: Prof. Dr. Jan
Born*
Phone: (49) (951) 863 580
Fax: (49) (951) 69028

Bayreuth Univ.
Geschwister-Scholl-Platz 3
Postfach 10 12 51
8580 Bayreuth
*Lehrstuhl f. Psychologie
Dept. Head: Prof. Dr.
Wiebke Putz-Osterloh*
Phone: (49) (921) 55700
Fax: (49) (921) 55753

Bielefeld Univ.
Universitätstrasse
4800 Bielefeld
*Oberstufen-Kolleg
Other Depts: Exp.
u-Angewandte
Psychologie*

**Benedikt-Kreutz
Rehab-Zentrum**
7812 Bad Krozingen

Berlin, Technische Univ.
Dovestrasse 1-5
1000 Berlin 10
*Psychologie, Inst. f.
Dept. Head: Prof. Dr.
Arnold Upmeyer*
Phone: (49) (30) 314 22370
Fax: (49) (30) 314 25274

Berlin Technische Univ.
Franklinstrasse 28/29 -
FR4-8
1000 Berlin 10
*Medienpädagogik und
Hochschuldidaktik, Inst.
Dept. Head: Prof. Dr.
Christine Holzkamp*
Phone: (49) (30) 314 25348

Bielefeld Univ.
Postfach 8640
Bielefeld 1
*Psychologie &
Sportwissenschaft,
Fak.f.*
Phone: (49) (521) 1064296
Fax: (49) (521) 1065844
Telex: 932362 UNIBI

Bonn Univ.
Römerstrasse 164
5300 Bonn 1
*Psychologie Inst.
Other Depts:
Pädagogosche*

**Braunschweig, Tech.
Univ.**
Spielmannstrasse 19a
3300 Braunschweig
Psychologie, Inst. f.

Bremen Univ.
Bibliothekstrasse
2800 Bremen 33
*Psychologie, Inst. f.
Other Depts: Studiengang
Psychologie FB9*

**Bundesanstalt f.
Arbeit**
Regensburgerstrasse 104
8500 Nürnberg 30
*Psychologischer Dienst
Dept. Head: Dr. Reinhard
Hilke*
Phone: (49) (911) 179 2446
Fax: (49) (911) 179 2123
Telex: 622 348 BA D

**Bundesinst. f. Ost/Int.
Studien**
Lindenbornstrasse 22
5000 Köln 30
*Dept. Head: Dr. Thomas
Kussmann*
Phone: (49) (221) 57570
Fax: (49) (221) 5747110

**Bundeswehr München
(UNIBWM), Univ. der**
Werner-Heisenberg-Weg
39
8014 Neubiberg
*Psychologie & Empirische
Pädagogik, Inst. f.
Dept. Head: Prof. Dr.
Wilfrid Ennenbach*
Phone: (49) (89) 600 43157

Bundeswehr, Univ. der
Postfach 70 08 22
D-2000 Hamburg 70
*Kognitionsforschung,
Inst. f.
Dept. Head: Prof. Dr.
Rainer H. Kluwe*
Phone: (49) (40) 6541 2863
Fax: (49) (40) 653 0413
Telex: 02 14952
Email: p-rain@
unibw.hamburg.de

**Burg Berghausen, Psy.
Inst.**
Lindenstrasse 51
4100 Duisburg 28

Bürgerhospital
Tunzhoferstrasse 14-16
7000 Stuttgart

**Central Inst. for Mental
Health**
POB 5970
6800 Mannheim

**Chirurgische Univ.
sklinik Heidelberg**
Ernst-Moro-Haus
Im Neuenheimer Feld 155
6900 Heidelberg
*Psychosoziale
Nachsorgeeinrichtung
Dept. Head: Prof. Dr.
Reinhold Schwarz*
Phone: (49) (6221) 563 088
Fax: (49) (6221) 565 250

**Christian-Albrechts-
Univ.**
Olhausenstrasse 40-60
2300 Kiel 1
Psychologie Inst.

Curschmann-Klinik
W-2408 Timmendorfer
Strand
Saunaring 6
*Dept. Head: Dr Thomas
Riedemann*
Phone: (49) (4503) 602127
Fax: (49) (4503) 602657

Darmstadt, Tech. Univ.
Steubenplatz 12
6100 Darmstadt
Psychologie Inst.

**Deutsche
Sporthochschule
Köln**
Carl-Diem-Weg 6
5000 Köln 41
*Psychologisches Inst.
Dept. Head: Dr. Jürgen R.
Nitsch*
Phone: (49) (221) 498
2550
Fax: (49) (221) 499 5235

**Deutschen Wirtschaft,
Inst. der**
Gustav-Heinemann-Ufer
84-9
5000 Köln 51
*Forschungsgruppe
PRODIS*

**Deutsches Inst. f. Int.
Päd. Forschung**
Schlossstrasse 29
6000 Frankfurt am Main
*Dept. Head: Prof. Dr.
Bernhard Kraak*
Phone: (49) (69) 770245
Fax: (49) (69) 770245
Telex: 4 17 0331

Dortmund Univ.
Postfach 500500
4600 Dortmund 50

**Duisburg
Gesamthochschule,
Univ.**
4100 Duisburg
Lotharstr. 65
Psychology, Dept. of

Düsseldorf Univ.
Moorenstrasse 5
4000 Düsseldorf
*LS f. Psychotherapie Ge.
14. 91
Other Depts:
Arbeitsmedizin Inst.*

Düsseldorf Univ.
Universität strasse 1
4000 Düsseldorf
*Psychologie Inst.
Other Depts:
Erziehungswissenschaft
Inst.*

Eichstätt, Kath. Univ.
Philos. -Pädagog. Fak.
Ostenstrasse 26-8
8078 Eichstätt
*Lehrstuhl Psychologie
II
Other Depts: FB
Sozialwesen*

**Erlangen-Nürnberg,
Univ.**
Bismarckstrasse 1
D-8520 Erlangen
*Lehrstuhl Psychologie I
Dept. Head: Prof. Dr.
Friedrich Lösel*
Phone: (49) (9731) 852
330
Fax: (49) (9731) 852646
Email: Loesel@cnve.
rrze.uni-erlangen.
dbp.de

**Erlangen-Nürnberg
Univ.**
Findelgasse 9
8500 Nürnberg
Sozialwissenschaft Inst.

**Erlangen-Nürnberg
Univ.**
Hindenburgstrasse 14
8520 Erlangen
*Psych. Inst., Lehrstuhl
III
Dept. Head: Prof. Dr. E.
Olbrich*
Phone: (49) (9131) 854744

**Erlangen-Nürnberg
Univ.**
Regensburgerstrasse 160
8500 Nürnberg 30
*Lehrstuhl f. Psychologie
IV, Psychologisches
Inst.
Dept. Head: Wolf D.
Oswald*
Phone: (49) (911) 530
2568
Fax: (49) (911) 4010584
Email: geronto@cnve.
rrze.uni-erlangen.dbp.de

**Ernst-Moritz-Arndt-
Univ.**
2200 Greifswald
Franz-Mehring-Strasse
47
*Sek.
Erziehungswissen-
schaften*

**Erz. Hochschule
Rheinland-Pfalz**
Grosse Bleiche 60-2
6500 Mainz
Fachbereich Sonderpäd

Essen Univ.
Universität strasse 11
4300 Essen

**Fachhochschule des
Bundes f. öffentliche
Verwaltung**
Seckenheimer
Landstrasse 16
6800 Mannheim 1
*Fachbereich
Arbeitsverwaltung*
Phone: (49) (621)
42090
Fax: (49) (621) 4209215

**Fachhochschule
Hagen**
Haldenerstrasse 182
5800 Hagen 1

**Fachhochschule
Kiel**
Diesterwegstrasse 20
2300 Kiel
FB Sozialwesen

**Fachhochschule
Köln**
Ubierring 46
5000 Köln 1
FB Sozial Psychologie

**Fachhochschule
Sozialwesen**
Pettenkoferstrasse
24-30
6800 Mannheim

**Fed. Highway Research
Inst.**
Brüderstrasse 53
5060 Bergisch
Gladbach
*Accident Research Divn.
Other Depts: Section on
Road Use Attitudes &
Behaviour; J. Pfafferett,
Phone: (49) (2204)
43421
Dept. Head: G. Kroj*
Phone: (49) (2204)
43456

Fern Univ.
Postfach 940
5800 Hagen 1
Arbeitsbereich
Psychologie
Schwerpunkt;
Psychologie sozialer
Prozesse
Dept. Head: Prof. Dr.
Helmut E. Lück
Phone: (49) (2331) 987
2776
Fax: (49) (2331) 987
2709

FH Bund.
Postfach 560
7480 Sigmaringen 1
FB Finanzen

FKH Hahnenholz III
Am Weinberg 12
3559 Hatzfeld-
Reddinghausen

Flugmedizinisches Inst.
der Luftwaffe
Postfach 172/KFL
8080 Fürstenfeldbruck

Forschungsinstitut f.
Psychotherapie
Christian-Belser-Strasse
79a
7000 Stuttgart 70

Forschungsinstitut f.
Anthropotechnik
Neuenahrerstrasse 20
D-5307 Wachtberg-
Werthhoven
Dept. Head: Dr. Heino
Widdel
Phone: (49) (228)
852490
Fax: (49) (228)
348953
Email: wid@
fatvax.fat.fgan.de

Forschung u.
Ausbildung in
Kommunikations-
therapie, Inst. f.
Rückerstrasse 9
8000 München 2

Frankfurt Univ.
Kettenhofweg 128
6000 Frankfurt
Psychologie, Inst. f.
Other Depts:
Psychoanalyse Inst.

Frederich-Alexander
Univ.
Hindenburgerstr. 14
D-8520 Erlangen
Psychology, Dept. of
Dept. Head: Dr J.
Brunstein

Freiburg, Univ.
Belfortstrasse 16
D-7800 Freiburg
Rehabilitations-
psychologie, Abt. f.
Other Depts:
Persönlichkeits-
psychologie; Phone: (49)
(761) 203 3622; Fax:
(49) (761) 203 3627
Dept. Head: Prof. Uwe
Koch
Phone: (49) (0761) 2033634
Fax: (49) (0761) 203 3300
Email: kania@
psychologie. uni-
freiburg.de

Freiburg Univ.
Niemensstrasse 10
7800 Freiburg
Psychologisches Inst.,
Allgemeine Psychologie
Dept. Head: Prof. Dr.
Hans Spada
Phone: (49) (761) 203 3628
Fax: (49) (761) 203 4164

Freie Univ. Berlin
Habelschwerdter Allee 45
1000 Berlin 33
Psychologie Fachbereich
Erziehungs- und
Unterrichtswissenschaften,
Inst. f.
Dept. Head: Prof. Dr. Ralf
Schwarzer
Phone: (49) (30) 838 5642
Fax: (49) (30) 838 6777

Freie Univ. Berlin
Rheinbabenalle 14
1000 Berlin 33
Sportpsychologie, Inst. f.
Dept. Head: Prof. Dr.
Hans-Gerhard Sack
Phone: (49) (30) 823 5057
Fax: (49) (30) 824 3731

Freie Univ. Berlin
Univ-klinikum
Charlottenburg
Platanenallee 23
1000 Berlin 19
Psych. u. Neurologie
Kind / Jugalt.
Dept. Head: Prof. Ulrike
Lehmkuhl
Phone: (49) (030) 30
038101
Fax: (49) (030) 30 44737

Friedrich-Schiller-
Univ.
D-O-6900 Jena
Leutragraben 1
UHH 19. OG
Psychologie, Inst. f.
Dept. Head: Dozent Dr.
Georg Eckhardt
Phone: (37) (78) 82 24221
Fax: (37) (78) 82 53252

Frühförderung
Coerrach
Zum Blauenblick 12
7850 Coerrach

Frühpädagogik,
Inst. f.
Arabellastrasse 1
8000 Müunchen 81

Georg-August-Univ.
Göttingen
Waldweg 26
3400 Göttingen
Pädagogische
Psychologie, Inst. f.
Dept. Head: Prof. Franz
Thurner
Phone: (49) (0551) 399289

Gerichtliche Psychiatr.
Klinik
3553 Haina
Dept. Head: Lutz
Gretenbord
Phone: (49) (4364) 563
1500
Fax: (49) (4964) 5691 511

German Air Force
8080 Fürstenfeldbruck
Airbase
Aerospace Medicine,
Inst.f.

Gesamthochschule
Kassel
Heinrich-Plettstrasse 40
3500 Kassel

Gesamthochschule
Wuppertal, Univ.
FB3
Gauss Strasse 20
5600 Wuppertal

Geschichte d. N.
Psychologie,Inst.
POB 2540
8390 Passau
Dept. Head: Prof. Dr.
Horst Gundlach
Phone: (49) (851) 509 632
Fax: (49) (851) 509 622

Giessen, Univ. of
Otto Behaghel Strasse 10
6300 Giessen
Fachbereich
Psychologie

Giessen, Univ. of
Kugelberg 62
D-6300 Giessen
Sport Psychology Dept.
Dept. Head: Dorothee
Alfermann
Phone: (49) (641) 702 5326
Fax: (49) (641) 702 5328

Giessener Inst. f. Ang.
Psych.
Dietrich-Bonhoeffer
Strasse 22
6300 Giessen

Göttingen Univ.
Calsarstrasse 73
3400 Göttingen
Päd. Seminar

Göttingen Univ.
Gosslerstrasse 14
3400 Göttingen
Psychologie, Inst. f.

Göttingen Univ.
Kinderklinik
Humboldtallee 38
3400 Göttingen

Hamburg, Univ. of
Von-Melle-Park 11
D-2000 Hamburg
General, Differential and
Applied Psychology,
Inst. of
Dept. Head: Prof. Kurt
Pawlik
Phone: (49) (40) 4123
4723
Fax: (49) (40) 4123 6591
Email: p01paw@
dhhdesy3

Hannover, Univ.
Bismarckstrasse 2
3000 Hannover 1
FB Erziehungswiss. 1
Dept. Head: Prof. Dr.
Joachim Tiedemann
Phone: (49) (511) 807 8356
Fax: (49) (511) 807 8555

Heidelberg, Univ.
Hauptstrasse 47-51
6900 Heidelberg
Psychologisches Inst.
Other Depts: Speech &
Situation, Prof. Dr. C. F.
Craumann; Centre for
Psychological Treatment
& Clinical Research,
Prof. Dr. Reiner
Bastine
Dept. Head: Prof. Dr.
Reiner Bastine
Phone: (49) (6221)
547349
Fax: (49) (6221) 547348
Telex: 461515 UNIHD
Email: b68@ dhdurzi

Heilpädagogisches
Heim
4194 Bedburg-Hau

Heilpädagogisches,
Inst. Pad. Hoch.
Olhausenstrasse 75
2300 Kiel

Heilpädagogisches
-ther. Kinderzentrum
Marienthalerstrasse 4-6
6761 Steinbach

Hildesheim, Univ.
Marienburger Platz 22
3200 Hildesheim
Dept. Head: Prof. Dr.
Peter Moltke
Phone: (49) (5121) 883 150
Fax: (49) (5121) 883 199

**Hirnverletzten-Vers.
krankenhaus**
Auf dem Sand 3
7400 Tübingen

Hochschule Bremen
Langemarckstrasse 116
2800 Bremen, FB 8

**Hochschule der
Bundeswehr**
Postfach 700822
2000 Hamburg 70
FB Päd. Allg. Psychologie

**Hochschule
Rheinland-Pfalz**
Industriestrasse 15
6740 Landau
*Päd. Forschung der
Erziehungswiss.*

Hohenheim, Univ.
Postfach 70 05 62
7000 Stuttgart 70
*Lehrstuhl f. Psychologie
Dept. Head: Prof. Dr.
Heinz Schuler*
Phone: (49) (711) 459 2654
Fax: (49) (711) 459 2652

Humbolt-Univ. zu Berlin
1020 Berlin
Oranienburger Strasse 18
*Sektion Psychologie
Other Depts: Sekt. Päd.
Wissens. bereich*

IPN
Olshausenstrasse 40
2300 Kiel

**J. W. Goethe Univ.
Frankfurt**
Kettenhofweg 128
6000 Frankfurt
Psychologie, Inst. f.
Phone: (49) (69) 798 3153
Fax: (49) (69) 798 8383

J. W. Goethe-Univ.
Heinrich-Hoffmann-strasse
10
6000 Frankfurt 70
Psychiatrie, Zentrum der

J. W. Goethe-Univ.
Postfach 111939
6000 Frankfurt am
Main 11
*Päd. Psychologie, Inst. f.
Dept. Head: Prof. Dr. H.
Giesen*
Phone: (49) (69) 798 2488
Fax: (49) (69) 798 3652

**Johannes-Gutenberg
Univ.**
Saarstrasse 21
6500 Mainz
Psychologie Inst.

Justus-Liebig Univ.
Otto-Behagelstrasse 10
6300 Giessen
*Psychology, Dept. of
Dept. Head: Prof. Dr. Gert
Haubeusak*
Phone: (49) (641) 702
5385
Fax: (49) (641) 702 3811
Telex: 176 419013

Karl-Marx Univ.
7030 Leipzig
Tieckstrasse 2
Section Psychologie

**Kassel,
Gesamthochschule**
Präsidialverwaltung
3500 Kassel
Mönchebergstr. 19
Psychology, Dept. of

**Kath. Fachhochschule
Mainz**
Saarstrasse 2
6500 Mainz

Kiel Univ.
Olshausenstrasse 40-60
2300 Kiel
*Psychologie, Inst. f.
Other Depts: Inst. Päd.
Naturwissensch.*

Kinderhaus München
Menzingerstrasse 139
8000 München 50

**Kinderklinik Univ.
Würtzburg**
Josef-Schneider-Strasse 2
8700 Würzburg

**Kinderneurologisches
Zentrum**
Hartmühlenweg 24
6500 Mainz

Kinderzentrum
Katharinenufer 9
5500 Trier

**Klinik u. Rehabz.
Lippoldsberg**
3417 Wahlsburg
Dept. Head: Jens Sinram
Phone: (49) (5572) 41225
Fax: (49) (5572) 41221

**Klinikum
Charlottenburg**
Spandauer Damm
1000 Berlin 19
Neurologische Abt.

**Klinikum
Charlottenburg f.
Kinder- und
Jugendspsychiatrie,Uni
v.**
Platanenallee 23
1000 Berlin 19

Klinikum der Univ.
Schleusenweg 2-16
6000 Frankfurt am Main

Klinikum Psychologie, Inst. f.
Kaulbachstrasse 93
8000 München 40

Koblenz-Landau, Univ.
Im Fort 7
W-6740 Laundau
Zentrum f. Emp.
Pädagogische
Forschung
Other Depts: Seminar
Psychologie
Dept. Head: Prof. Dr.
Reinhold S. Fager
Phone: (49) (634)
280229
Fax: (49) (634) 280101
Email: lfb999@ dkluni01

Koblenz, Univ. of
Rheinau 3
5400 Koblenz
Dept. Head: Prof. Dr.
Elisabeth Sander / Prof.
Dr. Manfred Koch
Phone: (49) (261) 91190
Fax: (49) (261) 37524

Köln, Univ. zu
Herbert-Lewinstrasse
2
5500 Köln 41
Psychologisches Inst.
Dept. Head: Prof. Dr.
Egon Stephan
Phone: (49) (221) 400
0167
Fax: (49) (221) 400 0167

Köln, Univ. zu
Herbert-Lewinstrasse
2
5500 Köln 41
Dept. Head: Prof. Dr.
Egon Stephan
Phone: (49) (221) 470
2571

Köln, Univ. zu
Richard Wagner Strasse
39
5000 Köln 1
Heilpädagogische
Psychologie, Sem. f.
Other Depts: Erzungs.
-Heilpädagog. Fak.
Dept. Head: Prof. Dr.
Gudula List
Phone: (49) (221) 470
4637

Köln Univ. zu
Richard Wagner Strasse
39
5000 Köln 41
Psychologisches Inst.
Dept. Head: Prof. Ulrich
Schmidt-Denter
Phone: (49) (221) 470
4474

Kommunikations-psychologie Inst.
Westring 10a
D-6740 Landau
Medienpädagogik
Phone: (49) (6341)
84076
Fax: (49) (6341) 280 101

Konfliktfor. u. Krisen-berat. Inst.
Taschnerstrasse 9
8000 München 19

Krankenhaus Hamburg, Univ.
Pav. 69 II Medizinische
Klinik
Martinistrasse 52
2000 Hamburg 20
Medizinische Psychologie
Abt.
Other Depts:
Psychomatische; Kinder
und Jugend-
psychiatrie

Krim. Forschungsinst. Niedersachsen
Leisewitzstrasse 41
3000 Hanover 1
Dept. Head: Dr. Margit E.
Oswald
Phone: (49) (511) 28 10
91
Fax: (49) (511)81 91 07

Lübeck, Medizinische Univ. zu
2400 Lübeck
Ratzeburger Allee 160
Medical Psychology, Dept.
of

Lübecker Inst. f. Angewandte Psychologie (LIAP)
Schwartaner Allee 2a
W-2400 Lübeck 1
Dept. Head: Dr. Friedrich
Balck
Phone: (49) (451)
42182

Mainz Univ.
Saarstrasse 21
6500 Mainz
Psychologie, Inst. f.
Other Depts:
Medizinsche
Psychologie

Mannheim Univ.
Schloss
6800 Mannheim 1
Lehrstuhl Psychologie
II
Other Depts: Leh.
Erziehungswissen-
schaft

Marburg Univ.
Gutenbergstrasse 18
3550 Marburg
FB Psychologie

Max-Planck-Inst.
Lentzeallee 94
1000 Berlin 33
Bildungsforschung
Dept. Head: Prof. Dr.
Paul B. Baltes
Phone: (49) (30) 829951
Fax: (49) (30) 8249939

Max-Planck-Inst.
Leopoldstrasse 24
8000 München 40
Psychologische Forschung
Dept. Head: Prof. Dr.
Wolfgang Prinz / Prof.
Dr. Franz E. Weinert
Phone: (49) (89) 386 021
Fax: (49) (89) 342 473
Email:
postmaster@mpipf.muenc
hen.mpg.dbp.de

Max-Planck-Inst. f.
Psychiatrie
Proj. Rauschmittel-
abhängigkeit
Parzivalstrasse 25
8000 München 40
Psychologie Abt.

Max-Planck-Inst. f.
Strafrecht
Günterstalstrasse 73
7800 Freiburg
Dept. Head: Prof. Dr.
Günther Kaiser
Phone: (49) (761) 7081
201
Fax: (49) (761) 7081 294

Medizinische Inst. f.
Umwelthygiene
Gurlitlstrasse 53
4000 Düsseldorf

Medizinische
Psychologie Inst.
Eberstrasse 14
7500 Karlsruhe

Medizinische
Psychologie Inst.
Martinistrasse 52
2000 Hamburg 20

Medizinische
Psychologie, Inst. f.
Friedrichstrasse 36
6300 Giessen

Medizinische
Psychologie, Inst. f.
Niemannsweg 147
2300 Kiel
Zentrum Nervenheil-
kunde
Dept. Head: Prof.
Wolf-Dieter Gerber
Phone: (49) (431) 597
2644
Fax: (49) (431) 597 2711

Medizinische
Psychologie, Inst. f.
Bahnhofstrasse 18a
3550 Marburg

Medizinischen Univ. zu
Lübeck
Ratzeburger Allee 160
D-2400 Lübeck 1
Medizinische
Psychologie
Dept. Head: Prof. Dr.
Fritz Schmielau
Phone: (49) (451) 500 6099

Mercedes-Benz AG
Postfach 60 02 02
7000 Stuttgart 60
Zentrales
Bildungswesen
Psychologischer
Dienst
Dept. Head: Dr. Wolfgang
Bachl
Phone: (49) (711) 17
59211
Fax: (49) (711) 17 59253

Modelprog. Psych. d.
Bundesreg.
Kamenzer Damm 1
1000 Berliln 46
AG Begleitforschung

MPI f. Psychiatrie
Psycholog.
Kraepelinstrasse 10
8000 München 40
Clinical Psychology Dept.
Dept. Head: Prof. Dr.
Hans-Ulrich Wittchen
Phone: (49) (89) 30622
546
Fax: (49) (89) 30622 200

München, Technische
Univ.
Lothstraße 17
8000 München 2
Lehrstuhl f. Pädagogik
Dept. Head: Prof.
Andreas Schelten
Phone: (49) (89) 2105
8651
Fax: (49) (89) 180431

München Univ.
Goethestrasse 31/I
D-8000 München 2
Medizinische Psychologie,
Inst. f.
Dept. Head: Prof. Dr.
Ernst Pöppel
Phone: (49) (89) 5996 650
Fax: (49) (89) 5996 615
Email: all@imp.med.
uni-muenchen.dbp.de

München Univ.
Leopoldstrasse 13
8000 München 40
Org. -u.
Wirtschaftspsychologie
Dept. Head: Prof. Dr.
Lutz von Rosenstiel
Phone: (49) (89) 2180 5201
Fax: (49) (89) 2180 5255

München Univ.
Leopoldstrasse 13
8000 München 40
Educational Psychology,
Inst. of
Dept. Head: Prof. Dr.
Kurt A. Heller
Phone: (49) (89) 2180 5148
Fax: (49) (89) 2180 5250
Telex: 529860
Email: dm0lrz01 user:
UB 35101.bitnet

München Univ.
Schellingstrasse 10
8000 München 40
Psychologie, Inst. f.
Phone: (49) (89) 2180 5207
Fax: (49) (89) 2180 5255

Münster Univ.
Bispinghof 3
4400 Münster
Erziehung Inst.

Münster Univ.
Lazarettstrasse 23
4400 Münster
Psychologie Inst.

Münster Univ.
Fliednerstrasse 21
4400 Münster
Fachbereich
Psychologie
Dept. Head: Prof. Dr.
Hanko Bommert
Phone: (49) (251) 83 4138
Fax: (49) (251) 83 2090

Münster, West. Wilh.
Univ.
Fliednerstrasse 21
4400 Münster
FB 21 Psychologie

Nervenklinik Spandau
Griesinger Strasse 27-33
1000 Berlin 20

Nervenklinik,
Univ.
Nussbaumstrasse 7
8000 München 2

Nervenklinik, Univ.
Niemannweg 147
2300 Kiel

Nervenklinik, Univ.
6650 Homburg/Saar
Kinder u. Jugendpsych,
Abt. f.

Nervenkrankenhaus
8770 Lohr am Main

Neuropädiatrische
Klinik
Landstrasse 1
7640 Kehl-Kork

Neurolog. Psychiat.
Klinik
Heugnerstrasse 40
5600 Wuppertal 2

Neurolog. Rehabz.
Godeshöhe
Waldstrasse 2-10
5300 Bonn

Neurolog. Univ.
klinik
Hansastrasse 9
7800 Freiburg

Oldenburg, Univ. of
Birkenweg 3
D-2900 Oldenburg
FB5-Arbeits & Org.
Psychologie
Dept. Head: Prof. Dr.
Friedhelm Nachreiner
Phone: (49) (441) 798
8240
Fax: (49) (441) 798
8333
Email: 010301@ dolunia

Oldenburg, Univ. of
POB 25 03
D-2900 Oldenberg
Psychology, Dept. of
Dept. Head: Dr. Eckart
Scheerer
Phone: (49) (441) 798
8224
Fax: (49) (441) 798 3000
Telex: 25 655 unol d
Email: 111977@
doluni1.bitnet

Osnabrück Univ.
Heger-Tor-Wall 12
4500 Osnabrück, FB 8
Dept. Head: Prof. Dr.
Peter Machemer
Phone: (49) (541) 969
4404
Fax: (49) (541) 969 4470

Päd. Hochschule
Keplerstrasse 87
6900 Heidelberg
Fach. Psychologie
Phone: (49) (6221) 477 530
Fax: (49) (6221) 477 432

Päd. Hochschule
Halle-Köthen
Lohmannstr 23
0-4370 Köthen
Dept. Head: Prof.
Manfred Baumann
Phone: (49) (00445) 690
Fax: (49) (37) 445 2781

Paderborn, Univ. of
Warburger Strasse 100
4790 Paderborn
Psychology, Dept. of
Dept. Head: Prof. M.
Wettler
Phone: (05251) 602902
Fax: (05251) 603243
Telex: 936776 unipb d
Email: brappl@
pbhrzt.uni-paderborn.de

Passau Univ.
Schustergasse 21
8390 Passau
Gesch. der Neueren
Psych. Inst.

Philipps Univ.
Gutenbergstrasse 18
3550 Marburg
FB Psychologie
Dept. Head: Dr. Dekan
Phone: (49) (6421) 283 674
Fax: (49) (6421) 284 884

Psychoanalyse, Inst. f.
Seuckenberganlage 15
6000 Frankfurt

**Psychiatrische Univ.
klinik**
Hauptstrasse 5
7800 Freiburg
Dept. Head: Prof. M.
Berger
Phone: (49) (761) 270 6501
Fax: (49) (761) 270 6523

**Psychiatrische Univ.
Klinik**
Berger Landstrasse 2
4000 Düsseldorf

Psychologie Inst.
Bundesallee 187
1000 Berlin 31

Psychologie Inst.
Steubenplatz 12
6000 Darmstadt

Psychologie Inst.
Gosslerstrasse 14
3400 Göttingen

Psychologie Inst.
Bingerstrasse 22
6500 Mainz 1
Entwick. u. Päd.
Psychologie

Psychologie, Inst. f.
Habelschwerdter Allee
45
1000 Berlin 33
FB Erziehungs-u.
Unterricht- swiss.

Psychologie, Inst. f.
Spielmannstrasse 12a
3300 Braunschwaig
Dept. Head: Prof. Dr.
Kurt Hahlweg
Phone: (49) (531) 391
3654
Fax: (49) (531) 391 8105

Psychologie, Inst. f.
Kaulbachstrasse 93
8000 München 40

Psychologie, Inst. f.
Wiedenmayerstrasse
46a
8000 München 22

**Psychologie
Landeskrankenhaus**
7102 Weinsberg
Kinder-u.
Jugendpsychiatrie Abt.
Dept. Head: Dr. Joachim
Jungmann
Phone: (49) (7134) 75 217
Fax: (49) (7134) 75 500

Psychologie, Seminar für
Rheinau 3-4
5400 Koblenz, EWH-Abt.

**Psychologisches
Beratungs. d. Landkr.
Konstanz**
Reichenaustrasse 34
7760 Radolfzell

**Psychologisches
Beratungstelle**
Kleemannstrasse 36
8490 Cham

**Psychologisches
Beratungstelle**
Viktoriastrasse 5
5632 Wermelskirchen

**Psychologisches
Beratungszentrum**
Martinstrasse 21
8700 Würzburg

Regensburg Univ.
Universitätsstrasse 31
8400 Regensburg
Psychologie, Inst. f.
Dept. Head: Prof. Dr.
Klaus E. Grossmann
Phone: (49) (941) 943 3814
Fax: (49) (941) 943 3872
Telex: 065658 unire d
Email: grossmann@vax1.
rz.uni-regensburg.dbp.de

**Rheinische
Braunkohlewerke AG**
HW Grefrath
5020 Frechen 5

**Rheinische
Friedrich-Wilhelms
Univ. Bonn**
5300 Bonn
Regina-Pacis-Weg 3

**Rheinische
Landesklinik Düren**
Meckerstrasse 15
5160 Düren

**Rheinische Landesklinik
und Hochschulklinik**
Hufelandstrasse 55
4300 Essen 1
Klinik f. Kinder- und
Jugendpsychiatrie
Dept. Head: Prof. Dr. Ch.
Eggers / Dr. Detlef Bunk
Phone: (49) (201) 7227 465
Fax: (49) (201) 7227 301
Email: tjp010@ de0hrz1a

Rhine State Clinic
Kaiser-Karl-Ring 20
D-5300 Bonn 1
Psychological Lab.
Dept. Head: Dr. Georg
Lamberti
Phone: (49) (228) 551
2168
Fax: (49) (228) 551 2720

Rostock, Univ.
0-2500 Rostock
August-Bebelstrasse 28
Pädagogische und
Rehabilitations
psychologic
Dept. Head: Prof. Erich
Kurth
Phone: (49) (378) 379
2476

Rostock, Univ.
0-2540 Rostock 45
Gehlsheimer Strasse 20
Nervenklinik und
Poliklinik
Dept. Head: Prof.
Hans-Dieter Rosler
Phone: (49) (3781) 36031

Ruhr-Univ.
Postfach 102148
4630 Bochum
Psychologie Inst.
Other Depts: Vegetative
Physiologie; Medizin
Psychologie; Lehrstuhl
Medizinische
Psychologie

RWTH Aachen
Jägerstrsse 17-19
D-5100 Aachen
Psychologie, Inst. f.
Dept. Head: Prof. Dr.
Dieter Heller
Phone: (49) (241) 806
012
Fax: (49) (241) 803 995

RWTH Aachen -
Medizinische Fak.
Pauwelstrasse 1
5100 Aachen
Medical Psychology, Inst.
of
Phone: (49) (241) 808 900
Fax: (49) (241) 875 992

Saarbrücken Univ.
6600 Saarbrücken 1
Sozialpsy. Forschung. f.
Entwick.

Saarlandes Univ.
Medizinische und Klin.
Psychologie
6650 Homburg
Fachrichtung 4. 20

Saarlandes, Univ. des
D-6600 Saarbrücken 11
FR Psychologie
Dept. Head: Prof. Dr.
Werner H. Tack
Phone: (49) (681) 302
2303
Fax: (49) (681) 302 4361

Seelische Gesundheit,
Zentralinstitut für
Postfach 12 21 20
D 6800 Mannheim 1
Dept. Head: Prof. Heinz
Häfner
Phone: (49) (621) 1703
739
Fax: (49) (621) 2 34 29

Seminar f. Pädagogik
Wendenring 1
3300 Braunschweig
Dept. Head: Prof. Dr.
Reiner Fricke
Phone: (49) (531) 391
2554
Fax: (49) (531) 391 3115
Email: I80204001@
dbstui.bitnet

Seminar f. Psychologie
Römerstrasse 164
5300 Bonn
Pädagogische Fak.
Dept. Head: Prof. Dr.
Dieter Dumke
Phone: (49) (228) 550
368

Siegen Univ.
Hölderlinstrasse 3
5900 Siegen

Sozial-psychiatrischer
Dienst
Erlanger Strasse 27
8580 Bayreuth

Sozial-psychol. Dienst
des Ldk
Wallstrasse 40
4410 Northeim

Sozialwissenschaften
Inst.
Fraenkelstrasse 28/9
1000 Berlin 10

Sozialwissenschaftlichen
Inst.
Lange Gasse 20
Postfach 3931
D-8500 Nürnberg
Lehrstuhl f. Psychologie
Dept. Head: Prof. Dr. J.
Franke
Phone: (49) (911) 530
2259
Fax: (49) (911) 530 2243

Sozio-therapeutische
Praxis
Friedrichstrasse 16
1000 Berlin 61

Stuttgart, Univ.
7000 Stuttgart 1
Keplerstr.7
Psychology, Dept. of

**Techn. Hochschule
Darmstadt**
Hochschulstrasse 1
6100 Darmstadt
Psychologie, Inst. f.

Techn. Univ.
Ernst-Reuter-Platz 7
1000 Berlin 10
*Humanwissenschaft in
Arbeit und
AusbildungInst. f.
Dept. Head: Prof. Dr.
Walter Volpert*
Phone: (49) (30) 314
25069

**Techn. Univ.
Braunschweig**
Bültenweg 74/75
3300 Braunschweig
*Seminar f. Psychologie
FB9*
Phone: (49) (531) 391
3493
Fax: (49) (531) 391 4577
Telex: 952526 tubsw

Techn. Univ. Dresden
Mommsenstrasse 13
8027 Dresden
*Psychologie, Inst. f.
Dept. Head: Prof. Dr.
Winfried Hacker*
Phone: (37) (351) 463
4695
Fax: (37) (351) 463 7110

**Test-u. Begabungs-
forschung, Inst. f.**
Koblenzer Strasse 77
5300 Bonn 2
*Dept. Head: Dr. Günther
Trost*
Phone: (49) (228) 820
900
Fax: (49) (228) 820 9038
Email: ext/meyer@
kmx&gmd.dbp.de

TH Darmstadt
Steubenplatz 12
6100 Darmstadt
Psychologie, Inst. f.

**Therapieforschung
Gemeinschaft Peterhof**
Buschmannweg 1-3
4130 Moers 2

**Therapieforschung,
Inst. f.**
Parzivalstrasse 25
8000 München 40
*Dept. Head: Dr. Gerhard
Bühringer*
Phone: (49) (89) 360804-0
Fax: (49) (89) 360804-69

Trier Univ.
Postfach 3825, 5500 Trier
*Psy. Info. und
Dokumentation
Other Depts: Klinik
Psychologie, Lehrstuhl f.
Dept. Head: Prof. Dr. Leo
Montada*
Phone: (49) (651) 201 2877
Fax: (49) (651) 201 2071

Tübingen, Univ.
Aussenstelle Weissenau
Rasthalde 3
7980 Ravensburg
*Dept. Head: Prof. Dr. B.
Preilowski*
Phone: (49) (751) 64988
Fax: (49) ('751) 64184
Email: e2prei@
dknkurz1.bitnet

Tübingen Univ.
Friedrichstrasse 21
7400 Tübingen 1
*Psychologisches Inst.
Dept. Head: Prof. Dr. W.
Stroebe*
Phone: (49) (7071) 292 412
Fax: (49) (7071) 293 363

Tübingen Univ.
Osanderstrasse 14
7400 Tübingen
*Kinder / Jung-psychiatrie
Abt.*

Tübingen Univ.
Psychologisches Inst.
Gartenstrasse 29
7400 Tübingen
*Klinische & Physiol.
Psychologie, Abt.
Dept. Head: Prof. Dr.
Niels Birbaumer*
Phone: (49) (7071) 294
219
Fax: (49) (7071) 295 956
Email: sipb101 mailserv.
zdv.uni-tubingen.de

Ulm Univ.
Am Hochstraess 8
7900 Ulm
*Psychotherapie, Abt.
Dept. Head: Prof. Dr.
Kaechele Horst*
Phone: (49) (731) 502
5661
Fax: (49) (731) 502
5662
Email: kaechele@
sip.medizin.uni-ulm.de

Ulm Univ.
Christian Belser Strasse
79a
7 Stuttgart 70
*Psychotherapy Research
Centre
Dept. Head: Prof. Dr.
Horst Kaechele*
Phone: (49) (711) 678
1400
Fax: (49) (711) 678 6902

**Umfragen, Meth. u.
Anal. Zentrum**
Postfach 5969
6800 Mannheim

Univ. - GH
Lotharstrasse 65
4100 Duisburg 1
Fachbereich 2,
Psychologie
Dept. Head: Prof. Dr.
Ulrich Raatz
Phone: (49) (203) 379 3790
Fax: (49) (203) 379 3167
Telex: 379 3167

Werner Otto Inst.
Postfach 12 21 20
D 6800 Mannheim 1
Der Ev. Stiftung Alsterdorf
Dept. Head: Dr. Herbert
Scheying
Phone: (49) (40) 507 3145
Fax: (49) (40) 507 3191

Wuppertal Univ.
Building S. -12. 05
Gaußstrasse 20
5600 Wuppertal 1
Psychology, Dept. of
Dept. Head: Prof.
Hartmut Häcker
Phone: (49) (202) 439 2289
Fax: (49) (202) 439 3320
Email: haickercyber@urz.
uni-wuppertal.dbp.de

Würzburg, Univ.
Wittelsbacherplatz 1
D-8700 Würzburg
Lehrstuhl f. Psychologie IV
Dept. Head: Prof. Dr.
Wolfgang Schneider

Würzburg Univ.
Domerschulstraße 13
D-8700 Würzburg
Psychologie, Inst. f.
Dept. Head: Prof.
Wilhelm Janke
Phone: (49) (931) 31842
Fax: (49) (931) 53624
Email: janke@vax.rz.
uni-wurzburg.dbp.de

Würzburg, Univ.
Röntgenring 11
D-8700 Würzburg
Psychologisches Inst.
III
Dept. Head: Prof. Otto
Heller
Phone: (49) (931) 31645
Fax: (49) (931) 571786
Email: haickercyber@urz.
uni-wuppertal.dbp.de

Zentrum Europa und
Dritte Welt (ZEDW)
Univ. des Saarlandes
D-6600 Saarbrücken 11
Im Fuchstälchen
Entwicklungspolitische
Forschung & Beratung
Dept. Head: Dr. H. W.
Schoenmeier
Phone: (49) (681) 302 2564
Fax: (49) (681) 302 2514

GHANA

Cape Coast, Univ. of
Univ. Post Office
Cape Coast
Psychology, Dept. of

Ghana, Univ. of
POB 84, Legon
Psychology, Dept. of
Dept. Head: Dr J. Y.
Opoku
Phone: (233) (21) 75381

Kumasi, Univ. of
Science & Tech.
Univ. PO, Kumasi
Psychology, Dept. of

GREECE

Aegean, Univ. of
Kanari 9
106 71 Athens
Psychology, Dept. of

Aristoteleio
Panepistimio
Thessalonikis
Univ. Campus
540 06 Thessaloniki
Psychology, Dept. of
Dept. Head: Prof.
Andreas Demetriou
Phone: (30) 31 992904
Fax: (30) 31 206138
Telex: 041 2181
Email: bczz04@ grtheun1

Athens, Univ. of
Panepistemiopolis
Athens 15784
Psychology, Dept. of
Dept. Head: Prof. James
Georgas
Phone: (30) (1) 7249000
Fax: (30) (1) 724 8979
Email: ppy10@ grathun1

Athinisin Ethnikon Kai
Kapodistriakon
Panepistimion
Odos Panepistimiou 30
106 79 Athens
Psychology, Dept. of

Crete, Univ. of
Rethymnon, Crete
Psychology, Dept. of
Dept. Head: Joannis N
Nestoros
Phone: (30) (831) 20014
Fax: (30) (831) 20013

Dimokriteio
Panepistimio Thrakis
Demokritos Str. 17
691 00 Komotini
Psychology, Dept. of

Ethniko Metsovio
Polytechneio
Odos 28 Octovriou 42
106 82 Athens
Psychology, Dept. of

Ioannina, Univ. of
451 00 Ioannina
Psychology, Dept. of
Phone: (30) (651) 21920
Fax: (30) (651) 21920

Panteios, Univ. of
Syngrou 136
Athens 17671
Psychology, Dept. of
Dept. Head: Prof. Stamos
Papastamou
Phone: (30) (1) 9232767
Fax: (30) (1) 9223690

Patras, Univ. of
26110 Patras
Psychology, Dept. of
Dept. Head: Prof. C. D.
Porpodas
Phone: (30) (061) 997629
Fax: (30) (061) 997629

GUAM

Guam, Univ. of
Mangilao, Guam 96923
Psychology, Dept. of
Dept. Head: Dr A. M.
Wylie
Phone: (1) (671) 734 9155
Fax: (1) (671) 734 3420
Email: socsci@
uog.pacific.edu.internet

GUATEMALA

Francisco Marroquin,
Univ. de
6 Calle Final
Zona 10
Guatemala City
Psychology, Dept. of

Mariano Gálvez de
Guatemala, Univ. de
Apdo Postal 1811
Guatemala
Psychology, Dept. of

Rafael Landívar,
Univ.
Vista Hermosa III
Zona 16
Apdo Postal 39 'C'
Guatemala
Psychology, Dept. of

San Carlos de
Guatemala, Univ.
Ciudad Univ.
Guatemala 12
Psychology, Dept. of

Valle de Guatemala,
Univ. del
Apdo Postal No. 82
01901 Guatemala
Psychology, Dept. of

GUINEA

Kankan, Univ. de
Ministère de l'Éducation
Nat.e
Kankan
Psychology, Dept. of

GUYANA

Guyana, Univ. of
Fac. of Education
POB 101110
Georgetown
Educational Research &
Development, Dept. of
Dept. Head: Gocool
Boodoo
Phone: (592) (2) 54841
Fax: (592) (2) 54885
Telex: (592) (2) 54841

HAITI

Haiti, Univ. d'État d'
10 rue Magloire Ambroise
Port-au-Prince
Ethnologie, Fac. d';
Psychologie, Dept. de
Dept. Head: Dr
Milchelange Momplaisir
Phone: (509) 224236

HONDURAS

Honduras, Univ. Nac. Aut. de
POB 3560
Tegucigalpa DC
Psychology, Dept. of

José Cecilio del Valle, Univ.
Apdo 917
Tegucigalpa
Psychology, Dept. of

HONG KONG

Asia Pacific Studies, Hong Kong Inst. of,
Shatin N. T.
Gender Research Programme
Dept. Head: Prof. Fanny
M. Cheung
Phone: (852) 609 7061

Caritas Family Service
Caritas House
2 Caine Rd

Child Assessment Clinic
9 Arran St.
Mongkok
Kowloon

Correctional Services
Guardian House
32 OI Kwan Rd
WANCHAI

Duchess of Kent Children's Hospital
12 Sandy Rd
Sandy Bay

Hong Kong Chinese Univ.
Shatin
N. T.
Psychology Dept.
Other Depts: Psychiatry
Dept. Head: Dr Kwok
Leung
Phone: (852) 609 6486
Fax: (852) 603 5019
Email: bo45746@
cucsc.bitnet

Hong Kong Polytechnic
Hung Hom
Kowloon
Applied Social Studies, Dept. of
Dept. Head: Diana Mak
Phone: (852) 766 5773
Fax: (852) 773 6558

Hong Kong Psychiatric Centre
6b Bonham Rd

Hong Kong, Univ. of
Pokfulam Rd
Psychology Dept.
Dept. Head: Prof. Henry
S. R. Kao
Phone: (852) 8592375
Fax: (852) 8583518
Telex: 71919 CEREB
Email: dpsychol@
hkucc.bitnet

Hong Kong, Univ. of
Community Medicine
Dept.
4/F Li Shu Fan Building
Sasson Rd
Behavioural Sciences Unit
Dept. Head: Dr Richard
Fielding
Phone: (852) 8199280
Fax: (852) 8559528
Email: hrmrfir@
hkucc.hku.hk

Kowloon Hospital
Argyle St. Kowloon
Psychiatric Unit

Lai Chi Kok Reception Centre
5 Butterfly Valley Rd
Lai Chi Kok
Kowloon

Matilda Hospital
Mt Kellett Rd
Handicapped Children's Centre

Psychological Service, School of
Osborn Barracks
200 Waterloo Rd
Kowloon

Sha Tsui Detention Centre
Lautau Island
Clinical Psychology Dept.

South Kwai Chung Polyclinic
Kwai Shing Circuit
N. T.
Psychiatric Centre

Sui Lam Psychiatric Centre
16. 5 M. S. Castle Peak
Rd, N. T.

United Christian
Hospital
130 Hip Wo St.
Kwun Tong, Kowloon
*Psychiatry, Dept. of
Dept. Head: Joyce Mok*
Phone: (852) 3496111
Fax: (852) 7727098

HUNGARY

Apáthy Children's
Hospital
Ida u 6, Budapest 1145

Bács-Kiskun County
Hospital
Izasáki út 5, Keckskemét

Ballassa János Hospital
Aurora u 22, Budapest
*Psych. Outpatient Guid.
Centre*

Bánki Donát Tech.
College
Népszínház u. 8
Budapest 1081
*Teacher Training Dept.
Dept. Head: László Tunkli*
Phone: (36) (1) 134 1337
Fax: (36) (1) 1336 761

Baranya County
Hospital
Légszeszgyár u 7, Pécs
Mental Health Dept.

Bárczi Gustáv Training
College for Teachers of
the Handicapped
1443 Pf. 146
Budapest VII
Damjanich u. 41-43
*Psychology, Inst. of
Dept. Head: Dr Ágnes
Lányi-Engelmayer*
Phone: (36) (1) 1425168
Fax: (36) (1) 1425168

Borsod County Hospital
Szentpéteri kapu 76
Miskolc 3500
*Child Psychiatric Unit
Dept. Head: Dr Istvan
Fedor*
Phone: (36) (46) 321211

Budai Children's
Hospital
Borbolya u 2
Budapest 1023

Budai Children's
Hospital
Feszty Arpád u 2
Budapest 1013
Neurosis & Psych. Dept.

Budapest, Tech. Univ.
Egry József u 1
Budapest H-1111
*Ergonomics &
Psychology, Dept. of
Dept. Head: Miklós
Antalovits*
Phone: (36) (361) 181
2567
Fax: (36) (361) 181 2567

Budapest Univ. of
Economics
Budapest 1093
Fövám tér 8
*Dept. of Education &
Economic Psychology
Dept. Head: István
Magyari-Beck*
Phone: (36) (1) 117 45 18
Fax: (36) (1) 117 4539

Central State Hospital
Kútvölgyi út 4
Budapest 1125

Child & Adolescent
Pstp. Clinic
Faludi u 5
Budapest 1131

Children's Hospital of
Madarász St.
Madarász u 22-4
Budapest 1131

Children's Hospital of
Budapest
Ali u 14, Budapest 1025
Neurosis Dept.

Child Psychiatric Amb.
Clinic
Tanácsköztársaság u 2
Szeged 6720

Child Psychiatry Dept.
Varga u 1, Debrecen 4024

Child Psychiatry
Service
Nagy Lu 4/c, Veszprém

City District Hospital
Csepel
Vénusz u 2-4
Budapest 1214
Mental Health Dept.

County Hospital
Kandia u 4/b
Debrecen 4027
Psychiatry Dept.

County Hospital
Komszomol tér 7
Kecskemét 6000
Child Psychiatry Dept.

County Hospital
Széchenyi u 27
Eger 3300
Psychiatry Dept.

County Hospital
Szentpéteri kapu 72-6
Miskolc 3501
*Child Psychology Unit
Dept. Head: Judith Füzi*
Phone: (36) (46) 321211

**Devlopmental &
Educational
Psychiatry Dept.**
Bogdánfy u 7/d
Budapest 1117

**Eötvös Lorend
Univ.**
Budapest VIII
Pollack M ter 10
POB 394
Budapest 1446
*Social Psychology, Dept.
of
Dept. Head: Gyorgy
Csepeli*
Phone: (36) (1) 266
5222
Fax: (36) (1) 266 3860

Eötvös Univ.
Izabella u 46
Budapest 1064
Dev. & Ed. Dept.

Eötvös Univ.
Károlyi Mihály u 10
Budapest 1053

Eötvös Univ.
Múseum krt 4
Budapest 1088
Comp. Phys. Dept.

Eötvös Univ.
Pf 4
Budapest 1378
Gen. Psychiatry Dept.

**Flór Ferenc
Hospital**
Semmelweis tér 1
Kerepestarcsa 2143
Budapest

**HC Teachers Training
College**
Bethlen tér 2
Budapest 1071

**Heim Pál Children's
Hospital**
Rottenbiller u. 26
Budapest 1077
*Mental Health Dept. &
Epilepsy Centre
Dept. Head: Dr Márta
Fohn*
Phone: (36) (1) 1424 527
Fax: (36) (1) 1382 888

**Heim Pál Children's
Hospital**
Ulloi út 86
Budapest 1089
*Dept. Head: Dr Tamás
Kolos*
Phone: (36) (1) 1330 378
Fax: (36) (1) 1334 553

**Hetényi Géza
Children's Hospital**
Vöröshadsereg útja 39-41
Szolnok 5004
Adolescent Dept.

**Hungarian Academy of
Science**
Szondy u 83-5
Budapest 106 8

**Hungarian Army Cent.
Hospital**
Róbert Károly krt 44
Budapest 1134

**Hungarian Army
Hospital No. 3**
Zengo u 10, Pécs-Hird

**Hungarian Rail, Health
Centre**
Baross tér 9
Budapest 1087

István Hospital
Nagyvárad tér 1
Budapest 1096
Neurosis Dept.

Jahn Ferenc Hospital
Vándor Sándor u 1
Budapest 1181
*Mentally Ill Outpatient
Centre*

János Polyclinics
Trefort u 3
Budapest 1088
*Mental-hygienic
Psychotherapeutic
Outpatient Dept.
Dept. Head: Dr Márta
Antalfai*
Phone: (36) 1 1180 544

**Janus Pannonius
Univ.**
Rókus u 7/a
Pécs 7624

**Jósa András Children's
Hospital**
Vöröshadsereg u 68
Nyiregyháza 4400

József Attila Univ.
Petőfi S. sgt. 30-34
Szeged H-6722
*Dept. of Psychology
Dept. Head: Dr. Ferenc
Erős*
Phone: (36) (62) 21034
Fax: (36) (62) 21034

**Judicial Observation &
Mental Hospital**
Kozma u 13
Budapest 1108

**Juhász Gyula Teachers'
Training College**
H-6722 Szeged,
Boldogasszony sgt. 8
6701 POB 396
*Psychology, Dept. of
Dept. Head: Tibor Balogh*
Phone: (36) (62) 10 244
Fax: (36) (62) 10 953

Korányi F. & S. Hospital
Alsó erdosor u 7
Budapest 1074

Korvin Ottó Hospital
Gorkij fasor 7-9
Budapest 1071

Kossuth Lajos Univ.
Kárpát u 12
Budapest 1133
Psychiatry Dept.

Kossuth Univ.
Debrecen 10
Pf 17 4010
Psych. Dept.

**Laboratory Research,
Nat. Inst. for**
Könyves Kálmán krt
48-52
Budapest 1087

Madarász Hospital
Faludi u 5
Budapest 1131
Child Pstp Dept.

**Mahart Lab. Ind.
Psychiatry**
Apáczai Csere János u 11
Budapest 1052

**Medical Rehabilitation,
Nat. Inst. for**
Szanatórium u 2
Budapest 1528

**Medical Rehabilitation,
Nat. Inst. for**
Szillassy út 6
Budapest 1121
*Psychosomatic & Pstp.
Dept.*

Military Hospital
Róbert Károly krt 44
Budapest 1134

Municipal Hospital
Kossuth u 34-6
Kalocsa 6301

Municipal Hospital
Petofi u 26-8
Esztergom 2500
Neur. Psychiatry Dept.

Municipal Hospital
Rákóczi út 125
Balassagyarmat 2660
Psychiatry Dept.

Municipal Hospital
Péterfy Sándor u 8-14
Budapest 1076

**Nervous Mental
Diseases, Nat. Inst.
for**
Hüvösvölgyi u. 116
Budapest 1021
*Clinical Psychology
Lab.
Dept. Head: Dr Szakács
Ferenc*
Phone: (36) (1) 176 0922
Fax: (36) (1) 176 3402

**Neurotics Outpatient
Centre**
21st District
Akadémia u 7
Budapest 1054

Péterfy S. St. Hospital
Péterfi S. u 5-7
Budapest 1076

Pécs, Med. Univ. of
Ifjúság útja 6
Pécs 7624
Surgical Clinic No. 1

Pécs, Med. Univ. of
Stigeti út 12
Pécs 7624
Philosophy Dept.

**Paediatrics, Nat. Inst.
of**
Tüzoltó u 7-9
Budapest 1094

**Polyclinic for Child
Psych.**
Markusovsky Hospital
Hámán Kató u 30
Szomathely 9701

**Postgraduate Med.
School**
Lahner u 26
Budapest 1046

**Postgraduate Med.
School**
Nyéki út 12
Budapest 1021
Psychiatry Dept.

**Postgraduate Med.
School**
Vöröshadsereg útja 116
Budapest 1021
Psychiatry Dept.

Psychiatric Rehab. Inst.
Intaháza-Mesteri 9551

**Psychochronography
Research Group &
Consultative Centre of
Conductive Education**
Huvosvolgyt Ut 35
Budapest 1026
Dept. Head: Károly Akos
Phone: (36) 17 61 470

**Public Health,
Hungarian Inst. of**
Gyáli út 2-6
Budapest 1097

**Railway-workers
Hospital**
Rudas László u 105-9
Budapest 1062

**Residential Inst. of
Education**
Victor Hugó u 18-22
Budapest 1132

Semmelweis Med. Univ.
Ballasse u 6
Budapest 1083
Psychiatry Clinic
Other Depts: Neurology

**Semmelweis Med.
Univ.**
Búkai János u 54
Budapest 1083
First Pediatric Clinic

**Semmelweis Med.
Univ.**
Budapest pf 370 1445
Ed. Tech. Inst.

Semmelweis Med. Univ.
Karolina út 27
Budapest 1113
Orthopedic Clinic

Speech Correction Inst.
Festetich u 3
Budapest 1087

Szeged, Med. Univ. of
Hunyadi János sgt 5
Szeged 6722
Philosophy Dept.

Szeged, Med. Univ. of
Pulcz u 1
Szeged 6724
Psychiatry Dept.

Szigetvár Hospital
Lening lkt. 7
Szigetvár 7900
Mental Health Dept.

Tata Hospital
November 7 tér 7
Tata 2890

Tétényi Hospital
Tétényi út 12-16
Budapest 1115

Tétényi St. Hospital
Jókai út 21-5
Budapest 1223
Psychiatry Dept.

**Therapy-Prevention
Centre**
Radnóti Miklós u 21/b
Budapest 1137
23rd District

**Tolna County
Hospital**
pf 85
Szeksárd 7100
Psychiatry Dept.

Ujpest Hospital
Arpád út 126
Budapest 1042
Child Psychiatry Dept.

**Zalaegerszeg-Pózva C.
Hospital**
Landorhegyi u 32
Zalaegerszeg 8900

ICELAND

Reykjavik Univ.
Borgarspitalinn
108 Reykjavic
*Clinical Psychology
Dept.*

INDIA

Agra Univ.
Paliwal Park
Agra 280004
Uttar Pradesh
Psychology, Dept. of

Alagappa Univ.
Alagappa Nagar
Karaikudi 523 004
Tamil Nadu
Psychology, Dept. of

**Aligarh Muslim
Univ.**
Aligarh
UP 202001
Psychology, Dept. of

Amravati Univ.
Amravati
Maharashtra 444604
Psychology, Dept. of

**Andhra Pradesh Open
Univ.**
6-3-645 Somajiguda
Hyderabad 500482
Andhra Pradesh
Psychology, Dept. of

Andhra Univ.
Waltair 530003
Andhra Pradesh
Psychology, Dept. of

Annamalai Univ.
Annamalai Nagar PO
Tamil Nadu 608002
Psychology, Dept. of

Arunachal Univ.
Doimukh PO, Itanagar
791112
Psychology, Dept. of

Avadh Univ.
Faizabad
Uttar Pradesh 224001
Psychology, Dept. of

**Awadhesh Pratap Singh
Univ.**
Rewa 486003
Madhya Pradesh
Psychology, Dept. of

Banaras Hindu Univ.
Varanasi 221005
Uttar Pradesh
Psychology, Dept. of

Banasthali Vidyapith
PO Banasthali Vidyapith
Rajasthan 304022
Psychology, Dept. of

Bangalore Univ.
Jnana Bharathi
Bangalore 560056
Karnataka State
*Psychology, Dept. of
Dept. Head: Dr Vinoda
Narayana Murthy*
Phone: (91) (812) 355036

**Barkatullah Vishwa
Vidyalaya**
Bhopal 462026 MP
*Psychology, Dept. of
Dept. Head: Misra
Girishwar*
Phone: (91) (755) 549563

Berhampur Univ.
Berhampur 760007
Ganjam
Orissa
Psychology, Dept. of

Bhagalpur Univ.
Bhagalpur 812007
Bihar
Psychology, Dept. of

Bharathiar Univ.
Coimbatore
Tamil Nadu 641046
*Psychology, Dept. of
Dept. Head: S.
Narayanan*
Phone: (91) (422) 42222
Telex: 855 488 unibin

Bharathidasan Univ.
Palkalaiperur
Tiruchirapalli
Tamil Nadu 620024
Psychology, Dept. of

Bhavnagar Univ.
Gaurishanker Lake Rd
Univ. Campus
Bhavnagar 364002
Gujurat
Psychology, Dept. of

**Bidhan Chandra Krishi
Viswa Vidyalaya**
Haringhata
POB Mohanpur 741252
Dist Nadia, West Bengal
Psychology, Dept. of

Bihar, Univ. of
Muzaffarpur
Bihar 843001
Psychology, Dept. of

Bombay, Univ. of
Univ. Rd
Fort, Bombay 400032
Psychology, Dept. of

Bundelkhand Univ.
Jhansi, UP 284003
Psychology, Dept. of

Burdwan, Univ. of
Burdwan 713104
West Bengal
Psychology, Dept. of

Calcutta, Univ. of
College St.
Calcutta, West Bengal
Psychology, Dept. of

Calicut, Univ. of
POB Calicut Univ.
Thenhipalam 673635
Kerala
Psychology, Dept. of
Dept. Head: Dr M. A.
  Faroqi
Phone: (91) (495) 80217
Telex: 804-243 UNIC - IN

CMC
Veliore 632002
Tamil Nadu
Psychiatry, Dept. of

Cochin, Univ. of
Univ. PO
Cochin, Kerala 682022
Psychology, Dept. of

Delhi, Univ. of
Delhi 110007
Psychology, Dept. of
Other Depts: Divn. of
  Applied Psychology
Dept. Head: Prof. Anima
  Sen
Phone: (91) (11) 7257725
Fax: (91) (11) 672427

Dibrugarh Univ.
Rajabheta
Dibrugarh 786004
Assam
Psychology, Dept. of

Dr Harisingh Gour Univ.
Gour Nagar, Sagar
Madhya Pradesh 470003
Psychology, Dept. of

Gauhati Univ.
Gauhati 781014, Assam
Psychology, Dept. of

Goa Univ.
Bambolim PO, Santa Cruz
Goa 403005
Psychology, Dept. of

Gorakhpur Univ.
Gorakhpur
Uttar Pradesh 273009
Psychology, Dept. of

Gujurat Ayurved Univ.
Jamnagar
Gujurat 361008
Psychology, Dept. of

Gujurat Univ.
Navrangpura
Ahmedabad 380009
Gujarat
Psychology, Dept. of

Gujurat Vidyapith
Ahmedabad 380014
Gujarat
Psychology, Dept. of

Gulbarga Univ.
Gulbarga
Karnataka 585106
Psychology, Dept. of
Dept. Head: Dr B.
  Krishna Murthy
Phone: (91) (8472) 23514

Gurukula Kangri
Vishwavidyalaya
Hardwar
Dist. Hardwar
UP 249404
Psychology, Dept. of

Guru Nanak Dev Univ.
Amritsar 143005
Psychology, Dept. of

Himachal Pradesh Univ.
Summer Hill
Shimla 171005
Psychology, Dept. of
Dept. Head: Prof. Sagar
  Sharma
Phone: (91) (177)
  3513-264

Hyderabad, Univ. of
Central Univ. PO
Hyderabad 500134
Psychology, Dept. of

Indara Kala Sangit
Univ.
Khairagarh 491881
Madhya Pradesh
Psychology, Dept. of

Jadavpur Univ.
PO Jadavpur Univ.
Calcutta 700032
Psychology, Dept. of

Jamai Millia Islamia
Jamai Nagar
New Dehli 110025
Psychology, Dept. of

Jawaharlal Nehru
Univ.
New Mhrauli Rd
New Dehli 110067
Psychology, Dept. of

Jodhpur, Univ. of
Jodhpur 342001
Rajasthan
Psychology, Dept. of

Kakatiya Univ.
Vidyaranyapuri
Warangal 500009
Psychology, Dept. of

Kalyani Univ.
Kalyani 741235
Nadia, West Bengal
Psychology, Dept. of

**Kameshwara Singh
Darghanga Sanskrit
Univ.**
Darbhanga
Bihar 846004
Psychology, Dept. of

Karnatak Univ.
Dharwad
Karnataka 580003
Psychology, Dept. of

Kashmir, Univ. of
Hazratbal
Srinagar 190006
Jammu & Kashmir
Psychology, Dept. of

Kerala, Univ. of
Trivandrum 69503
Kerala
Psychology, Dept. of

Kumaun Univ.
Nainital 263001
Uttar Pradesh
Psychology, Dept. of

Kurukshetra Univ.
Kurukshetra 132119
Haryana
Psychology, Dept. of

Kuvempu Univ.
Shimoga District
Karnataka 577115
Psychology, Dept. of

**Lalit Narayan Mithila
Univ.**
POB 13 Kameshwarnagar
Darbhanga 846004
Bihar
Psychology, Dept. of

Lucknow, Univ. of
Badshah Bagh
Lucknow 226007
UP
Psychology, Dept. of

Madras, Univ. of
Chepauk
Triplicane PO
Madras 600005
Tamil Nadu
Psychology, Dept. of

**Madurai-Kamaraj
Univ.**
Palkalai Nagar
Madurai 625021
Tamil Nadu
Psychology, Dept. of

Magadh Univ.
Bodh-Gaya 824234
Bihar
Psychology, Dept. of

**Mah. Sayajirao Univ. of
Baroda**
Baroda 390002
Gujarat
Psychology, Fac. of

**Maharshi Dayanand
Univ.**
Rohtak 124001
Haryana
Psychology, Dept. of

**Mahatma Ghandi
Univ.**
Kottayam 686562
Kerala
Psychology, Dept. of

**Mahatma Phule Krishi
Vidyapeeth**
Rahuri 413722
Ahmednagar District
Maharashtra
Psychology, Dept. of

Mangalore Univ.
Mangalaganotri 574199
DK Karnataka
Psychology, Dept. of

Manipur Univ.
Canchipur
Imphal, Manipur 795003
Psychology, Dept. of

Marathwade Univ.
Aurangabad (Deccan)
Maharashtra 431004
Psychology, Dept. of

Meerut Univ.
Meerut 250005
Uttar Pradesh
Psychology, Dept. of

**Mohan Lal Sukhadia
Univ.**
Pratap Nagar
Udaipur Rajasthan
Psychology, Dept. of

Mysore, Univ. of
POB 407
Mysore, Karnataka
Psychology, Dept. of

Nagarjuna Univ.
Nagarjuna Nagar 522510
Andhra Pradesh
Psychology, Dept. of

Nagpur, Univ. of
Rabindranath Tagore
Marg
Nagpur 440001
Maharashtra
Psychology, Dept. of

North Bengal, Univ. of
PO North Bengal Univ.
Raja Rammohunpur
Darjeeling District
West Bengal 734430
Psychology, Dept. of

North-Eastern Hill Univ.
Shillong, Meghalaya
Psychology, Dept. of

North Gujurat Univ.
Rajmahel Rd
POB 21
Patan 384265
North Gujrat
Psychology, Dept. of

Osmania Univ.
Hyderabad 500007
Andhra Pradesh
Psychology, Dept. of

Panjab Univ.
Chandigarh 160014
Union Territory
Psychology, Dept. of

Patna Univ.
Patna, Binhar State
Psychology, Dept. of

Poona, Univ. of
Ganeshkhind
Pune 411007
Maharashtra
Psychology, Dept. of

Punjabi Univ.
Patiala 147002
Punjab
Psychology, Dept. of
Dept. Head: Dr Agya Jit
Singh
Phone: (91) 822161

Rabindra Gharati Univ.
6/4 Dwarakanath Tagore
Lane
Calcutta 700050
Psychology, Dept. of

Rajasthan, Univ. of
Gandhi Nagar
Jaipur 320004
Psychology, Dept. of

Ranchi Univ.
Ranchi 834008, Bihar
Psychology, Dept. of

Ravishankar Univ.
Raipur 492010
Madhya Pradesh
Psychology, Dept. of

Rohilkhand Univ.
Bareilly
Uttar Pradesh 243001
Psychology, Dept. of

Roorkee, Univ. of
Roorkee
Uttar Pradesh 247667
Psychology, Dept. of

Sambalpur Univ.
PO Jyoti Vihar
Burla, Sambalpur 768017
Orissa
Psychology, Dept. of

**Sampurnanand
Sanskrit Univ.**
Varanasi 221002
Uttar Pradesh
Psychology, Dept. of

Sardar Patel Univ.
Vallabh Vidyanagar
388120
Kaira
Gujarat
Psychology, Dept. of
Dept. Head: Dr Pramod
Kumar
Phone: (91) (2692) 30310

Saurashtra Univ.
Univ. Campus
Kalawad Rd
Rajkot 360 005
Gujarat
Psychology, Dept. of
Dept. Head: Dr D. J.
Bhatt

Shivaji Univ.
Vidyanagar
Kolhapur 416004
Maharashtra
Psychology, Dept. of

**Shri Krishnadevaraya
Univ.**
Sri Venkateswarapuram
PO
Anantapur 515003
Andhra Pradesh
Psychology, Dept. of

South Gujarat Univ.
PB 49
Surat 395007, Gujarat
Psychology, Dept. of

**Sri Sathya Sai Inst. of
Higher Learning**
Prasanthinilayam
Anantapur District
Andhra Pradesh 515134
Psychology, Dept. of

Sri Venkateswara Univ.
Tirupati 517502
District Chittoor
Andhra Pradesh
Psychology, Dept. of

Tamil Univ.
Palace Buildings
Thanjavur
Tamil Nadu 613001
Psychology, Dept. of

**Tilak Maharashtra
Vidyapeeth**
Vidyapeeth Bhavan
Gultekdi
Pune 411037
Psychology, Dept. of

Tripura Univ.
PO Agartala College
Agartala 799004, Tripura
Psychology, Dept. of

Utkal Univ.
PO Vani Vihar
Bhubaneswar 751004
Orissa
*Centre of Advanced
Study in Psychology
Dept. Head: Dr Ajit K.
Mohanty*
Phone: (91) 674 53639

Vidyasagar Univ.
Subasnagar
Midnapore, West Bengal
Psychology, Dept. of

Vikram Univ.
Ujjain 456010
Madhya Pradesh
Psychology, Dept. of

Visva-Bharati
PO Santiniketan
Birbhum, West Bengal
Psychology, Dept. of

INDONESIA

17 Agustus 1945, Univ.
Jl. Teuku Cik Ditiro 46
Jakarta
Psychology, Dept. of

Airlangga, Univ.
Jl. Darmawangsa 1
Surabaya
Psychology, Dept. of

Andalas, Univ.
Jl. Perintis Kemerdekaan
77
Padang, West Sumatra
Psychology, Dept. of

Cenderawasih Univ.
Jl. Sentani
Abepura
Jayapura
Irian Jaya
Psychology, Dept. of

Diponegoro, Univ.
Jl. Imam Barjo
Sh. 1-3
POB 270
Semarang
Psychology, Dept. of

Gadjah Mada, Univ.
Bulaksumur
Yogyakarta 55281
Psychology, Dept. of

Haluoleo, Univ.
Jl. S. Parman
Kendari
Psychology, Dept. of

HKBP Nomensen Univ.
Jl. Sutomo 4A
POB 134
Medan
Psychology, Dept. of

**Ibn Khaldun Bogor
Univ.**
Jl. Laksamana
Martadinata 2-4
POB 74, Bogor
Psychology, Dept. of

Ibn Khaldun, Univ.
Jl. Pemuda
Kav. 97, POB 224
Rawamangun
Jakarta, Timur
Psychology, Dept. of

**Indonesia Atma Jaya,
Univ. Kat.**
POB 2639 Dak
Jl. Jendral Sudirman 51
Semanggi
Jakarta 12930
Psychology, Dept. of

Indonesia, Univ. Kristen
Jl. Mayjen Sutoyo
Cawang, Jakarta 13630
Psychology, Dept. of

Indonesia, Univ. of
Fac. of Psychology
Jl. Salemba Raya 4
Jakarta
*Applied Psychology, Inst.
of
Dept. Head: Dr
Soesmalijah Soewondo*
Phone: (62) (21) 3105078
Fax: (62) (21) 3105077

**Islam Indonesia
Cirebon, Univ.**
Jl. Kapten Samadikun 31
Cirebon
Psychology, Dept. of

Islam Indonesia, Univ.
Jl. Cik Ditiro
POB 56
Yogyakarta, Java
Psychology, Dept. of

Islam Jakarta, Univ.
Jl. Prof. Muh. Yamin 57
Jakarta
Psychology, Dept. of

Islam Riau, Univ.
Jl. Prof. M. Yamin SH
No. 69
Pekanbaru, Riau
*Psychology, Dept. of
Other Depts: Medicine
Dept. Head: H. Rawi
Kunin Sh*
Phone: (62) 33667

Jambi, Univ.
Jl. Prof. Sri Soedewi
Masjchun Sofwan
Jambi
Psychology, Dept. of

Jayabaya, Univ.
Jl. Jenderal A. Yani
By-Pass
Jakarta
Psychology, Dept. of

Jember, Univ.
Jl. Veteran 3
Jember
East Java
Psychology, Dept. of

Jenderal Soedirman,
Univ.
Kampus UNSOED
 Grendeng
POB 15
Purwokerto
Central Java
Psychology, Dept. of

Krisnadwipajana,
Univ.
Jl. Tegal 10
Jakarta
Psychology, Dept. of

Lambung Mangkurat,
Univ.
Kampus UNLAM
Jl. Brigjen H. Hasan
 Basry
Banjarmasin 70123
South Kalimantan
Psychology, Dept. of

Lampung Univ.
Kampus UNILA
Gedong Meneng
Kedaton
Bandar Lampung
Psychology, Dept. of

Maranatha, Univ.
Kristen
Jl. Cihampelas 169
Bandung 40131
Psychology, Dept. of

Mataram, Univ.
Jl. Pendidikan 37
Mataram
Nusa Tenggara Barat
Kotak Pos 20
Psychology, Dept. of

Muhammadiyah
Malang, Univ.
Jl. Bandung 1
Malang
Psychology, Dept. of

Muhammadijah, Univ.
Jl. Limau 1
Keb. Baru
Jakarta
Psychology, Dept. of

Mulawarman, Univ.
Kampus Gn. Kelua
Samarinda
Psychology, Dept. of

Nasional Univ.
Jl. Sawo Manila Pejaten
Pasar Minggu
Jakarta Selatan
Psychology, Dept. of

Nusa Cendana, Univ.
Jl. Adi Sucipto
Penfui
Kupang
Nusa Tengara Timur
Psychology, Dept. of

Padjadjaran, Univ.
Jl. Dipati Ukur 35
Bandung 40132
Java
Psychology, Dept. of

Pakuan, Univ.
Jl. Pakuan
POB 353
Bogor
Psychology, Dept. of

Palangkaraya, Univ.
Kampus UNPAR
Tunjung Nyaho
Jl. Yos Sudarso-Palangka
 Raya
Kalimantan Tengah
Psychology, Dept. of

Pancasila, Univ.
Srengseng Sawah
Pasar Minggu
Jakarta Selatau 12640
Psychology, Dept. of

Parahyangan, Univ.
Katolik
Jl. Ciumbuleuit 94
Bandung 40142
Psychology, Dept. of

Pattimura Ambon, Univ.
POB 95
Jl. Ir. M. Putuhena
Kampus Poka
Ambon
Psychology, Dept. of

Petra Christian Univ.
Jl. Siwalankerto 121-131
POB 5304
Surabaya 60002
Psychology, Dept. of

Riau, Univ.
Jl. Pattimura 9
Pekanbaru 28131
Sumatra
Psychology, Dept. of

Satya Wacana, Univ.
Kristen
Jl. Diponegoro 52-60
Salatiga 50711
Central Java
Psychology, Dept. of

Sebelas Maret, Univ.
Jl. Ir. Sutami 36A
Surakarta
Psychology, Dept. of

Sriwijaya, Univ.
Jl. Jaksa Agung R.
 Suprapto
Palembang
South Sumatra
Psychology, Dept. of

Sumatera Utara, Univ.
Jl. Univ. 9
Kampus USU
Medan 20155
Psychology, Dept. of

Syiah Kuala, Univ.
Jl. Darusalam
Banda Aceh
Psychology, Dept. of

Tanjungpura, Univ.
Jl. Imam Bonjol
POB 50
Pontianak
Kalbar
Psychology, Dept. of

Terbuka, Univ.
Jl. Terbang Layang/Pelita
Pondok Cabe
Ciputat POB 6666
Jakarta 10001
Psychology, Dept. of

Tjokroaminoto Surakarta Univ.
Jl. Kusumojudan
Surakarta
Psychology, Dept. of

Trisakti Univ.
Jl. Kiyai Tapa
Grogol
Jakarta 114400
Psychology, Dept. of

Udayana, Univ.
Jl. Jendral Sudirman
POB 105
Denpasar, Bali
Psychology, Dept. of

IRAN

Al-Zahra Univ.
Vanak
Teheran 19934
Psychology, Dept. of

Bu-Ali Sina Univ.
POB 211
Hamadan
Psychology, Dept. of

Gilan, Univ. of
POB 401
Rasht
Psychology, Dept. of

Isfahan, Univ. of
Isfahan
Psychology, Dept. of

Mashhad, Ferdowsi Univ. of
Mashhad
Psychology, Dept. of

Mazandaran Univ.
POB 416
Babolsar
Psychology, Dept. of

Razi Univ.
Bakhtaran
Psychology, Dept. of

Shadeed Bahonar Univ.
POB 133
Kerman
Psychology, Dept. of

Shadid Beheshti Univ.
Shahid Chamran Ave.
Evin
19834 Teheran
Psychology, Dept. of

Shadid Chamran Univ.
Ashwaz
Khuzestan
Psychology, Dept. of

Shiraz Univ.
Zand Ave
Shiraz
Psychology, Dept. of

Sistan & Baluchistan, Univ.
POB 98135-987
Zahedan
Psychology, Dept. of

Tabriz Univ.
Tabriz 711-51664
Psychology, Dept. of

Teheran, Univ. of
Enghelab Ave.
Teheran 14174
Psychology, Dept. of

Urmi, Univ. of
POB 165, Urmia 57135
Psychology, Dept. of

IRAQ

Al-Mustansiriya Univ.
POB 14022
Waziriya, Baghdad
Psychology, Dept. of

Baghdad, Univ. of
POB 12
Jadiriya, Baghdad
Psychology, Dept. of

Basrah, Univ. of
Basrah
Psychology, Dept. of

Mosul, Univ. of
Mosul
Psychology, Dept. of

Salahaddin, Univ. of
Arhil
Psychology, Dept. of

IRELAND

Abha-na-Scáil
79 Moorefield Drive
Newbridge
Co. Kildare

**Adam & Eve
Counselling Centre**
4 Merchant's Quay
Dublin 8

**Alzheimer's Research
Clinic**
7 Lower Dublin Rd
Tuam, Co. Galway
*Dept. Head: Terence F.
Connors*
Phone: (353) (93) 28929
Fax: (353) (93) 28159

Beaumont Hospital
POB 1297
Beaumont Rd
Dublin 9
Neurosciences, Dept. of
*Dept. Head: Hugh
Staunton*
Phone: (353) (1) 377755
Fax: (353) (1) 3767982

Beaumont Hospital
POB 1297
Beaumont Rd
Dublin 9
Cardiology Dept.
*Dept. Head: Dr John
Horgan*
Phone: (353) (1) 377755
Fax: (353) (1) 376740

**Brothers of Charity
Services**
Ardsallagh, Roscommon
*Assessment & Advisory
Centre*

**Brothers of Charity
Services**
Belmont Park Hospital
Waterford

**Brothers of Charity
Services**
Lota
Glanmire, Co. Cork

**Brothers of Charity
Services**
Midwestern Region
Bawnmore
Co. Limerick
*Dept. Head: John F.
Toomey*
Phone: (353) (61) 412288
Fax: (353) (61) 412389

**Brothers of Charity
Services**
Pastoral Centre
Killarney
Co. Kerry

**Brothers of Charity
Services**
Woodlands Centre
Renmore
Co. Galway
*Dept. Head: Patrick
McGinley*
Phone: (353) (91) 55241
Fax: (353) (91) 52362

**Castleknock Child &
Family Ctr**
Castleknock
Dublin

**Children's Assessment
& Treatment Centre**
Cork Spastic Clinic
Ballintemple
Co. Cork

**Child Development &
Assessment Clinic**
Ballymun Rd
Dublin 9
*Dept. Head: Michael J.
Murphy*
Phone: (353) (1) 375171
Fax: (353) (1) 374062

Child Guidance Clinic
James' Green
Kilkenny

Child Study Centre
St Vincent's Centre
Navan Rd
Dublin 7
*Dept. Head: Dympna
Walsh*
Phone: (353) (1) 383881
Fax: (353) (1) 385496

City of Dublin VEC
25 Temple Rd
Dartry
Dublin 4
*Schools Psychological
Service*

**Cluain Mhuire Fam.
Psych. Serv.**
Newtownpark Ave.
Blackrock
Co. Dublin

Cope Foundation
Bonnington
Montenotte
Co. Cork
*Dept. Head: Richard
O'Callaghan*
Phone: (353) (21) 507131
Fax: (353) (21) 507580

Córas Iompair Éirann
Transport House
Batchelor's Walk
Dublin 1
Medical Dept.

**Cork Polio & Gen.
Aftercare Assn.**
Bonnington
Montenotte
Co. Cork

County Clinic
Cavan
*Dept. Head: Rory B.
Tierney*
Phone: (353) (49) 31822
Fax: (353) (49) 61877

Dublin City Univ.
Dublin 9
*Dept. Head: Prof. John
Hurley*
Phone: (353) (1) 7045 224
Fax: (353) (1) 7045 222
Telex: 360830
Email: hurleyj@ dcu.ie

**Dublin Well Woman
Centre, The**
73 Lower Leeson St
Dublin 2
*Dept. Head: Rita
Burtenshaw*
Phone: (353) (1) 789204
Fax: (353) (1) 768949

**Economic & Social
Research Inst.**
4 Burlington Rd
Dublin 4

Education, Dept. of
Talbot St.
Dublin 1
Psychological Service

ESRI
4 Burlington Rd
Dublin 4

Good Counsel College
New Ross
Co. Wexford

**Lyradoon Family
Centre**
65 Lower Salthill
Galway

Marriage & Family Inst.
6 North Frederick St.
Dublin 1

Mater Dei Inst.
Clonliffe Rd
Dublin 3
Counselling Centre

Mater Hospital
North Circular Rd
Dublin 7
*Child & Fam. Psychiatry
Dept.*

**Mentally Handicapped
Children's Assn.**
Galway Association
The Halls
Quay St, Galway
*Dept. Head: Frances
Smyth*
Phone: (353) (91) 62379
Fax: (353) (91) 62379

**Mhuire Child & Family
Centre**
Newtownpark Ave.
Blackrock, Co. Dublin

**Nat. Rehabilitation
Board**
24-25 Clyde Rd
Ballsbridge
Dublin 4
Dept. Head: Trevor James
Phone: (353) (1) 684181
Fax: (353) (1) 685029

**Nat. Rehabilitation
Board**
Cathedral Rd
Cavan

**Nat. Rehabilitation
Board**
High St.
Tullamore
Co. Offaly

Newcastle Hospital
Greystones
Co. Wicklow

**North Western Health
Board**
Health Clinic
Cleveragh Rd, Sligo

Regional Hospital
Cork
Psychiatric Unit

Regional Hospital
Co. Galway
Psychiatric Unit

**Regional Technical
College**
Athlone, Co. Westmeath
Dept. Head: John Cusack
Phone: (353) (902) 72647
Fax: (353) (902) 74529

**Sandymount, Eastern
Health Board**
POB 41a
1 James' St. Dublin 8
*Healthcare / Psychosomatic
Unit*

**Royal College of
Surgeons in Ireland**
Mercer Building
Mercer St. Lower
Dublin 2
*Psychology, Dept. of
Dept. Head: Prof. Ciaran
O'Boyle*
Phone: (353) (1) 780200
Fax: (353) (1) 780934

Rutland Centre Ltd
Knocklyon House
Knocklyon Rd
Templeogue, Dublin 14

Sacred Heart Home
40 Lower Drumcondra Rd
Dublin 9

Sisters of La Sagesse
Cregg House
Sligo
*Dept. Head: Patrick A
Scallan*
Phone: (353) (71) 77229
Fax: (353) (71) 77439

Spina Bifida Association
Scoil Mochua
Nangor Rd
Clondalkin
Co. Dublin

St Anne's Children's Centre
Taylor's Hill
Co. Galway
Dept. Head: Kevin Fitzpatrick
Phone: (353) (91) 21755

St Anne's Hospital & Clinic
Shanakiel
Sunday's Well
Co. Cork

St Bonaventure's
Capuchin Friary
Victoria Cross
Co. Cork

St Brendan's Hospital
Eastern Health Board
POB 418, Dublin 7
Psychology Dept.

St Brigid's Hospital
Ballinasloe, Co. Galway

St Canice's Psychiatric Hospital
Kilkenny

St Frances' Clinic
The Children's Hospital
Temple St. Dublin 1
Dept. Head: Patricia Smyth
Phone: (353) (1) 741751
Fax: (353) (1) 748355

St Francis Day Hospital
Grange Rd
Raheny, Dublin 5
Eastern Health Board

St Garvan's Vocational School
3 Great Denmark St.
Dublin 1

St James' Hospital
James' St.
Dublin 8
Psychiatric Unit

St John of God Admin. Centre
Stillorgan
Co. Dublin

St John of God Centre
Islandbridge
Dublin 8

St John of God Child & Fam. Ctr
59 Orwell Rd
Rathgar, Dublin 6

St Joseph's Hospital
Mulgrave Rd
Limerick

St Joseph's Occ. Therap. College
Rochestown Ave.
Dún Laoghaire
Co. Dublin

St Joseph's Special School
Ferryhouse
Clonmel
Co. Tipperary

St Michael's House
Upper Kilmacud Rd
Stillorgan
Co. Dublin
Research Dept.
Dept. Head: Patricia Noonan Walsh
Phone: (353) (1) 2885805
Fax: (353) (1) 2988729

Stewart's Hospital
Palmerstown
Dublin 20
Dept. Head: Dr Timothy O'Callaghan
Phone: (353) (1) 6264444

Trinity College
25 Westland Row
Dublin 2
Psychology Dept.
Dept. Head: Dr Ray Fuller
Phone: (353) (1) 7021886
Fax: (353) (1) 712006
Telex: 93782 TCD EI
Email: rfuller@vax1.tcd.ie

University College
Belfield
Dublin 4
Psychology, Dept. of

University College
Cork
Applied Psychology Dept.
Dept. Head: Prof. Max Taylor
Phone: (353) (21) 276871
Fax: (353) (21) 270439
Telex: (353 (21) 76050 UNIC EI
Email: stay8016@iruccvax.ucc.ie

University College
University Rd
Galway
Psychology, Dept. of
Dept. Head: Prof. Martin McHugh
Phone: (353) (91) 24411
Fax: (353) (91) 21355

ISRAEL

Abarbanel Hospital
Bat-Yam 59100

Assaf Harofe Hospital
Jabotinski St. 16, Holon

Bar-Ilan Univ.
Ramat-Gan 52900
Psychology Dept.
Other Depts: Education
Dept. Head: Shaul Fox
Phone: (972) (3) 5318539
Fax: (972) (3) 5351825
Telex: 361311
Email: fy1000@ barilan

Beilinson Hospital
Petach-Tikva
Pediatric Endocrinology
Inst.
Dept. Head: Avinoam A.
Galatzer
Phone: (972) (3) 9377763
Fax: (972) (3) 9225108

Beilinson Hospital
Petach-Tikva
Psychology Dept.
Other Depts: IVF
Genicology Dept: Dr
Yehudith Achmon
Dept. Head: Maya
Lerman
Phone: (972) (3) 9377683

Ben Gurion Univ.
POB 653
Beer Sheva
84105
Behavioral Sciences Dept.
Other Depts: Health
Sciences
Dept. Head: Joseph
Tzelgou
Phone: (972) (57) 461770
Fax: (972) (57) 32766
Email: kdaf100@ bgunve

Center for Education in
the Kibbutz
Oranim
Kiryat - Tivon

Child Youth & Fam.
Therapy Clinic
Ministry of Health
5 Jerusalem St.
Haifa
Dept. Head: Mr Ilan
Madar
Phone: (972) (4) 666402

Community Mental
Health Centre
36 Yeffet St.
Yaffo 68030
Dept. Head: Amnon
Wolfinger
Phone: (972) (3) 815577
Fax: (972) (3) 824227

Eitanim Hospital
Doar Na Shimshon
99790 Jerusalem
Adolescent Unit
Dept. Head: Dr Miguel D.
Schestatzky
Phone: (972) (2) 343211
Fax: (972) (2) 340084

Everyman's Univ.
16 Klausner St.
Tel Aviv

Ezrat Nashim Herzog
Mental Health Ctr
POB 35300
Jerusalem 91351
Dept. Head: Dr Gaby
Shefler
Phone: (972) (2)
374505
Fax: (972) (2) 536075

Gehah Psychiatric
Hospital
POB 102
Petach-Tikya 49100
Dept. Head: Maya
Lerman
Phone: (972) (3)
9258258

Haifa Univ.
Haifa 31905
Ray D. Wolfe Ctr for
Study of Psychological
Stress
Other Depts: Social
Work
Dept. Head: Prof. Shlomo
Breznitz
Phone: (972) (4) 240169
Fax: (972) (4) 342104

Hebrew Univ.
Mount Scopus
91905 Jerusalem
Psychology Dept.
Other Depts: Education
Dept. Head: Prof. Benny
Shanon
Phone: (972) (2) 883444
Fax: (972) (2) 322545
Telex: 25391

Hof Hagalil Clin.
Centre
Shderot Hagaaton 50
Naharia

Ichlov Hospital
Tel Aviv

Israel Defence Army
POB 01172
Tzahal
Psychology Dept.

Israel Inst. for Social
Research
Washington str 30
Jerusalem

Jerusalem Inst. for
Social Research
Radak str 20
Jerusalem

Kaplan Hospital
Rehovot
Mental Health Clinic

Kfar-Shaul Hospital
Jerusalem

Kibbutz Child & Family Clinic
Psych. Inst. of Family
Therapy
Derech Namir 147
POB 48154
Tel Aviv 61480
*Dept. Head: Dr Mordecai
Kaffman*

Medical Corp. Mental Health Dept.
POB 02149
I. D. F.

Mental Health Clinic
31 Achad Haam St.
Petach - Tikva 49507
*Dept. Head: Dr J.
Strich*
Phone: (972) (3) 9312098

Mental Health Clinic
Ramat-Chen. Hazvi 9 St.
Tel Aviv

Mental Hospital
Nes Ziona

Municipal Psych. Educ. Services
Hill St. 27
Jerusalem

Psychology Developmental Center
Kadoshev Kahir 36/30
Holon

Psychological Services
6 Mevo Palyam St.
Jerusalem

Rambam Hospital
Haifa
Psychiatry Dept.

Rehabilitation of Brain Injured, Nat. Inst. for
89 Itzhak Sadeh St.
Tel Aviv 67228
Dept. Head: Dan Hoofien
Phone: (972) (3) 5624777

Social Psych. Clinic/Kibbutzim
Haifa Rd 147
Seminar Hakibuzim
Tel Aviv

Szold Inst.
Colombia str 9
Kiryat Menachem
Jerusalem 96503

Talbich Hospital & Clinic
14 Disraeli St. Jerusalem

Tel Aviv Univ. Medical School
Loewenstein Hospital
Rehab. Center
POB 3 Raanana

Tel Aviv Univ.
Tel Aviv 69978
Psychology Dept.
Other Depts: Education
Dept. Head: Prof.
Nehemia Friedland
Phone: (972) (3) 6409693
Fax: (972) (3) 6409547
Email: nehemia@ taunos

Tel-Hashomer Hospital
Tel-Hashomer
Psychiatric Dept.

Weizmann Inst. Rehovot.
8 Meonot Shine, 76100

Youth Aliyah/Jewish Agency
Kaplan str 10, Tel-Aviv

Zfat Hospital
Community Stress
Prevention Ctr.
POB 1, Merkaz
Habriut
Kiryat Shmona 10200
*Educational Psychology
Unit*
*Dept. Head: Dr Mooli
Lahad*
Phone: (972) (6) 948827
Fax: (972) (6) 950740

ITALY

Bologna, Univ. of
V. Berti Pichat 5
40127 Bologna
Psychology, Dept. of
Phone: (39) (51) 243200
Fax: (39) (51) 243086
Email: g77a@ icineca

Cagliari, Studi, Univ.
09100 Cagliari
Ist. di Psicologia
Dept. Head: Prof.
Marcello Lostia
Phone: (39) (70) 291204

Calabria, Univ. di
87100 Cosenza
Dpto. Educazione

Catt. Psicologia
c/o Clin. Psichiatr. Pisa

Catt. Psicologia
V. XXIV Maggio 21
98100 Messina

Centro Salesiano Orient.
V. Marconi 22
31021 Mogliano Veneto

Centro terapia integrativa
V. Giusti 3, 00185 Roma

Città Univ.
00100 Roma
Ist. Psicologia

Dip. Psicol. Svil. e Soc.
V. B. Pellegrino 26
35100 Padova
Dept. Head: Remo Job
Phone: (39) (49) 8761411
Fax: (39) (49) 8755025
Email: psico.06@
unipad.unipd.it

Dpto. Psicologia
V. le Castro Pretorio 20
00185 Roma

Fac. Educazione
V. Cremolino 141
00166 Roma

Gregoriana, Univ.
Piazza Pilotta 4
00187 Roma
*Dept. Head: Bartholomew
Kiely*
Phone: (39) (6) 6701
5305
Fax: (39) (6) 6701 5413

Ist. di Psicologia CNR
V. Marx, 15
I-00137 Roma
*Dept. Head: Domenico
Parisi*
Phone: (39) (6) 86894596
Fax: (39) (6) 824737
Email: ip@ irmkant.bitnet

Ist. Fisiol. Umana
V. Gramsci 14, Parma

Ist. Politico Amm.
V. G. Petroni 33
Bologna

Ist. Psicologia
V. Pergola 48
Firenzi

Ist. Psicologia
V. Festa del Perdono 7
20122 Milano
*Dept. Head: Prof.
Giuseppe Mosconi*
Phone: (39) (2) 58307009
Fax: (39) (2) 58303842

Ist. Psicologia
V. F. Sforza 23
20122 Milano
*Dept. Head: Prof.
Marcello Cesa-Bianchi*
Phone: (39) (2) 799082
Fax: (39) (2) 784581
Email: psicme@imiucca.
csi.2inimi.it.bitnet

Ist. Psicologia
V. Porta di Massa
Napoli

Ist. Psicologia
V. Università 7, Trieste

Ist. Psicologia
V. Saffi 15, Urbino

**Milano, Univ. degli
Studi di**
Via Festa del Perdono 7,
20122 Milan
Social Psychology, Dept. of

Milan, Cat. Univ. of
Largo A. Gemelli 1
20123 Milano
*Psychology, Dept. of
Dept. Head: Assunto
Quadrio*
Phone: (39) (2) 72342284
Fax: (39) (2) 72342210
Email: catel@ imicilea

**Modena, Univ. degli
Studi**
Via Università 4
41100 Modena
Psychology, Dept. of

Osp. Civ.
Neuropsichiatria
33100 Udine

Osp. Maggiore
26013 Crema (CR)
Centro Discinetici

**Padua, Univ. degli Studi
di**
Via 8 Febbraio 9
35122 Padua
*General Psychology, Dept.
of*

**Pavia, Univ. degli Studi
di**
Corso Strada Nuova 65
27100 Pavia
Psychology, Dept. of

Pisa Univ.
V. Galvani 1
56100 Pisa
Lab. Psicologia

**Psicologia Generale,
Dpto. di**
Piazza Capitaniato
35100 Padova
*Dept. Head: Prof.
Erminio Gius*
Phone: (39) (49) 8756303
Fax: (39) (49) 660090

**Reparto di
Psicopedagogia
CNR**
V. U. Aldrovandi 18
00197 Roma
*Dept. Head: Francesco
Tonucci*
Phone: (39) (6) 3221198
Fax: (39) (6) 3217090

Servizio Psicoferapia
Policlinico, 37134 Verona
Dept. Head: O. Siciliani
Phone: (39) (45) 8203224

**Siena, Univ. degli
  Studi**
Banchi di Sotto 55
53100 Siena
*Advanced School of
  Psychology*

Studi, Univ.
70100 Bari
Ist. Psicologia

**Trabattoni-Ronzoni,
  Presidio
  Ospedaliero**
Via Verdi 2
20038 Seregno
Milano

**Trento, Univ. degli
  Studi**
V. Verdi 26, 38100 Trento

**Trieste, Univ. degli
  Studi di**
Paizzale Europa 1
34127 Trieste
Psychology, Dept. of

**Urbino, Univ. degli
  Studi di Urbino**
Via Saffi 2
61029 Urbino
*Other Depts: Evolutionary
  Educational; & Social
  Psychology*

Verona, Univ. di
Policlinico
37134 Verona
*Servizio Psicologia
  medice*
*Dept. Head: Antonio
  Balestrieri*
Phone: (39) (45) 585633
Fax: (39) (45) 585871

JAMAICA

Consortium Graduate School of Social Sciences
Mona, Kingston 7
Psychology, Dept. of

Social & Economic Res. Inst.
Mona, Kingston 7
Psychology, Dept. of

West Indies, Univ. of
Mona, Kingston 7
School of Education
Dept. Head: Dr Don Robotham
Phone: (809) 977 3315
Fax: (809) 927 2163

JAPAN

Aichi Gakuin Univ.
Fac. of Letters
Nissin-cho
Aichi-gun
Aichi 470-01
Psychology Dept.
Dept. Head: Tomio Miyama
Phone: (81) (5617) 3 1111
Fax: (81) (5617) 3 8179
Email: chino@
  dpc.aichi-gakuin.ac.jp

Aichi Prefectural Univ.
Fac. of Literature
Takada-cho
Mizuho-ku
Nagoya 467
Psychology Lab.

Aichi Univ. of Education
Fac. of Education
Igaya-cho, Kariya 448
Psychology Dept.
Other Depts: Special Education

Aichigakuin Univ.
College of General Education
Nisshin-cho
Aichi-gun
Aichi 470-01
Psychology Dept.
Dept. Head: Hisato Kawamura
Phone: (81) (5617) 3 1111
Fax: (81) (5617) 3 1860

Air, Univ. of
Liberal Arts Fac.
Wakaba
Chiba 260
Development & Education Dept.

Akita Univ.
Fac. of Education
Tegatagakuen-cho
Akita 010
Psychology Dept.

Aoyama Gakuin Univ.
College of Literature
Shibuya
Shibuba-ku
Tokyo 150
Psychology Dept.

Ashiya Univ.
Fac. of Education
Rokurokuso-cho
Ashiya 659
Psychology Dept.

ATR Auditory & Visual Perception Research Labs.
2-2 Hirari-dai,
Seika-cho
Soraku-gun, Kyoto 619-02
Cognitive Processes Dept.
Other Depts: Speech & Hearing; Visual Perception
Dept. Head: Katsunori Shimohara
Phone: (81) (77) 495 1440
Fax: (81) (77) 495 1408
Email: katsu@
  atr-hr.atr.co.jp

Bukkyo Univ.
Kitahananobo-cho
Kita-ku, Kyoto 603
Psychology, Lab. of
Dept. Head: Prof. Chizuko Sugita
Phone: (81) (75) 491 2141
Fax: (81) (75) 493 9040

Bunkyo Univ.
Fac. of Human Sciences
Minami-ogishima
Koshigaya 343
Psychology Dept.
Other Depts: Educational Psychology

Chiba Univ.
Fac. of Letters
Yayoi-cho, Inage-ku
Chiba 263
Psychology, Dept. of
Other Depts: Educational Psychology; Early Childhood Education; Special Education
Dept. Head: Takayoshi Aoki
Phone: (81) (43) 251 1111
Fax: (81) (43) 256 7032
Email: miyano@
  psych.1.chiba-u.ac.jp

Chukyo Univ.
Fac. of Letters
Yagotohonmachi
Showa-ku
Nagoya 466
Psychology Dept.
Other Depts: Sociology;
  Computer & Cognitive
  Sciences
Dept. Head: Kanao Yahiro
Phone: (81) (52) 832
  2151
Fax: (81) (52) 835 7144

Chuo Univ.
Fac. of Literature
Higashinakano
Hachioji 192-03
Psychology Dept.

Disabled, Nat.
Rehabilitation Center
for
4-1 Namiki
Tokorozawa 359
Research Inst.

Doshisha Univ.
Fac. of Letters
Karasuma-Imadegawa
Kamigyo-ku
Kyoto 602
Psychology, Dept. of
Dept. Head: Yoshinori
  Matsuyama
Phone: (81) (75) 251
  4095
Fax: (81) (75) 251 3059

Ehime Univ.
Fac. of Law &
  Literature
Bunkyo-cho
Matsuyama 790
Psychology Dept.
Dept. Head: Terufumi
  Sakane
Phone: (81) (899) 24 7111
Fax: (81) (899) 22 5369

Electro-communications,
Univ. of
Chofugaoka 1-5-1
Chofu 182
Psychology Lab.
Dept. Head: Takehisa
  Takizawa
Phone: (81) 0424 83 2161
Fax: (81) 0424 89 6974

Fukui Univ.
Fac. of Education
Bunkyo
Fukui 910
Psychology Dept.
Other Depts:
  Neuropsychology

Fukuoka Univ. of
Education
Fac. of Education
Akama
Munakata
Fukuoka 811-41
Psychology Dept.

Fukushima Univ.
School of Education
Asakawa
Matsukawa-machi
Fukushima 960-12
Educational Psychology
  Dept.

Gakushuin Univ.
1-5-1 Mejiro
Toshima-ku
Tokyo 171
Dept. Head: Hiyoshi
  Nakamura
Phone: (81) (3) 3986 0221
Fax: (81) (3) 5992 1005

Gifu Univ.
Fac. of General
  Education
Yanagido
Gifu 501-11
Psychology Dept.

Group Dynamics, Inst.
for
Nishinippon Shinbun
  Kaikan
1-4-1 Tenjin
Chuo-ku, Fukuoka 810

Hamamatsu Univ.
School of Medicine
Handa-cho
Hamamatsu 431-31
Psychology Dept.
Dept. Head: Aiko Satow
Phone: (81) (53) 435 2321
Fax: (81) (53) 435 1626

Hirosaki Univ.
College of Liberal Arts
Bunkyo-cho
Hirosaki 036
Psychology Dept.

Hiroshima Shudo Univ.
Fac. of Humanities &
  Sciences
Numata-cho
Asaminami-ku
Hiroshima 731-31
Psychology Dept.

Hiroshima Univ.
Fac. of Integ. Arts &
  Sciences
Higashisenda-machi
Naka-ku, Hiroshima 730
Behavioural Sciences
  Dept.
Dept. Head: Tadao Hori
Phone: (81) (82) 241 1221
Fax: (81) (82) 244 5170

Hiroshima Univ.
Fac. of Education
Shitami
Saijo
Higashihiroshima 724
Psychology Dept.
Other Depts: Early
  Childhood Research

Hiroshima Univ.
Fac. of Education
Fukuyama Campus
Midori-machi
Fukuyama 720
Psychology Lab.

**Hiroshima Women's
Univ.**
Fac. of Home
 Economics
Ujinahigashi
Minami-ku
Hiroshima 734
Child Study Dept.

Hokkaido Univ.
Fac. of Education
Kita-11
Nishi-7, Kita-ku
Sapporo 060
*Developmental
 Psychology Dept.
Other Depts: Clinical
 Psychology*

Hokkaido Univ.
Fac. of Letters
Kita-10
Nishi-7, Kita-ku
Sapporo 060
*Dept. of Human
 Behaviouristics
Dept. Head: Prof. Dr
 Shiro Imai*
Phone: (81) (11) 716
 2111
Fax: (81) (11) 726 0919
Email: suto@
 hubs.hokudai.ac.jp

**Hokkaido Univ. of
Education**
Fac. of Education
Ainosato
Kita-ku
Sapporo 002
*Educational Psychology
 Dept.*

**Hyogo College of
Medicine**
College Hospital
Mukogawa-cho
Nishinomiya 663
*Clinical Psychology
 Dept.
Other Depts: Science of
 Behaviour*

Ibaraki Univ.
College of General
 Education
Bunkyo
Mito 310
*Psychology Dept.
Other Depts: Education
 Psychology
Dept. Head: Munehiko,
 Matsui; Miyoko, Aritomi*
Phone: (81) (292) 26 1621
Fax: (81) (292) 27 0960

**Industrial Products
Res. Inst.**
Human Factors Research
 Dept.
Higashi
Tsukuba
Ibaragi 305
*Physiological Informatics
 Div.
Other Depts: Sensory
 Informatics Divn.*

**International Christian
Univ.**
College of Liberal Arts
Osawa
Mitaka
Tokyo 181
*Psychology Dept.
Other Depts: Educational
 Psychology; Graduate
 School of Education
Dept. Head: Kazuo
 Hara*
Phone: (81) (422) 33 3150
Fax: (81) (422) 34 6982

Iwate Univ.
Fac. of Education
Ueda
Morioka, Iwate 020
*Psychology Dept.
Other Depts: Behavioural
 Sciences
Dept. Head: Prof.
 Masakazu Sugawara*
Phone: (81) (196) 23 5171
Fax: (81) (196) 54 4214

**Japan Color Research
Inst.**
3-1-19 Nishi-azabu
Minato-ku, Tokyo 106
*Psychological Research
 Lab.*

Japan Women's Univ.
Mejirodai
Bunkyo-ku, Tokyo 112
*Psychology Dept.
Other Depts: Child
 Study; Education*

Kagawa Univ.
Fac. of Education
Saiwai-cho, Takamatsu
Psychology Dept.

Kagoshima Univ.
Fac. of Education
Korimoto
Kagoshima 890
Psychology Dept.

Kanazawa Univ.
Fac. of Letters
Kakuma-Machi
Kanazawa
Ishikawa-ken 920
*Psychology Dept.
Other Depts: Education
 Psychology*
Phone: (81) (762) 64 5302
Fax: (81) (762) 5362
Email: ab0713@
 jpnknzw1.bitnet

Kansai Univ.
Fac. of Letters
Yamate-cho, Suita 564
Psychology Dept.
Other Depts: Industrial
Psychology

Keio Univ.
Fac. of General Education
Hiyoshi
Kohoku-ku
Yokohama 223
Psychology Lab.
Dept. Head: Shigemasa
Sumi
Phone: (81) (45) 563 1111
Fax: (81) (45) 563 1650
(psychology)

Keio Univ.
Fac. of Letters
Mita
Minato-ku, Tokyo 108
Psychology Dept.

Kinjo Gakuin Univ.
Fac. of Home Economics
Omori 2
Moriyama-ku
Nagoya 463
Child Development Dept.

Kobe College
Fac. of Literature
Dept. of Intercultural
  Studies
Okadayama
Nishinomiya 662
Psychology Lab.
Other Depts: Child
Development Studies

Kobe Univ.
Fac. of Letters
Tsurukabuto
Nada-ku, Kobe 657
Psychology Dept.
Other Depts: Dev. / Educ.
Psychology

Kobe Women's Univ.
Fac. of Letters
Higashi Suma Aoyama
Suma-ku, Kobe 654
Psychology Dept.

Kochi Univ.
Fac. of Humanities
Akebono-cho, Kochi 780
Psychology Dept.

Komazawa Univ.
Fac. of Literature
Komazawa
Setagaya-ku, Tokyo 154
Psychology Dept.

Konan Univ.
Fac. of Literature
Okamoto
Higashinada-ku, Kobe
Psychology Dept.

Konan Women's Univ.
Fac. of Letters
Morikita-cho
Higashinada-ku, Kobe
  658
Psychology Dept.
Dept. Head: Prof. Yasuo
Matsuyama
Phone: (81) (78) 431 0391
Fax: (81) (78) 412 7177

Kumamoto Univ.
Fac. of General Education
KurokamiK
Kumamoto 860
Psychology Dept.
Dept. Head: Tatsuo Tone
Phone: (81) 096 344 211
Fax: (81) 096 345 8907

Kwansei Gakuin Univ.
School of Humanities
Uegahara
Nishinomiya 662
Psychology Dept.
Other Depts: Education

**Kyoto Inst. of
Technology**
Fac. of Engineering &
  Design
Gosho-Kaido-cho
Matsugasaki, Sakyo-ku
Kyoto 606
Psychology Laboratories
Other Depts: Health Care
Service Center
Dept. Head: Prof. Dr
Munehira Akita
Phone: (81) (75) 791 3211
Fax: (81) (75) 723 2851
Email: C51666@
  jpnkudpc.bitnet

Kyoto Prefectural Univ.
Fac. of Letters
Shimogamohangi-cho
Sakyo-ku, Kyoto 606
Social Welfare Dept.

**Kyoto Tachibana
Women's College**
Yamada-cho Ooya
Yamashina-ku, Kyoto 607
Psychology Dept.

**Kyoto Univ. of
Education**
Fac. of Education
Fukakusa Fujinomori-cho
Fushimi-ku, Kyoto 612
Educ. Psychology Lab.
Other Depts: Career
Guidance; Infant
Education; Psychology
of Physical Education

Kyoto Univ.
College of Liberal Arts &
  Sci.
Nihonmatsu-cho
Sakyo-ku
Kyoto 606
Psychology Dept.
Other Depts: Educational
Psychology

Kyoto Univ.
Kanrin
Inuyama
Aichi 484
Psychology, Dept. of;
  Primate Research Inst.
Dept. Head: Dr Shozo
  Kojima
Phone: (81) (568) 61 2891
Fax: (81) (568) 62 2428
Email: kojima@
  pri.kyoto-u.ac.jp

Kyoto Women's Univ.
Fac. of Literature
Kitahiyoshi-cho
Imakumano,
  Higashiyama-ku
Kyoto 605
Psychology Dept.
Other Depts: Child
  Psych / Dev. Disorders
  Inst.

Kyushu Inst. of Design
Fac. of Design
Shiobaru
Minami-ku
Fukuoka 815
Visual Communication
  Design Dept.

Kyushu Univ.
Fac. of Literature
Hakozaki
Higashi-ku
Fukuoka 812
Psychology Dept.
Other Depts: Education
  Psychology
Dept. Head: Katsuya
  Matsunaga
Phone: (81) (92) 641 1101

Kyushu Univ.
Fac. of General Education
Ropponmatsu
Fukuoka 810
Psychology Dept.

Meijigakuin Univ.
College of Liberal
  Arts
Shirokanedai
Minato-ku
Tokyo 108
Psychology Dept.
Other Depts: Teacher
  Education
Dept. Head: Prof.
  Shinichi Jinbo
Phone: (81) (3) 3448
  5258
Fax: (81) (3) 3448 5202

Meijigakuin Univ.
General Education, Dept.
  of
1518 Kamikurata-cho
Totsuka-ku
Yokohama 244
Psychology, Lab. of
Dept. Head: Yasuhiro
  Hanada
Phone: (81) (45) 863
  2084
Fax: (81) (45) 863
  2067

Meisei Univ.
Fac. of Humanities &
  Social Science
Hodokubo
Hino
Tokyo 191
Psychology / Pedagogy
  Dept.
Dept. Head: Takashi
  Ogawa
Phone: (81) (425) 91
  5111
Fax: (81) (425) 91 8181

Mie Univ.
Fac. of Education
Kamihama-cho
Tsu 514
Educational Psychology
  Dept.

**Miyagi Univ. of
Education**
Fac. of Education
Aoba
Aramaki
Sendai 980
Educational Psychology
  Dept.
Other Depts: Special
  Education

Miyazaki Univ.
Fac. of Education
Miyazaki 889-21
Psychology Dept.
Dept. Head: Iwao
  Takayama
Phone: (81) (985) 58
  2811
Fax: (81) (985) 58 2892
Email: e14101u@muipc.
  miyazaki-u.ac.up

**Mukogawa Women's
Univ.**
Fac. of Letters
Ikebiraki-cho
Nisinomiya 663
Educational Psychology
  Dept.
Other Depts: Child
  Education

Nagasaki Univ.
Fac. of Liberal Arts
Bunkyo-machi
Nagasaki 852
Psychology Dept.
Other Depts:
  Educational
  Psychology

Nagoya City Univ.
College of General
  Education
Mizuho-cho
Mizuho-ku
Nagoya 467
Psychology Dept.

**Nagoya Inst. of
Technology**
Humanities & Social
  Science Dept.
Gokiso-cho
Showa-ku
Nagoya 466
Psychology Lab.

Nagoya Univ.
College of General
  Education
Furo-cho
Chikusa-ku
Nagoya 464-01
Psychology Dept.
*Other Depts: Educational
  Psychology; Aero-Space
  Psychology*

**Nagoya Women's
Univ.**
Takimiya-cho
Tenpaku-ku
Nagoya 468
Fac. of Literature

Nanzan Univ.
Fac. of Literature
Yamazato-cho
Showa-ku
Nagoya 466
Psychology Dept.

Nara Univ. of Education
Fac. of Education
Takabatake-cho
Nara 630
Psychology Dept.

Nara Univ.
Fac. of Social Research
Misasagi-cho
Nara 631
Social Psychology Dept.
*Dept. Head: Kiyoshi
  Maiya*
Phone: (81) (742) 44 1251
Fax: (81) (742) 41 0650

Nara Women's Univ.
Fac. of Letters
Kitauoya-Nishimachi
Nara 630
Psychology Dept.

Nihon Univ.
College of Humanities &
  Sciences
3-25-40 Sakurajosui
Setagaya-ku, Tokyo 156
Psychology, Dept. of
*Dept. Head: Kensuke
  Murai*
Phone: (81) (3) 3329 1151
Fax: (81) (3) 3303 9899

Niigata Univ.
Fac. of Humanities
Ikarashi
Niigata 950-21
Psychology Dept.
*Other Depts: Educational
  Psychology*

**Notre Dame Seishin
Univ.**
Fac. of Home Economics
Ifuku-cho
Okayama 700
Child Welfare Dept.
*Dept. Head: Keiichi
  Hamano*
Phone: (81) (862) 55 3257
Fax: (81) (862) 55 7663

Ochanomizu Univ.
Fac. of Letters &
  Education
Ohtsuka
Bunkyo-ku, Tokyo 112
Psychology Dept.
Other Depts: Child Study

Oita Univ.
Fac. of Education
Dannoharu
Oita 870-11
Psychology Dept.

Okayama Univ.
Fac. of Letters
Tsushima-naka
Okayama 700
Psychology Dept.
*Other Depts: Educational
  Psychology*
*Dept. Head: Dr Keiichi
  Mitani*
Phone: (81) (862) 51
  7401
Fax: (81) (862) 53 1449

Osaka City Univ.
Fac. of Letters
Sugimoto
Sumiyoshi-ku
Osaka 558
Psychology Dept.
*Other Depts: Child &
  Clinical Psychology*
*Dept. Head: Takehiro
  Ueno*
Phone: (81) (6) 605 2380
Fax: (81) (6) 605 2355
Email: d54323@
  jpnkudpc.bitnet

**Osaka Prefecture, Univ.
of**
College of Int. Arts &
  Sciences
Gakuencho
Sakai 593
Human Sciences Inst.
*Dept. Head: Masahiko
  Kirimura*
Phone: (81) (722) 52
  1161
Fax: (81) (722) 55 2981
Email: e01074@
  sinet.ad.jp

Osaka Univ.
College of General
  Education
Machikaneyama
Toyonaka 560
Psychology Dept.

Osaka Univ.
Fac. of Human Sciences
1-2 Yamadaoka
Suita, Osaka 565
General Psychology Dept.
Other Depts: Comp. / Dev.
Psychology; Behavioural
Psychology; Social
Psychology; Industrial
Psychology; Biological
Anthropology;
Ethological Studies;
Educational Psychology;
Behavioural Engineering
Dept. Head: Yoshiaki
Nakajima
Phone: (81) (6) 877 5111
Fax: (81) (6) 878 1032

Osaka Univ. of Education
Fac. of Education
Minami-Kawabori-cho
Tennoji-ku, Osaka 543
Psychology Dept.

Osaka Univ. of Foreign Studies
Fac. of Foreign Studies
Aomadani, Minoo 562
Psychology Dept.
Dept. Head: Mariko
Osaka
Phone: (81) (727) 28 3111

Osaka Women's Univ.
Daisen-cho
Sakai 590
Human Relations Dept.

Otemon Gakuin Univ.
Fac. of Letters
Nishi-Ai
Ibaraki 567
Psychology Dept.
Dept. Head: Prof.
Tadaaki Fujimoto
Phone: (81) (726) 43 5421
Fax: (81) (726) 43 5427

Police Science, Nat. Res. Inst.
6 Sanbancho
Chiyoda-ku
Tokyo 102
Crime Prevention &
Juvenile Delinquency
Dept.
Other Depts: Psychology
Dept. Head: Kanehiro
Hoshino
Phone: (81) (3) 3261 9986
Fax: (81) (3) 3221 1245

Psychiatric Research Inst.
Kamikitazawa
Setagaya-ku
Tokyo 156
Clinical Psychology Divn.

Rikkyo Univ. (St Paul's)
Fac. of General Education
Nishi-Ikebukuro
Toshima-ku
Tokyo 171
Psychology Dept.
Other Depts: Industrial
Relations
Dept. Head: Prof. Dr
Masada Wataru
Phone: (81) (3) 3985 2641
Fax: (81) (3) 3985 2641

Rissho Univ.
Fac. of Letters
Oosaki
Shinagawa-ku
Tokyo 141
Philosophy Dept.

Ritsumeikan Univ.
Fac. of Social Sciences
Tojiin Kitamachi
Kita-ku
Kyoto 603
Psychology Dept.
Other Depts: Educational
Psychology

Ryukoku Univ.
Fac. of Literature
Shichijo-Ohmiya
Shimokyo-ku
Kyoto 600
Psychology Lab.

Ryukyus Univ.
College of Law & Letters
Sembaru
Nishihara-cho
Okinawa 903-01
Psychology Dept.
Other Depts: Educational
Psychology

Sacred Heart Univ.
Fac. of Letters
Hiroo
Sibuya-ku, Tokyo 150
Psychology Lab.
Other Depts: Human
Relations

Saga Univ.
Fac. of Education
Honjo, Saga 840
Psychology Dept.
Other Depts:
Neuropsychology

Saitama Univ.
Fac. of Education
Shimo-ohkubo
Urawa 338
Educational Psychology
Dept.

Sapporo Medical College
School of Medicine
Minami-1
Nishi-17, Chuo-ku
Sapporo 060
Psychology Dept.
Dept. Head: Yoshio
Sugiyama
Phone: (81) (11) 611 2111
Fax: (81) (11) 613 7949

Science of Labour, Inst. for
2-8-14 Sugao
Miyamae-ku
Kawasaki 213
Work Physiology & Psych. Div.

Seijo Univ.
Fac. of Arts & Letters
Seijo
Setagaya-ku
Tokyo 157
Mass Communication Dept.
Dept. Head: Masao Miyaji
Phone: (81) (3) 3482 1181 469
Fax: (81) (3) 3482 7740

Seiwa College
Education Dept.
Okadayama
Nishinomiya 665
Child Psychology Lab.

Senshu Univ.
School of Literature
Higashi-Mita
Tama-ku
Kawasaki 214
Psychology, Dept. of
Dept. Head: Tatsuo Kinjoh
Phone: (81) (44) 911 1015
Fax: (81) (44) 922 4175
Email: thl0255@
jpnsens.bitnet

Shiga Univ.
Fac. of Education
Hiratsu
Otsu 520
Psychology Dept.

Shimane Univ.
Fac. of Law & Literature
Nishikawatsu-cho
Matsue 690
Psychology Dept.

Shinshu Univ.
Allied Medical Sciences School
Nishi-nagano
Nagano 380
Psychology Dept.

Shinshu Univ.
Fac. of Education
Nishi-nagano
Nagano 380
Educational Psychology Dept.
Other Depts: Special Education; Early Childhood Education

Shirayuri College
Fac. of Letters
1-25 Midorigaoka
Chofu-shi
Tokyo 182
Developmental Psychology, Graduate Dept. of
Dept. Head: Hiroshi Azuma
Phone: (81) (3) 3326 5050
Fax: (81) (3) 3326 4942
Email: azumah@
tansei.cc.u-tokyo.ac.jp

Shizuoka Univ.
Fac. of Education
Ooya
Shizuoka 422
Psychology Dept.
Other Depts: Social Psychology
Dept. Head: Takeji Uchiyama
Phone: (81) (54) 237 111

Sophia Univ.
Fac. of Literature
Kioi-cho
Chiyoda-ku
Tokyo 102
Psychology Dept.

Special Education, Nat. Inst. of
2360 Nobi
Yokosuka
Kanagawa-ken 239
Emotionally Disturbed, Dept. of Educ. for
Other Depts: Education for Mentally Retarded, Multiple Handicapped, Speech & Hearing Handicapped
Dept. Head: Dr Yoshikata Atumi
Phone: (81) (468) 48 4121
Fax: (81) (468) 49 5563

Tamagawa Univ.
Tamagawa Gakuen
Machida 194
Fac. of Literature

Teikoku Women's Univ.
Fac. of Domestic Science
Toda-cho
Moriguchi 570
Psychology Dept.

Teikyo Univ.
Fac. of Letters
Otsuka
Hachioji 192-03
Psychology Dept.
Dept. Head: Prof. Hiroto Katori
Phone: (81) (426) 74 6798
Fax: (81) (426) 76 0388

Tohoku Gakuin Univ.
Ichinazaka
Izumi-ku
Sendai 981-31
Psychology, Dept. of
Phone: (81) (22) 375 1183
Fax: (81) (22) 375 4040
Email: lpsycho@izcc.
tohoku-gakuin.ac.jp

Tohoku Univ.
Fac. of Arts & Letters
Kawauchi
Aoba-ku, Sendai 980
Psychology Dept.
Dept. Head: Kinya
Maruyama
Phone: (81) (22) 222 1800
Fax: (81) (22) 265 8028
Email: hatayama@
jpntuvmo.bitnet

Tohoku Univ.
Fac. of Education
Kawauchi
Aoba-ku, Sendai 980
Educational Psychology
Dept.
Other Depts: Mental
Retardation; Science for
the Visually
Handicapped;
Audiology / Speech
Science

Tokai Univ.
Research Inst. of
Civilization
Kitakaname
Hiratsuka 259-12
Psychology Dept.
Other Depts: Mass
Communnication;
Information Society
Study; Education

Tokiwa Univ.
Fac. of Human Science
Miwa, Mito 310
Psychology Dept.

Tokushima Univ.
College of General
Education
Minami-johsanjima
Tokushima 770
Psychology Dept.
Other Depts: Behavioural
Science

Tokyo Metropolitan
Inst. of
Gerontology
35-2 Sakae-cho
Itabashi-ku
Tokyo 173
Psychology, Dept. of
Dept. Head: Yoshiko
Shimonaka
Phone: (81) (3) 3964 3241
Fax: (81) (3) 3579 4776

Tsukuba Univ.
Tennodai 1-1-1
Tsukuba City 305
Psychology, Inst. of

Waseda Univ.
Mikajima
TokorozawaS
aitama 359
Basic Human Sciences,
School of
Dept. Head: Prof. Yutaka
Haruki
Phone: (81) (3) 3203
4141
Fax: (81) (3) 3203 7718

Waseda Univ.
Mikajima
Tokorozawa
Saitama 359
Sports Sciences, Dept. of
Dept. Head: Prof. Masao
Ueda
Phone: (81) (3) 3203 4141
Fax: (81) (3) 3203 7718

Waseda Univ.
Mikajima
Tokorozawa
Saitama 359
Human Sciences, School
of
Dept. Head: Prof. Kageyu
Noro
Phone: (81) (3) 3203 4141
Fax: (81) (3) 3203 7718

Waseda Univ.
Toyama 1-24-1
Shinjuku-ku
Tokyo 162
Health Sciences,
Dept. of
Dept. Head: Prof. Kageyu
Noro
Phone: (81) (3) 3203
4141
Fax: (81) (3) 3203 7718

Waseda Univ.
Toyama 1-24-1
Shinjuku-ku
Tokyo 162
Psychology, Dept. of
Dept. Head: Prof.
Masatoshi Tomita
Phone: (81) (3) 3203
4141
Fax: (81) (3) 3203
7718

Waseda Univ.
Toyama 1-24-1
Shinjuku-ku
Tokyo 162
School of Letters
Dept. Head: Prof.
Yasutomo Ishii
Phone: (81) (3) 3203
4141
Fax: (81) (3) 3203 7718

JORDAN

Al-Quds Open Univ.
POB 77
Um Summaq
Amman
Psychology, Dept. of

An-Najah Nat. Univ.
POB 7
Nablus
West Bank
Via Israel
Psychology, Dept. of

Bethlehem Univ.
POB 9, Bethlehem
West Bank, Via Israel
Psychology, Dept. of

Birzeit Univ.
POB 14, Birzeit
West Bank, Via Israel
Psychology, Dept. of

Hebron Univ.
POB 40 Hebron
West Bank
Via Israel
Psychology, Dept. of

Jordan, Univ. of
Amman
Psychology, Dept. of

Yarmouk Univ.
POB 566
Irbid
Psychology, Dept. of

KAZAKHSTAN

**Karaganda Met.
Combine Tech.
Univ.**
Temirtau Pr. Lenina 34
472300
Psychology, Dept. of

**Karaganda State
Univ.**
Univ.skaya ul. 28
Karaganda
470074
Psychology, Dept. of

**Kazakh S. M. Kirov
State Univ.**
Ul. Timiryazeva 46
Alma-Ata
480121
Psychology, Dept. of

Kirgiz State Univ.
Ul. Frunze 537
Frunze
720024
Kirgiz
Psychology, Dept. of

KENYA

Egerton Univ.
POB 536
Njoro
Psychology, Dept. of
Other Depts:
Education

Kenyatta Univ.
POB 43844
Nairobi
Educational Psychology,
Dept. of
Dept. Head: Dr Shashi K.
Bali
Phone: (254) (2) 810901
Fax: (254) (2) 810759
Telex: (254) (2) 25483

Moi Univ.
POB 3900
Eldoret
Psychology, Dept. of

Nairobi Univ.
POB 30197
Nairobi
Education & Psychology
Dept.

KOREA, DEMOCRATIC PEOPLE'S REPUBLIC OF

Kim il Sung Univ.
Daesong District
Pyongyang
Psychology, Dept. of

KOREA, REPUBLIC OF

Ajou Univ.
Suweon 170
Gyeong-gi
Psychology, Dept. of

Andong Nat. Univ.
388 Song cheon dong
Angong
Kyung-buk
460-380
Psychology, Dept. of

Chonbuk Nat. Univ.
664-14 Deoglin-dong 1-
ga
Jeonju
Chonbuk
Psychology, Dept. of

Chonnam Nat. Univ.
300 Yong Bong Dong
Buk-Gu
Kwangju
500-757
Psychology, Dept. of

Chosun Univ.
375 Seosuk-dong
Kwangju
Chollanam-do
500
Psychology, Dept. of

Chung-ang Univ.
221 Huksuk-dong
Dongjak-ku
Seoul 151
Psychology, Dept. of
Dept. Head: Sang Chin
Choi
Phone: (82) (2) 810
2107
Fax: (82) (2) 816 9938

**Chungbuk Nat.
Univ.**
48 Gaesin-dong
Cheongju-si
Chungbuk
310
Psychology, Dept. of

Chungnam Nat. Univ.
Taejon
Chungnam
302-74
Psychology, Dept. of
Dept. Head: Kim, Kyo
Heon
Phone: (82) (11) 42 821
6368
Fax: (82) (11) 42 823 4520

Dan Kook Univ.
San 8 Hannam-dong
Yongsan-gu
Seoul
Psychology, Dept. of

Dong-a Univ.
1, 3-ga Dongdaeshin-
dong
Seo-gu
Pusan
600
Psychology, Dept. of

**Dongduck Women's
Univ.**
23-1 Wolgok-dong
Sungbuk-ku
Seoul
136-714
Psychology, Dept. of

Dongguk Univ.
26 3-ga
Pil-dong
Chung-gu
Seoul
Psychology, Dept. of

**Duk Sung Women's
Univ.**
419 Sang Mun-dong
Dobong-gu
Seoul
132-714
Psychology, Dept. of

Ewha Woman's Univ.
11-1 Daihyun-dong
Seodaimoon-gu
Seoul
Psychology, Dept. of

Hanyang Univ.
17 Haengdang-dong
Sungdong-gu
Seoul
133
Psychology, Dept. of

Hong-ik Univ.
72-1 Sangsu-dong
Mapo-gu
Seoul 121
Psychology, Dept. of

Inha Univ.
253 Yonghyun-dong
Nam-gu
Inchon
175-46
Psychology, Dept. of

Kangweon Nat. Univ.
192-1 Hyoja-dong
Chuncheon 200
Kangweon-do
Psychology, Dept. of
*Dept. Head: Sung Youl
Hong*
Phone: (82) (361) 50
6850

Keimyung Univ.
2139 Taemyung-dong
Daegu
705-701
Psychology, Dept. of

Kon-kuk Univ.
93-1 Mojin-dong
Seongdong-gu
Seoul
131-439
Psychology, Dept. of

Kookmin Univ.
861-1, Chongnung-
dong
Songbuk-ku
Seoul
136
Psychology, Dept. of

Korea Univ.
1, 5-ga, Anam-dong
Sungbuk-gu
Seoul
*Behavioural Science
Research Inst.*
*Dept. Head: Prof. Man
Young Lee*
Phone: (82) (2) 923
9203
Fax: (82) (2) 920 1192

Korea Univ.
1, 5-ga, Anam-dong
Sungbuk-gu
Seoul
Psychology, Dept. of
*Dept. Head: Prof.
Chang-Yil Ahn*
Phone: (82) (2) 920 1192
Fax: (82) (2) 920 1192

**Kyungpook Nat.
Univ.**
1370 Sankyuk-dong
Pug-ku Taegu
702-701
Psychology, Dept. of
*Dept. Head: Dr.
Young-Sun Jin*
Phone: (82) (2) (53) 950
5244
Email: ysjin@
bh.kac.kr

Pusan Nat. Univ.
30 Jangjeon-dong
Dongnae-gu
Pusan
Psychology, Dept. of

Seoul City Univ.
8-3 Junong-dong
Dong-daemun-ku
Seoul 131
Psychology, Dept. of

Seoul Nat. Univ.
Sinlim-dong
Kwanak-gu
Seoul
151
Psychology, Dept. of

Seoul Woman's Univ.
126 Kongnung
2-dong
Nowon-gu
Seoul
139-744
Psychology, Dept. of

Sogang Univ.
CPO 1142
Seoul 121
Psychology, Dept. of

Sookmyung Women's Univ.
53-12 Chungpa-dong 2-ga
Yongsan-gu, Seoul 140
Psychology, Dept. of

Soong Sil Univ.
1-1 Sangdo 1 dong
Dongjak-ku
Seoul 156-743
Psychology, Dept. of

Sung Kyun Kwan Univ.
53, 3-ga
Myungryun-dong
Chongro-gu
Seoul 110-745
Psychology, Dept. of

Won Kwang Univ.
344-2 Sinyong-dong
Iri
Chollabuk-do
Psychology, Dept. of

Yeungnam Univ.
Gyongsan 532
Psychology, Dept. of

Yonsei Univ.
134 Shinchon-
dong
Sudaemoon-gu
Seoul
Psychology, Dept. of

KUWAIT

Kuwait Univ.
POB 23558
Psychology Dept.
Dept. Head: Dr Mostafa
Ahmad Torki
Phone: (965) 4830157
Fax: (965) 4837108

LAO PEOPLE'S DEMOCRATIC REPUBLIC

Sisavangvong Univ.
Ministry of Education
Lane Xang Ave.
Vientiane
Psychology, Dept. of

LATVIA

Latvia, Univ. of
Raina blvd. 19
Riga LV-1098
Practical Psychology, Dept. of
Dept. Head: Ivan Michailov
Phone: (7) (132) 217 492
Fax: (7) (132) 225 039

Latvia, Univ. of
Raina blvd. 19
Riga LV-1098
Psychology, Dept. of
Phone: (7) (132) 217 492
Fax: (7) (132) 225 039

Riga Technical Univ.
Kalku str. 1
226355 Riga
Psychology, Dept. of

LEBANON

American Univ. of Beirut
Beirut
Psychology Dept.

Beirut Arab Univ.
Tarik El-Jadidé
POB 5020
Beirut
Psychology, Dept. of

Libanaise, Univ.
Place du Musée
Beirut
Psychology, Dept. of

Saint-Esprit de Kaslik, Univ. de
Jounieh
Psychology, Dept. of

Saint-Joseph, Univ. de
rue de Damas
BP 293
Beirut
Psychology, Dept. of

LESOTHO

Lesotho National Univ.
PO Roma 180
Dept. Head: Prof. Benson Charles Nindi
Phone: (266) 340601
Fax: (266) 34000
Telex: 4303LO

LIBERIA

Liberia, Univ. of
POB 9020
Monrovia
Psychology, Dept. of

LIBYAN ARAB JAMAHIRIYA

Al-Fateh Univ.
POB 13040 Tripoli
Psychology, Dept. of

Bright Star Univ. of Technology
POB 858
Mersa-El-Brega
Psychology, Dept. of

Garyounis, Univ. of
POB 1308
Benghazi
Psychology, Dept. of

Sebha Univ.
POB 18758
Sebha
Psychology, Dept. of

LITHUANIA

Vilnius Univ.
Univ.o 3
Vilnius
232734
Psychology, Dept. of

Vytautas the Great Univ.
Laisves Ave. 53
Kaunas
233000
Psychology, Dept. of

LUXEMBOURG

Centre de Réadaptation
Route d'Arlon 82
Capellen

Centre Univ. de Luxembourg
162A ave de la Faiencerie
1511 Luxembourg
Psychology, Dept. of

MACEDONIA, FORMER YUGOSLAV REPUBLIC OF

Bitolj, Univ.
97000 Bitola
Bulevar '1 Maj' b. b.
Psychology, Dept. of

Skopje, Univ. 'Kiril i Metódij' vo
91000 Skopje
POB 576
Bulevar 'Krste Misirkov'
b. b.
Psychology, Dept. of

MADAGASCAR

Antananarivo, Univ. de
Campus Univ.e d'Ankatso
BP 566
101 Antananarivo
Psychology, Dept. of

Fianarantsoa, Univ. de
BP 1264
301 Fianarantsoa
Psychology, Dept. of

Toamasina, Univ. de
BP 591
501 Toamasina
Psychology, Dept. of

MALAWI

Malawi, Univ. of
POB 280
Zomba
Psychology, Dept. of
Dept. Head: Dr. Stuart Carr
Phone: (265) 523 102
Fax: (265) 523225
Telex: 44742 CHANCOL MI

MALAYSIA

International Islamic Univ.
POB 70, Jl. Sultan
46700 Petaling Jaya
Selangor
Psychology, Dept. of
Dept. Head: Prof.
Shamsur Rehman Khan
Phone: (60) (3) 7555322
Fax: (60) (3) 7579598
Telex: ISLAMU MA 37161
Email: general@ mpi.nl

Kebangsaan Malaysia, Univ.
43600 Bangi, Selangor
Psychology, Dept. of

Malaysia, Nat. Univ. of
Bangi
Selangor
Psychology, Dept. of

Malaysia, Univ. Pertanian
43400 Serdang
Selangor Darul Ehsan
Psychology, Dept. of

Malaysia, Univ. Sains
Minden
11800 Penang
Psychology, Dept. of

Malaysia, Univ. Utara
Sintok
06010 Changlun
Kedah
Psychology, Dept. of

Malaya, Univ. of
Lembah Pantai
59100 Kuala Lumpur
Psychology, Dept. of

Malaya, Univ. of
Kuala Lumpur 22-11
Fac. of Education

Sains Malaysia Univ.
Penang
Psychiatry Dept.

MALTA

Malta, Univ. of
Msida
Psychology, Dept. of
Dept. Head: Dr. Alfred Darmanin
Phone: (356) 336451
Fax: (356) 336450
Telex: 407 HIEDUC MW

MAURITANIA

Nouakchott, Univ. de
BP 798, Nouakchott
Psychology, Dept. of

MAURITIUS

Mauritius, Univ. of
Réduit
Psychology, Dept. of

MEXICO

Anáhuac, Univ.
Apdo 10-844
Mexico 11000 DF
Psychology, Dept. of

Antonio Narro, Univ. Aut. Agraria
Buenavista
Saltillo
Coahuila
Psychology, Dept. of

Baja California, Univ. Aut. de
Apdo Postal 459
Avda Alvaro Obregón y
    Julian Carrillo s/n
21100 Mexicali
Baja California
Psychology, Dept. of

Bajio, Univ. del
Apdo Postal 444
371150 Léon
Gto
Psychology, Dept. of
Dept. Head: Dra. Leticia
    Garcia de Pejenaute
Phone: (52) (471) 7 17
40
Fax: (52) (471) 18 55 11

Bellavista, Univ.
Campostella 126
Iztapalapa 09860

Carmen, Univ. Aut. del
Calle 31 x 56 s/n
24176 Ciudad del Carmen
Camp.
Psychology, Dept. of

Chapingo, Univ. Aut. del
Domicilio conocido
56230 Chapingo
Edo de México
Psychology, Dept. of

Chiapas, Univ. Aut. de
Poniente Sur 118
29050 Tuxtla Gutiérrez
Chiapas
Psychology, Dept. of

Chihuahua, Univ. Aut. de
Apdo Postal 324
31000 Chihuahua
Chih.
Psychology, Dept. of

Ciudad Juárez, Univ. Aut. de
Apdo Postal 1594-D
Avda López Mateos 20
32300 Ciudad Juárez
Chihuahua
Psychology, Dept. of

Coahuila, Univ. Aut. de
Blvd Constitución y
    Durango
Apdo Postal 308
25280 Saltillo
Coahuila
Psychology, Dept. of

Col. Copilco Univ.
Odontologia 85
04360 México DF

Col. Educación
Calle 1 No. 9
México 21 DF
Manzana XII

Colima, Univ. de
Avda Univ. 333
Apdo Postal 134
28000 Colima
Col.
Psychology, Dept. of

Edif. Cuba/902
Integración
    Latinoamericana
Col. Copilco
México 21 DF

Edif. E. Eento
Av. Univ. 1810
Col. Romero de Terreros
Coyoacán
04310 México DF

Golfo, Univ. del
Obregón 203 Pte
89000 Tampico
Tamps
Psychology, Dept. of

Guadalajara, Univ. Aut. de
Apdo Postal 1-440
44100 Guadalajara
Jalisco
Psychology, Dept. of

Guadalajara, Univ. de
Avda Juárez No. 974
Sector Járez
44100 Guadalajara
Jalisco
Psychology, Dept. of

Guanajuato, Univ. de
Lascuráin de Retana 5
36000 Guanajuato
Psychology, Dept. of

Guerrero, Univ. Aut. de
Abasolo 33
03900 Chilpancingo
Guerrero
Psychology, Dept. of

Hidalgo, Univ. Aut. de
Abasolo No. 600
Centro
42000 Pachuca
Hidalgo
Psychology, Dept. of

Iberoamericana, Univ.
Prolongación Paseo de la
    Reforma 880
Col. Lomas de Santa Fé
01210 México DF
Psychology, Dept. of
Other Depts:
    Psychological
    Counselling

Intercontinental, Univ.
Insurgentes Sur 4135
14000 México DF
Psychology, Dept. of

Jan de Dios Batiz,Univ.
Edif. 33-A-302, Av. IPN
Col. Lindavista
07300 México DF

**Juárez del Estado de
Durango, Univ.**
Constitución 404
Sur
34000 Durango
Psychology, Dept. of

Las Americas, Univ. de
Apdo Postal 100
72820 Santa Catarina
Mártir
Puebla
Psychology, Dept. of

Loma Hermosa, Univ.
Edif. 31-A Depto. 201
Col. Irrigación
11500 México DF

Lomas Becerra, Univ.
Edif. 11-101
Col. Mixcoac
01470 México DF

**Metropolitana, Univ.
Aut.**
Apdo Postal 325
Del. Cuauhtémox
06000 México, DF
Psychology, Dept. of

**México, Univ. del Valle
de**
Tehuantepec 250
Colonia Roma Sur
Del. Cuauhtémoc
06760 México, DF
Psychology, Dept. of

**México, Univ. Femenina
de**
Avda Constituventes 151
11850 México DF
Psychology, Dept. of

México, Univ. la Salle de
Benjamin Franklin 47
Col. Condesa
Del. Cuauhtémoc
06140 México, DF
Psychology, Dept. of

**México, Univ. Nacion.
Aut. de**
Del. Coyoacán
04510 México DF
Psychology, Dept. of

**México, Univ. Aut. del
Estado**
Constituventes 100
Oriente
50000 Toluca
Edo de México
Psychology, Dept. of

**Michoacana de San
Nicolás de Hidalgo,
Univ. de**
Edif. 'TR'
Ciudad Univ.
58030 Morelia, Michoacán
Psychology, Dept. of

Montemorelos, Univ. de
Apdo 16
Montemorelos
Nuevo León
Psychology, Dept. of

Monterey, Univ. de
Apdo 4442
C. P. 66250, San Pedro
Garza García
Nuevo León
Psychology, Dept. of

**Morelos, Univ. Aut. del
Estado de**
Avda Univ. 1001
Col. Chamilpa
62210 Cuernavaca
Morelos
Psychology, Dept. of

Motolinia AC, Univ.
Cerrado de Ameyalco 227
Col. del Valle
03100 México DF
Psychology, Dept. of

Nayarit, Univ. Aut. de
Ciud. de la Cultura
Amado Nervo
63190 Tepic, Nayarit
Psychology, Dept. of

Norest, Univ. Aut. del
Monclova 1561
Col. República
25280 Saltillo, Coahuila
Psychology, Dept. of

**Oaxaca, Univ. Aut.
Benito Juarez**
Apdo 76
Ciudad Univ.
68120 Oaxaca
Psychology, Dept. of

Oxtopulco Univ.
Av. Unidad 1815-C.
Depto. 606
04310 México DF

Panamericana, Univ.
Augusto Rodin 498
Col. Mixcoac
03910 México DF
Psychology, Dept. of

**Puebla, Benemerita
Univ. Aut de**
4 Sur No. 104
72000 Puebla
Pue.
Psychology, Dept. of

**Puebla, Univ. Pop. Aut.
del Estado de**
21 Sur 1103
72160 Puebla
Pue.
Psychology, Dept. of

Querétaro, Univ. Aut. de
Centro Universitario
Cerro de las Campanas
76010 Querétaro
Qro.
Psychology, Dept. of

Regiomontana, Univ.
Villagrán 238 Sur
Apdo Postal 243
64000 Monterrey
NL
Psychology, Dept. of

Salesiana, Univ.
Calle Colegio Salesiano
35, Co
11320 Mexico DF

San Luis Potosí, Univ. Aut. de
Alvaro Obregón 64
78000 San Luis Potosí
SLP
Psychology, Dept. of

Sinaloa, Univ. Aut. de
Apdo Postal 1919
Calle Angel Flores s/n
80000 Culiacán
Sinaloa
Psychology, Dept. of

Sonora, Univ. de
Apdo Postal 336 y 106
83000 Hermosillo
Sonora
Psychology, Dept. of
*Dept. Head: Jose Angel
Vera Noriega*
Phone: (52) (621) 17 47 81
Fax: (52) (621) 17 47 75

Sudeste, Univ. Aut. del
Apdo Postal 204
Ciudad Univ.
24030 Campeche
Camp.
Psychology, Dept. of

Tabasco, Univ. Juárez Aut. de
Carretera a Frontera
Zona de la Cultura
86020 Villahermosa
Tabasco
Psychology, Dept. of

Tamaulipas, Univ. Aut. de
Apdo Postal 186
87000 Ciudad Victoria
Tamaulipas
Psychology, Dept. of

Tlaxcala, Univ. Aut. de
Apdo Postal 19
90000 Tlaxcala
Psychology, Dept. of

Unidad Candelaria de los Patos
15810 México DF
Manzana 1 Edif. F Depto. 11

Unidad Habitacional Santa Fe
01170 México
Manzana 5 Grupo 1 Ent. Depto. 2

Unidad San Juan de Aragón
Av. 475 No. 107
Sección 7, México 14 DF

Veracruzana, Univ.
Zona Univ.
Lomas del Estadio
Jalapa, Ver.
Psychology, Dept. of

Xochicalco, Univ.
Av. López Mateos y
Castillo s/n
Encenada
Baja California
Centro de Estudios

Yucatán, Univ. Aut. de
Apdo 415
Calles 57 por 60
97000 Mérida
Yucatán
Psychology, Dept. of

Zacatecas, Univ. Aut. de
Jardin Juarez 147
98000 Zacatecas
Psychology, Dept. of

MOLDAVIA

Moldavian State Univ.
Ul. Livezilor 60
Kishinev
277014
Psychology, Dept. of

MONGOLIA

Mongolian State Univ.
POB 377
Ulan Bator
Psychology, Dept. of

MONTENEGRO

Titogradu, Univ. 'V. Vlahovic' u
81000 Titograd
POB 105
Cetinjski put b. b.
Psychology, Dept. of

MOROCCO

Cadi Ayyad, Univ. de
Ave Prince My Abdellah
BP S 511
Marrakech
Psychology, Dept. of

Hassan II, Univ. de
BP 9167
19 rue Tariq Bnou Ziyad
Casablanca
Psychology, Dept. of

Ibnou Zohr, Univ. de
Agadir
Psychology, Dept. of

Mohamed I, Univ. de
BP 524, Oujda
Psychology, Dept. of

Mohammed V, Univ. de
BP 554, 3 rue Michlifen
Agdal, Rabat
Psychology, Dept. of

Quaraouyine, Univ.
BP 60, Fès
Psychology, Dept. of

Sidi Mohamed Ben Abdellah Univ.
BP 2626
ave. des Alm
ohades
Fès
Psychology, Dept. of

MOZAMBIQUE

Eduardo Mondlane, Univ.
CP 257
Maputo
Psychology, Dept. of

MYANMAR

Mandalay, Univ. of
University Estate
Mandalay
Psychology, Dept. of

Mawlamyine Univ.
Mawlamyine
Mon State
Psychology, Dept. of

Yangon, Univ. of
Mein University Estate
University PO, Yangon
Psychology, Dept. of

NEPAL

**Mahendra Sanskrit
Viswavidyalaya**
Beljhundi, Dang
Psychology, Dept. of

Tribhuvan Univ.
POB 3757
Kirtipur, Kathmandu
Psychology, Dept. of
Dept. Head: Prof. Dr.
Ayan Bahadur Shrestha
Phone: (977) (1) 213277

NETHERLANDS

Amsterdam, Univ. van
ANC, Meibergdreef 15
1005 AZ Amsterdam
Medische Psychologie

Amsterdam, Univ. van
Roetersstraat 15
1018 WB Amstyerdam
Psychology, Fac. of
Dept. Head: R. K. Popma
Phone: (31) (20) 525 6228
Fax: (31) (20) 525 6710

Amsterdam, Vrije Univ.
De Boelelaan 1109
1021 HV Amsterdam
Clinical Psychology Dept.
Dept. Head: Prof. T. L.
Holdstock
Phone: (31) (20) 5483852
Fax: (31) (20) 6426275

Amsterdam, Vrije Univ.
De Boelelaan 1111
1081 HV Amsterdam
Cognitive Psychology,
Dept. of
Dept. Head: Prof. A. F.
Sanders
Phone: (31) (20) 5483868
Fax: (31) (20) 6426275
Email: ineke@ psy.vu.nl

N-O

Amsterdam, Vrije Univ.
Van de Boechorststr 1
1081 HV Amsterdam
Developmental
Psychology, Dept. of
Dept. Head: Willem Koops
Phone: (31) (20) 5486973
Fax: (31) (20) 6425075
Email: v73usteg@
hasarall

Amsterdam, Vrije Univ.
De Boelelaan 1111
1081 HV Amsterdam
Psychophysiology, Dept. of
Dept. Head: Prof. J. F.
Orlebeke
Phone: (31) (20) 5483863
Fax: (31) (20) 6426275
Email: alies@ psy.vu.nl

Amsterdam, Vrije Univ.
De Boelelaan 1081
1081 HV Amsterdam
Social Psychology, Dept. of
Dept. Head: Prof. G. R.
Semin
Phone: (31) (20) 5485543
Fax: (31) (20) 6429863
Email: v73usops@
hasarall

Amsterdam, Vrije Univ.
De Boelelaan 1111
1081 HV Amsterdam
Theoretical Psychology,
Dept. of
Dept. Head: Prof. J. F. H.
van Rappard
Phone: (31) (20) 5484446
Fax: (31) (20) 6426275
Email: ineke@ psy.vu.nl

**Amsterdam, Vrije
Univ.**
De Boelelaan 1081
1081 HV Amsterdam
Work & Organizational
Psychology, Dept. of
Other Depts: Medical
Psychology; Child
Psychology
Dept. Head: Prof. P. J.D.
Drenth
Phone: (31) (20)
5485502
Fax: (31) (20) 6425625
Email: v73umuij@
hasara11

Brabant, Kath. Univ.
POB 90153
LE Tilburg
Sociale Wetenschappen,
Fac. der

**Buro Slachtofferhulp
Rotterdam**
Westersingel 6
3014 GM Rotterdam

**Clientenbond in de
Geestelijke
Gezondheidszorg**
POB 645
3500 AP Utrecht

Delft, Tech. Univ.
Kanaalweg 2B
2628 Delft
Psychology, Dept. of
Dept. Head: Prof. J. H.
Andriessen
Phone: (31) (15) 783720
Fax: (31) (15) 782950

Dercksen Centrum
Centrum voor
Psychiatrische
Deeltijdbehandeling
POB 71526
1008 DA Amsterdam

Eindhoven
Psycholigisch Inst.
Edenstraat 29-31
5611 JN Eindoven

Eindhoven Univ. of
Technology
Den Dolech 2
Postbus 513
5600 MB Eindhoven
Psychology, Dept. of
Other Depts: Psychologie
en Taal en Techniek;
Sociale Psychologie
Dept. Head: Prof. J. H.
Midden
Phone: (31) (40)
472889
Fax: (31) (40) 449875

Erasmus Univ.
Rotterdam
Burgemeester Oudlaan
50
POB 1738
3000 DR Rotterdam
Psychology, Dept. of
Other Depts:
Geneeskunde en
Gezondheidsweten-
schappen, Fac. der

Gelders Inst. voor
Welzijn en
Gezondheid
POB 9043
6500 KC Nijmegen

GG & GD Amsterdam
POB 20244
1000 HE Amsterdam
Psychologische Afdeling

GGD Rotterdam e. o.
POB 70032
3000 LP Rotterdam
Afdeling Openbare
Geestelijke
Gezondheidszorg

Groningen, Rijksuniv.
Grote Kruisstraat 2/1
9712 TS Groningen
Psychology, Dept. of
Other Depts: Medische
Psychologie
Dept. Head: Prof. P. M. G.
Emmelkamp
Phone: (31) (50) 636303
Fax: (31) (50) 636304

Humanistiek, Univ. voor
Postbus 797
3500 AT Utrecht
Psychology, Dept. of

Kath. Theolog Univ.
Heidelberglaan 2
3584 CS Utrecht
Psychology, Dept. of

Kinderkliniek
Beatrix-Irene
Aarnoudstraat 59
Rotterdam
Dept. Head: P. Wester

Landbouw Univ.
Wageningen
POB 8130
6700 EW Wageningen
Psychology, Dept. of

Leiden, Rijksuniv.
Wassenaarseweg 52
2333 AK Leiden
Sociale Wetenschappen -
Psychologie
Other Depts: Functieleer
en Theoretishce
Psychologie; Klinische,
Gezondheids- en
Persoonlijkheidspsycholo-
gie; Methoden en
Technieken;
Ontwikkelings- en
Onderwijspsychologie;
Sociale en
Organisatiepsychologie

Leiden, Rijksuniv.
Stationsweg 46
POB 9500
2300 RA Leiden
Psychology, Dept. of
Dept. Head: Stan Maes
Phone: (31) (71) 27 37
37
Fax: (31) (71) 27 36 19
Email: smelik@
rulfsw.leidenuniv.nl

Leiden, State Univ. of
Hooigracht 15
2312 KM Leiden
Psychology, Inst. of

Limburg Univ.
POB 616
6200 MD Maastricht
Medical Psychology, Dept.
of
Other Depts:
Neuropsychologie en
Psychobiologie
Dept. Head: Prof. A.
Appels
Phone: (31) (43) 881484
Fax: (31) (43) 670952

Limburg Rijksuniv.
POB 616
6200 MD Maastricht
Mental Health Sciences /
Experimental
Psychopathology, Dept.
of
Dept. Head: Prof. M. A.
van der Hout
Phone: (31) (43) 221592
Fax: (31) (43) 60962
Email: afm.verwey@
ggk@ Rulimburg. nl

Limburg, Rijksuniv.
POB 616
6200 MD Maastricht
Onderwijsontwikkeling
en Onderwijsresearch

Mass Communication & PR
Heidelberglaan 1
NL-3508 TC Utrecht
Psychology, Dept. of
Dept. Head: Prof. Jo
Groebel
Phone: (31) (30) 534720
Fax: (31) (30) 531619
Email: mcsecr@ f
sw.ruu.nl

Max-Planck Inst. f.
Psycholinguistik
Wundtlaan 1
6525 XD Nijmegen
Dept. Head: Wolfgang
Klein; Willem Levelt
Phone: (31) (80) 521911
Fax: (31) (80) 521213
Email: general@ mpi.nl

Medisch
Kleuterdagverblijf
Tesinkweide
Postbus 10021
7504 PA Enschede
Dept. Head: G. L. G.
Couturier
Phone: (31) (53) 285555
Fax: (31) (53) 285556

Medisch Opvoedkundig
Bureau
Luybenstraat 23-5
5211 BS 's-
Hertogenbosch

Nederlands Centrum
voor Geestelijke
Volksgezondheid
POB 5103
3502 JC Utrecht

Nederlands Inst. voor
Sociaal Sexuologisch
Onderzoek
POB 5018
3501 JA Utrecht

Nederlands Inst. voor
Zorg en Welzijn
POB 19152
3501 DD Utrecht

Nederlands Vereniging
voor Ambulante
Geestelijke
Gezondheidszorg
POB 8400
3503 RK Utrecht
College voor Arbeidszaken

Nijmegen, Kath. Univ.
Montessorilaan 3
POB 9104
6500 HE Nijmegen
Psychology, Dept. of
Other Depts: Cultuur en
Godsdienstpsychologie;
Klinische Psychologie
en Persoonlijkheidsleer;
Ontwikkelingspsychologie;
Psychologie van Arbeid en
Bedrijf; Psychologische
Functieleer; Sociale
Psychologie; Vergelijkende
en Fysiologische
Psychologie
Dept. Head: Dr A.C.J.
Nolet
Phone: (31) (80) 61 26 00
Fax: (31) (80) 61 59 38

Noordelijk Inst. voor
Toegepaste
Psychologie en
Bdrijfswetenschappen
A-weg 5A
97715 CS Groningen

Nw. Psychiatrische
Kliniek
Academisch Ziekenhuis
Oostersingel 59
9713 EZ Groningen
Clinical Psychology Dept.
Phone: (31) (50) 614187
Fax: (31) (50) 614187

Onderzoek naar
Psycho-Sociale Stress,
Inst. voor
Hollandseweg 1
6706 KN Wageningen

Open Univ.
Postbus 2960
6401 DL Heerlen
Psychology, Dept. of
Dept. Head: J. Von
Grumbkow
Phone: (31) (45)
762293
Fax: (31) (45) 711486
Telex: (31) (45) 56559

Provinciale Stichting
voor de Geestelijke
Gezondheidszorg
Limburg
POB 411
6200 AK Maastricht

Psychologisch Buro
Burgemeester
Lambooylaan 11
1217 LB Hilversum
Dept. Head: Dr A.
Eppink

Psychologisch
Marktonderzoek, Inst.
voor
Sloterkade 133
1058 HM Amsterdam

Psycho-therapeutisch
Centrum De
Viersprong
De Beeklaan 2
4611 EP Halsteren

RIAGG (Mental health
service organisation)
Almelo e. o.
Hanzelaan 1
7600 AJ Almelo
Afdeling Preventie

**RIAGG
Amsterdam-Noord**
Staatenjachtstraat 2
1034 EC Amsterdam

RIAGG Arnhem
POB 726
6800 AS Arnhem

RIAGG Breda
Baronielaan 165
4818 PG Breda

RIAGG Centrum West
Mathenesserlaan 208
3014 HH Rotterdam

**RIAGG Centrum-
Oudwest Amsterdam**
Keizersgracht 477
1017 DC Amsterdam

RIAGG de Hagen
Hengeloseweg 24
7511 JC Enschede
Afdeling Preventie

RIAGG Dordrecht
M. H. Trompweg 225 E
3317 BS Dordrecht

RIAGG Drenthe
POB 10029
9400 CA Assen

RIAGG Flevoland
Kempenaar 03-25
8242 BD Lelystad
*Afdeling Preventie en
Dienstverlening*

RIAGG Friesland
POB 932
8901 BS Leeuwarden

**RIAGG Gooi en
Vechtstreek**
Middenweg 20
1217 HW Hilversum

RIAGG Groningen
Westerkade 6
7918 AP Groningen

RIAGG Ijsselland
POB 390
7400 AJ Deventer

RIAGG Leiden
POB 1172
2302 BO Leiden

RIAGG Maastricht
Parallelweg 45-47
6221 BD Maastricht

RIAGG Midden-Holland
Ronsseweg 225
2803 ZB Gouda

RIAGG Midden-Limburg
Hornerheide 1
6085 NM Horn

RIAGG Nijmegen
Groesbeekseweg 3
6524 CJ Nijmegen

RIAGG Noordhage
Prinsengracht 71
2512 EK Den Haag

**RIAGG Noord-
Limburg**
POB 368
5900 AJ Venlo

**RIAGG Noord-
Limburg**
POB 9001
5900 MB Venlo

RIAGG Oost-Gelderland
Vondellaan 2
6901 ME Zevenaar

RIAGG Oost
Linaeushof 6
1098 KH Amsterdam

**RIAGG Rijnmond
Noord-Oost**
POB 4450
3006 AL Rotterdam

RIAGG Rivierenland
Abtmanstraat 24
4001 MC Tiel

**RIAGG Rotterdam Zuid
e. o.**
Van Swietenlaan 80
3083 DZ Rotterdam

RIAGG Stad Utrecht
Tolsteegsingel 2a
3882 AC Utrecht

RIAGG Veluwe
Akademiestraat 14
3841 ES Harderwijk

**RIAGG West
Friesland**
Lambert Meliszweig 1
1622 AA Hoorn

**RIAGG Westelijk
Mijnstreek**
Stationsplein 12
6131 AT Sittard

**RIAGG Westelijk
Noord-Brabant**
Laan van Belgie 55
4701 CJ Roosendaal

**RIAGG Westelijk
Utrecht**
Nieuwe Houtenseweg 2
3524 SH Utrecht

RIAGG Westhage
Verhulstplein 14
2517 SC Den Haag

RIAGG Zeeland
Loskade 17
4331 HW Middelburg

RIAGG Zuid-Holland Noord
POB 1172
2302 BD Leiden

RIAGG Zuid-Kennemerland
Stolbergstraat 14
2012 EP Haarlem

RIAGG Zuid-Nieuwwest Amsterdam
Oldenaller 1
1081 HJ Amsterdam

RIAGG Zuidhage
Leggelostraat 85
2541 HR Den Haag

RIAGG Zuidoost
Ganzenhoef 5a
1103 JA Amsterdam

Rijkspsychologische Dienst
Prins Mauritslaan 1
2582 LK Den Haag

Stichting Interventie en Onderzoek o. h. Terrein v. Geestelijke Gezondheidszorg
POB 503
3500 AM Utrecht

Tilburg Univ.
POB 90153
5000 LE Tilburg
Psychology, Dept. of
Dept. Head: Dr H. F. M.
Peeters
Phone: (31) (13) 662270
Fax: (31) (13) 662370
Telex: (31) (13) 55426

Toegepaste Psychologie, Inst. voor
Beethovenstraat 154
1077 JV Amsterdam

Twente, Univ.
POB 217
7500 AE Enschede
Psychology, Dept. of
Other Depts:
Sociaal Management,
Organisatiesociologie en
Psychologie
Dept. Head: Prof. O.
Wiegman
Phone: (31) (53)
893287
Fax: (31) (53) 356695
Telex: 44200
Email: o.wiegman@
wmw.utwente.nl

Utrecht, Rijksuniv.
Heidelberglaan 8
POB 80125
3508 TC Utrecht
Social Sciences, Fac.
of
Other Depts: Clinical &
Health Psychology;
Social &
Organisational
Pyschology
Dept. Head: Prof. J. D.
Ingleby
Phone: (31) (30)
534700
Fax: (31) (30) 531619

Utrecht, Rijksuniv.
Akademische
Ziekenhuis
Heidelberglaan 100
3584 CX Utrecht
Geneeskunde, Fac. der
Other Depts: Foniatrie;
Medische
Psychologie;Klinische
Psychologie en
Gezondheid;
Ontwikkelings-
psychologie;Sociale en
Organisatie-
psychologie

Utrecht, Rijksuniv.
Willem Pompe Inst.
Janskerkhof 16
3512 BM Utrecht
Rechtsgeleerdheid, Fac.
der
Other Depts:
Strafrechtsweten-
schappen;
Forensische Psychiatrie
en Psychologie

NEW ZEALAND

Auckland Univ.
POB 2175
Auckland
Psychology Dept.
Dept. Head: Michael C.
Corballis
Phone: (64) (9) 373
7999
Fax: (64) (9) 373 7450
Email: mikec@
ccu1.aukuni.ac.nz

Canterbury Univ.
Christchurch 1
Psychology Dept.
Dept. Head: Prof. K. T.
Strongman
Phone: (64) (3)
667001
Fax: (64) (3) 642181

Carrington Hospital
Private Bag
Carrington Rd
Point Chevalier
Auckland 2

Christchurch School of Medicine
Christchurch
Hospital
Private Bag
Christchurch
Psychological Medicine
Dept.

Educational Research, New Zealand Council for
POB 3237
Wellington
Dept. Head: Ian Livingstone
Phone: (64) (4) 384 7939
Fax: (64) (4) 384 7933
Email: contra@ matai.vuw.ac.nz

Massey Univ.
Palmerston North
Psychology Dept.
Other Depts: Human Resources; Statistics
Dept. Head: Prof. Andrew Lock
Phone: (64) (6) 356 9099
Fax: (64) (6) 350 5611
Email: psychsec@ massey.ac.nz

Otago Univ.
POB 56
Dunedin
Psychology Dept.
Other Depts: Preventative & Social Medicine; Psychological Medicine
Dept. Head: Prof. K. G. White
Phone: (64) (3) 479 7645
Fax: (64) (3) 479 8335
Email: kgwhite@ otago.ac.nz

Porirua Hospital
Private Bag
Porirua
Psychology Dept.

Victoria Univ.
Private Bag
Wellington
Psychology Dept.

Waikato Univ.
Hamilton
Psychology Dept.
Dept. Head: Dr Michael Hills
Phone: (64) (7) 856 2889
Fax: (64) (7) 856 2158
Email: psyc3093@ waikato.ac.nz

Wellington Hospital
Wellington
Psychological Medicine Dept.

Wellington School of Medicine
Private Bag, Wellington
Psychological Medicine Dept.
Other Depts: Community Health

NICARAGUA

Centroamericana, Univ.
Apdo 69, Managua
Psychology, Dept. of
Dept. Head: Gustavo Pineda Chávez
Phone: (505) (2) 670352
Fax: (505) (2) 670106

Ingenieria, Univ. Nac. de
Apdo 5595, Managua
Psychology, Dept. of

Nicaragua, Univ. Nac. Aut. de
Recinto Univ. 'Ruben Dario', Managua
Psychology, Dept. of

NIGERIA

Ahmadu Bello Univ.
Zaria
Educational Psychology Dept.

Fed. Univ. of Technology
P. M. B. 1526
Owerri

Ibadan, Univ. of
Ibadan, Oyo State
Psychology Dept.
Other Depts: Guidance & Counselling

Ife Univ.
Ile-Ife
Psychology Dept.

Jos Univ.
P. M. B. 2084
Jos
Psychology Dept.

Lagos, Univ. of
Akoka
Yaba
Psychology, Dept. of
Dept. Head: Prof. Bamidele Adepeju Folarin
Phone: (234) (1) 821180

Niamey, Univ. de
BP 237
Niamey
Psychology, Dept. of

Nigeria, Univ. of
Enugu Campus
Anambra State
Psychological Medicine Dept.

Nigeria, Univ. of
Nsukka
Psychology Dept.
Dept. Head: Dr Bernice N Ezeilo
Phone: (234) (42) 771911

Obafemi Awolowo Univ.
Osun State
Psychology Dept.

Ondo State Univ.
Ado-Ekiti
Ondo State
Psychology Dept.

NORWAY

Bergen Univ.
Aarstadvn. 21
5000 Bergen
Clinical Neuropsychology
Dept.

Bergen Univ.
Eisteinsgate 3
5000 Bergen
Social Psychology
Dept.

Bergen Univ.
Hans Tanksgate 11
5000 Bergen
Nursing Science Inst.

Bergen Univ.
Sydnesplass 13
5000 Bergen
Psychology, Fac. of
Other Depts: Biological &
  Medical Psychology;
  General Psychology;
  Clinical Psychology;
  Psychosocial Science;
  Applied Education
Dept. Head: Prof. Geir
  Nielsen
Phone: (47) (5) 212091
Fax: (47) (5) 325809

Berglund Treatment
Centre
9020 Tromsdalen
Dept. Head:
  Lundesgaard Anders
Phone: (47) (83) 94100

Dikemark Hospital
POB 95
1385 Solberg

Family Guidance
Centre
Råhuset boks 178
1301 Sandvika
Dept. Head: Inger Brun
Phone: (47) (2) 473 733

Family Service
Centre
Akershus County
Oscarsgate 30
0352 Oslo 3

Gaustad Psychiatric
Hospital
POB 24
Gaustad
0320 Oslo 3

Lier Psychiatric
Hospital
3401 Lier

Lillehammer Hospital
2600 Lillehammer
Psychiatric Clinic

Mental Health
Counselling Centre
Drammensvn. 51
0271 Oslo 2

National Hospital,
The
0027 Oslo 1
Psychosomatic Med. Dept.
Dept. Head: Prof. Ivar
  Reinvang
Phone: (47) (2) 86 81 40
Fax: (47) (2) 86 81 49

Norwegian State
College of Local
Government & Social
Work
Trernveien 12
0957 Oslo 9
Phone: (47) (2) 16 43 10
Fax: (47) (2) 16 36 16

Occupational Health,
National Inst. of
POB 8149 Dep.
0033 Oslo 3
Physiology, Dept. of
Other Depts: Medicine,
  Dept. of
Dept. Head: Nina K.
  Vøllestad
Phone: (47) (2) 46 68 50
Fax: (47) (2) 60 90 32

Ørje Treatment Centre
Eikeliveien 45, 1870 Ørje

Oslo, Univ. of
POB 1104 Blindern
N-0317 Oslo
Neurophysiology, Dept.
  of
Dept. Head: Arild Njå
Phone: (47) (2) 85 10 00
Fax: (47) (2) 85 12 49
Email: terjesa@
  pons.uio.no

Oslo, Univ. of
POB 1094
Blindern, N-0317 Oslo
Psychology, Inst. of
Phone: (47) (2) 85 52 34
Fax: (47) (2) 85 44 19

Østfold School of
Nursing
Borgarveien 18
1600 Fredrikstad

Östmarka Hospital
POB 3008 Lade
N-7002, Trondheim
Psychiatry & Behaviour,
  Dept. of
Dept. Head: K. Gunnar
  Götestam
Phone: (47) (4) 92 17 22
Fax: (47) (4) 92 18 22
Email: gunnar.gotestam@
  unit.no

**Psychiatric Nursing,
Nat. School of**
Nestaasen
8000 Bodø

**Psychiatry Service,
Askøy Centre**
POB 50
5300, Kleppestø

**School Psychology
Service Ctr**
Ullensaker County
2050 Jessheim
*Dept. Head: Tor
Jakobsen*
Phone: (47) (6) 97 10 10
Fax: (47) (6) 97 02 12

Solli Sanatorium
Osveien 15
5050 Nesttun

**Stavanger College of
Education**
POB 2521
Ullandhaug
N-4004 Stavanger
*Reading Research,
Ctr. for*

Tromso Univ.
Breivika III
9000 Tromso
Psychology Dept.

**Trondheim State
College of Social
Work**
Lade Gaard
7040 Trondheim
*Dept. Head: Ove
Gustavsson*
Phone: (47) (7) 920566
Fax: (47) (7) 922552

Trondheim, Univ. of
7055 Dragvoll
Psychology, Dept. of
*Dept. Head: Arnulf
Kolstad*
Phone: (47) (7) 511960
Fax: (47) (7) 511920

**Trondvik Psychiatric
Hospital**
5934 Kyrkjebø

**Underwater Technology
Centre**
POB 6, 5034 Laksevaag

OMAN

Sultan Qaboos Univ.
POB 6281
Ruwi, Muscat
Psychology, Dept. of

PAKISTAN

Aga Khan Univ.
Stadium Rd
POB 3500
Karachi 74800
Psychology, Dept. of

Allama Iqbal Open Univ.
Sector H-8
Islamabad
Psychology, Dept. of

Azad Jammu & Kashmir Univ.
Muzaffarabad
Psychology, Dept. of

Baluchistan, Univ. of
Sariab Rd
Quetta
Psychology, Dept. of

Karachi, Univ. of
Univ. Campus
Karachi 32
Psychology, Dept. of

Peshawar Univ.
Peshawar
NWFP
Psychology, Dept. of

Psychology, Nat. Inst. of
Centre of Excellence
Quaid-i-Azam Univ.
Islamabad
Psychology, Dept. of
Dept. Head: Dr Pervaiz Naeem Tariq
Phone: (51) 824337
Fax: (51) 821397

Punjab, Univ. of the
1 Shahrah-e-al-Beruni
Lahore 2
Psychology, Dept. of

Sind, Univ. of
Jamshoro
District of Dadu
Psychology, Dept. of

PANAMA

Panamá, Univ. de
Ciudad Univ.
El Cangrejo, Apdo
  Estafeta Univ.
Panamá City
Psychology, Dept. of
Dept. Head: Dr Octavio Méndez Pereira

Santa Maria La Antigua, Univ. of
Apdo 6-1696
El Dorado, Panamá 6
Psychology Dept.
Dept. Head: Maria Eugenia de Aleman
Phone: (507) 36 1868
Fax: (507) 36 1472

Santa Maria La Antigua, Univ. of
Apdo 6-1696
El Dorado, Panamá 6
Urban Research & Social Promotion. CIPSU, Center for
Dept. Head: Carlos Castro
Phone: (507) 36 1311
Fax: (507) 36 1472

PAPUA NEW GUINEA

National Research Inst.
POB 5854, Boroko
National Capital District

Papua New Guinea Inst. of Med. Research
POB 60
Goroka
Eastern Highlands
  Province

Papua New Guinea Studies, Inst. of
POB 1432
Boroko
National Capital District
Pyschology Dept.

Papua New Guinea Univ.
POB 320
Univ. Post Office
National Capital
  District
Psychology, Dept. of

Papua New Guinea Univ. of Technology
Private Mail Bag
Lae
Psychology, Dept. of

PARAGUAY

Nuestra, Univ. Cat. de
CC1718
Asuncion

PERU

Altiplano, Univ. Nac. del
Avda Ejercito No 329
Apdo 291
Puno
Psychology, Dept. of

Amazonia Peruana, Univ. Nac. de la
Apdo 496
Iquitos
Loreto
Psychology, Dept. of

Cajamarca, Univ. Nac. de
Apdo 16
Jr Lima 549
Cajamarca
Psychology, Dept. of

Cayetano Heredia, Univ. Peruana
Apdo 5045
Lima 100
Psychology, Dept. of

Centro del Peru, Univ. Nac. del
Calle Real 160
Apdo 77
Huancayo
Junín
Psychology, Dept. of

Federico Villarreal, Univ. Nac.
Calle Carlos Gonzalez 285
San Miguel
Lima
Psychology, Dept. of

Inca Garcilaso de la Vega Univ.
Avda Arequipa 3610
San Isidro
Lima
Psychology, Dept. of

Jorge Basadre Grohmann, Univ. Nac.
Casilla 316
Tacna
Psychology, Dept. of

Libertad, Univ. Nac. de la
Independencia 431
Of. 203
Trujillo
Psychology, Dept. of

Lima, Univ. de
Avda Javier Prado Este s/n
Monterrico
Apdo 852
Lima 100
Psychology, Dept. of

Pacífico, Univ. del
Avda Salaverry 2020
Jesós María
Apdo 4683
Lima 11
Psychology, Dept. of

Pedro Ruiz Gallo, Univ. Nac.
8 de Octubre 637
Apdo 557
Lambayeque
Psychology, Dept. of

Piura, Univ. Nac. de
Cusco 323
Apdo 295
Piura
Psychology, Dept. of

Pont. Univ. Cat. del Peru
Avda Univ. Cda 18
Apdo 1761
Lima 32
Especialidad de Psicologia
Dept. Head: Marcia de la Flor
Phone: (51) (14) 622540
Fax: (51) (14) 611785
Email: psicol@ pucp.pe

Ricardo Palma, Univ.
Avda Prolongación Benavides
Cdra 54
Urb. Las Gardenias
Surco, Lima
Psychology, Fac. of

Sagrado Corazón, Univ. Fem. del
Avda Los Frutales s/n
Monterrico
Apdo 3604
Lima
Psychology, Dept. of

San Agustin, Univ. Nac. de
Santa Catalina 117
Apdo 23
Arequipa
Psychology, Dept. of

San Antonio Abad, Univ. Nac. de
Avda de la Cultura s/n
Apdo 367
Cusco
Psychology, Dept. of

San Cristobal de Huamanga, Univ. Nac. de
Apdo 220, Avacucho
Psychology, Dept. of

San Marcos de Lima, Univ. Nac. Mayor de
Avda República de Chile 295
Of. 506
Casilla 454, Lima
Psychology, Dept. of

San Martín de Porres Univ.
Calle Bolívar 348
Miraflores, Lima
Psychology, Dept. of

San Martin, Univ. Nac. de
Martínez de Compagñón 527
Apdo 239
Tarapoto
Psychology, Dept. of

PHILIPPINES

Adamson Univ.
900 San Marcelino
Manila
College of Liberal Arts

AFP Medical Centre
V. Luna, Quezon City
NP Service Ward

Armed Forces Medical Centre
V. Luna Rd, Quezon City
Neuropsychiatric Services

Assumption College
San Lorenzo Drive
San Lorenzo, Makati

Ateneo de Manila Univ.
POB 154, Manila
Psychology Dept.
Other Depts: Central Guidance Bureau

Colegio de San Juan de Letran
151 Muralla St.
Intramuros

Cupertino Ctr/Special Children
Mangyan Rd
La Vista
Loyola Heights
Quezon City

De La Salle Univ.
2401 Taft Ave.
Manila
Psychology Dept.
Other Depts: Counselor Education - Dr Naomi Ruiz
Dept. Head: Marita D. Bernardo
Phone: (63) (2) 50 46 11
Fax: (63) (2) 52 23 661

Far Eastern Univ.
Nicanor Reyes St.
Manila
Psychology Dept.

Greenhills Creative Child Ctr.
Room 208 PCIB Building
Ortigas Ave.
Greenhills

Makati Medical Centre
Room 321, Third Floor
Makati

Manila Electric Co.
Ortigas Ave.
Pasig
Metro Manila
1602
Psychological Services Divn.
Dept. Head: Elena Villahermosa Morada
Phone: (63) (2) 631 22 22

Maryknoll College Foundation Inc.
Katipuunan Rd
Quezon City
Behavioural Sciences Dept.

National Bureau of Investigation
Taft Ave.
Manila
Neuropsychiatric Services

National Center for Mentally Retarded
Elsie Gaches Village
Alabang
Muntinlupa

National Mental Hospital
Mandaluyong

Ng. Manila Hospital
Pres. Quirino Ave.
Manila

Philippine Christian Univ.
1648 Taft Ave.
Manila
Guidance & Counselling Office

Philippines/Visayas, Univ. of
Miagao
Iloilo
Psychology Program
Dept. Head: Ida Siason
Phone: (63) (33) 81511
Fax: (63) (514) 398 8432

Philippine Womens' Univ. Ext.
EDSA
Quezon City

Philippines, Univ. of the
Diliman, Quezon City
Psychology Dept.

Philippines, Univ. of the
PGH Health Sciences Centre
Manila
Psychiatry Dept.

Psychodynamic Syst. R&P Centre
R. Poblete Building
17 Gil J. Puyat St.
Makati

San Sebastian College
C. M. Recto
Manila

Silliman Univ.
Dumaguete City
Negros Oriental
Psychology Dept.

**Social Services & Dev.,
Min. of**
Batasan Pambansa
  Complex
Quezon City
Bureau of Rehabilitation

St Joseph's College
295 E. Rodriguez
Quezon City

St Louis Univ.
2600 Baguio City
*Psychological Reasearch
Unit
Dept. Head: Marlene C.
Beunaventura*
Phone: (63) 442 2793

St Paul Univ.
Tuguegarao, Cagayan
*Dept. Head: Sister Fé C.
Maniquis*
Phone: (63) (446) 1863

UERMMM Centre
Aurora Blvd, Quezon City
Neuropsychiatry Dept.

**Valdez NP Screening &
Test Ctr.**
3rd Ave., Front Gate 2
Santolan Rd, Quezon City

**Veterans Memorial
Med. Centre**
Hilaga Ave., Quezon City

**Western Mindanao
State Univ.**
Zamboanga City
Psychology Centre

**Western Philippines
Colleges**
M. H. del Pilar
Batangas City
*Behavioural Sciences
Dept.*

POLAND

**Adama Mickiewicza W.
Poznanii, Uniw. im**
60-568 Poznan
Ul. Szamarzewskiego 89
*Psychology, Dept. of
Dept. Head: Prof. Tomasz
Maruszewski*
Phone: (48) (61) 04 84 24
Email: psymar@plpuam11

Gdanski, Uniw.
80-952 Gdansk
Ul. Bazynskiego 1A
Psychology, Dept. of

Jagiellonski, Uniw.
31-007 Cracow, Golebia 13
*Psychology, Dept. of
Dept. Head: Adam J.
Niemczynski*
Phone: (48) (12) 22 10 33
Fax: (48) (12) 21 77 10
Telex: 032 22 97 PL UJ
Email: upniemcz@
  11plkrcy

Lódzki, Uniw.
90-131 Lódz, Narutowicza
Psychology, Dept. of

Lubelski, Kat. Uniw.
20-950 Lublin
al. Raclawickie 14
Psychology, Dept. of

**Marii Curie-
Sklodowskiej**
20-031 Lublin
Plac. Marii
  Curie-Sklodowskiej
Psychology, Dept. of

**Mikolaja Kopernika W
Toruniu Uniw.**
87-100 Torun
Ul. Gagarina 11
Psychology, Dept. of

**Nencki Inst. of
Experimental Biology**
3 Pasteur str.
02-093 Warsaw
*Psychophysiology, Lab. of
Other Depts:
  Neurophysiology
Dept. Head: Anna
  Grabowska*
Phone: (48) (22) 659 85 71
Fax: (48) (22) 22 53 42
Telex: (48) (22) 81 48 92

Silesian Uniw.
Katowice, Tyszki 53
Psychology Inst.

Slaski, Uniw.
40-007 Katowice
Bankowa 12
Psychology, Dept. of

Szczecinski Uniw.
70-540 Szczecin.
Ul. Korsarzy 1
Psychology, Dept. of

Warsaw Uniw.
Stawki 5/7, Warsaw
*Psychology Inst.
Dept. Head: Prof.
  Stanislaw Mika*
Phone: (48) (22) 31 11 65
Fax: (48) (22) 31 11 65
Telex: (48) (22) 26 75 20
Email: qzl00@ plearn

Warsaw, Uniw.
00-325 Warsaw
Krakowske Przedmiescie
Psychology, Fac. of

PORTUGAL

Açores, Univ. dos
Rua da Ma. De Deus
9502 Ponta Delgada
(Açores) Codex
Psychology, Dept. of

Algarve, Univ. do
Qt. da Penha, 8000 Faro
Psychology, Dept. of

Aveiro, Univ. de
3800 Aveiro
Psychology, Dept. of

Beira Interior, Univ. da
Rua Marquês de Avila e
Bolama, 6200 Covilh.
Psychology, Dept. of

Coímbra, Univ. de
Paco das Escolas, Coímbra
Psychology, Dept. of

Colegio Valsassina
Quinta das Teresinhas
1900 Lisboa

Évora, Univ. de
Largo dos Colegiais 2
Apdo 94
7001 Évora Codex
Educational Sciences Dept.
Dept. Head:
  ManuelPatrício
Phone: (351) (66) 25572
Fax: (351) (66) 28407
Telex: (351) (66) 18771
  UNIEVR P

Inf. D. Henrique, Univ.
Porto.
Av. Rodrigues de Freitas
4000 Porto
Psychology, Dept. of

Lisboa, Univ. Técnica de
Estrade da Costa-Cruz
  Quebrada
1499 Lisboa
Sport Psychology, Lab. of
Dept. Head: Antònio
  Paula-Brito
Phone: (351) (1) 4196777
Fax: (351) (1) 4151248
Telex: 62430 UTISEF-P

Lisboa, Univ. de
Alameda da Univ. e
1699 Lisbon
Codex
Psychology, Dept. of

Lisboa, Univ. Nova de
Praça do Príncipe Real
  26
1200 Lisbon
Codex
Psychology, Dept. of

Lusíada, Univ. e
Rua da Junqueira 194
1300 Lisbon
Codex
Psychology, Dept. of

Minho, Univ. do
Largo do Paço
4719 Braga
Codex
Psychology, Dept. of

Porto, Univ. do,
R. Das Taipas, 76
4000 Porto
Psicologia Cognitiva,
  Centro de
Dept. Head: Amâncio C.
  Pinto
Phone: (351) (2) 31 50 07
Fax: (351) (2) 20 04 27 7

Porto, Univ. do
Rua Das Taipas, 76
4000 Porto
Psicologia e de ciências
  da educacao, Fac. de
Phone: (351) (2) 31 02 30
Fax: (351) (2) 20 04 27 7

Portuguesa, Univ.
Cat.
Palma de Cima
1600 Lisbon
Codex
Psychology, Dept. of

Trás-Os-Moontes E Alto
Douro, Univ. de
POB 202
5001 Vila Real Codex
Psychology, Dept. of
Dept. Head: Maria
  Adelaide Pires
Phone: (351) (59) 32 16 76
Fax: (351) (59) 74 48 0

PUERTO RICO

Bayamón Central Univ.
POB 1725
Bayamón
PR 00621
Psychology, Dept. of

Inter-American Univ. of
Puerto Rico
POB 3255
San Juan PR 00936
Psychology, Dept. of

Puerto Rica, Univ. de
Mayaguez 00680
Social Sciences, Dept. of
Dept. Head: Jaime
  Gutierrez-Sanchez
Phone: (809) 833 5143
Fax: (809) 265 1225
Email: j_gutierrez@
  upr1.upr.clu.edu

Puerto Rico, Cath. Univ.
of
Ponce, PR 00732
Psychology, Dept.. of

Puerto Rico, Univ. de
Apdo 23345
Recinto de Rio Piedras
Rio Piedras
00931
Psychology Dept.
Dept. Head: Ilsa
  Echegaray
Phone: (809) 764 0000
Fax: (809) 764 4173

Sacred Heart, Univ. of the
POB 12383
Loiza Station
Santurce
PR 00914
Psychology, Univ. of
Dept. Head: Maria Elisa
  Santona
Phone: (809) 728 1515
Fax: (809) 728 1515

Turabo, Univ. del
Apdo 1091
Caguas
00625-1091

QATAR

Quatar, Univ. of
POB 2713
Doha
Psychology, Dept. of
Other Depts: Mental
  Hygiene: Prof Dr Kafafi
  Alaa-Deen
Dept. Head: Prof. Dr.
  El-Sheikh Soliman el
  Khodri
Phone: (974) 892783
Fax: (974) 835111
Telex: 4630 UNIVSTY DH

ROMANIA

Al I. Cuza Iasi, Univ.
Iasi, Calea 23 August 11
Psychology, Dept. of

Brasov, Univ. din
2200 Brasov
Bd. Gh. Gheorghiu-Dej 29
Psychology, Dept. of

Bucuresi, Univ.
Bucharest
Bd. M. Kogalniceanu 64
Psychology, Dept. of

Cluj-Napoca, Univ.
3400 Cluj-Napoca
Str. M. Kogalniceanu 1
Psychology, Dept. of

Craiova, Univ. din
1100 Craiova
Str.Al I.Cuza 13, Jud. Dolj
Psychology, Dept. of

Galati, Univ. din
6200 Galati
Bd. Republicii 47
Psychology, Dept. of

Timisoara, Univ. din
1900 Timisoara
V. Parvan 4
Psychology, Dept. of

RUSSIAN FEDERATION

Altai State Univ.
Ul. Dimitrova 66
656099 Barnaul
Psychology, Dept. of

Astrakhan Pedagogical Inst.
20a Tatishcheva str.
414050 Astrakhan
Psychology, Dept. of

Bashkirsky State Univ.
3a October Revolution Str.
450000 Ufa
Psychology, Dept. of

Belgorod State Pedagogical Inst.
12 Zhdanov Str.
308007 Belgorod
Psychology, Dept. of

Bryansk State Pedagogical Inst.
14 Bezhizkays Str.
241036 Bryansk
Psychology, Dept. of

Buryatsky State Pedagogical Inst.
24a Smolin Str.
670000 Ulan/Ude
Psychology, Dept. of

Checheno-Ingush State Univ.
Ul. Sheripova 32
Groznyi
364907 Checheno-Ingush
Psychology, Dept. of

Cheliabinsk State Pedagogical Inst.
69 Lenin Ave.
454080 Cheliabinsk
Psychology, Dept. of

Cheliabinsk State Univ.
Ul. Br. Kashirinykh 129
454136 Cheliabinsk
Psychology, Dept. of

Chuvash IN Ulyanov State Univ.
Moskovskii pr. 15
428015 Cheboksary
Psychology, Dept. of

Complex Social Investigations, Research Inst. of
60 Krasnaya Str.
190000 St Petersburg
Social Psychology, Lab. of

Dagestan State Univ.
Sovetskaya ul. 8
Makhachkala
367025 Dagestan
Psychology, Dept. of

Far Eastern State Univ.
Ul. Sukhanova 8
690600 Vladivostok
Primorskogo Kraya
Psychology, Dept. of

Gorkii State Univ.
Pr. Gagarina 23
603600 Gorkii
Psychology, Dept. of

Irkutsk State Pedagogical Inst.
6 N. Naberezhnaya
664653 Irkutsk
Psychology, Dept. of

Irkutsk State Univ.
Ul. K. Marksa 1
664003 Irkutsk 3
Psychology, Dept. of

Ivanovo State Univ.
39 Ermak Str. 153377
Ivanovo
15337 Ivanovo
Psychology, Dept. of

Kabardino-Balkar State Univ.
Ul. Chernyshevskogo 173
360004 Kabardino-Balkar
Psychology, Dept. of

Kaliningrad State Univ.
Ul. A. Nevskogo 14
236041 Kaliningrad
Psychology, Dept. of

Kalinin State Univ.
Ul. Zhelyabova 33
170000 Kalinin
Psychology, Dept. of

Kalmyk State Univ.
Ul. Pushkina 11
358000 Elista
Psychology, Dept. of

Kaluga State Pedagogical Inst.
26a Stepan Razin Str.
248023 Kaluga
Psychology, Dept. of

Kamchatsky State Pedagogical Inst.
4 Pogranitchnaya Str.
683032 Petropavlovsk /
Kamchatsky
Psychology, Dept. of

Kazan State Pedagogical Inst.
1 Mezhlauka Str.
420021 Kazan
Psychology, Dept. of

Kazan State Univ.
18 Lenin Str.
420008 Kazan
Creative Personality
Psychology, Lab. of
Other Depts:
Psychological Problems
of High School

Kemerovo State Univ.
Krasnaya ul. 6
650043 Kemerovo
Psychology, Dept. of

Khabarovsk State Pedagogical Inst.
68 Marx Str.
680030 Khabarovsk
Psychology, Dept. of

Kostroma State Pedagogical Inst.
14 First of May Str.
156601 Kostromo
Psychology, Dept. of

Krasnoyarsk State Pedagogical Inst.
79 Lebedev Str.
660017 Krasnoyarsk
Psychology, Dept. of

Krasnoyarsk State Univ.
Pr. Svobodnyi 79
660062 Krasnoyarsk
Psychology, Dept. of

Kuban State Univ.
149 Libkneht Str.
350750 Krasnodar
Psychology, Dept. of

Kurgan State Pedagogical Inst.
63 Sovietskaya Str.
640000 Kurgan
Psychology, Dept. of

Kursk State Pedagogical Inst.
33 Radishev Str.
305416 Kursk
Psychology, Dept. of

Kuybyshev State Univ.
Ul. Akademika Pavlova 1
443086 Kuybyshev
Psychology, Dept. of

Lipetsck State Pedagogical Inst.
42 Lenin Str.
398020
Lipetsck
Psychology, Dept. of

Magnitogorsk State Pedagogical Inst.
114 Lenin Str.
455043 Magnitogorsk
Psychology, Dept. of

Mari Univ.
Pl. Lenina 1
Yoshkar-Ola
424001 Mari
Psychology, Dept. of

Mordovsky State Univ.
68 Bolshevistskaya
Str
430000 Saransk
Psychology, Dept. of

Moscow MV Lomonosov State Univ.
Leninskie gory
117234 Moscow
Psychology, Dept. of

Moscow State Pedadogogical Univ.
3 Novospassky Lane
109172 Moscow
Psychology, Dept. of

Moscow State Univ.
18 Marx Ave
103009 Moscow
Psychology, Dept. of

N. Novgorod State Pedagogical Inst.
1 Ulianov Str.
603005 N. Novgorod
Psychology, Dept. of

N. Novgorod State Univ.
23 Gagarin Ave.
603600 N. Novgorod
Applied Psychology, Lab. of

N. Tagil State Pedagogical Inst.
57 Krasnogvardeiskaya Str.
622009 N. Tagil
Psychology, Dept. of

North-Osetin State Univ.
Ul. Vatutina 46
Ordzhonikidze
362000 North-Osetia
Psychology, Dept. of

North-Osetin State Univ.
46 Watutina Str.
362040 Wladikavkaz
Psychology, Dept. of

Novgorod State Pedagogical Inst.
Settlement Antonovo
173014 Novgorod
Psychology, Dept. of

Novosibirsk State Pedagogical Inst.
28 Wiluiskaya Str.
630126 Novosibirsk
Psychology, Dept. of

Novosibirsk State Univ.
Ul. Pirogova 2
630090 Novosibirsk
Psychology, Dept. of

Omsk State Pedagogical Inst.
4a Partizanskaya Str.
644099 Omsk
Psychology, Dept. of

Omsk State Univ.
77 Pr. Mira 55A
644077 Omsk
Psychology, Dept. of

Orel State Pedagogical Inst.
39a Komsomolskaya Str.
302001 Orel
Psychology, Dept. of

Orenburg State Pedagogical Inst.
1 Gagarin Str.
460021 Orenburg
Psychology, Dept. of

Patrice Lumumba People's Friendship Univ.
Ul. Ordzhonikidze
3117302 Moscow
Psychology, Dept. of

Penza State Pedagogical Inst.
37 Lermontov Str.
440026 Penza
Psychology, Dept. of

Perm A. M. Gorkii State Univ.
Ul. Bukireva 15
614600 Perm.
Psychology, Dept. of

Perm State Pedagogical Inst.
24 Marx Str.
614000 Perm
Psychology, Dept. of

Petrozavodsk OV Kuusinen State Univ.
Pr. Lenina 33
Petrozavodsk
185640 Karelia
Psychology, Dept. of

Piatigorsk State Pedagogical Inst. of Foreign Languages
9 Kalinin Ave.
357533 Piatigorsk
Psychology, Dept. of

Pskov State Pedagogical Inst.
2 Lenin Square
180560 Pskov
Psychology, Dept. of

RAE Psychologogical Inst.
18 Marx Ave
103009 Moscow
Psychology, Dept. of

Riazin State Pedagogical Inst.
46 Svoboda Str.
390000 Riazin
Psychology, Dept. of

Rostov State Pedagogical Inst.
33 Engels Str.
344082 Rostov/Don
Psychology, Dept. of

Rostov State Univ.
105 Engels Str.
344711 Rostov/Don
Psychology, Dept. of

Russian Academy of Sciences
13 Yaroslavskaya str.
129366 Moscow
Psychology, Inst. of

Saratov State Pedagogical Inst.
82 Michurin Str.
410601 Saratov
Psychology, Dept. of

Saratov State Univ.
83 Astrakhanskaya Str.
410601
Saratov
Psychology, Dept. of
Other Depts: Engineering
Psychology

Smolensk State
Pedagogical Inst.
4 Przhevalsky Str
214000 Smolensk
Psychology, Dept. of

St. Petersburg State
Inst. of Physical
Training
35 Decabristov
Str.
190121 St. Petersburg
Psychology, Dept. of

St. Petersburg State
Pedagogical
Institute.
48 River Moika
Embankment
191186 St. Petersburg
Psychology, Dept. of

St Petersburg Univ.
7/9 University
Embankment
199034 St Petersburg
PsychologyS, Dept. of

Stavropol State
Pedagogical Inst.
1 Pushkin Str.
355009 Stavropol
Psychology, Dept. of

Syktyvkar State
Univ.
Oktyabrskii
Pr. 55
Syktyvkar
167001 Komi
Psychology, Dept. of

Tobolsk State
Pedagogical Inst.
58 Znamensky Str.
626100 Tobolsk
Psychology, Dept. of

Tomsk V. V Kuibyshev
State Univ.
Pr. Lenina 36, Tomsk
Psychology, Dept. of

Tver State Univ.
33 Zhekyabova Str.
170013 Tver
Psychology, Dept. of

Tyumen State Univ.
Ul. Semakova 10
625610 Tyumen 3
Psychology, Dept. of

Udmurtsky State Univ.
69 Krasnogeroiskaya Str.
426037 Izhevsk
Psychology, Dept. of

Urals A. M. Gorkii State
Univ.
Pr. Lenina 51
620083 Sverdlovsk
Psychology, Dept. of

Ussuryisk State
Pedagogical Inst.
35 Nekrasov Str.
692500 Ussuryisk
Psychology, Dept. of

Viatka State
Pedagogical Inst.
111 Lenin Str.
610002 Viatka
Psychology, Dept. of

Volgograd State
Pedagogical Inst.
27 Lenin Ave.
400013 Volgograd
Psychology, Dept. of

Volgograd State
Univ.
30 Prodolnaya Str.
400062 Volgograd
Pedagogy & Psychology,
Dept. of

Vologda State
Pedagogical Inst.
6 Orlov Str.
160000 Vologda
Psychology, Dept. of

Voronezh State
Pedagogical Inst.
86 Lenin Str.
394611 Voronezh
Psychology, Dept. of

Voronezh State
Univ.
Univ. skaya Pl. 1
294693 Voronezh
Psychology, Dept. of

Yakutsk State Univ.
Ul. Belinskogo 58
Yakutsk
677891 Yakut ASSR
Psychology, Dept. of

Yaroslavl State
Pedagogical Inst.
108 Respublikanskaya Str
150000 Yaroslavl
Psychology, Dept. of

Yaroslavl State Univ.
14 Sovietskaya Str.
150000 Yaroslavl
Psychology, Dept. of

RWANDA

Rwanda, Univ.
Nationale du
BP 56
Butare
Psychology, Dept. of

SAUDI ARABIA

Islamic Univ.
POB 170
Medina
Psychology, Dept. of

Islamic Univ. of Imam
Muhammad Ibn
Saud
POB 5701
Riyadh
Psychology, Dept. of

King Abdulaziz Univ.
POB 1540
Jeddah 21441
Psychology, Dept. of

King Faisal Univ.
POB 1982
Dammam
Psychology, Dept. of

King Saud Univ.
POB 2454
Riyadh 11451
Psychology, Dept. of

Riyadh Military
Hospital
SWC 2A
POB 7897
Riyadh 11159
Psychiatry, Dept. of
Dept. Head: Dr Mohamed
Osman Ahmed El
Marazki
Phone: (966) (1) 477 7714
Fax: (966) (1) 478 6088

Riyadh Univ.
Riyadh
Psychology Dept.

Umm Al-Qura Univ.
POB 407/715
Mecca
Psychology, Dept. of

S

Umm Al-Qura Univ.
Taif Campus
Al-Saddad Rd
Shihar
Taif
Psychology, Dept. of

SERBIA

Belgrade, Univ. of
Vojvode Stepe 305
11000 Beograd
Traffic Psychology &
Ergonomics, Lab. of
Dept. Head: Prof. Staniša
Miloševic
Phone: (38) (11) 493 211
Fax: (38) (11) 466 294
Telex: 72928 SFBGD yu

Beogradu, Univ.
Umetnosti u
11000 Belgrade
Vuka Karadzia 12
Psychology, Dept. of

Kragujevcu, Univ. S.
Markovic u
34000 Kragujevac
Trg Avnoja 1
Psychology, Dept. of

Nisu, Univ. u
18000 Nis
Trg Bratstva i
Jedinstva 2
Psychology, Dept. of

Pristina, Univ. u
M. Tito 53
38000 Pristina
Psychology, Dept. of

SINGAPORE

Singapore, National
Univ. of
10 Kent Ridge Crescent
Singapore 0511
Social Work &
Psychology, Dept. of
Dept. Head: Dr S. Vasoo
Phone: (65) 7723811
Fax: (65) 7781213

SLOVAK REPUBLIC

Centrum poradensko-
psychologickych
sluzieb
Rybny trh
929 01 Dunajská
Streda
Psychological
Counselling Centre for
Individuals, Couples &
Families
Dept. Head: Dr Irena
Pálffyová
Phone: (42) (7) 09 256 66

Ceskoslovenská Atátna
autom obilová
doprava
ul. Cs. armády 24
974 67 Banská Bystrica

Child Psychology &
Patopsych, Research
Inst. of
Záhradnícka 93
821 08 Bratislava
Other Depts: Child Center
Dept. Head: Vladimír
Dockal
Phone: (42) (7) 288 311
Fax: (42) (7) 288313

Detsky diagnosticky
ústav
Slovinská 1
821 04 Bratislava

**Filozofická fak. UK
Bratislava**
Gondova 2
818 01 Bratislava
Psychological Inst.
*Other Depts: Theory &
methodology of
psychology; Counselling
Psychology; Ethology &
comparative psychology
Dept. Head: Dr. Dušan
Fabián*
Phone: (42) (7) 564 718
Fax: (42) (7) 516 49

**Katedra inziniersko-
humanitnych vied**
SVST
Pionierksa 15
831 02 Bratislava

**Katedra
psychologickych filoz.
fak. UPJS**
040 01 Košice

**Katedra
psychologickych vied
UK**
Gondova 2
818 01 Bratislava
*Dept. Head: Dr. Teodor
Kollárik*
Phone: (42) (7) 581 29
Fax: (42) (7) 516 49

**Krajská ped-psy.
poradna**
Mládeznícka 34
974 00 Banská Bystrica

**Krajská ped-psy.
poradna**
Zádielska 1.
041 32 Košice

KUNZ
902 18 Pezinok
Psychiatric Dept.

KUNZ
Mickiewiczova 13
813 69 Bratislava

KUNZ
nám. L. Svobodu 1
975 17 Banská Bystrica
Neurologické odd.

KUNZ
Psychiatric Dept.
935 61 Hrinovce

**Mapp hl. mesta SR
Bratislava**
Vajanského nábr. 17
811 02 Bratislava

**Nemocnice s
poliklinikou, Fak.**
Rastislavova 43, Košice

**Nemocnice s
poliklinikou Staré
Mesto**
Bezrucova 3
815 26 Bratislava
Dept. Head: Dr Ivan Štúr
Phone: (42) (7) 490 841

Nitrianskej Univ.
Tr A. Hlinku 1
949 01 Nitra
*Psychology Dept. in
Pedagogical Fac.
Dept. Head: Dr Ivan
Szabó*
Phone: (42) (87) 285 36
Fax: (42) (87) 411 243

**Obvodná ped-psy.
poradna**
Hubeného 25, Bratislava

**Okresná manzelská a
predmanzelská
poradna**
Gottwaldova 37
071 01 Michalovce

**Okresná ped-psy.
poradna**
Gottwaldova 29
010 01 Zilina

**Okresná ped-psy.
poradna**
Hlavná ul. 32/4
929 01 Dunajská Streda
*Dept. Head: Dr Margita
Némethová*
Phone: (42) (7) 09 268 02

**Okresná ped-psy.
poradna**
Mierová 1, Levice

**Okresná ped-psy.
poradna**
Mierové nám. 9
911 01 Trenin 1

**Okresná ped-psy.
poradna**
Rimavská Sobota
Amfiteáter
979 01 Rimavská Sobota

**Okresná ped-psy.
poradna**
Safárikova 38
924 00 Galanta
Phone: (42) (707) 23 34
Fax: (42) (707 52 60

**Okresná ped-psy.
poradana**
Stúrova 25
066 01 Humenné

**Okresná ped-psy.
poradna**
Stúrova 37
031 01 Liptovsky Mikulá.

**Okresná ped-psy
poradna**
T. Sevenka 9
080 86 Prešov

Okresná ped-psy.
poradna
ul. Febr. vítazstva 38
955 01 Topolany

Okresná ped-psy.
poradna
ul. M. S. Trnavského
2
917 01 Trnava

Okresná ped-psy.
poradna
ul. Tarasa Sevenka 9
080 86 Preov

Okresny ústav
národného zdravia
Komenského ul.
031 01 Liptovsky
Milusáš.
*detské odd. nemocnice s
poliklinikou*

Okresny ústav
národného zdravia
Nemocnica s
poliklinikou
965 01 Ziar nad
Hronom

Okresny ústav
národného zdravia
OUNZ Psychiatrická
ambulancia
058 01 Poprad
*Dept. Head: Netocny
Otakar*

Okresny ústav
národného zdravia
ul. Mieru 35
979 01 Rimavská
Sobota

OUNZ
022 16 Cadca
*Psychologická
ambulancia*

P.J. Šafárika, Univ.
Moyzesova 50
040 01 Košice
*Katedra psychológie FF
Dept. Head: Dr Ján
Ferjencik*
Phone: (42) (95) 236 85
Fax: (42) (95) 766 95

Pedagag. fak. Banská
Bystrica
Tajovského 40
975 49 Banská Bystrica

Pedagog. fak. UK
Moskovská 3
813 34 Bratislava
*Dept. Head: Prof.
Ladislav Pož ár*
Phone: (42) (7) 254 879
Fax: (42) (7) 585 05

Pedagog.-psychol.
poradna
Brnenská 47
817 12 Bratislava
*Dept. Head: Dr. Eugen
Kolenyi*
Phone: (42) (7) 375582

Pedagog.-psychol.
poradna
Tomašikova 5
052 01 Spišska Nova Ves
Phone: (42) (965) 23981

Pedagog.-psychol.
poradna mesta
Bratislava
Legionárska 4, Bratislava

Pedagog.-psychol.
poradna mesta
Bratislava
Záhradnícka 93
821 08 Bratislava
*Dept. Head: Dr Gabriel
Rovan*
Phone: (42) (7) 21 29 00

Pedagog.-psychol.
poradna mesta Košíc
Karpatská 8
041 32 Košice
*Psychological counselling
& training
Dept. Head: Katarína
Mankovicová*
Phone: (42) (95) 559 31

Pedopsychiatrická
ambulancia
Mestsky ústav národného
zdravia
pol. Sever
Komenského 37/A
040 01 Košice

Podnikové riaditeľstvo
CSAD
Odd. psych a soc
Stanicné
nám. 9
041 46 Košice

Preventive & Clinical
Medicine, Inst. of
Limbová 14
833 01 Bratislava
*Dept. Head: Dr Eva
Šovcíková*
Phone: (42) (7) 373 560
Fax: (42) (7) 373 906
Telex: (42) (7) 992 79

Psychiatrická klinika
FN
Mickiewiczova 13
813 69 Bratislava

Psychologická
ambulancia NsP
052 80 Spiska Nová
Ves

Psychologická
ambulancia OUNZ
017 01 Povazská
Bystrica

Psychologicky ústav UK
Gondova 2
818 01 Bratislava

**Slovenská vysoká škola
technická**
Pionierska 15
831 02 Bratislava

**Social & Biological
Communications SAV,
Dept. of**
Šancova
813 64 Bratislava
*Dept. Head: Dr. Jana
Plichtoyá*
Phone: (42) (7) 495480
Fax: (42) (7) 497989
Email: plichtová@
kvsbk.savba.cs

**Spolocenskovedny
ústav SAV**
Karpatská 5
040 01 Košice

**Ústav exp. psych.
Slovenskaj akadémie
vied**
Dúbravská Cesta 9
813 64 Bratislava
*Dept. Head: Dr. Michal
Strízenec*
Phone: (42) (7) 378 3417
Fax: (42) (7) 378 3427

**Ústav národného
zdravia mesta
Bratislavy**
Limbova 3
833 05 Bratislava
Neurochirurgickáklinika

**Ústav sociálnej
starostlivosti**
968 01 Nová Bana -
Hrabiny
*pre telesne postihnuitú
mládez*

**Ústav sociálnej
starostlivosti pre
telesne
postihnutú mládež**
Mokrohájska 3
844 08 Bratislava

**Útvar Zboru Nápravnej
vychovy SSR**
Chorvátska 1
812 29 Bratislava

**Útvar Zboru Nápravnej
vychovy SSR**
Pribinova 1, Košice

**Vyskumny ústav
bezpecnosti práce**
Štefánikova ul. 47
814 35 Bratislava

**Vyskumny ústav
jadrovych elektrár"ní**
Okružná 5, Trnava

**Vyskumny ústav
pedagogicky**
Kutlíková 17
852 55 Bratislava
*Dept. Head: Dr Karol
Kollírik*
Phone: (42) (7) 824 814
Fax: (42) (7) 821 584

**Vyskumny ústav práce
a sociálních vecí**
Mierová 23
827 48 Bratislava
*Labour an Social Affairs,
Research Inst.*
*Dept. Head: Ferdinand
Vykopal*
Phone: (42) (7) 238 620
Fax: (42) (7) 235 789

**Vyskumny ústav
reumatickych chorôb**
Kúpelny ostrov 20
921 01 Pieštany

**Vyskumny ústav
telesnej kultúry UK**
Nábr. L. Svobodu 9
814 69 Bratislava

**Vysoká vojenská
pedagogická škola**
Kutuzovova 8
832 28 Bratislava
Psychology, Dept. of
*Dept. Head: Prof. Gustáv
Dianiška*
Phone: (42) (7) 2799

**Závody ťazkého
strojárstva**
Ústav technologie a
racionalzácie
Nevädzova 5
826 13 Bratislava

SLOVENIA

Ljubljania, Univ. of
Aškerceva 12
61000 Ljubljana
Psychology, Dept. of
Dept. Head: Drago Zagar
Phone: (38) (61) 150 001
Fax: (38) (61) 159 337
Email: deptpsych.lj@
uni-lj.si

SOMALIA

Somali National Univ.
POB 15
Mogadishu
Psychology, Dept. of

SOUTH AFRICA

**Anglo American Test
Centre**
POB 87, Welkom 9460
*Dept. Head: Mr H. J.
Trytsman*
Phone: (27) (171) 52000
Fax: (27) (171) 52001

Cape Town Univ.
Rondebosch 7700
Psychology Dept.
Other Depts: Education;
Graduate School of
Business
Dept. Head: Prof. Peter
du Preez
Phone: (27) (21) 650 3430
Fax: (27) (21) 650 3726
Telex: 5 21439
Email: heather@
uctvax.uct.as.za

Centre for Labour &
Community Research
POB 11504, Johannesburg

Durban-Westville Univ.
Private Bag X54001
Durban 4000
Industrial Psychology
Dept.
Dept. Head: Prof. E.
Thomson
Phone: (27) (31) 820 2126
Fax: (27) (31) 820 2383
Telex: 6-23228 SA

Durban-Westville Univ.
Private Bag X54001
Durban 4000
Psychology Dept.
Dept. Head: Prof. B. A.
Balkisson
Phone: (27) (31) 820 2423
Fax: (27) (31) 820 2866
Telex: 6-23228 SA
Email: ipeterse@
daisy.ee.und.ac.za

Education & Culture
Dept.
Private Bag X04, Ulundi

Elizabeth Donkin
Hospital
Private Bag X6024
Port Elizabeth 6000

Fort Hare Univ.
Private Bag X1314
Alice 5700
Psychology Dept.
Other Depts: Industrial
Psychology

Groote Schuur Hospital
Ward C13
Observatory 7295
Psychiatry Dept.

Human Resources,
Group for
POB 32410
Braamfontein 2017
Organization
Development Divn.
Dept. Head: Dr J. Van
Rooyen
Phone: (27) (11) 339 4451
Fax: (27) (11) 403 2353

Human Resources,
Group for
Private Bag X41
Pretoria 0001
Human Development
Divn.
Other Depts:
Environmental
Management Divn.
Dept. Head: R. F.
Skawran
Phone: (27) (12) 202 2968
Fax: (27) (12) 202 2994
Telex: 321710 SA

Human Resources,
Group for
Private Bag X41
Pretoria 0001
Human Development
Strategies Divn.
Dept. Head: Dr J. S. van
der Walt
Phone: (27) (12) 202 2169
Fax: (27) (12) 202 2994
Telex: 321710 SA

Human Resources,
Group for
Private Bag X41
Pretoria 0001
Dept. Head: Dr K. F.
Mauer
Phone: (27) (12) 2022001
Fax: (27) (12) 2022994
Telex: 321710 SA

Manpower, Dept. of
Private Bag X117
Pretoria 0001

Natal, Univ. of
POB 17039
Congella 4013
Psychiatry Dept.
Other Depts: Medically
Applied Psychology
Dept. Head: Prof.
Lourens Schlebusch
Phone: (27) (31) 250 4324
Fax: (27) (31) 250 4322

Natal Univ.
King George V Ave.
Durban 4001
Psychology Dept.
Dept. Head: Ronald Miller
Phone: (27) (31) 816 2527
Fax: (27) (31) 816 2618

Natal Univ.
POB 375
Pietermaritzburg 3200
Psychology, Dept. of
Dept. Head: Prof. P. A.
Sharratt
Phone: (27) (331) 955369
Fax: (27) (331) 955599
Telex: 643719

National Education
Dept.
Educational Auxiliary
Services
Private Bag X122
Pretoria 0001

North Univ.
Private Bag X1106
Sovenga 0727
Psychology Dept.
Other Depts: Industrial
Psychology

Orange Free State Univ.
POB 339
Bloemfontein 9300
Psychology Dept.
Other Depts: Psychiatry;
Psychopedagogics;
Industrial Psychology
Dept. Head: Prof.
Sebastian J. Wessels
Phone: (27) (51) 401 2340
Fax: (27) (51) 475719

Port Elizabeth, Univ. of
POB 1600 Port Elizabeth
Psychology Dept.
Other Depts: Industrial
Psychology
Dept. Head: Prof. Josua
P. P. Fullard
Phone: (27) (41) 504 2354
Fax: (27) (41) 504 2574
Telex: 243342

Potchefstroom Univ. for
C. H. E.
Vaaltrianglecampus
POB 1174 Vanderbijlpark
Psychology Dept.

Potchefstroom Univ. for
C. H. E.
Potchefstroom 2520
Psychology Dept.
Other Depts:
Psychotherapy /
Counseling; Industrial
Psychology
Dept. Head: Prof. M. P.
Wissing
Phone: (27) (14) 899 1721
Fax: (27) (14) 899 2799
Telex: (95) 3-46019

Pretoria Univ.
Pretoria 5
Psychology Dept.
Other Depts: Personnel
Management; Graduate
Business School;
Orthopedagocis
Dept. Head: Prof. W. J.
Schoeman
Phone: (27) (12) 420 2329
Fax: (27) (12) 420 2185
Telex: 3-22723

Rand Afrikaans Univ.
POB 524
Auckland Park 2006
Psychology Dept.
Other Depts: Industrial
Psychology; Child &
Adult Guidance;
Human Resources;
Education Psychology;
Bureau for Student
Counselling.
Dept. Head: Prof. Dave
Beyers
Phone: (27) (11) 489 3130
Fax: (27) (11) 489 2797

Rhodes Univ.
POB 94 Grahamstown
Psychology Dept.
Dept. Head: Prof. David
J. A. Edwards
Phone: (27) (461) 22023
Fax: (27) (461) 25049

South Africa, Univ. of
POB 392 Pretoria
Psychology Dept.
Other Depts: Behavioural
Sciences; Industrial
Psychology; Empirical
Education; Health
Psychology
Dept. Head: Prof.
Wilhelm J. Jordaan
Phone: (27) (12) 429 8088
Fax: (27) (12) 429 3414

South Africa Medical
Univ.
P. O.
Medunsa 0204
Clinical Psychology Dept.

Stellenbosch Univ.
Stellenbosch 7600
Psychology Dept.
Other Depts: Industrial
Psychology; Educational
Psychology
Dept. Head: Prof. J. A. Le
Roux
Phone: (27) (2231) 773466
Fax: (27) (2231) 774336
Telex: (95) 520383

Transkei Univ.
Private Bag X1
Unitia
Transkei
Psychology Dept.

Vaal Triangle Technikon
Private Bag X021
Vanderbijlpark 1900
Student Counselling Dept.
Dept. Head: C. P. de Jager
Phone: (42) (16) 852221
Fax: (42) (16) 312640

Valkenberg Hospital
Private Bag X1
Observatory 7935
Dept. Head: Dr Quarta
du Toit
Phone: (27) (21) 470050
Fax: (27) (21) 476041

Venda Univ.
Private Bag X2220
Sibase
Republic of Venda
Clinical Psychology
Dept. Head: Prof. A.
Stricken
Phone: (27) (159) 21071
Fax: (27) (159) 331694

Vista Univ.
Private Bag X613
Port Elizabeth 6000
Psychology Dept.

**Western Cape,
Univ. of**
Private Bag X17
Bellville 7530
*Industrial Psychology
Dept.*
*Dept. Head: Prof. Dan M.
Steyn*
Phone: (27) (21) 959 2585
Fax: (27) (21) 959 2578

**Western Cape,
Univ. of**
Private Bag X17
Bellville 7530
Psychology Dept.
*Dept. Head: Rachel
Prinsloo*
Phone: (27) (21) 959 2283
Fax: (27) (21) 959 2755

**Western Cape,
Univ. of**
Private Bag 17
Bellville 7530
*Educational Psychology,
Dept. of*
*Dept. Head: Dr Sandy
Lazarus*
Phone: (27) (21) 959
2282
Fax: (27) (21) 9592647

**Witwatersrand
Univ.**
POB WITS 2050
Psychology Dept.
Other Depts: Education
*Dept. Head: Prof. S. D.
Bluen*
Phone: (27) (11) 716 2407
Fax: (27) (11) 403 1926
Email: 144sdbs@
witsvma.wits.ac.za

Zululand Univ.
Private Bag X1001
Kwadlangezwa 3886
Psychology Dept.
*Other Depts: Industrial
Psychology: Education
Psychology: Dr P. T.
Sibaya*
*Dept. Head: Prof. Stephen
David Edwards*
Phone: (27) (351) 93911
Fax: (27) (351) 93735
Telex: SA 631311

SPAIN

**Academia de la Policia
Nal.**
Carretera de Canillas 53
Madrid 33

Agustiniano, Colegio
c/ Pez Austral 13 Bis.
Madrid 30

Alava, Colegio Univ. de
c/ Carretera de Lasarte s/n
Vitoria, Alava

Alicante, Univ. de
Campus de San Juan
Alicante
Health Psychology Dept.
*Dept. Head: Prof. Jesús
Rodríguez-Marín*
Phone: (34) (9) 6 565 98 11
Fax: (34) (9) 6 594 00 15

**ALPE- ELS
Tremolenchas s/n,
Colegio**
La Garriga (Barna 26)
Privado, América 9

**Bachill. M. Juan de
Avila, Inst.**
Ronda Calatrava s/n
Ciudad
Real

Barcelona, Univ. de
C/ Adolf Florensa s/n
08028 Barcelona
*Psicología Bàsica, Dpto
de*
*Other Depts: Psicología
Social; Psicología
Personalidad;
Psicología
Metodologia;
Psicología Evolutiva;
Psicología
Psiquiatria.*
*Dept. Head: Miguel Serra
Raventos*
Phone: (34) (3) 449 71
84
Fax: (34) (3) 334 72 90

Barcelona Univ.
Letras, Fac. de
Plaza Imperial
Tarraco
Tarragona
Sección de Psic.

**Barcelona, Univ.
Autónoma de**
Letras, Fac. de
Bellaterra
Barcelona
*Psi Exp. y Psicofisiol.,
Dpto de*

**Barcelona, Univ.
Autónoma de**
Edifici B
08193 Bellaterra
Barcelona
*Health Psychology, Dept.
of*
*Dept. Head: Josep M.
Blanch*
Phone: (34) (3) 581
1326
Fax: (34) (3) 581 2324
Telex: 52040 EDUCI E
Email: ilps1@
ccuab1.uab.es

Cc. de la Educación
Santiago de Compostela
Filosofía, Fac. de

Cc. de la Educación
Alto Zorroaga, S.Sebastian
Pedagogia Exp., Dpto de

Centro d'Assistencia
Prim. La Pau
Ampordá s/n
Barcelona 20

Centro de Diag. y
Orient. Terap.
c/ Real 2, Toledo

Centro de Salud Mental
c/ Comte Vilardaga s/n
Edificio Júpiter
Sant. Feliu de Llobregat
Barcelona

Complutense, Univ.
Somosaguas
Fac. de Psicologiá
Madrid 11
Psicología Exper., Dpto de

Coruña, Colegio Univ.
de La
A Zapateira, s/n
15071 - La Coruña
Fac. de Humanidades
Dept. Head: Fernando del
Valle-Inclán Alsina
Phone: (34) (81) 10 00 00
Fax: (34) (81) 10 41 29

Coruña, Colegio Univ.
de La
A Zapateira, s/n
15071 - La Coruña
Psicología Evolutiva y de
la Educación, Dpto de
Dept. Head: Alfonso
Barca Lozano
Phone: (34) (81) 10 00 00
Fax: (34) (81) 10 41 29

Dr Castany Hospital
Psiquiátrico
Salt, Gerona

Educ. a Distancia, Univ.
Nac. de
Apdo 50. 487
Madrid
Psicología Basica I, Dpto
de
Dept. Head: Jose Luis
Fernandez Trespalacios
Phone: (34) (1) 398 62 20
Fax: (34) (1) 543 89 46
Telex: (34) (1) 478 44

Educ. a Distancia, Univ.
Nac. de
Fac. de Psicología
Ciudad Univ.
Madrid 3
Ps. de la Personalidad,
Dpto de
Dept. Head: Jose
Bermudez
Phone: (34) (91) 398 62 50
Fax: (34) (91) 543 89 46

Educ. Especial SILOE,
Colegio de
Carretera de Torregrosa
s/n
Mollerusa (Lérida)

Escuela Univ. de F. P. de
EGB
c/ Geólogo F. H. Pacheco 1
Huerta del Rey
Valladolid 14

Escuela Univ. de F. P. de
EGB
Po. de Ronda 47
La Coruña

Escuela Univ. de
Magisterio
Carretera de Ronda 34
Almeria

Escuela Univ. del Prof.
de EGB
Pablo Montesino
c/ Santisma Trinidad
37
Madrid 3

Escuela Univ. Prof. EGB
Sta Ma
Ronda de Toledo 9
Madrid 5

Fem. Sta. Teresa de
Jesús, Colegio
Hermanas Carmelitas
Orense
Psicóloga, Dpto de

Fundación Jimenez
Diaz
Cliníca Ntra.
Sra/Concepción
Avda. RR. Catolicos 2
Madrid 28040
Dept. Head: P. Perez
Garcia
Phone: (34) (1) 549
9398
Fax: (34) (1) 549 4764

Granada Univ.
Fac. de Fa. y Letras
Granada
Psi. Social, Dpto de

Hospital Central Cruz
Roja
Avda. Reina Victoria 26
Madrid 3
Servicio Psiquiatria

Hospital Cliníc y
Provincial
c/ Villarrdel 170
08036 Barcelona
Dept. Head: Teodoro
Marcos
Phone: (34) (3) 454 60
00

**Hospital Clínico
Barcelona**
Fac. de Medicina
Casanova 143
Barcelona 36
*Cat. de Psiquiatria y
Psid. Med.*

Hospital Clínico Univ.
Avda. Dr. Febriani s/n
Sevilla
*Psiq. y Psic. Medica, Dpto
de*

**Hospital de la VOT de S.
Francisco**
c/ San Bernabé 13
Madrid 5
Sección de Conductores

**Hospital de
Rehabilitación**
c/ Francisco Silvela 40
Madrid

**Hospital Inst. San
José**
Carabanchel Alto
Madrid 28

**Hospital Psi. Infantil La
Atalaya**
Ciudad
Real

**Hospital Psi. Nueastra
Sen. del Pilar**
Zaragoza

**Hospital Psi. Ramón
Alberca**
El Palmar, Murcia

Hospital Psi. Regional
Oviedo
Servicio de Psicología

Hospital Psi. Santa Faz
San Juan, Alicante

Hospital Psi. Toledo
Covarrubias No. 7
Madrid 10

Insp. de EGB, SOEV
c/ Marqués del Turia
78-7a
Valencia

**L'Arjau Equip.
Psicoterapeutic**
c/ López i Puigcerver
8-2oa
Palamos, Gerona

La Laguna Univ.
Filosofia y Cc. de la
Educ., Fac.
La Laguna, Tenerife
*Psi. Pers. y Anormalidad,
Dpto*

**Las Palmas de Gran
Canaria,Univ. de**
Calle Alfonso XIII 2
35003 Las Palmas
Canary Islands
*Psychology & Sociology,
Dept. of*

**Les Illes Balears, Unive.
de**
Miquel dels Sants Oliver2
07071 Palma de
Mallorca
Psychology, Dept. of

M. Peleteiro, Colegio
San Pedro de Mezonzo 27
Santiago de Compostela
La Coruña

**Madrid, Univ.
Autónoma de**
Psicología, Fac. de
Campus de Cantoblanco
Madrid 34
*Diag. Psic. y Med., Dpto
de*

Madrid, Univ. de
Psicología, Fac. de
Somosaguas
Madrid 11
Psicología Exp., Dpto de

**Madrid, Univ. Politéc.
de**
c/ Conde de Xiquena 6
Madrid 4
*Cc. de la Educacion, Inst.
de*

Malaga, Univ. de
Campus de Teatino
29071 Malaga
*Basic Psychology, Dept. of
Dept. Head: Prof. Juan
Ant. Mora*
Phone: (34) (95) 213 10 89
Fax: (34) (95) 213 26 21

Murcia, Univ. de
Espinardo
Murcia
*Filosofia y Cc. Educ.,
Fac. de*

Murcia, Univ. de
Filosofia, Fac. de
Cc. de la Educación
Murcia
Psicología Social, Dpto de

Navarra Univ.
Pio XII s/n
Pamplona
Clínica Univ.

**Nuestra Sa. del
Recuerdo, Colegio**
Plaza Duque de Pastrana
5
Madrid 16
Orientación, Dpto de

Orense, Colegio Univ. de
c/ General Franco 35
Orense

**Orientacion Ed. y Prof.,
Inst. de**
Urbanización
Monteprincipe
A4. No. 32 Boadilla del
Monte
Madrid

Oviedo, Univ. de
Calle San Francisco 3
33003 Oviedo
Psychology, Dept. of

**Palma de Mallorca,
Univ.**
Filosofia, Fac. de y Letras
Cta. Valldemosa km. 7. 6S
Palma de Mallorca
Psicología, Dpto de

**Pedagogia. Terap., Inst.
Nac. de**
c/ General Oraá 55
Madrid

Pinadell, Inst.
c/ Baucels 12
Barcelona

**Pontificia de
Salamanca Univ.**
c/ Compañia
Salamanca
*Dept. Head: Luis Jimenez
Diaz*
Phone: (34) (923) 21 77 66
Fax: (34) (923) 26 24 56
Email: compañia5@
37008salamanca

**Psicología de O. E. y
Profesional, Inst.**
c/ General Franco 10
A2o Drcha. Lugo

Psicología, Fac. de
Avd. Blasco Ibañez 21
Valencia 10
Psicología Dif., Dpto de

Psicología, Fac. de
Zona Univ. Pedralbes
Barcelona 28
*Psicología Exper., Dpto
de*

**Pub. Juan Ramón
Jiminez, Colegio**
Carretera Villaverde
s/n
Leganés

Salamanca, Univ. de
Po. Canalejas 169
Salamanca
*Metodologia Educ., Dpto
de*

Salamanca, Univ. de
Cc. de la Educación
Filosofia, Fac. de
Plaza de Anaya 1
Salamanca
Psicología, Sección de

**Santiago de
Compostela, Univ.
de**
Filosofia, Fac. de
Cc. de la Educación
Santiago de
Compostela
*Psicología Fisiologica,
Dpto*

**Santiago de
Compostela, Univ. de**
La Coruña
Psicología Evol., Dpto de

Sevilla, Univ. de
Avda. Ciudad Jardin 22
Sevilla
U. del Magisterio

St Louis Univ.
Vintia 3
28003 Madrid
Social Sciences, Dept. of

Valencia, Univ. de
c/ Gascè Oliag 12 - 1o
Valencia
*Psi. Med. de Trafico, Inst.
de*

Valencia, Univ. de
Fac. Psicología
Avda. Blasco Ibañez 21
46010 Valencia
*Metodologia, Dpto de;
Psicobiologia Y
Psicología Social
Other Depts:
Psicología Basica;
Personalidad,
Evaluacion ü
Tratamientos
Psicologicos; Psicología
Evolutiva Y de la
Educacion*
Phone: (34) (9) 386 44
73
Fax: (34) (9) 386 46 68

SRI LANKA

Buddhist/Pali Univ.
214 Bauddhaloka
Mawatha
Colombo 7
Psychology, Dept. of

Colombo, Univ. of
94 Cumaratunga
Munidasa Mawatha
Colombo 3
Psychology, Dept. of

Eastern Univ.
Vantharumoolai
Chenkaladi
Psychology, Dept. of

Jaffna, Univ. of
Thirunelvely, Jaffna
*Psychiatry, Dept. of
Dept. Head: Dr D. J.
Somasundaram*

Kelaniya, Univ. of
Dalugama, Kelaniya
Psychology, Dept. of

Moratuwa, Univ. of
Katubedda, Moratuwa
Psychology, Dept. of

**Open Univ. of Sri
Lanka**
POB 21
Nawala, Nugegoda
Psychology, Dept. of

Peradeniya, Univ. of
Univ. Park
Peradeniya
Psychology, Dept. of

Ruhuna, Univ. of
Matara
Psychology, Dept. of

**Sri Jayewardenepura,
Univ. of**
Gangodawila, Nugegoda
Psychology, Dept. of

SUDAN

Ahfar Univ. for Women
POB 167, Omdurman
Psychology, Dept. of

Cairo Univ.
POB 1055
Khartoum
Psychology, Dept. of

Gezira, Univ. of
POB 20
Wad Medani
2667 Khartoum
Psychology, Dept. of

Juba, Univ. of
POB 82
Juba
Psychology, Dept. of

Khartoum, Univ. of
POB 321
Khartoum
Psychology, Dept. of

Omdurman Ahlia Univ.
POB 786
Omdurman
Psychology, Dept. of

**Omdurman Islamic
Univ.**
POB 382
Omdurman
Psychology, Dept. of

SWAZILAND

Swaziland, Univ. of
Private Bag 4
Kwaluseni
Education, Dept. of
Dept. Head: Dr A. B.
Shongwe
Phone: (268) (9268)
84011
Fax: (268) (9268) 55270
Telex: 2087 WD

SWEDEN

Avesta lasarett
Psykiatriska
mottagningen
774 00 Avesta

Barnpsyk. Klin.
Danderyds sjukhus
182 88 Danderyd

Gothenburg Univ.
Box 14158
400 20 Gothenburg
Psychology, Dept. of
Dept. Head: Prof. Trevor
Archer
Phone: (46) (31)
634694
Fax: (46) (31) 634628

Hogskolan Halmstad
Box 7014
300 07 Halmstad

Hogskolan i Boras
Box 874, 501 15 Boras
Psychology, Dept. of

Hogskolan i Jonkoping
Box 1026
551 11 Jonkoping

Hogskolan i Karlstad
Bos 9501
650 09 Karlstad
Psychology, Dept. of

Hogskolan i Skovde
Box 264
541 26 Skovde

**Hogskolan i
Sundsvall/Harnosand**
Box 860
851 24 Sundsvall
Psychology, Dept. of

Hogskolan i Vaxjo
Box 5035
35005 Vaxjo

Linkoping Univ.
58183 Linkoping
Education & Psychology,
Dept. of
Dept. Head: Håkan Hult
Phone: (46) (13) 282156
Fax: (46) (13) 282145

**Lulea Univ. of
Technology**
S-95187 Lulea
Psychology, Dept. of
Dept. Head: Kjell Ohlsson
Phone: (46) (920) 91030
Fax: (46) (920) 91030
Telex: 80447
Email: kjell.ohlsson@
arb.luth.se

Lund Univ.
Paradisgatan 5 P
S-223 50 Lund
Psychology, Dept. of
Other Depts: Cognitive
Psychology; Personality
& Developmental
Psychology; Work
Science; Environmental
Psychology; Gerontology;
Neuropsychology.

Malmö School of
Education
Lund Univ. Box 23501
S-200 45 Malmö
Educational &
Psychological Research,
Dept. of
Dept. Head: Barbro
Eneskär
Phone: (46) (40) 325 000
Fax: (46) (40) 325 210

Occupational Health,
National Inst. of
S-171 84 Solna
Psychology, Dept. of
Dept. Head: Prof.
Francesco Gamberale
Phone: (46) (8) 730 9100
Fax: (46) (8) 730 9051
Telex: 15816 ASBSKY S

Orebro, Univ. of
Box 923
701 30 Orebro
Psychology & Education,
Dept. of
Dept. Head: Auders Agrell
Phone: (46) (19) 301110
Fax: (46) (19) 330130
Email: auders.agrell@
hoe.se

Psykiatriska
verksamheten
Trädgårdsg 20
951 35 Luleå

Psykologiska Inst.
Paradisg 5
223 50 Lund

Psykologiska Klin.
Bollnäs sjukhus
821 00 Bollnäs

Psykolog- verksam
heten
St Persg. 7
753 20 Uppsala

Stockholm Univ.
S-106 91 Stockholm
Psychology, Dept. of
Other Depts: Education
Dept. Head: Prof. Lars
Nystedt
Phone: (46) (8) 162000
Fax: (46) (8) 159342
Telex: 105199
UNIVERS
Email: devine@
psychology.su.se

Umeå, Univ. of
901 87 Umeå
Psychology, Dept. of
Other Depts: Psychiatry;
Applied Psychology
Dept. Head: Prof.
Lars-Göran Nilsson
Phone: (46) (90)
166402
Fax: (46) (90) 166695
Email: psy@ seumdc51

Uppsala Univ.
Box 1225
751 42 Uppsala
Clinical Psychology, Dept.
of
Other Depts: Applied
Psychology
Dept. Head: Asst Prof.
Outi Lundén
Phone: (46) (18) 182107
Fax: (46) (18) 182123

Växjö Univ
POB 5035, 350 05 Växjö
Psychology, Dept. of

SWITZERLAND

Basel Univ.
Bernoullistrasse 16
CH-4056 Basel
Psychologie, Inst. f.
Dept. Head: Prof. G.
Steiner
Phone: (41) (61) 267 3528
Fax: (41) (61) 267 3526
Email: steiner3@
urz.unibas.ch

Bern Univ.
Lampenstrasse 4
CH-3008 Bern
Psychol. Inst.

Bern Univ.
Waldheimstrasse 6
CH-3012
Päd. Psychologie Abt.

Child & Adolescent
Psychiatry, Dept. of
Freiestrasse 15
8028 Zürich
Dept. Head: Prof. H. -C.
Steinhausen
Phone: (41) (1) 251 9694
Fax: (41) (1) 251 0292
Email: k722920@
czhrzula

Clinique de Pédiatrie
30 Blvd. de la Cluse
1205 Genève

EPFL
Centre-Est
1015 Lausanne

FPSE
3 place de l'Université
1211 Genève 4

Friburg, Univ.
Rte des Fougères
1700 Fribourg
Psychologisches Inst.
Dept. Head: Prof. Oswald
Huber
Phone: (41) (37) 219262
Fax: (41) (37) 219290

Fribourg Univ.
rue St-Michel 14
Fribourg
Psychologisches Inst.

Genève, Univ. de
CH-1211
Genève
Psychology Dept.

Genève, Univ. II de
24 rue Général Dufour
1200 Genève

Neuchâtel Univ.
Pierre-A-Mazel 7
2000 Neuchatel
Psychologie Appliqueé,
Groupe de
Dept. Head: Prof. Michel
Rousson
Phone: (41) (38) 21 14
85
Fax: (41) (38) 21 10 85

Neuropsychologische
Abteilung
Vogelsangstrasse 52
8006 Zürich

Psychiatrische Univ.
Klinik
Wilh. -Kleinstrasse 27
4025 Basel

Psychiatrische Univ.
Klinik
Bollingenstrasse 111
3072 Ostermundigen
BE

Psychiatrische Univ.
Klinik
Postfach 68
CH - 8029 Zürich
Forschungsdirektion
Dept. Head: Jules Angst
Phone: (41) (1) 384 26 13
Fax: (41) (1) 383 51 14

Psychologie, Inst. f.
Missionsstrasse 24
Basel

Psychologisches Inst.
Gesellschaftsstrasse 49
3008 Bern
Dept. Head: Prof. Norbert
Semmer
Phone: (41) (31) 65 40 11
Fax: (41) (31) 65 82 12

Schweizer
Föderationsinstitut f.
Technologie
CH-8092 Zürich

Servizio medico
psicologico
Via Bramantino 27
6600 Locarno

Swiss Fed. Inst. of
Technology
Nelkenstrasse 11
CH-8092 Zürich
Work & Organizational
Psychology Unit
Dept. Head: Prof.
Eberhard Ulich
Phone: (41) (1) 254 7070
Fax: (41) (1) 362 5205

Univ. Hospital
Vogelangstrasse 52
CH-8006 Zürich

Univ. Kinderklinik
Freiburgstrasse 23
3010 Bern

Univ Klinik
Murtenstrasse 21
3010 Bern
Socialpsych.

Verein. Schweizer Tech.
Inst.
ETH-Zentrum
Turnerstrasse 1
CH-8092 Zürich
Verh. Wiss. Inst.

Verhaltenswissenschaft
Inst.
Turnerstrasse 1
8092 Zürich

Zürich, Univ.
Zürichbergstrasse 43
CH-8044 Zürich
Psychologisches Inst.
Other Depts:
Anthropological,
General, Applied,
Methodological;
Social & Clinical
Psychology
Phone: (41) (1) 257
2101
Fax: (41) (1) 261 12 68

SYRIA

Al-Baath Univ.
POB 77
Homs
Psychology, Dept. of

Aleppo, Univ. of
Aleppo
Psychology, Dept. of

Damascus, Univ. of
Damascus
Psychology, Dept. of

Tishreen Univ.
Lattakia
Psychology, Dept. of

TAIWAN

Central Univ., Nat.
Chung-Li
Psychology, Dept. of

Cheng Kung Univ., Nat.
1 Ta-Hsueh Rd
Tainan 70701
Psychology, Dept. of

Chengchi Univ., Nat.
Wenshan 11623
Taipei
Psychology, Dept. of

Chiao Tung Univ., Nat.
1001 Ta Hsueh Rd
Hsinchu
Psychology, Dept. of

Chinese Culture Univ.
Hwa Kang
Yangmingshan
Taipei
Psychology, Dept. of

Chung Yuan Christ. Univ.
Chung Li 32023
Psychology, Dept. of

Chunghsing Univ., Nat.
250 Kuokuang Rd
Taichung
Psychology, Dept. of

Feng Chia Univ.
100 Wenhwa Rd
Seatwen
Taichung
Psychology, Dept. of

Fu-Jen Cath. Univ.
Hsinchuang 242
Taipei
Psychology, Dept. of

T

Taiwan Inst. of Tech., Nat.
43 Keelung Rd
Sec. 4
Taipei
Psychology, Dept. of

Taiwan Normal Univ., Nat.
162 Ho-Ping E Rd
Sec. 1
Taipei 10610
Educational Psychology & Counseling, Dept. of
Phone: (886) (2) 351 1263
Fax: (886) (2) 341 3865

Taiwan Univ., Nat.
1 Roosevelt Rd IV
Taipei
Psychology, Dept. of

Tamkang Univ.
151 Ying-Chuan Rd
Tamsui
Taipei 25137
Psychology, Dept. of

Tsing Hua Univ., Nat.
101 Kuang Fu Rd
Sec. 2
Hsinchu
Psychology, Dept. of

Tunghai Christian Univ.
Taichung
Psychology, Dept. of

THAILAND

Asian Inst. of Technology
POB 2754
Bangkok 10501
Psychology, Dept. of
Dept. Head: Songram Chowslipa
Phone: (66) (053) 221699
Fax: (66) (53) 221595

Chiang Mai Univ.
130 Huay Kaew Rd
Muang District
Chiang Mai 50002
Psychology, Dept. of

Chulalongkorn Univ.
Phyathai Rd
Bangkok 10330
Psychology, Dept. of

Dhurakijpundit Univ.
110/1-4 Prachacheun Rd
Bangkhen
Bangkok 10210
Psychology, Dept. of

Kasetsart Univ.
Bangkhen
Bangkok 10900
Psychology, Dept. of

Khon Kaen Univ.
123 Friendship Highway
Khon Kaen 40002
Psychology, Dept. of

King Mongkut's Inst. of Tech.
Chalongkrung Rd
Ladkrabang District
Bangkok 10520
Psychology, Dept. of

**Maejo Inst. of Agric.
Tech.**
Chiang Mai 50290
Psychology, Dept. of

Mahidol Univ.
198/2 Trok Wat
Saowakhon
Bang Yikhan, Bangkok
Noi
Bangkok 10700
Psychology, Dept. of

Payap Univ.
LPO Chiang Mai 101
Chiang Mai 50000
Psychology, Dept. of
*Dept. Head: Tussaneeya
Wongchant*
Phone: (66) (53) 241255
Fax: (66) (53) 241983

Prince of Songkla Univ.
Hat-Yai
Songkla 90110
Psychology, Dept. of

Ramkhamhaeng Univ.
Ramkhamhaeng Rd
Huamark
Bangkok 10240
Psychology, Dept. of

Siam Univ.
235 Petchkasem Rd
Phasi-Charoen
Bangkok 10160
Psychology, Dept. of

Silpakorn Univ.
31 Na-Phralan Rd
Bangkok 10200
Psychology, Dept. of

Srinakharinwirot Univ.
Prasarn Mitr Rd
Sukhumwit 23
Bangkok 10110
Psychology, Dept. of

**Sukhothai
Thammathirat Open
Univ.**
9/9 Moo 9 Tambol
Bangpood, Pakkred
Nonthaburi 11120
Psychology, Dept. of

Thammasat Univ.
2 Prachand Rd
Bangkok 10200
Psychology, Dept. of

TOGO

Bénin, Univ. de
BP 1515, Lomé
Psychology, Dept. of

TRINIDAD

West Indies, Univ. of the
St Augustine Campus
St Augustine, Trinidad
Psychology, Dept. of

TUNISIA

**Centre d'Etudes et de
Recherches
Economiques et
Sociales (CERES)**
23, rue d'Espagne, Tunis
Psychologie, Dépt. de
Phone: (216) (1) 343 237

Sfax, Univ. de
Route de l'Aéroport, Sfax
Psychology, Dept. of

Tunis I, Univ. de
Fac. des Sciences
Humaines et Sociales
94, Bd. du 9 Avril, Tunis
Psychologie, Dépt. de
*Dept. Head: Dr Chafik
Ghorbel*
Phone: (216) (1) 260 950
Fax: (216) (1) 567 551

Tunis II, Univ. de
29 rue Asdrubal
1002 Tunis
Psychology, Dept. of

TURKEY

Akdeniz Univ.
07003 Antalya
Psychology, Dept. of

Anadolu Univ.
Yunus Emre Kampüsü
26470 Eskisehir
Psychology, Dept. of

Ankara Univ.
Tandogan, Ankara
Psychology, Dept. of

Atatürk Univ.
Erzurum
Psychology, Dept. of

Bilkent Univ.
Lojmanlar
Blok 20 No: 5-6
Ankara
*Psychological
Counseling & Research
Center*
*Dept. Head: Dr Nesrin H.
Sahin*
Phone: (90) (4) 266 40 40
Fax: (90) (4) 266 41 27

Bogazici Univ.
80815 Bebek
Istanbul
Psychology, Dept. of
*Other Depts: Educational
Science*
*Dept. Head: prof Dr
Cigdem Kagitcibasi*
Phone: (90) (1) 263 1500
Fax: (90) (1) 265 6357
Telex: (90) (1) 26411
BOUN TR
Email: kagit@ trboun

Cukurova Univ.
Balcali Campus, Adana
Psychology, Dept. of

Cumhuriyet Univ.
58140 Campus-Sivas
Psychology, Dept. of

Dicle Univ.
21280 Diyarbakir
Psychology, Dept. of

Dokuz Eylül Univ.
Cumhuriyet Bul 144
35210 Alsancak, Izmir

Ege Univ.
Bornova, Izmir
Psychology, Dept. of
Dept. Head: Prof. Sefik
Uysal

Erciyes Univ.
PK 275, Kayseri
Psychology, Dept. of

Firat Univ.
23119 Elazig
Psychology, Dept. of

Gazi Univ.
Besevler, Ankara
Psychology, Dept. of

Gaziantep Univ.
POB 300, Gaziantep
Psychology, Dept. of

Hacettepe Univ.
Hacettepe Parki
Beytepe, Ankara
Neurol. Sci. & Psychology
Inst.
Dept. Head: Dr Hüsnü
Arici

Inönü Univ.
Malatya
Psychology, Dept. of

Istanbul Teknik Univ.
Ayazaga
Istanbul
Psychology, Dept. of

Istanbul Univ.
Beyazit
Istanbul
Psychology, Dept. of

Karadeniz Teknik
Univ.
61080 Trabzon
Psychology, Dept. of

Marmara Univ.
Kayisdagi Caddesi
Fikirtepe
Kadivöy
Istanbul
Psychology, Dept. of

Middle East Technical
Univ.
06531 Ankara
Psychology, Dept. of
Dept. Head: Prof. Olcay
Imamoglu
Phone: (90) (4) 210 10 00
Fax: (90) (4) 286 95 80
Telex: (90) (4) 42761

Mimar Sinan Univ.
Findikli
80040 Istanbul
Psychology, Dept. of

Ondokuz Mayis Univ.
University Campus
Kurupelit, Samsun 55139
Psychology, Dept. of

Psychological
Research, Inst. for
Or-An Sehri
Ü Yasar Sok No: 43/1
Cankaya
Ankara
Dept. Head: Dr Bail
Sehin
Phone: (90) (4) 287 80
46

Selçuk Univ.
Vali Izzetbey
Caddessi
42050 Konya
Psychology, Dept. of

Trakya Univ.
22030 Edirne
Psychology, Dept. of

Uludag Univ.
Rektörlügü Görükle
Kampüsü
16120 Bursa
Psychology, Dept. of

Yüzüncü Yil
Univ.
Van
Psychology, Dept. of

Yildiz Univ.
Yildiz
Istanbul
Psychology, Dept. of

TURKMENISTAN

Turkmen A. M Gorkii
State Univ.
Pr. Lenina 31
Ashkhabad
744014 Turkmen
Psychology, Dept. of

UGANDA

Makerere Univ.
POB 7062, Kampala
Psychology, Dept. of
Dept. Head: Dr John C.
Munene
Email: j.munene@
mukla.gn.apc.org

UKRAINE

Dnepropetrovsk State Univ.
Pr. Gagarina 72
Dnepropetrovsk 320625
Psychology, Dept. of

Donetsk State Univ.
Ul. Univ. skaya 24
Donetsk 340055
Psychology, Dept. of

Kharkov AM Gorkii State Univ.
Pl. Dzerzhinskogo 4
Kharkov, 310077

Kiev TG Shevchenko State Univ.
17 Vladimirskaya ul. 64
Kiev, 252601
Psychology, Dept. of

Lvov Ivan Franko State Univ.
Lvov. Univ. skaya ul. 1
290602
Psychology, Dept. of

Odessa State Univ.
Ul. Petra Velikogo 2
Odessa, 270057

Simferopol MV Frunze St. Univ.
Yaltinskaya ul. 4
Simferopol 333036
Psychology, Dept. of

Uzhgorod State Univ.
Ul. M. Gorkogo 46
Uzhgorod 294000

Zaporozhe State Univ.
Ul. Zhukoyskogo 66
Zaporozhe 330600

UNITED ARAB EMIRATES

United Arab Emirates Univ.
POB 15551, Al Ain

UNITED KINGDOM OF GREAT BRITAIN AND NORTHERN IRELAND

Aberdeen, Univ. of
Kings College
Aberdeen AB9 2UB
Psychology Dept.
Dept. Head: Prof. Jan B.
Deregowski
Phone: (44) (224) 272227
Fax: (44) (224) 273426
Telex: 73458 uniabn g
Email: j.b.deregowski@
uk.ac.abdn.

Aberystwyth, Univ. Coll. of
Aberystwyth
Dyfed SY23 2AX
Education Dept.
Dept. Head: Prof. Gareth
Elwyn Jones
Phone: (44) (970) 622103
Fax: (44) (970) 622122
Telex: 35181 ABYUCW G

Addenbrookes Hospital
Level 4, Hills Rd
Cambridge
CB2 2QQ
Family Research, Ctr for
Phone: (44) (223) 334510
Fax: (44) (223) 334748

Addenbrookes Hospital
Level 4, Hills Rd
Cambridge CB2 2QQ
Psychiatry Dept.
Dept. Head: Prof. E. S.
Paykel
Phone: (44) (223) 336965
Fax: (44) (223) 336968
Telex: (44) (223) 81240

Airedale General Hospital
Steeton
Nr Keighley
W. Yorkshire
BD20 6TD
Clinical Psychology Dept.
Dept. Head: Dr Rooshmie
Bhagat
Phone: (44) (535) 652511
Fax: (44) (535) 655129

Alder Hey Children's Hospital
Eaton Rd
Liverpool
L12 2AP
Psychology Dept.
Dept. Head: Jean
Sambrooks
Phone: (44) (51) 252 5586
Fax: (44) (51) 228 0328

All Saint's Hospital
Chatham
Kent
ME4 5NG
Psychology Dept.
Dept. Head: F. K. Cutler
Phone: (44) (634) 407311
Fax: (44) (634) 817347

Anglia Polytechnic Univ.
Victoria Rd South
Chelmsford
Essex CM1 1LL
Health Management &
Social Work, Dept. of
Dept. Head: Dr Roy
Stephens
Phone: (44) (245) 493131
Fax: (44) (245) 490835
Formerly: Anglia
Polytechnic

Argyll & Bute Hospital
Lochgilphead, Argyll
Paisley PA31 8LD
Psychology Dept.
Dept. Head: Charles
Anthony Prior
Phone: (44) (546) 604904

Ashworth Hospital
School Lane
Maghull
Liverpool
LS31 1BD
Psychology Dept.
Phone: (44) (51) 473 0303

Astley Ainslie Hospital
Grange Loan
Edinburgh
EH9 2HL
Clinical Psychology Dept.
Dept. Head: David A.
Johnson
Phone: (44) (31) 447 6271
Fax: (44) (31) 452 8405

Aston Hall Hospital
Community Health
  Services
Aston on Trent
Derby DE7 2AL
Clinical Psychology, Dept.
of
Dept. Head: Joe Beswick
Phone: (44) (332) 792412
Fax: (44) (332) 792039

Aston Univ.
Aston Triangle
Birmingham
B4 7ET
Psychology Divn.
Other Depts: Ethnic
Relations Research Unit
Dept. Head: Dr R. B.
Stammers
Phone: (44) (21) 359 3611
Fax: (44) (21) 359 6384
Telex: 336997 UNIAST G
Email: stammersrb@
  uk.ac.aston

Atkinson Morleys
Hospital & Wolfson
Rehabilitation Centre
Copse Hill
London
SW20 0NE
Psychiatric Research Unit
Dept. Head: Dr T. M.
McMillan
Phone: (44) (81) 946 7711
Fax: (44) (81) 947 8389

Ballamona Hospital
Braddan
Isle of Man
Psychology Dept.

Bangor, Univ. Coll. of
North. Wales
Gwynedd
LL57 2DG
Psychology, Dept. of
Dept. Head: Prof. C.
Fergus Lowe
Phone: (44) (248) 382629
Fax: (44) (248) 364412
Email: pss001@
  bangor.vaxa

Banstead Hospital
Sutton
Surrey
SM2 5PA
Psychology Dept.

Barking College of
Technology
Dagenham Rd, Romford
Essex RM7 0XU
Occupational Psychology
Unit

Barnsley Hall Hospital
Bromsgrove
Worcs. B61 0EX
Clinical Psychology Dept.
Dept. Head: Joanne Smith
Phone: (44) (527) 75252
Fax: (44) (527) 570096

Barrow Hospital
Barrow Gurney
Bristol BS19 3SG
Psychology Dept.
Dept. Head: Dr Moira
Hamlin / Dr Rosie Corke
Phone: (44) (275) 392811

Basildon Hospital
Basildon
Essex SS16 5NL
Psychology Dept.
Dept. Head: David
Fewtrell
Phone: (44) (268) 533911
Fax: (44) (268) 287649

Basingstoke College of
Technology
Worting Rd
Basingstoke RG21 1TN
General Studies Dept.
Dept. Head: John J.
Rogers
Phone: (44) (256) 54141
Fax: (44) (256) 810007

Basingstoke District
Hospital
Psychiatric Divn.
Park Prewett
Basingstoke
Hants. RG24 9LZ
Psychology Dept.

Bath, Univ. of
Claverton Down
Bath BA2 7AY
Psychology, Dept. of
Other Depts: Social
Sciences
Dept. Head: Prof. Harry
Collins / Dr Helen
Hastie
Phone: (44) (225) 826826
Fax: (44) (225) 826381
Telex: 449097

Bedford College
Regent's Park
London NW1
Psychology Dept.

Bedford General
Hospital
South Wing, Weller Wing,
Kempston Rd
Bedford MK42 9DJ
Psychology Dept.

Belfast City Hospital
Windsor House
Lisburn Rd
Belfast BT9 7AB
Clinical Psychology, Dept.
of
Dept. Head: Dr A.
Desmond Poole
Phone: (44) (232) 329241
Fax: (44) (232) 326614

Belfast, Queen's Univ. of
10 Lennoxvale
Malone Rd
Belfast BT9 5BY
Psychology Dept.
Other Depts: Education;
Mental Health; Social
Studies
Dept. Head: Prof. K.
Brown
Phone: (44) (232) 245133
Fax: (44) (232) 664144
Email: psychology@ qub

Bellsdyke Hospital
Larbert
Stirlingshire FK5 4SF
Psychology Dept.
Dept. Head: Ruth Salter
/ Roisin Hall
Phone: (44) (324) 556131
Fax: (44) (324) 562343

Bethel Hospital
Bethel St.
Norwich NR2 1NR
Child & Family Centre

Bethlem Royal Hospital
Monks Orchard Rd
Beckenham
Kent BR3 3BX
Phone: (44) (81) 777 6611
Fax: (44) (81) 777 1668

Bexley Hospital
Old Bexley Lane
Bexley
Kent DA5 2BW
Psychology Dept.
Dept. Head: Peter
Cummins
Phone: (44) (322) 526282
Fax: (44) (322) 555491

Billinge Hospital
Billinge
Nr. Wigan
Lancs. WN5 7ET
Psychology Dept.
Dept. Head: Dr Graham
Spratt
Phone: (44) (695) 626181
Fax: (44) (695) 626181

Birch Hill Hospital
Birch Rd
Rochdale OL16 9QN
Clinical Psychology Dept.
Dept. Head: Dr L. E.
Burns
Phone: (44) (706) 755797
Fax: (44) (706) 755130

Birkbeck College
London, Univ. of
Malet St.
London
WC1E 7HX
Psychology Dept.
Dept. Head: Prof. William
Marslen-Wilson
Phone: (44) (71) 631 6207
Fax: (44) (71) 631 6270

Birkbeck College
London, Univ. of
Malet St.
London
WC1E 7HX
Occupational Psychology
Dept.
Dept. Head: Prof. David
Guest
Phone: (44) (71) 631 6392
Fax: (44) (71) 631 6392

Birmingham, Univ. of
Edgbaston
Birmingham, B15 2TT
Psychology, School of
Other Depts: Accident
Research Unit
Dept. Head: Prof. G. W.
Humphreys
Phone: (44) (21) 414 4932
Fax: (44) (21) 414 4897
Email: thomasgv@
uk.ac.bham.ibm3090

Birmingham, Univ. of
Dudley Rd Hospital
Birmingham B18 7QH
RSU Research Unit

Bolton General Hospital
Minena Rd, Farnworth
Bolton BL4 0JR
Clinical Psychology, Dept.
of
Dept. Head: Kerry H.
McCullough
Phone: (44) (204) 390675

Bolton Inst. of Higher Education
Deane Rd, Bolton
Lancs. BL3 5AB
Dept. Head: Alec Ragley
Phone: (44) (204) 28851
Fax: (44) (204) 399074

Bournemouth Univ.
Talbot Campus
Fern Barrow, Poole
Dorset BH12 5BB
Nursing, Health &
Community Studies,
Dept. of
Other Depts: Psychology
Dept. Head: J. Gosby &
S. Hume
Phone: (44) (202) 524111
Fax: (44) (202) 513293
Formerly; Bournemouth
Polytechnic

Bradford, Univ. of
26 Pemberton Drive
Bradford BD7 1RA
Interdisciplinary Human
Studies
Dept. Head: Roger Fellows
Phone: (44) (274) 383986
Fax: (44) (274) 720494

Brain Injury Rehab. &
Development, Ctr. for
131 Main Rd, Broughton
Chester CH4 0NR
Phone: (44) (244) 532047
Fax: (44) (244) 538723

Brandesburton Hospital
Brandesburton, Driffield
North Humberside
YO25 8QT
Clinical Psychology Dept.

Branksome Clinic
Layton Rd, Parkstone
Poole, Dorset
District Psychology Dept.

Brighton, Univ. of
Hillbrow
1 Denton Rd, Eastbourne
E. Sussex BN20 7SR
Chelsea School of Human
Movement
Dept. Head: Prof.
Elizabeth B. Murdoch
Phone: (44) (273) 643700
Fax: (44) (273) 643700
Formerly: Brighton
Polytechnic

Brighton, Univ. of
D Block
Falmer, Brighton
E. Sussex BN1 9PH
Community Studies,
Dept. of
Dept. Head: A. D. Hadley
Phone: (44) (273) 600900
Fax: (44) (273) 643473

Bristol, Univ. of
8 Woodlands Rd
Bristol BS8 1TN
Psychology, Dept. of
Dept. Head: W. P.
Robinson
Phone: (44) (272) 288450
Fax: (44) (272) 288588

Bristol, Univ. of
College of St Matthias
Fishponds
Bristol
Dept. Head: Dr Mary N.
Haslum
Phone: (44) (272) 656261

Broadgate Hospital
Walkington, Beverley
North Humberside
Psychology Dept.

Broadmoor Hospital
Crowthorne
Berks
RG11 7EG

Broakchall Hospital
Old Langho
Blackburn BB6 8AZ

Bromley Cross Clinic
Chapeltown Rd
Bromley Cross
Bolton, Lancs.

Brookwood Hospital
Knaphill, Woking
Surrey GU21 2RQ

Broughton Hospital
Broughton
Nr Chester
Psychology Dept.
Dept. Head: Judy
Thomson
Phone: (44) (244) 520350
Fax: (44) (244) 538314

Brunel, The Univ. of
West London
Uxbridge
Middx. UB8 3PH
Human Sciences, Dept. of
Dept. Head: Prof. John T.
E. Richardson
Phone: (44) (895) 274000
Fax: (44) (895) 232806
Telex: 261173 G
Email: john.richardson@
uk.ac.brunel

Buckingham, The Univ.
of
Hunter St, Buckingham
Bucks. MK18 1EG
Psychology, Dept. of
Dept. Head: Prof. Len
Evans
Phone: (44) (280) 814080
Fax: (44) (280) 822245

Burton Rd Hospital
Dudley
West Midlands
Psychology Dept.

Calderstones Hospital
Whalley
Nr. Blackburn
Lancs.
BB6 9PE
Psychology Dept.
Dept. Head: Tim Lister
Phone: (44) (254) 822121
Fax: (44) (254) 823023

Cambridge Inst. of
Educ.
Shaftesbury Rd
Cambridge CB2 2BX

Cambridge, Univ. of
Free School Lane
Cambridge
CB2 3RF
Centre for Family
Research
Dept. Head: Martin P. M.
Richards
Phone: (44) (223) 334510
Fax: (44) (223) 334748
Email: sr25@
phx.cam.ac.uk

Cambridge, Univ. of
Dept. of Education
17 Trumpington St.
Cambridge
CB2 1PT
Educational Psychology
Dept. Head: Prof. D.H.
Hargreaves
Phone: (44) (223) 33288
Fax: (44) (223) 332876

Cambridge, Univ. of
Downing St.
Cambridge CB2 3EB
Exp. Psychology Dept.
Dept. Head: Prof. N. J.
Mackintosh
Phone: (44) (223) 333550
Fax: (44) (223) 333564
Email: rgf10@
uk.ac.cam.phy

Cardiff Inst. of Higher
Education
Llandaff Centre
Western Ave.
Cardiff
Psychology Section
Dept. Head: Dr P. J.
Harris
Phone: (44) (222) 551111
Fax: (44) (222) 578084

Cardiff, Univ. of Wales
College of
POB 901
Cardiff
CF1 3YG
Psychology, School of
Dept. Head: Prof. H. D.
Ellis
Phone: (44) (222) 874007
Fax: (44) (222) 874007

Carlton Hayes Hospital
Forest Rd
Narborough, Leics.
Psychology Dept.
Dept. Head: Christopher
Stowers
Phone: (44) (533) 863481

Castel Hospital for
Nervous Disorders
Castel, Guernsey

Cefn Coed Hospital
Cockett, Swansea
West Glamorgan
Psychology Dept.
Dept. Head: Dr Paul D.
G. Harris
Phone: (44) (792) 561155
Fax: (44) (792) 580740

Central Hospital
Hatton, Warwick
Clinical Psychology Dept.
Dept. Head: Adrian
Newell
Phone: (44) (926) 496241

Central Lancashire,
Univ. of
Heatley St
Preston
Lancs.
PR1 2TQ
Psychology, Dept. of
Dept. Head: Peter Young
Phone: (44) (772) 201201
Fax: (44) (772) 892902
Email: young.p@
uk.ac.lancsp.pi
Formerly: Lancashire
Polytechnic

Charing Cross &
Westminster Medical
School
Fulham Palace Rd
London
W6 8RF
Psychiatry Dept.
Other Depts: Neurology
Dept. Head: Prof. S. R.
Hirsch
Phone: (44) (81) 846 7390
Fax: (44) (81) 846 7390

Chelmsley Hospital
Marston Green
Birmingham
B37 7HL
Psychology Dept.
Dept. Head: Jill Dagnan
Phone: (44) (21) 779 6981

Chelsea College
London, Univ. of
552 Kings Rd
London
SW10
Nursing Studies Dept.

Chelsea College
London, Univ. of
Bridges Place
London
SW6 4HR
Science Education Centre

**Child & Family
Guidance Centre**
Broadfield Rd, Knowle
Bristol, BS4 2UH

**Child & Family Psych.
Clinic**
130 Hempstead Rd
Watford
Herts. WD1 3LG

Child Guidance Centre
Springwood House
Polmaise Rd, Stirling

Child Guidance Clinic
Whitehall Cottage
Whitehall Lane
Grays
Essex RM17 6SH
Dept. Head: Y. P. Gupta
Phone: (44) (375) 374749

Child Health, Inst. of
Guildford St.
London
WC1
Behavioural Sciences Unit
*Dept. Head: Prof. P.
Graham*
Phone: (44) (71) 405 9200
Fax: (44) (71) 829 8657

**Child Psychology
Service**
12 Grange Rd
West Bromwich
West Midlands
B70 8PD
Dept. Head: P. E. Watts
Phone: (44) (21) 553 7411

City General Hospital
Newcastle Rd
Stoke-on-Trent
ST4 6DQ
Clinical Psychology Dept.
Phone: (44) (782) 718922
Fax: (44) (782) 718001

City of London, Univ. of
Old Castle St.
London E1 7NT
Psychology Dept.
Dept. Head: L. Currie
Phone: (44) (71) 283 1030
Fax: (44) (771) 247 7782

City Univ., The
Walmsley Building
Northampton Square
London EC1V 0HB
Psychology Divn.
*Dept. Head: Dr James
Hampton*
Phone: (44) (71) 477 8504
Fax: (44) (71) 477 8581
Email: hampton@
city.ac.uk

City Univ., The
Northampton Square
London EC1V 0HB
*Soc. Science &
Humanities Dept.*
*Dept. Head: Dr Steve
Miller*
Phone: (44) (71) 477 8502
Fax: (44) (71) 477 8580
Email: hampton@
city.ac.uk

Claybury Hospital
Woodford Bridge, Essex
Psychology Dept.

**Cleveland Health
Authority**
22 Belle Vue Grove
Middlesbrough
Clinical Psychology Dept.

Clifton Hospital
Shipton Rd, York
*Clinical Psychology
Services*
*Dept. Head: Dr Anne
Pattie*
Phone: (44) (904) 645165

**Clinical & Comm.
Psychology Dept.**
Church Lane
Heavitree
Exeter
EX2 5SH
*Dept. Head: Dr
Christopher Williams*
Phone: (44) (392) 403172
Fax: (44) (3392) 403186

**Clinical Psychology,
Dept. of**
Elmhill House
Cornhill Rd
Aberdeen
AB9 2ZY
*Dept. Head: J. Stephen
Bell*
Phone: (44) (224) 681818
Fax: (44) (224) 646201

**Clinical Psychology
Dept.**
Furness Mount
4 Holmesdale Gardens
Hastings
East Sussex,
TN34 1LY
*Dept. Head: Dr Robert
Wycherley*
Phone: (44) (424) 435066

**Clinical Psychology
Partnership**
Denethorpe
Stockton Rd
Ryhope
Sunderland SR2 0NE
*Dept. Head: Dr Per O. G.
Svanberg*
Phone: (44) (91) 521 0541
Fax: (44) (91) 523 7683

Coldeast Hospital
Sarisbury Green
Southampton
SO3 6ZD
Clinical Psychology Dept.

Coney Hill Hospital
Coney Hill
Gloucester
GL4 7Q1
Clinical Psychology Dept.

Coventry Univ.
Priory St.
Coventry
CV1 5FB
Health & Social Studies,
School of.
Dept. Head: Prof. Norma
Reid
Phone: (44) (203) 838491
Fax: (44) (203) 258597
Telex: 931 210 2228 CPG
Formerly: Coventry
Polytechnic

Craig Dunian Hospital
Highland Health Board
Inverness
IV3 6JU
Clinical Psychology Dept.

Cranage Hall Hospital
Holmes Chapel
Crewe
Cheshire
Clinical Psychology Dept.

Cranfield Inst. of Tech.
Cranfield
Beds.
MK43 0AL
Applied Psychology, Dept.
of
Dept. Head: Dr Helen
Muir
Phone: (44) (234) 750111
Fax: (44) (234) 750192
Telex: 825072 CITECH G

Crichton Royal Hospital
Johnson House
Bankend Rd
Dumfries
Psychology Services Dept.

Darenth Park Hospital
Dartford
Kent
DA2 6LZ
Psychology Dept.

De Montfort Univ.
Scaptoft Campus
Leicester LE7 9SU
Human Communication,
Dept. of
Dept. Head: Prof. P.
Grunwell
Phone: (44) (533) 551551
Fax: (44) (533) 577866
Formerly: Leicester
Polytechnic

Dene Barton
9 Dene Rd
Morton Fitzwarren
Taunton
Somerset TA4 3DF
Dept. Head: Madeleine
Thomas
Phone: (44) (823) 432136
Fax: (44) (823) 433423

Derby, Univ. of
Western Rd
Mickleover
Derby
DE3 5GX
Health & Community
Studies, Inst. of
Dept. Head: Dr Patrick
McGhee
Phone: (44) (332) 62226
Fax: (44) (332) 514323
Formerly: Derbyshire
College, H.E.

Digby Stuart College
Roehampton Lane
London SW15 5PM
Psychology Dept.
Dept. Head: Dr Eileen
Pickard
Phone: (44) (81) 876 8273

Dingleton Hospital
Melrose
Roxburghshire Scotland

Dundee, Univ. of
Dundee DD1 4HN
Psychology, Dept. of
Dept. Head: Prof.
Nicholas Emler
Phone: (44) (382) 307622
Fax: (44) (382) 29993
Email: pc07@uk.ac.
dundee.primeb.janet

Durham, Univ. of
South Rd
Durham DH1 3LE
Psychology Dept.
Dept. Head: Prof. A. W.
Young
Phone: (44) (91) 374 2610
Fax: (44) (91) 374 3741
Telex: 537351 DURLIB G
Email: m.s.hall@
uk.ac.durham

Ealing College of
Higher Educ.
St Mary's Rd
London W5

East Anglia, Univ. of
Keswick Hall
Norwich NR4 6TL
Education, School of

East London, Univ. of
Arthur Edwards Building
The Green
Romford Rd
London E15 4LZ
Psychology Dept.
Dept. Head: Dr Keith
Phillips
Phone: (44) (81) 590 7722
Fax: (44) (81) 849 3625
Email: a46kp@ pel
Formerly: Polytechnic of
East London

East Somerset Clinical Psychology Dept.
Rosebank, Priory Park
Glastonbury Rd, Wells
Somerset, BA5 1TH
Dept. Head: Colin A. Shorvon
Phone: (44) (749) 670445
Fax: (44) (749) 679487

Eaves Lane Hospital
Eaves Lane, Chorley
Lancs PR6 0TT
Clinical Psychology Dept.

Edinburgh, Univ. of
2 Buccleuch Place
Edinburgh EH8 9LW
Human Communication Research Centre
Dept. Head: Prof. Keith Stenning
Phone: (44) (031) 650 4444
Fax: (44) (031) 650 4587
Email: k.stenning@ed.ac.uk

Edinburgh, Univ. of
7 George Square
Edinburgh EH8 9JZ
Psychology Dept.
Dept. Head: Prof. Robert Grieve
Phone: (44) (31) 650 3441
Fax: (44) (31) 650 6512
Telex: 727442 UNIVED G

Education, Inst. of
25 Woburn Square
London WC1H 0AA
Educational Psychology & Special Educational Needs, Dept. of
Dept. Head: Dr Brahm Norwich
Phone: (44) (71) 580 1122
Fax: (44) (71) 612 6304
Email: teephjb@uk.ac.ioe

Education Research, Nat. Foundation for
The Mere
Upton Park
Slough
SL1 2DQ
Assessment & Measurement Dept
Dept. Head: C. Whetton
Phone: (44) (753) 574123
Fax: (44) (753) 691632

Education Research, Nat. Foundation for
The Mere
Upton Park
Slough
SL1 2DQ
Curriculum Studies Dept.
Dept. Head: D. Foxman
Phone: (44) (753) 574123
Fax: (44) (753) 691632

Educational Psychology Service
Eastview
Ayton St.
Newcastle upon Tyne
NE6 2DB
Child & Family Guidance Service
Dept. Head: Keith A. Herbert
Phone: (44) (91) 265 6632
Fax: (44) (91) 261 7934

Ely Hospital
Cowbridge Rd West
Ely
Cardiff
CF5 5XE
Psychology Dept.
Dept. Head: Dr David Whitlow
Phone: (44) (222) 562323
Fax: (44) (222) 578717

Essex County Hospital
Essex Rivers Healthcare Trust
Lexden Rd
Colchester
CO3 3NB
Dept. Head: Wendy MacKay
Phone: (44) (206) 853535
Fax: (44) (206) 560372

Essex, Univ. of
Victoria Rd South
Chelmsford
Essex
CM1 1LL
Social Science Fac.

Exeter, Univ. of
Washington Singer Laboratories
Exeter
EX4 4OG
Psychology Dept.
Dept. Head: Prof. J. Richard Eiser
Phone: (44) (392) 264626
Fax: (44) (392) 264623
Email: p.webley@uk.ac.exeter

Extra Mural & Adult Educ. Dept.
57/61 Oakfield Ave.
Glasgow
G12 8LW

Fairfield General Hospital
Bury
Lancs.
BL9 7TD
Clinical Psychology Dept.

Fairleigh Hospital
Flax Bourton
Bristol
BS19 3QZ
Clinical Psychology Dept.

Fairmile Hospital
Wallingford
Berks
Clinical Psychology, Dept.
of
Dept. Head:
A. C. Keddie
Phone: (44) (491) 651281

Farnborough Hospital
Bassetts Starts Hill Rd
Orpington
Kent
BR6 7AR
Psychology Dept.
Other Depts: Psychiatry

Fieldhead Hospital
Inchthorpe Lane
Wakefield
W. Yorks.
Psychology Dept.

Fleming Nuffield Unit
Burdon Terrace
Newcastle upon Tyne
NE2 3AE
Nuffield Psychology
Unit
Phone: (44) (91) 281 6177

Frenchay Hospital
Bristol
BS16 1LE
Neurological Rehab.
Unit

Friern Hospital
Friern Barnet Rd
London
N11 3BP
Psychology Dept.
Other Depts:
Neuropsychology Unit

Frimley Park Hospital
Frimley
Surrey
Psychology Dept.

Gartnaval Royal
Hospital
3 Whittinghame Gardens
Glasgow
G12 0AA
Psychology Dept.
Dept. Head: Dr Gerald
Greene
Phone: (44) (41) 334 6241
Fax: (44) (41) 337 2408

George Eliot Hospital
Combe House
Nuneaton
Warwickshire
CV10 7DJ
Psychology Dept.
Dept. Head: Peter Watson
Phone: (44) (203) 350111
Fax: (44) (203) 350727

Glamorgan, Univ. of
Pontypridd
Mid-Glamorgan
CF37 1DL
Humanities & Social
Sciences, School of
Dept. Head: Dr Frances
Mannsaker
Phone: (44) (443) 482551
Fax: (44) (443) 480558

Glasgow, Univ. of
2 Lilybank Gardens
Glasgow
G12 8RZ
Public Health, Dept. of
Dept. Head: Prof. James
McEwen
Phone: (44) (41) 339 8855
Fax: (44) (41) 330 5018

Glasgow, Univ. of
6 Whittinghame Gardens
Gt Western Rd
Glasgow
G12 0AA
Psychological Medicine
Dept.

Glasgow, Univ. of
Adam Smith Building
Glasgow G12 8RT
Psychology Dept.
Dept. Head: P. J.
O'Donnell
Phone: (44) (41) 330 4688
Fax: (44) (41) 339 8889
Email: mbox@
psy.glasgow.ac.uk

Glenside Hospital
Stapleton
Bristol BS16 1DD
Psychology Dept.

Gogarburn Hospital
Glasgow Rd
Edinburgh EH12 9BJ
Psychology Dept.

Goldsmith's College
London, Univ. of
New Cross
London SE14 6NW
Psychology Dept.
Dept. Head: Prof. Ruth
Campbell
Phone: (44) (81) 692 7171
Fax: (44) (81) 691 4765
Email: psycho@
uk.ac.lon.gold

Goodmayes Hospital
Barley Lane
Ilford
Essex IG3 8XJ
Psychology Dept.
Dept. Head: Dr Morris
Nitsun
Phone: (44) (081) 590
6060
Fax: (44) (081) 599 4852

Gorseinon Hospital
Brynawel Rd, Gorseinon
Swansea SA4 2UU
Community Handicap
Team

Graylingwell Hospital
Chichester
West Suxssex
PO19 4PQ
Psychology Dept.

Greaves Hall Hospital
Banks
Nr. Southport
Merseyside
Psychology Dept.

Greenwich, Univ. of
Riverside House
Beresford St.
London
SE18
Business Admin. School
Phone: (44) (081) 316 8000
Fax: (44) (081) 316 8845
Formerly: Thames Polytechnic

Gulson Hospital
Gulson Rd
Coventry
CV1 2HR
Clinical Psychology Service
Dept. Head: Dr Marcia L. Davis
Phone: (44) (203) 844061

Guy's Hospital
York Clinic
St Thomas Street
London
SE1 9RT
Psychology Dept.
Other Depts: Adult Mental Health; Child Psychology; Learning Disability; AIDS & HIV
Dept. Head: Isobel Morris
Phone: (44) (71) 955 4933
Fax: (44) (71) 6910

Gwent Psychology Services
St Cadoc's Hospital
Caerleon
Gwent
NP6 1XQ
Psychology Dept.
Dept. Head: Alan D. Wright
Phone: (44) (633) 421121
Fax: (44) (633) 430184

Hairmyres Hospital
East Kilbride, Scotland
G75 8RG
Dept. Head: Dr Jim White
Phone: (44) (3352) 20292

Harmston Hall Hospital
Harmston
Nr. Lincoln
Lincolnshire
LN5 9SR
Clinical Psychology Dept.

Harperbury Hospital
Harper Lane
Radlett
Herts. WD7 9HZ
Psychology Dept.

Hartwood Hospital
Hartwood
Shotts
Lanarkshire
ML7 4LA

Hellingly Hospital
Hailsham
E. Sussex
BN27 4ER
Psychology Dept.

Heriot-Watt Univ.
31-35 Grassmarket
Edinburgh
EH1 2HT
Business Organisation Dept.

Hertfordshire, Univ. of
College Lane
Hatfield, Herts.
AL10 9AB
Psychology Dept.
Dept. Head: Prof. Ben Fletcher
Phone: (44) (707) 279612
Fax: (44) (707) 285073
Telex: 262413
Formerly: Hatfield Polytechnic

High Royds Hospital
Menston, Ilkley
W. Yorkshire
LS29 6AQ
Psychology Dept.

HM Prison Gartree
Market Harborough
Leics.
Psychology Dept.

HM Prison Maidstone
County Rd
Maidstone
Kent
Psychology Unit

HM Prison Wormwood Scrubs
POB 757
DuCane Rd
London W12 0AE
Psychology Unit
Dept. Head: M.C. Smith
Phone: (44) (81) 743 0311
Fax: (44) (81) 749 5655

HM Young Offenders Inst. & Remand Centre
Bedfont Rd
Feltham
Middx. TW13 4ND
Psychology Dept.
Dr Pam Wilson
Phone: (44) (81) 890 0061
Fax: (44) (81) 844 1551

Hollymoor Hospital
Northfield
BirminghamB31 5EX
Psychology Dept.

Holywell Hospital
60 Steeple Rd, Antrim
N. Ireland BT41 2RJ
Clinical Psychology Dept.
Dept. Head: Dr Robin
Davidson
Phone: (44) (8494) 65211
Fax: (44) (8494) 61803

Home Office Prison Dept.
89 Eccleston Square
London SW1
Adult Offender
Psychology Unit

Hospitals for Sick
Children, The
Great Ormond St.
London WC1 3JH
Psychology, Dept. of
Other Depts:
Psychological Medicine
Dept. Head: Dr R. G.
Lansdown
Phone: (44) (71) 405 9200
Fax: (44) (71) 829 8657

Huddersfield, Univ. of
Queensgate
Huddersfield HD1 3DH
Behavioural Sciences Dept.
Dept. Head: Prof. Nigel
Lemon
Phone: (44) (484) 422 288
Fax: (44) (484) 516151
Telex: 518299 HUDPOL G
Formerly: The Polytechnic
of Huddersfield

Hull, Univ. of
26 Newland Park, Hull
Nth Humberside HU5 2DW
Ergonomics Research
Group

Hull, Univ. of
Hull
Yorkshire HU6 7RX
Psychology Dept.
Other Depts: Nursing
Studies Dept.
Dept. Head: Prof. D.
Bartram
Phone: (44) (482) 465388
Fax: (44) (482) 465599

Humberside, Univ. of
Inglemire Ave.
Hull HU6 7LU
Behavioural Science,
Dept. of
Dept. Head: Dr K.J.B.
Jones
Phone: (44) (482) 440550
Faxc: (44) (482) 449624
Formerly: Humberside
Polytechnic

Hurstwood Park
Neurological Ctr.
Lewes Rd
Haywards Heath RH 16
4EX
Phone: (44) (444) 441881
FAx: (44) (444) 417995

Ida Darwin Hospital
Fulbourn
Cambridge CB1 5EE
Psychology Dept.
Dept. Head: Suzanne
Collins
Phone: (44) (223) 218762
Fax: (44) (223) 881561

Island Clinical
Psychology Service
The Gables
Halberry Lane
Fairlee, Newport
Isle of Wight, PO30 2ER
Dept. Head: Fiona C.
Kennedy
Phone: (44) (983) 521464

John Radcliffe Hospital
Oxford
OX3 9DU
Paediatric Psychology,
Dept. of
Dept. Head: Dr John
Richer
Phone: (44) (865) 220953
Fax: (44) (865) 69223

Jordanhill College of
Educ.
Southbrae Drive
Glasgow G13 1PP
Psychology Dept.

Keele, Univ. of
Keele
Staffs.
ST5 5BG
Psychology Dept.
Dept. Head: Angus
Gellatly
Phone: (44) (782) 583380
Fax: (44) (782) 613847
Telex: 36113 UNKLIB G
Email: psa31@
uk.ac.keele.seq1

Kent at Canterbury,
Univ. of
Canterbury
Kent CT2 7LZ
Social & App. Psychology
Inst.
Dept. Head: Prof. G. M.
Stephenson
Phone: (44) (227) 764000
Fax: (44) (227) 763674
Email: gms1@ ukc.ac.uk

Kerrier Community
Team
12 Penventon Terr.
Redruth
Cornwall
Psychology Dept.
Dept. Head: Frank Baker
Phone: (44) (209) 219251

**Kidderminster General
Hospital**
Bewdley Rd
Kidderminster
Worcs. DY11 6RJ
Clinical Psychology Dept.

**Kings College Hospital
Med. School**
Denmark Hill
London SE5
*Psychological Medicine,
Dept. of*
Phone: (44) (71) 326 3181
Fax: (44) (71) 326 3445

Kingston Hospital
Wolverton Ave.
Kingston upon Thames
KT2 7QB
Psychology Dept.

Kingston Univ.
Kingston Hill
Kingston-on-Thames
Surrey KT2 7LB
Psychology Dept.
*Formerly: Kingston
Polytechnic*

Knowle Hospital
Fareham PO17 5NA
Psychology Dept.

Lancaster, Univ. of
Bailrigg
Lancaster LA1 4YF
Psychology Dept.
*Dept. Head: Prof. P. E.
Morris*
Phone: (44) (524) 65201
Fax: (44) (524) 841710
Telex: 65111 LANCUL G
Email: psa004@
lancs.cent1.ac.uk

Langdon Hospital
Dawlish, Devon
The Butler Clinic

Larchwood Lodge
Colwell Rd
Haywoods Heath
West Sussex RH16 4EZ
Clinical Psychology Dept.

Le Bas Centre
St Saviours Rd
St Helier
Jersey, Channel Islands
*Clinical Psychology, Dept.
of*
Dept. Head: A. I. Berry
Phone: (44) (534) 89933
Fax: (44) (534) 30353

Lea Castle Hospital
Wolverley, Kidderminster
Worcs. DY10 3PP
Psychology Dept.

**Leeds Metropolitan
Univ.**
Calverley St
Leeds
LS1 3HE
*Health & Social Care,
Fac. of*
Dept. Head: S. Sayers
Phone: (44) (532) 832600
Fax: (44) (532) 833124
*Formerly: Leeds
Polytechnic*

Leeds, Univ. of
15 Hyde Terrace
Leeds
LS2 9LT
Psychology Dept.
*Other Depts: Education;
Management Studies;
Psychiatry*
*Dept. Head: Dr Peter
Davies*
Phone: (44) (532) 335724
Fax: (44) (532) 335749
Telex: 556473 UNILDS G
Email: psc6mtc@
uk.ac.leeds.cmsi

**Leicester General
Hospital**
Hadlay House
Gwendolen Rd
Leicester
*Medical Psychology, Dept.
of*
*Dept. Head: Christine
Cordle*
Phone: (44) (533) 490490

Leicester, Univ. of
Univ. Rd
Leicester
LE1 7RH
Psychology, Dept. of
*Dept. Head: Prof. G. M.
Davies*
Phone: (44) (533) 522170
Fax: (44) (533) 522067
Telex: 347250 LEICUN G

**Leicestershire County
Council**
Collegiate House
College St.
Leicester LE2 0JX
*Educational Psychology
Service*
Dept. Head: John Wallis
Phone: (44) (533) 555051
Fax: (44) (533) 557824

Lennox Castle Hospital
Glasgow G65 7LB
Psychology Dept.

Leverndale Hospital
510 Crookston Rd
Glasgow G53
Psychology Dept.
*Dept. Head: Angus M.
Scott*
Phone: (44) (41) 882 6255
Fax: (44) (41) 882 8086

Lister Hospital
Stevenage Herts.
Clinical Psychology Dept.

**Little Plumstead
Hospital**
Little Plumstead
Norwich
NR13 5EW
Psychology Dept.
Dept. Head: P. E. Morgan
Phone: (44) (603) 713355

**Liverpool City College
of H. E.**
Liverpool Rd
Prescoot L34 1NP
Psychology Dept.

**Liverpool John Moores
Univ.**
Trueman Bldg
15-21 Webster St
Liverpool L3 2ET
Psychology, Centre for
Alex Harrop
Phone: (44) (051) 231
4035
Fax: (44) (051) 709 0172
Formerly: The Liverpool
Polytechnic

Liverpool, Univ. of
POB 147
Liverpool L69 3BX
Psychology Dept.
Other Depts: Clinical
Psychology
Dept. Head: Prof. Andrew
R. Mayes
Phone: (44) (51) 794 2957
Fax: (44) (51) 794 2945
Telex: 627095 UNILPL G

**Llanfrechfa Grange
Hospital**
Cwmbran
Gwent
Psychology Dept.

London Hospital
Eastmount St.
London E1

London Hospital
Medical College
Turner St.
London E1 2AD
Psychiatry Dept.

**London School of
Economics**
Houghton St.
London WC2A 2AE
Social Psychology Dept.
Dept. Head: Prof. Robert
M. Farr
Phone: (44) (71) 955 7712
Fax: (44) (71) 242 0392
Telex: 24655 BLPES G
Email: jackson@
uk.ac.lse.vax

Long Grove Hospital
Horton Lane
Epsom
Surrey KT19 8PU
Psychology Dept.
Other Depts: Regional
Adolescent Unit

**Loughborough Univ. of
Technology**
Loughborough
Leics. LE11 3TU
Social Sciences Dept.
Other Depts: Human
Sciences: Prof. Ken
Eason; Physical
Education & Sports
Sciences: Prof. C.
Williams
Dept. Head: Prof. Peter
Golding
Phone: (44) (509) 223390
Fax: (44) (509) 238277
Telex: 34319

**Luton & Dunstable
Hospital**
Dunstable Rd
Luton
Farringdon Wing

Lynfield Mount Hospital
Heights Lane
Bradford BD9 6DP
Clinical Psychology Dept.

Magee College
Ulster, Univ. of
Northlands Rd
Londonderry BT48 7JL
Occupational Psychology
Dept.
Dept. Head: Prof. Chris
Brotherton
Phone: (44) (504) 265621
Fax: (44) (504) 269800

Magee College
Ulster, Univ. of
Londonderry
Northern Ireland
BT48 7JL
Psychology Dept.
Dept. Head: Prof. Julian
C. Leslie
Phone: (44) (504) 265621
Fax: (44) (504) 260737

Maiden Law Hospital
Lanchester
Co. Durham
DH7 0QM
Clinical Psychology Dept.
Dept. Head: W. M.
Jellema
Phone: (44) (207) 503456

Maindiff Court Hospital
Abergavenny
Gwent
NP7 8NF
Psychology Dept.

**Manchester Area
Health Auth.**
Rusholme Health Centre
Walmer St.
Manchester
M14 5
Clinical Psychology Dept.

Manchester, Inst. of Science & Technology Univ. of (UMIST)
POB 88
Manchester M60 1QD
Occupational / Organ. Psychology
Dept. Head: Prof. Ivan Robertson
Phone: (44) (61) 200 3509
Fax: (44) (61) 200 3505

Manchester Metropolitan Univ.
Hathersage Rd
Manchester M13 0JA
Psychology & Speech Pathology Dept.
Dept. Head: Dr B. Banister
Phone: (44) (61) 247 2591
Fax: (44) (61) 224 0893

Manchester, Univ. of
Psychiatry & Behavioural Science, School of
Withington Hsop.
Manchester M20 0LR
Clinical Psychology, Dept. of
Prof. N. Tarrier
Phone: (44) (61) 447 4058
Fax: (44) (61) 445 9263

Manchester, Univ. of
Oxford Rd
Manchester
M13 9PL
Psychology Dept.
Other Depts: Hester Adrian Research Centre; Education
Dept. Head: Dr Peter Meudell
Phone: (44) (61) 275 2553
Fax: (44) (61) 275 2588
Email: janet@
psy.man.ac.uk

Mapperley Hospital
Nottingham Univ.
Nottingham
NG3 6AA
Psychology Dept. Prof. Unit

Masson House
Pastures Hospital
Mickleover
Derby
DE3 5DO
Psychology Dept.
Dept. Head: Hilary Howell
Phone: (44) (332) 624581

Meanwood Park Hospital
Tongue Lane
Leeds
LS6 4QB
Psychology Dept.
Dept. Head: M. Potts
Phone: (44) (532) 758721
Fax: (44) (532) 745172

Medical Centre
Lordship Lane
London
N17
Child Guidance Clinic

Medical Research Council
17 Gordon St.
London
WC1H 0AH
Cognitive Development Unit
Dept. Head: Prof. John Morton
Phone: (44) (71) 387 4692
Fax: (44) (71) 383 0398
Email: i.morton@
uk.ac.ucl

Memorial Hospital
Hollyhurst Rd
Darlington
Co. Durham DL3 6HX
Psychology, Dept. of
Dept. Head: Charles Burdett
Phone: (44) (325) 743566
Fax: (44) (325) 464037

Mid Wales Hospital
Talgarth
Powys LO3 0DS
Psychology Dept.

Middlesex Hospital
Wolfson Building
Riding House St.
London W1N 8AA
Psychiatry (Medical Psychology), Dept. of
Dept. Head: Dr Stanton Newman
Phone: (44) (071) 380 9475
Fax: (44) (071) 323 1459

Middlesex Univ.
Queensway
Enfield
Middx. EN3 4SF
School of Psychology
Dept. Head: Prof. Elizabeth A. B. Sykes
Phone: (44) (81) 362 5343
Fax: (44) (81) 805 0702
Telex: 8954762
Formerly: Middlesex Polytechnic

Middlewood Hospital
Sheffield 6
MRC Unit

Moorhaven Hospital
Bittaford
Ivybridge
S. Devon PL21 0EX
Psychology Dept.

**MRC Applied
Psychology Unit**
15 Chaucer Rd
Cambridge
CB2 2EF
Other Depts:
Psychophysiology
Section
*Dept. Head: Dr Alan D.
Baddeley*
Phone: (44) (223) 355294
Fax: (44) (223) 359062

**MRC Cognitive
Development Unit**
17 Gordon St
London WC1H 0AII
*Dept. Head: Dr John
Morton*
Phone: (44) (71) 387 4692
Fax: (44) (71) 383 0398

MRC Cyclotron Unit
Hammersmith Hospital
DuCane Rd
London W12 0HS
Phone: (44) (81) 740 3162
Fax: (44) (81) 743 3987

**MRC Inst. of Hearing
Research**
Univ. of Nottingham
University Park
Nottingham
NG7 2RD
Phone: (44) (602) 223431
Fax: (44) (602) 423710

**MRC Social &
Community
Psychiatric Unit**
De Crespigny Park
London
SE5 8AF
*Psychiatry, Inst. of
Dept. Head: Prof. Julian
Leff*
Phone: (44) (71) 703 5411
Fax: (44) (71) 703 0458

**MRC Unit Dev. & Int. of
Behaviour**
Madingley
Cambridge CB3 8AA
*Animal Behaviour
Sub-Dept.
Dept. Head: Dr E. B.
Keverne*
Phone: (44) (954) 210301
Fax: (44) (954) 210247

**Muckamore Abbey
Hospital**
Antrim
Northern Ireland
Psychology Dept.

Napier Univ.
10 Colinton Rd
Edinburgh EH10 5DT
*ISS (Psychology),
Dept. of
Dept. Head: John Troy*
Phone: (44) (31) 455 2522
Fax: (44) (31) 447 0968
Email: peteh@
uk.ac.napier.prime

Napsbury Hospital
London Colney, St Albans
Herts AL2 1AA
Psychology Dept.

National Hospital
2 Wakefield St
London WC1 1PG
Phone: (44) (71) 837 0113
Fax: (44) (71) 713 0861
*College of Speech
Sciences*

National Hospital
Queen Square
London WC1N 3BG
*Psychology Dept.
Dept. Head: Prof.
Elizabeth K. Warrington*
Phone: (44) (71) 837 3611
Fax: (44) (71) 829 8720

**National Temperance
Hospital**
Hampstead Rd
London NW1
*Psychology Dept
Dept. Head: John Cape*

Nene College
Moulton Park
Northampton NN2 7AL
*Psychology Dept.
Dept. Head: Dr Gillian N.
Penny*
Phone: (44) (604) 735500
Fax: (44) (604) 720636

Netherne Hospital
POB 150, Coulsdon
Surrey CR3 1YE
Psychology Dept.

**Neurology &
Neurosurgery, Nat.
Hospital for**
Queens Square
London WC1N 3BG
*MRC Human Movement
& Balance Unit*

New Cross Hospital
Wolverhampton
West Midlands
WV10 0QP
Clinical Psychology Dept.

**New Possibilities NUS
Trust**
Turner Village Hospital
Turner Rd
Colchester CO1 5JP
Dept. Head: Felicity Arrell
Phone: (44) (206) 844840

New Univ. of Ulster
Coleraine
N. Ireland
BT52 1SA
*Psychology Dept.
Other Depts: Education*

Newcastle General Hospital
Westgate Rd
Newcastle NE4 6BE
Sir Martin Roth Young People's Unit
Other Depts: Regional Neuropsychological Ctr.
Dept. Head: Finlay Graham
Phone: (44) (91) 273 0404
Fax: (44) (91) 226 1734

Newcastle Mental Health Trust
St Nicholas Hospital
Jubilee Rd, Gosforth
Newcastle-upon-Tyne
NE3 3XT
Dept. Head: Graham Payne
Phone: (44) (91) 213 0151
Fax: (44) (91) 213 0821

Newcastle-upon-Tyne, Univ. of
Medical School
Framlington Place
Newcastle-upon-Tyne
NE2 4HH
Clinical Psycho-pharmacology Unit
Dept. Head: Dr C.H. Ashton
Phone: (44) (91) 222 6000
Fax: (44) (91) 261 1182

Newcastle-upon-Tyne, Univ. of
Newcastle-upon-Tyne
NE1 7RU
Psychology, Dept. of
Dept. Head: Prof. M. J. Snowling
Phone: (44) (91) 222 6000
Fax: (44) (91) 261 1182
Telex: 53654 UNINEW G
Email: ken.nott@
uk.ac.newcastle

Newton Abbot Hospital
East St.
Newton Abbot, Devon
Psychology Dept.
Dept. Head: Dr Ian Bennon
Phone: (44) (626) 54321

North Devon District Hospital
Raleigh Park, Barnstaple
Devon EX31 4JB
Clinical Psychology, District Dept. of
Dept. Head: Dorothea Hoefert
Phone: (44) (271) 22442
Fax: (44) (271) 75008

North London, Univ. of
Ladbroke House
62-66 Highbury Grove
London N5 2AD
Health Studies, School of
Other Depts: Applied Social Studies
Dept. Head: Susan Pike
Phone: (44) (71) 607 2749
Fax: (44) (71) 753 5166
Telex: (44) (71) 25228
  PNLG
Formerly: The Polytechnic of North London

North Manchester General Hospital
Delauney's Rd
Crumpsall
Manchester M8 6RB
Psychology Dept.

North Wales Hospital
Denbigh
Clwyd LL16 5SS
Psychology Dept.
Dept. Head: Alan Coupar
Phone: (44) (745) 812871

Northowram Hospital
Halifax
W. Yorkshire
HX3 7SW
Clinical Psychology Dept.
Dept. Head: Simon Gelsthorpe
Phone: (44) (422) 201101

Northumberland Health Authority
St George's Hospital
Morpeth
Northumberland
NE62 2NU
District Psychology Service
Dept. Head: Dr Roger Paxton
Phone: (44) (670) 512121
Fax: (44) (670) 511637

Northumbria at Newcastle, Univ. of
Ellison Building
Ellison Place
Newcastle upon Tyne
NE1 8ST
Psychology Divn.
Phone: (44) (91) 232 6002
Fax: (44) (91) 235 8017
Formerly: Newcastle Polytechnic

Nottingham Trent Univ.
Burton St.
Nottingham
Applied Social Studies Dept
Dept. Head: Dr Alex McGlaughlin
Phone: (44) (602) 418418
Fax: (44) (602) 486808
Telex: 377534 POLNOT G
Formerly: Nottingham Polytechnic

Nottingham, Univ. of
Nottingham NG7 2RD
Psychology Dept.
Dept. Head: Prof. C. I.
Howarth
Phone: (44) (602) 484848
Fax: (44) (602) 590339
Telex: 37346 UNINOT G
Email: crd@psyc.nott.ac.uk

Nuffield Clinic
Lipson Rd, Plymouth
Children's Section

Occupational Therapy
College
Victoria Rd, Huyton
Liverpool L36 5SB

Ockenden Hospital
Sth Ockenden, Essex
Psychology Dept.

Open Univ.
Gardiner Building
Milton Keynes MK7 6AA
Psychology Dept.
Dept. Head: Gillian Cohen
Phone: (44) (908) 652962
Fax: (44) (908) 653744
Telex: 825061
Email: gm.cohen@
uk.ac.open.acs.vax

Open Univ. in Wales
24 Cathedral Rd
Cardiff CF1 9SA

Orkney Islands
Authority
Education Dept.
Orkney Islands Council
Kirkwall
Orkney KW15 1NY
Psychological Service
Dept. Head: Peter J.
Shearer
Phone: (44) (856) 873535
Fax: (44) (856) 874615

Oxford Brookes Univ.
Gipsy Lane
Headington
Oxford
OX3 OBP
Psychology Dept.
Dept. Head: Dr G.
Carnibella
Phone: (44) (865) 819770
Fax: (44) (865) 819073

Oxford, Univ. of
Warneford Hospital
Headington
Oxford OX3 7JX
Psychiatry, Dept. of
Other Depts: Pschiatry
Dept.
Dept. Head: Prof. M. G.
Gelder
Phone: (44) (865) 26482
Fax: (44) (865) 793101

Oxford, Univ. of
South Parks Rd
Oxford
OX1 3UD
Exp. Psychology Dept.
Dept. Head: Prof. L.
Weiskrantz
Phone: (44) (865) 271444
Fax: (44) (865) 310447
Email: weiskrantz@
uk.ac.oxford.vax

Paisley, Univ. of
High St.
Paisley PA1 2BE
Applied Social Studies,
Dept. of
Dept. Head: Prof. John
Foster
Phone: (44) (41) 848 3766
Fax: (44) (41) 848 3891
Formerly: Paisley College

Park Day Hospital
Orphan Drive
Liverpool L6 7UN

Park Hospital for
Children
Old Rd, Headington
Oxford OX3 7LQ

Park Lane Hospital
Maghull Lane
Maghull
Liverpool L31 1HW
Psychology Dept.

Park Prewett Hospital
Basingstoke
Hants.
Psychology Dept.

Parkside Hospital
Victoria Rd
Macclesfield
Cheshire
SK10 3JF
Young People's Unit

Pastures Hospital
Mickleover
Derby DE3 5OQ
Psychology Dept.
Phone: (44) (332) 513921

Peterborough District
Hospital
Little Gables
Thorpe Rd, Peterborough
Clinical Psychology Dept.
Dept. Head: Bob George
Phone: (44) (733) 67451

Plymouth, Univ. of
Drake Circus
Plymouth PL4 8AA
Psychology, Dept. of
Dept. Head: Dr Fraser
Reid
Phone: (44) (752) 233157
Fax: (44) (752) 233176
Email: p02108@
uk.ac.psw.pa
Formerly: Polytechnic
South West

Portsmouth, Univ. of
King Charles St.
Portsmouth PO1 2ER
Psychology, Dept. of
Other Depts: Social
Studies
Dept. Head: Prof. Ray Bull
Phone: (44) (705) 827681
Fax: (44) (705) 877155
Formerly: Portsmouth
Polytechnic

Preston Hall
Maidstone
Kent ME20 7NJ
Clinical Psychology, Dept.
of
Dept. Head: John M.
Pinschof
Phone: (44) (622) 710161
Fax: (44) (622) 719802

Prestwich Hospital
Bury New Road, Prestwich
Manchester M25 7BI
Clinical Psychology Dept.

Princess Alexandra
Hospital
Hamstel Rd, Harlow
Essex CM20 1QX
Psychology Dept.

Prudhoe Hospital
Prudhoe,
Northumberland
NE42 5NT
Psychology Dept.

Psychiatry, Inst. of
De Crespigny Park
London SE5 8AF
Psychology Dept.
Dept. Head: Prof. Jeffrey
A. Gray
Phone: (44) (71) 701 7255
Fax: (44) (71) 703 5796
Email: jgray@
uk.ac.lon.psych.uk

Psychological Service,
School of
Liscard Municipal Office
52 Seaview Rd
Wallasey
Merseyside L45 4FY

Queen Elizabeth II
Hospital
East Herts NHS Trust
Howlands
Welwyn Garden City
Herts. AL7 4HQ
Psychology Dept.
Phone: (44) (707) 328111
Fax: (44) (707) 373359

Queen Elizabeth
Psychiatric Hosp, The
Mindelsohn Way
Vincent Drive
Edgbaston
Brimingham
B15 2QZ
Dept. Head: June Brown
Phone: (44) (21) 627 2870
Fax: (44) (21) 627 2970

Queen Margaret College
Clerwood Terrace
Edinburgh EH12 8TS
Manag. & Social Science
Dept.
Dept. Head: Prof. Alistair
Ager (Malawi Univ.)
Phone: (44) (31) 317 3000
Fax: (44) (31) 317 3256

Radcliffe Infirmary
Woodstock Road
Oxford
OX2 6HE
Phone: (44) (865) 224570
Fax: (44) (865) 224303

Rae Hospital
Wroughton
Swindon Wilts.
NPC Princess Alexandra's

Rainhill Hospital
Prescot
Merseyside L35 4PQ
Psychology Dept.
Other Depts: Reg.
Alcoholism Treatment
Unit

Rampton Hospital
Retford
Notts. DN22 0PD
Psychology Dept.
Dept. Head: John E.
Hodge
Phone: (44) (777) 248321
Fax: (44) (777) 248442

Rauceby Hospital
Sleaford
Lincs.
Psychology Dept.

Ravenscraig Hospital
Inverkip Rd
Greenock
PA16 9HA
Dept. Head: David
Martinage
Phone: (44) (475) 33777

Reading, Univ. of
3 Earley Gate
Whiteknights
Reading RG6 2AL
Psychology Dept.
Dept. Head: Prof. R. Davis
Phone: (44) (734) 318529
Fax: (44) (734) 314404
Telex: 847813 RULIB G
Email: sxsmrtin@
uk.ac.rdg.susssysi

Richards Hospital
Chichester Health
Authority
Chichester
West Sussex
PO19 4SE
Clinical Psychology Dept.

**Rivermead
Rehabilitation Ctr.**
Abingdon Rd, Oxford
Phone: (44) (865) 240321
Fax: (44) (865) 200185

**Rochdale Health
Authority**
160 Birch Rd, Rochdale
Lancs. OL16 9QN
Clinical Psychology Dept.

Roehampton Inst.
Digby Stuart College
Roehampton Lane
London SW15 5PH
Psychology, Dept. of
*Dept. Head: Dr Eileen
Pickard*
Phone: (44) (81) 876 8273
Fax: (44) (81) 878 2446

Rosehill Rehab. Unit
Lower Warberg Rd
Torquay
TQ1 1QY
Phone: (44) (803) 291909

Rosslynlee Hospital
Roslin
Midlothian
EH25 9QE

**Rotherham District
Gen. Hospital**
Moorgate Rd
Oakwood
Rotherham S600 2UD
Clinical Psychology Dept.

Royal Albert Hospital
Lancaster LA1 5AJ
Clinical Psychology Dept.

Royal Cornwall Hospital
Treliske, Truro
Cornwall
TR1 3LJ
Social Work Dept.

Royal Cornhill Hospital
Elmhill Hse., Cornhill Rd
Aberdeen AB9 2ZY
Clinical Psychology Dept.
*Dept. Head: J. Stephen
Bell*
Phone: (44) (224) 681818
Fax: (44) (224) 646201

**Royal Devon & Exeter
Hospital**
Barrack Rd
Exeter EX2 5DW
Child Development Centre

**Royal Dundee Liff
Hospital**
Dundee DD2 5NF
Clinical Psychology Dept.

**Royal Edinburgh
Hospital**
Morningside Terrace
Edinburgh EH10 5HF
Clinical Psychology Dept.

Royal Free Hospital
Pond St.
London NW3 2QG
Academic Dept. Psychiatry

**Royal Group of
Hospitals**
Grosvenor Rd
Belfast BT12 6BE
Child Psychiatry Dept.
*Dept. Head: Patricia M.
Donnelly*
Phone: (44) (232) 235340
Fax: (44) (232) 235340

**Royal Hallamshire
Hospital**
Floor O, Glossop Rd
Sheffield S10 2JF
Univ. Psychiatry Dept.
*Dept. Head: Prof. A.
Jenner*
Phone: (44) (742) 766222

**Royal Holloway Univ. of
London, The**
Egham Hill, Egham
Surrey TW20 0EX
Psychology Dept.
*Dept. Head: Prof. Michael
W. Eysenck*
Phone: (44) (784) 443526
Fax: (44) (784) 434347

**Royal Hospital for Sick
Children**
Yorkhill
Glasgow G3 8SJ
*Child & Fam. Psychology
Dept.*

**Royal Liverpool
Hospital**
POB 147
Liverpool L69 3BX
Psychiatry Dept.

**Royal Manchester
Children's Hospital**
Hospital Rd
Pendlebury
Nr. Manchester M27 1HA
The Agnew Unit

**Royal Scottish National
Hospital**
Larbert
Stirlingshire
Area Psychology Services

Royal United Hospital
Combe Park, Bath, Avon
Hillview Psychiatric Unit

**Royal Victoria
Infirmary**
Queen Victoria Rd
Newcastle upon Tyne
NE1 4LP
Clinical Psychology Dept.
Other Depts: Psychiatry
Phone: (44) (91) 232 5131
Fax: (44) (91) 232 1193

Royal Western Counties Hospital
Starcross, Exeter
Devon
EX6 8PU
Clinical Psychology Dept.

Runwell Hospital
Wickford, Essex
Psychology Dept.

Sale & Brooklands Hospital
Charlton Drive, Sale
Cheshire, M33 2BL
Clinical Psychology Dept.

Salford Health Authority
Prestwich Hospital
Bury New Rd
Prestwich
Manchester M25 7BI
Clinical Psychology Dept.
Dept. Head: Alan Tatham
Phone: (44) (61) 773 9121
Fax: (44) (61) 773 8186

Salford, Univ. Coll,
Frederick Rd
Salford M6 6PU
Health Studies, Ctr. for
Dept. Heads: Jeff Lucas
& David Ashcroft
Phone: (44) (61) 736 6541
Fax: (44) (61) 745 8386

School Psychological Service
Avon Approach, Castle St.
Salisbury, Wilts.
Education Dept.

School Psychology Service
Goffs Park House
Horsham Rd,
Crawley
W. Sussex. RH11 8PB

Scunthorpe General Hospital
Cliff Gardens
Scunthorpe
S. Humberside
DN15 7BH
Clinical Psychology Dept.
Dept. Head: Dr B. B. Hart
Phone: (44) (724) 282282
Fax: (44) (724) 282282

Severalls Hospital
NE Essex Mental Health Trust
2 Boxted Rd
Colchester
Essex
CO4 5HG
Psychology Dept.
Dept. Head: David Dickinson
Phone: (44) (206) 852271
Fax: (44) (206) 844435

Sheffield Hallam Univ.
36 Collegiate Crescent
Sheffield
S10 2BP
Cultural Studies, School of
Dept. Head: Peter Hartley
Phone: (44) (742) 532637
Fax: (44) (742) 532430
Telex: 54680 SHPOLY G
Formerly: Sheffield Polytechnic

Sheffield Hallam Univ.
36 Collegiate Crescent
Sheffield
S10 2BP
Health & Community Studies, School of
Dept. Head: John Hattersley
Phone: (44) (742) 532543
Fax: (44) (742) 532430
Telex: 54680 SHPOLY G

Sheffield Health Authority
Argyll Hse, Williamson Rd
Sheffield S11 9AR
Consulting & Clinical Psychology
Other Depts: Area Psychology
Dept. Head: Dr Glenys Parry
Phone: (44) (742) 852222
Fax: (44) (742) 508438

Sheffield, Univ. of
POB 603
Sheffield S10 2TN
Psychology Dept.
Other Depts: Artificial Intelligence Vision Research; MRC/ESCC Social & Applied Psychology: Prof. Peter Warr
Dept. Head: Prof. John P. Frisby
Phone: (44) (742) 768555
Fax: (44) (742) 766515
Email: pclac@
uk.ac.sheffield.primea

Shenley Hospital
Shenley Radlett
Herts. WD7 9HB
Psychology Dept.

Social Paed. & Obst. Res. Unit
64 Oakfield Ave.
Glasgow G12 8LS

South Bank Univ.
Borough Rd
London SE1 0AA
Human & Social Studies Dept.
Phone: (44) (71) 928 8989
Fax: (44) (71) 261 9115
Formerly: South Bank Polytechnic

**South Manchester Univ.
Hospital**
West Didsbury
Manchester M20 8LR
Psychiatry Dept.

South Western Hospital
Landor Rd, London SW4
Psychiatric Day Hospital

**Southampton General
Hospital**
Shirley
Southampton SO9 4XY
Neuropschology, Dept. of
Dept. Head: Dr Narinder
Kapur
Phone: (44) (703) 796576
Fax: (44) (703) 794148

Southampton, Univ. of
Highfieldon
Southampton SO9 5NH
Psychology Dept.
Dept. Head: Prof. A. Gale
Phone: (44) (703) 592612
Fax: (44) (703) 593939

Springfield Hospital
61 Glenburnie Rd
London SW17 7DJ
Psychology Dept.

St Andrew's Hospital
Billing Rd
Northampton NN1 5DG
Occupational Therapy
School
Dept. Head: C. G. Long
Phone: (44) (604) 29696
Fax: (44) (604) 232325

St Andrews, Univ. of
St Andrews, Fife
Scotland KY16 9JU
Psychology, Dept. of
Dept. Head: Dr D. Heeley
Phone: (44) (334) 76161
Fax: (44) (334) 77441

St Ann's Hospital
Portchester Rd
Nottingham
NG3 6LF
Area Psychology Dept.

St Augustine's Hospital
District Psychology
  Service
Chartham
Canterbury
Kent, CT4 7LL
Psychology Dept.
Dept. Head: Dr Simon
Hewson
Phone: (44) (227) 738382
Fax: (44) (227) 730067

St Bernards Hospital
Uxbridge Rd, Southall
Middx.
UB1 3EU

St Clement's Hospital
Foxhall Rd, Ipswich
IP3 8LS
Clinical Psychology
Services
Dept. Head: Clive A. Sims
Phone: (44) (473) 720077

St Clements Hospital
2a Bow Rd
London
E3 4LL

St Crispin's Hospital
Beechwood House
Duston
Northampton NN5 6UN
Area Psychology Dept.

St David's Hospital
Carmarthen
Dyfed SA31 3HB
Psychology Dept.
Dept. Head: Ian C. R.
Taylor
Phone: (44) (267) 237481

**St Edward's
Hospital**
Cheddleton
Leek
Staffs.
ST13 7EB
Clinical Psychology
Dept.
Dept. Head: Edward
John Calvert
Phone: (44) (538) 360421
Fax: (44) (538) 360611

St Francis Hospital
Haywards Heath
West Sussex
Clinical Psychology
Dept.

**St Georges Hospital
Med. School**
London, Univ. of
Cranmer Terrace
London
SW17 0RE
Psychology Dept.
Other Depts: Regional
Forensic Services; Child
Psychiatry
Dept. Head: Prof. Andrew
Steptoe
Phone: (44) (81) 672
  9944
Fax: (44) (81) 767 2741

St James Hospital
Locksway Rd
Milton
Portsmouth PO4 8LD
Psychology Dept.

**St James Univ.
Hospital**
Beckett St.
Leeds
LS9 7TF
Clinical Psychology Dept.
Other Depts: Child
Psychiatry

St John's Hospital at Howden
Howden Rd West
Livingston
West Lothian EH54 6PP
Clinical Psychology Dept.
Dept. Head: Prof.
* Nicholas Emler*
Phone: (44) (382) 307622
Fax: (44) (382) 29993
Email: pc07@uk.ac.
  dundee.primeb.janet

St Lawrence's Hospital
Bodmin, Cornwall
Clinical Psychology Dept.
Dept. Head: Dr Tony
* Wainwright*
Phone: (44) (208) 73281
Fax: (44) (208) 77370

St Lawrence's Hospital
Coulsdon Rd, Caterham
Surrey CR3 5YA
Psychology Dept.

St Luke's Hospital
Crosland Moor
Huddersfield
HD4 5RQ
Clinical Psychology Dept.

St Mary's Hospital
Burghill
Hereford HR4 7RF
Psychology Dept.

St Mary's Hospital
Dean Rd
Scarborough
N. Yorkshire

St Mathew's Hospital
Burntwood
Walsall, W. Midlands
Psychology Dept.
Dept. Head: T. J. Walton
Phone: (44) (543) 685511
Fax: (44) (543) 673860

St Nicholas Hospital
Parkwood House
Gosforth, Newcastle

St Thomas' Hospital
Lambeth Palace Rd
London SE1 7EX
Psychiatry, Divn. of
Phone: (44) (71) 928 9292
Fax: (44) (71) 633 0661

Staffordshire Univ.
College Rd
Stoke on Trent ST4 2DE
Pyschology Divn.
Dept. Head: Dr Marian
* Pitts*
Phone: (44) (782) 744531
Fax: (44) (782) 746553
Formerly: Staffordshire
Polytechnic

Stallington Hospital
Blythe Bridge
Stoke on Trent, Staffs
Clinical Psychology Dept.

Stanley Rd Hospital
H. Gwynne Jones Centre
Aberford Rd
Wakefield, Yorkshire
Clinical Psychology Dept.
Dept. Head: Dr Iain
* Burnside*
Phone: (44) (924) 375217

State Hospital
Carstairs Junction
Lanark ML11 8RP
Clinical Psychology Dept.
Dept. Head: Maureen Y.
* Morison*
Phone: (44) (555) 840293
Fax: (44) (555) 840308

Stepping Hill Hospital
Stockport
Cheshire SK2 7JE
Clinical Psychology Dept.

Stirling, Univ. of
Stirling FK9 4LA
Psychology Dept.
Dept. Head: Prof. Roger
* J. Watt*
Phone: (44) (786) 767640
Fax: (44) (786) 767641

Stone House Hospital
Dartford
Kent DA2 6AU
Psychology Dept.

Stranmillis College
Belfast BT9 5DY
Education Dept.

Strathclyde, Univ. of
Turnbull Building
155 George St.
Glasgow
G1 1RD
Psychology, Dept. of
Dept. Head: Prof. Hugh
* C. Foot*
Phone: (44) (41) 552 6307
Fax: (44) (41) 552 6307
Telex: 77472 UNSLIB G

Stratheden Hospital
Cupar
Fife KY15 5RR
Psychology Dept.

Sulley Hospital
Sully
Sth Glamorgan, Wales

Sunderland, Univ. of
Pasteur Bldg
Chester Rd
Sunderland
SR1 3SD
Psychology Section
Dept. Head: Dr J.L. Smith
Phone: (44) (91) 5152506
Fax: (44) (91) 5152502
Formerly: Sunderland
Polytechnic

Surrey, Univ. of
Guildford
Surrey GU2 5XH
Psychology Dept.
Other Depts: Adult
  Education Dept.
Dept. Head: Prof. Glynis
  Breakwell
Phone: (44) (483) 509175
Fax: (44) (483) 32813
Telex: 859331

Sussex, Univ. of
Brighton BN1 9QH
Cognitive & Computing
  Sciences, School of
Dept. Head: Prof. Gerald
  Gazdar
Phone: (44) (273) 678030

Sussex, Univ. of
Brighton BN1 9QG
Experimental Psychology
  Dept.
Dept. Head: Dr A. J.
  Parkin
Phone: (44) (273) 678058
Fax: (44) (273) 678433
Email: sec@ uk.ac.
  sussex.epvax.janet

Sussex, Univ. of
Brighton BN1 9QN
Psychology Dept.
Dept. Head: Prof. George
  Butterworth
Phone: (44) (273) 606755
Fax: (44) (273) 678534

**Swansea, Univ. College
of**
Singleton Park
Swansea SA2 8PP
Psychology Dept.
Other Depts: Education
Dept. Head: Dr D. J.
  Osborne
Phone: (44) (792) 295281
Fax: (44) (792) 295679

Swinton Hospital
Partington Lane
Swinton
Manchester
M27 3NA
Psychology Dept.

Tamworth Day Hospital
35 Hospital St.
Tamworth
Staffs.
Clinical Psychology Dept.
Dept. Head: Declan
  McNicholl
Phone: (44) (827) 54504

Tavistock Clinic
Tavistock Centre
120 Belsize Lane
London
NW3 5BA
Developmental
  Psychopathology
  Research Unit
Other Depts: Adult;
  Children's
Dept. Head: Prof. R. P.
  Hobson
Phone: (44) (71) 435 7111
Fax: (44) (71) 431 5382

Teeside, Univ. of
Borough Rd
Middlesborough
Cleveland TS1 3BA
Social & Policy Studies
Phone: (44) (642) 342344
Fax: (44) (642) 342067
Formerly: Teeside
  Polytechnic

Thames Valley Univ.
St Mary's Rd
London W5
Psychology Divn.
Phone: (44) (81) 579 5000
Fax: (44) (81) 566 1353
Formerly: Polytechnic of
  West London

**Thomas Coram
Research Unit**
27-28 Woburn Square
London
WC1H OAA
Dept. Head: Prof. Harry
  McGurk
Phone: (44) (71) 612 6927

Towers Hospital
Humberstone
Leicester
Psychology Dept.

Turner Village Hospital
Turner Rd
Colchester
Essex
Psychology Dept.

Uffculme Clinic
Queensbridge Rd
Moseley
Birmingham
B13 8QD
Psychology Dept.

**Ulster at Coleraine,
Univ. of**
Cromore Rd, Coleraine
Co. Londonderry
N. Ireland
BT52 1SA
Psychology Dept.
Dept. Head: Prof. Julian
  C. Leslie
Phone: (44) (265) 44141
Fax: (44) (265) 40904

**Ulster at Coleraine,
Univ. of**
Cromore Rd, Coleraine
Co. Londonderry
N. Ireland
BT52 1SA
Social Psychology Divn.
Dept. Head: Dr R. Wilson
Phone: (44) (265) 44141
Fax: (44) (265) 40904

Ulster at Jordanstown, Univ. of
Shore Rd, Newtownabbey
County Antrim
BT37 0QB
Psychology Dept.
Other Depts:
Occupational
Psychology; Social &
Health Sciences; Social
Skills Centre
Dept. Head: Prof. Julian
C. Leslie
Phone: (44) (232) 363151
Fax: (44) (232) 362806

University College Hospital
115 Gower St.
London
WC1E 6JJ
Medical School

University College London
Gower St.
London WC1E 6BT
Psychology Dept.
Dept. Head: Prof. R. J.
Audley
Phone: (44) (71) 387 7050
Fax: (44) (71) 436 4276
Email: n.preston@
ucl.ac.uk

University Hospital
Floor A South Block
Nottingham NG7 2UH
Psychiatry Dept, Behav.
Science
Dept. Head: Prof. E.
Szabadi
Phone: (44) (602) 709 336
Fax: (44) (602) 790 167

Upton Hospital
Albert St.
Slough SL1 2BJ
Psychology Dept.

UWIST
Llwyn-y-Grant Rd
Penylan
Cardiff CF3 7AW
Applied Psychology Dept.

Victoria Hospital
Blackpool FY3 8NR
Clinical Psychology Dept.

Wales College of Cardiff, Univ. of
POB 901
Cardiff CF1 3YG
Psychology, School of
Dept. Head: Prof. H. D.
Ellis
Phone: (44) (222) 874007
Fax: (44) (222) 874858
Email: ellish@
uk.ac.cardiff

Wales College of Medicine, Univ. of
Heath Park
Cardiff CF4 4XN
Nursing Studies, School
of
Dept. Head: Dr Paul
Morrison
Phone: (44) (222) 743298
Fax: (44) (222) 743298
Email: morrisonpa@
cardiff.ac.uk

Walton Hospital
Chesterfield
North Derbyshire
Psychology Dept.

Warley Hospital
Warley Hill, Brentwood
Essex CM14 5HQ

Warlingham Park Hospital
Warlingham
Surrey CR3 9YR
Psychology Dept.

Warneford Hospital
Headington
Oxford OX3 7JX
Clinical Psychology Dept.
Other Depts: Pschiatry
Dept. Head: Dr John Hall
Phone: (44) (865) 226430
Fax: (44) (865) 226507

Warwick, Univ. of
Coventry CV4 7AL
Psychology Dept.
Dept. Head: Prof. Gregory
V. Jones
Phone: (44) (203) 523096
Fax: (44) (203) 524225

West Cumberland Hospital
Whitehaven
Cumbria CA28 8JG
Clinical Psychology Dept.
Dept. Head: Dr Nigel
Roberts
Phone: (44) (946) 693181

West Dorset Healthcare District
10 Cornwall Rd
Dorchester
Dorset DT1 1RT
Psychology Services
Dept. Head: Peter Daw
Phone: (44) (305) 266011

West London Inst. of Higher Education
Borough Rd
Isleworth TW7 5DU

West of England, Bristol, Univ. of the
Coldharbour Lane
Frenchay, Bristol
Business Studies Dept.
Phone: (44) (272) 656261
Fax: (44) (272) 583758
Formerly: Bristol
Polytechnic

West Park Hospital
Horton Lane, Epsom
Surrey KT19 8PB
Psychology Dept.
Phone: (44) (372) 727811

Westminster, Univ. of
32-8 Wells St.
London W1
Business Studies School
Phone: (44) (71) 580 2020
Fax: (44) (710 436 7367
*Formerly: The Polytechnic
of Central London*

Whitchurch Hospital
Whitchurch
Cardiff
Clinical Psychology Dept.
*Dept. Head: Prof. Ray
Hodgson*
Phone: (44) (222) 521118
Fax: (44) (222) 522161

Whitecroft Hospital
Sandy Lane
Newport
Isle of Wight
Psychology Dept.

Whiteley Wood Clinic
Woodfindin Rd
Sheffield S10
Psychology Dept.

Whittingham Hospital
Preston, Lancs.
Psychology Dept.

Windsor Hospital
Hurworth St
Falkirk
FK1 5EW
Clinical Psychology Dept.

Winsley Hospital
Winsley Hill
Limpley Stoke
Bath BA3 6HF

Winterton Hospital
Sedgefield
Stockton on Tees
Cleveland
TS31 3EJ
Clinical Psychology Dept.
*Dept. Head: Esmé J.
Davies*
Phone: (44) (740) 20521
Fax: (44) (740) 22646

Winwick Hospital
Nr. Warrington
Cheshire WA2 8RR
Psychology Dept.

Withington Hospital
West Didsbury
Manchester M20 8LR
Psychiatry Dept.

Wolverhampton, Univ. of
62-68 Lichfield St
Wolverhampton WV1 1DJ
Health Sciences, School of
*Dept. Head: Dr Kevin
Hogan*
Phone: (44) (902) 28525
Fax: (44) (902) 321161
*Formerly:
Wolverhampton
Polytechnic*

Woodlands Rd Clinic
Middlesbrough TS1 3BL
*Psychology & Counselling
Service*
Dept. Head: R. P. Webster
Phone: (44) (642) 247311

**Wrexham Maelor
Hospital**
Croesnewydd Rd
Wrexham LL13 7TD
Paediatrics, Dept. of
*Dept. Head: Peter L.
Appleton*
Phone: (44) (978) 291100
Fax: (44) (978) 261243

York, Univ. of
Heslington
York
YO1 5DD
Psychology Dept.
*Dept. Head: Prof. Andrew
Ellis*
Phone: (44) (904)
433190
Fax: (44) (904) 433181
Email: lja1@
york.vaxa

UNITED STATES OF
AMERICA

**Abilene Christian
Univ.**
ACU Station
Abilene
Texas 79699
Psychology, Dept. of

Adelphi Univ.
Garden City
New York 11530
Psychology, Dept. of
*Dept. Head: David S.
Gorfein*
Phone: (1) (516)   877
4750
Fax: (1) (516) 877 4191
Email: gorfein@
auvax1.adelphi.edu

**Advanced Study, Inst.
for**
Olden Lane
Princeton
New Jersey 08540
Psychology, Dept. of

Akron, The Univ. of
Akron
Ohio 44325-4301
Psychology, Dept. of
*Dept. Head: Dr Paul E.
Levy*
Phone: (1) (216) 972 7280

Alabama at Birmingham, Univ. of
Univ. Station
Birmingham
Alabama
35294
Psychology, Dept. of
Dept. Head: Carl E. McFarland, Jr.
Phone: (1) (205) 934 3850

Alabama, Univ. of
POB 870348
Tuscaloosa
Alabama
35487-0348
Psychology, Dept. of
Dept. Head: Carl B. Clements
Phone: (1) (205) 348 1913
Fax: (1) (205) 348 8648

Albany, State Univ. of New York
1400 Washington Ave.
Albany
New York 12222
Psychology, Dept. of
Other Depts: Counseling Psychology
Dept. Head: Shirley C. Brown
Phone: (1) (518) 442 4820
Fax: (1) (518) 442 4867

Alcorn State Univ.
Lorman
Mississippi 39096
Psychology, Dept. of

Alfred Adler Inst. of Chicago
618 South Michigan Ave.
Chicago
Illinois 60605
Dept. Head: Mark Stone
Phone: (1) (312) 294 7100

Alfred Univ.
Alfred
New York 14802
Psychology, Dept. of
Dept. Head: Dr Eugene A. Lovelace
Phone: (1) (607) 871 2213
Fax: (1) (607) 871 2342
Email: flovelace@ceramics.bitnet

American Univ.
Washington DC
20016-8062
Psychology, Dept. of
Dept. Head: Carol Weissbrod
Phone: (1) (202) 885 1710

Andrews Univ.
Berrien Springs
Michigan 49104
Psychology, Dept. of

Angelo State Univ.
ASU Station
San Angelo
Texas 76909
Psychology, Dept. of

Arizona State Univ.
Temple
Arizona 85287
Psychology, Dept. of
Dept. Head: J. J. Braun
Phone: (1) (602) 965 3326

Arizona, Univ. of
Psychology Building
Tucson
Arizona 85721
Psychology, Dept. of
Dept. Head: Alfred W. Kaszniak
Phone: (1) (602) 621 7447
Fax: (1) (602) 621 9306
Email: kaszniak@ccit.arizona.edu

Arkansas, Univ. of
216 Memorial Hall
Fayetteville
Arkansas 72701
Psychology, Dept. of
Dept. Head: David A. Schroeder
Phone: (1) (501) 575 4256
Fax: (1) (501) 575 2642

Arts, Univ. of the
Broad & Pine St.s
Philadelphia
Pennsylvania 19102
Psychology, Dept. of

Ashland Univ.
Ashland
Ohio 44805
Psychology, Dept. of

Auburn Univ.
4082 Haley Center
Auburn
Alabama 36849
Psychology, Dept. of
Other Depts: Counseling & Counseling Psychology
Dept. Head: William L. Hopkins
Phone: (1) (205) 826 4412

Austin Peay State Univ.
Clarksville
Tennessee 37044
Psychology, Dept. of
Dept. Head: Stuart B. Bonnington
Phone: (1) (615) 648 7234
Fax: (1) (615) 648 7475
Email: bonningtons@apsu

Baltimore, Univ. of
1420 North Charles St.
Baltimore
Maryland 21201
Psychology, Dept. of

Baruch College
City Univ. of New York
17 Lexington Ave.
New York
10010
Dept. Head: Prof. Walter
Reichman
Phone: (1) (212) 387 1500
Fax: (1) (212) 387 1554

Baylor Univ.
Box 97334
Waco
Texas 76798
Psychology, Dept. of
Dept. Head: Jim H.
Patton
Phone: (1) (817) 755 2961
Fax: (1) (817) 755 2673

Bemidji State Univ.
1500 Birchmont Drive NE
Bemidji
Minnesota 56601-2699
Psychology, Dept. of
Dept. Head: Dr James M.
Rafferty
Phone: (1) (218) 755
2880
Fax: (1) (218) 755 4048

Biola Univ.
13800 Biola Ave.
La Mirada
California 90639
Rosemead School of
Psychology
Dept. Head: Keith
Edwards
Phone: (1) (213) 944 0351

Black Hills State
Univ.
Spearfish
South Dakota 57799
Psychology, Dept. of
Dept. Head: Walt Cook
Phone: (1) (605) 642 6609
Fax: (1) (605) 642 6214

Bloomsburg
Univ.
Bloomsburg
Pennsylvania 17815
Psychology, Dept. of

Boston College
Chestnut Hill
Massachusetts 02167
Counseling,
Developmental
Pyschology & Research
Methods, Dept. of
Dept. Head: Dr Mary E.
Walsh
Phone: (1) (617) 552
4078
Fax: (1) (617) 552 0812
Email: walsh@
bcvms.bitnet

Boston Univ.
147 Bay State Rd
Boston
Massachusetts 02215
Psychology, Dept. of

Bowie State
Univ.
14000 Jericho Park Rd
Bowie
Maryland 20715
Adler-Dreikurs Inst.
Dept. Head: Dr Henry
Ryamond
Phone: (1) (301) 464
7261
Fax: (1) (301) 464 9350

Bowling Green State
Univ.
Bowling Green
Ohio 43403
Psychology, Dept. of
Dept. Head: Charles J.
Cranny
Phone: (1) (419) 372
2031
Fax: (1) (419) 372 6013

Brandeis Univ.
415 South St.
Waltham, Massachusetts
02254-9110
Psychology, Dept. of
Dept. Head: Malcolm
Watson
Phone: (1) (617) 736 3300
Fax: (1) (617) 736 3291
Email: watson@
brandeis.bitnet

Brigham Young Univ.
Provo
Utah 84602
Psychology, Dept. of
Dept. Head: David V.
Stimpson
Phone: (1) (801) 378 4287

Brown Univ.
89 Waterman St.
Providence
Rhode Island 02912
Psychology, Dept. of
Dept. Head: Jack C.
Wright
Phone: (1) (401) 863 2727
Fax: (1) (401) 863 1300

Bryn Mawr College
Bryn Mawr
Pennsylvania 19010
Psychology, Dept. of
Dept. Head: Matthew
Yarczower
Phone: (1) (215) 645 5010

Bucknell Univ.
Lewisburg
Pennsylvania 17837
Psychology, Dept. of
Other Depts: Program in
Animal Behavior
Dept. Head: Douglas
Candland
Phone: (1) (717) 524 1200
Email: dcandlan@
bucknell

California Inst. of Integral Studies
765 Ashbury St.
San Francisco
California 94117
Psychology, Dept. of
Dept. Head: Robert Rosenbaum
Phone: (1) (415) 753 6100
Fax: (1) (415) 759 1169

California School of Professional Psychology: Berkey/Alameda
1005 Atlantic Ave.
Alameda
California 94501
Professional School
Dept. Head: Edward F. Bourg
Phone: (1) (415) 523 2300

California School of Professional Psychology: Fresno
1350 M St.
Fresno
California 93721
Professional School
Dept. Head: W. Gary Cannon
Phone: (1) (209) 486 8420

California School of Professional Psychology: Los Angeles
2335 Beverly Blvd
Los Angeles
California 90057
Professional School
Dept. Head: Connell F. Persico
Phone: (1) (213) 483 7034

California School of Professional Psychology: San Diego
6212 Ferris Square
San Diego
California 92121
Professional School
Dept. Head: Joanne E. Callaghan
Phone: (1) (619) 452 1664

California, Univ. of, Berkeley
Berkeley
California 94720
Psychology, Dept. of
Dept. Head: Ervin Hafter
Phone: (1) (415) 642 1382

California, Univ. of, Davis
152 Young Hall
Davis
California 95616
Psychology, Dept. of
Dept. Head: Prof. Lawrence V. Harper
Phone: (1) (916) 752 0770
Fax: (1) (916) 752 5660

California, Univ. of, Los Angeles
405 Hilgard Ave.
Los Angeles
California 90024-1563
Psychology, Dept. of
Dept. Head: J. Arthur Woodward
Phone: (1) (213) 825 2961

California Univ. of, Pennsylvania
California
Pennsylvania 15419
Psychology, Dept. of

California, Univ. of, Riverside
Riverside
California 92521
Psychology, Dept. of
Dept. Head: Carol Tomlinson-Keasey
Phone: (1) (714) 787 5242

California, Univ. of, San Diego
0109 La Jolla
California 92093
Psychology, Dept. of
Other Depts: Cognitive Science
Dept. Head: Laura E Schreibman
Phone: (1) (619) 534 8557
Fax: (1) (619) 534 7190
Email: pharp@ ucsd.edu

California, Univ. of, Santa Barbara
Santa Barbara
California 93106
Psychology, Dept. of
Dept. Head: Richard E. Mayer
Phone: (1) (805) 961 2858

Callier Center for Comm. Disorders
1966 Inwood Rd, Dallas
Texas 75235-7298
Psychology, Dept. of
Dept. Head: M. Teresa Nezworksi
Phone: (1) (214) 905 3034
Fax: (1) (214) 905 3022

Campbell Univ.
Buie's Creek
North Carolina 27506
Psychology, Dept. of

Capital Univ.
East Main St., Columbus
Ohio 43209

Carnegie Mellon Univ.
5000 Forbes Ave.
Pittsburgh
Pennsylvania 15213
Psychology, Dept. of
Dept. Head: David
Klahr
Phone: (1) (412) 268 3151
Email: klahr@
psy.cmu.edu

Case Western Reserve
Univ.
2040 Adelbert
Cleveland
Ohio 44106
Psychology, Dept. of

Catholic Univ. of
America, The
620 Michigan Ave., N. E.
Washington DC 20064
Psychology, Dept. of
Dept. Head: Dr James H.
Howard
Phone: (1) (202) 319 5750
Fax: (1) (202) 319 6263

Central Florida, Univ.
of
POB 2500
Orlando
Florida 32816
Psychology, Dept. of
Dept. Head: Richard D.
Tucker
Phone: (1) (407) 823 2216

Central Michigan
Univ.
Sloan Hall
Mount Pleasant
Michigan 48859
Psychology, Dept. of
Dept. Head: Michael A.
Kent
Phone: (1) (517) 774 3001
Email: 377cjbb@
cmuvm.bitnet

Central Missouri State
Univ.
Warrensburg
Missouri 64093
Psychology, Dept. of

Central State Univ.
Edmond
Oklahoma 73034
Psychology, Dept. of

Central State Univ.
Wilberforce
Ohio 45384
Psychology, Dept. of

Central Washington
Univ.
Ellensburg
Washington 98926
Psychology, Dept. of

Charleston, Univ. of
2300 MacCorkle Ave. SE
Charleston
West Virginia 25304
Psychology, Dept. of
Dept. Head: Dr Martha
S. Spiker
Phone: (1) (304) 357 4772
Fax: (1) ((304) 357 4715

Cheyney Univ. of
Pennsylvania
Cheyney
Pennsylvania 19319
Psychology, Dept. of

Chicago School of
Professional
Psychology
806 South Plymouth
Court
Chicago
Illinois
60605
Dept. Head: Jeffrey C.
Grip
Phone: (1) (312) 786 9443

Chicago, Univ. of
5835 South Kimbark
Ave.
Chicago, Illinois 60637
Educational &
Developmental
Psychology, Dept. of
Dept. Head: Susan C.
Levine
Phone: (1) (312) 702
1511

Chicago, Univ. of
5848 South University
Ave.
Chicago, Illinois 60637
Psychology, Dept. of
Dept. Head: Thomas R.
Trabasso
Phone: (1) (312) 702
8829
Fax: (1) (312) 702 0886
Email: gwen@cicero.
spc.uchicago.edu

Cincinnati, Univ. of
Mail Location 376
Cincinnati, Ohio 45221
Psychology, Dept. of
Dept. Head: Robert M.
Stutz
Phone: (1) (513) 556 6680
Fax: (1) (513) 556 1907
Email: stutz@
ucbeh.san.uc.edu

Claremont Graduate
School
130 East Ninth St.
Claremont
California 91711
Psychology, Graduate
Dept. of
Dept. Head: Dale E.
Berger
Phone: (1) (714) 621 8084
Fax: (1) (714) 621 8390
Email: cgspsych@
cgsvax.claremont.edu

Clarion Univ. of Pennsylvania
Clarion
Pennsylvania 16214
Psychology, Dept. of

Clark Univ.
950 Main St.
Worcester
Massachusetts 01610
Psychology, Dept. of
Dept. Head: James D.
Laird
Phone: (1) (508) 793 7273
Fax: (1) (508) 793 7780

Clarkson Univ.
Potsdam
New York 13676
Psychology, Dept. of
Dept. Head: Dr A. E.
Linkins
Phone: (1) (315) 268 6544
Fax: (1) (315) 268 6670
Email: biology@ clvm

Clemson Univ.
Clemson
South Carolina 29634
Psychology, Dept. of

Colorado State Univ.
Fort Collins
Colorado 80523
(1) (303) 491 6363
Psychology, Dept. of

Colorado, Univ. of, at Boulder
Muenzinger 244
Box 345, Boulder
Colorado 80309-0345
Psychology, Dept. of
Dept. Head: John S.
Werner
Phone: (1) (303) 492 8662
Fax: (1) (303) 492 2967
Email: info@
  psych.colorado.edu

Columbia Univ.
Morningside Heights
New York NY 10027
Psychology, Dept. of

Connecticut, Univ. of
406 Babbidge Rd, Storrs
Connecticut 06269-1020
Psychology, U-20, Dept. of
Dept. Head: Ronald
Growney
Phone: (1) (203) 486 3515
Fax: (1) (203) 486 2760

Cornell Univ.
Uris Hall
Ithaca, New York 14853
Psychology, Dept. of
Other Depts: Human
Development & Family
Studies; Neurobiology &
Behavior; Cognitive
Studies Program;
Modern Languages &
Linguistics; Industrial
& Labor Relations
Dept. Head: Bruce P.
Halpern
Phone: (1) (607) 255
  3834
Fax: (1) (607)) 255 8433

Corpus Christi State Univ.
6300 Ocean Drive
Corpus Christi
Texas 78412
Psychology, Dept. of

Creighton Univ.
Omaha
Nebraska 68178
Psychology, Dept. of
Dept. Head: Nancy
Walker Perry
Phone: (1) (402) 280 2821
Fax: (1) (402) 280 4748
Email: nperry@
  creighton.edu

Dakota State Univ.
Madison
South Dakota 57042
Psychology, Dept. of

Dakota Wesleyan Univ.
Mitchell
South Dakota 57301-4398
Psychology, Dept. of

Dallas Univ.
1845 E. Northgate Drive
Irving, Texas 75062-4799
Psychology, Dept. of
Dept. Head: Dr Robert
Kugelmann
Phone: (1) (214) 721 5349
Fax: (1) (214) 721 5130

Dartmouth College
Gerry Hall, Hanover
New Hampshire 03755
Psychology, Dept. of
Dept. Head: George
Wolford
Phone: (1) (603) 646 3181

David Lipscomb Univ.
Nashville
Tennessee 37204-3951
Psychology, Dept. of

Dayton, Univ. of
Dayton, Ohio 45469

Delaware, Univ. of
Newark
Delaware 19716-2577
Psychology, Dept. of
Other Depts: Educational
Studies; Individual &
Family Studies;
Business Management
Dept. Head: Ralph V.
Exline
Phone: (1) (302) 831 2271
Fax: (1) (302) 831 3645
Email: ayr00051@
  vm.udel.edu

Delta State Univ.
Cleveland
Mississippi 38733

Denison Univ.
Granville
Ohio 43023-0603
Psychology, Dept. of
Dept. Head: Rita Snyder
Phone: (1) (614) 587 6338
Fax: (1) (614) 587 6417
Email: snyder@
cc.denison.edu

Denver, Univ. of
230 South Gaylord,
Denver
Colorado 80208-0208
Professional Psychology,
School of
Dept. Head: Nelson F.
Jones
Phone: (1) (303) 871 3626

Denver, Univ. of
Univ. Park, Denver
Colorado 80208
Psychology, Dept. of
Dept. Head: Harry Gollob
Phone: (1) (303) 871 2478
Email: hgollob@
denver.du.edu

DePaul Univ.
2219 North Kenmore
Chicago, Illinois 60614
Psychology, Dept. of
Dept. Head: Sheldon
Cotler
Phone: (1) (312) 341 8275

Derner Inst. of
Advanced
Psychological Studies
Garden City
New York 11530
Dept. Head: George
Stricker
Phone: (1) (516) 228 7941

Detroit, Univ. of
4001 West McNichols Rd
Detroit, Michigan 48221
Psychology, Dept. of
Dept. Head: Robert P.
O'Neil
Phone: (1) (313) 927 1267

Dickinson State Univ.
Dickinson, N. Dakota
58601
Education & Psychology,
Divn. of
Dept. Head: Dr Douglas
A. LaPlante
Phone: (1) (701) 227 2151
Fax: (1) (701) 227 2006

Drew Univ.
Madison, NJ 07940
Psychology, Dept. of

Drexel Univ.
32nd & Chestnut St.s
Philadelphia, PA 19104
Psychology, Dept. of
Dept. Head: Charles
Golden
Phone: (1) (215) 895 2455

Duke Univ.
Durham
North Carolina 27706
Psychology, Dept. of
Dept. Head: Gregory R.
Lockhead
Phone: (1) (919) 660 5713
Fax: (1) (919) 660 5726
Email: dgreg@
dukemvs.bitnet

Duquesne Univ.
600 Forbes Ave.
Pittsburgh, PA 15282
Psychology, Dept. of
Dept. Head: Richard T.
Knowles
Phone: (1) (412) 434 6520
Fax: (1) (412) 434 5197

East Carolina Univ.
Greenville
North Carolina 27858
Psychology, Dept. of
Dept. Head: Rand B.
Evans
Phone: (1) (919) 757 6800
Fax: (1) (919) 757 6283
Email: pssmarti@
ecuvm1.bitnet

East Central Univ.
Ada
Oklahoma 74820
Psychology, Dept. of
Dept. Head: Roy T.
Maxwell
Phone: (1) (405) 332 8000

East Tennessee State
Univ.
Johnson City
Tennessee 37614
Psychology, Dept. of
Dept. Head: James S.
Perry
Phone: (1) (615) 929 4424
Fax: (1) (615) 929 5770

East Texas State Univ.
Commerce, Texas 75428
Psychology & Special
Education, Dept. of
Dept. Head: Glenn P.
Fournet
Phone: (1) (903) 886
5597
Fax: (1) (903) 886 5156

Eastern Michigan
Univ.
Ypsilanti
Michigan 48197
Psychology, Dept. of
Dept. Head: Kenneth
Rusiniak
Phone: (1) (313) 487
1155
Fax: (1) (313) 481 1095

Eastern New Mexico Univ.
Portales
New Mexico 88130
Psychology, Dept. of
Dept. Head: David J.
Marx
Phone: (1) (505) 562 2263
Fax: (1) (505) 562 2523

Eastern Washington Univ.
Cheney
Washington 99004
Psychology, Dept. of

Edinboro Univ.
Meadville St. Edinboro
Pennsylvania 16444
Psychology, Dept. of

Emory Univ.
Kilgo Circle
Atlanta
Georgia 30322
Psychology, Dept. of
Dept. Head: Howard A.
Rollins
Phone: (1) (404) 727 7438
Fax: (1) (404) 727 0372
Email: howard@
fsl.psy.emory.edu

Fairleigh Dickinson Univ.
1000 River Rd
Teaneck
New Jersey 07666
Psychology, Dept. of
Dept. Head: Dr Juliana
Lachenmeyer
Phone: (1) (201) 692 2300

Fayetteville State Univ.
1200 Murchison Rd
Fayetteville
North Carolina 28301
Psychology, Dept. of

Ferris State Univ.
901 South State St.
Big Rapids
Michigan 49307
Psychology, Dept. of

Fielding Inst., The
2112 Santa Barbara St.
Santa Barbara
California 93105
Psychology, Dept. of
Dept. Head: Ronald A.
Giannetti
Phone: (1) (805) 687 1099

Findlay, Univ. of
1000 North Main St.
Findlay
Ohio 45840
Psychology, Dept. of

Fisk Univ.
17th Ave. North
Nashville
Tennessee 37208-3051
Psychology, Dept. of
Dept. Head: Carrell P.
Horton
Phone: (1) (615) 329 8610

Florida Atlantic Univ.
Boca Raton
Florida 33431
Psychology, Dept. of
Dept. Head: Ingrid B.
Johnson
Phone: (1) (407) 367
3360

Florida International Univ.
Univ. Park & North
Miami Campuses
Miami
Florida 33199
Psychology, Dept. of
Dept. Head: Paul W. Foos
Phone: (1) (305) 348
2882

Florida State Univ.
Tallahassee
Florida 32306-1051
Psychology, Dept. of
Dept. Head: Dr George E.
Weaver
Phone: (1) (904) 644
2040
Fax: (1) (904) 644 7739
Email: weaver@ f
su.bitnet

Florida, Univ. of
114 Psychology
Building
Gainesville
Florida 32611
Psychology, Dept. of
Dept. Head: Robert D.
Sorkin
Phone: (1) (904) 392
0601
Fax: (1) (904) 392 7985
Email: ufpsych@
nervm.nerdc.ufl.edu

Fordham Univ.
Fordham Rd
Bronx
New York 10458
Psychology, Dept. of
Dept. Head: Dr Nancy A.
Busch-Rossnagel
Phone: (1) (212) 579
2173
Fax: (1) (212) 933 1061
Email: busch@
fordmurh.bitnet

George Mason Univ.
Fairfax
Virginia 22030
Behavioral & Cognitive
Studies, Ctr. for
Dept. Head: Dr Edwin
Fleishman
Phone: (1) (703) 993
1356
Fax: (1) (703) 993 1367

George Mason Univ.
Fairfax, Virginia 22030
Psychology, Dept. of
Dept. Head: Jane M.
Flinn
Phone: (1) (703) 993 1342
Fax: (1) (703) 993 1359

Forest Inst. of
Professional
Psychology: Alabama
2611 Leeman Ferry Rd
Huntsville
Alabama 35801
Programs in Clinical
Psychology
Dept. Head: Dr Edwin E.
Wagner
Phone: (1) (205) 536 9088
Fax: (1) (205) 533 7405

Forest Inst. of
Professional
Psychology: Hawaii
46-005 Kawa St.
Kaneohe
Hawaii 96744
Programs in Clinical
Psychology
Dept. Head: Terri Needels
Phone: (1) (808) 247 2117

Forest Inst. of
Professional
Psychology: Illinois
200 Glendale St., Wheeling
Illinois 60090
Dept. Head: Sandra Stern
Phone: (1) (708) 215 7870

Forest Inst. of
Professional
Psychology: Missouri
1322 South Campbell
Springfield
Missouri 65807
Dept. Head: Richard H.
Cox
Phone: (1) (417) 831 7902

Frostburg State
Univ.
College Ave.
Frostburg
Maryland 21532
Psychology, Dept. of

Fuller Theological
Seminary
180 North Oakland Ave.
Pasadena
California 91101
Psychology, Graduate
School of
Dept. Head: Dr Archibald
D. Hart
Phone: (1) (818) 584 5505
Fax: (1) (818) 584 9630

Furman Univ.
Greenville
South Carolina 29613
Psychology, Dept. of
Dept. Head: Dr Elaine C.
Nocks
Phone: (1) (803) 294 2206
Fax: (1) (803) 294 3001
Email: nocks@
frmnvax1.bitnet

Gannon Univ.
Univ. Square
Erie
Pennsylvania 16541
Psychology, Dept. of

George Peabody
College of Vanderbilt
Univ.
Box 512, Nashville
Tennessee 37203
Psychology & Human
Development, Dept. of
Dept. Head: Howard M.
Sandler
Phone: (1) (615) 322 8141
Fax: (1) (615) 343 9494
Email: campbepw@
vuctrvax

George Washington
Univ.
2125 G St.
Washington DC 20052
Psychology, Dept. of
Dept. Head: Paul J.
Poppen
Phone: (1) (202) 994
6320

Georgetown Univ.
306a White Gravenor
Building
Washington DC 20057
Psychology, Dept. of
Dept. Head: Fr Daniel C.
O'Connell, S. J.
Phone: (1) (202) 687
4042
Fax: (1) (202) 687 6050

Georgia State Univ.
Univ. Plaza
Atlanta
Georgia 30303
Psychology, Dept. of
Dept. Head: Walter F.
Daves
Phone: (1) (404) 651
2456

Georgia, Univ. of
402 Aderhold Hall
Athens
Georgia 30602
Counseling & Human
Development, Dept. of
Dept. Head: Dr Arthur M.
Horne
Phone: (1) (706) 542
1812
Fax: (1) (706) 542 4130
Email: chubert@
uga.cc.edu

Gonzaga Univ.
Spokane
Washington 99258-0001
Psychology, Dept. of

Hahnemann Univ.
Broad & Vine St.s
Philadelphia
Pennsylvania 19102
Mental Health Sciences,
Dept. of
Dept. Head: Leonard R.
Derogatis
Phone: (1) (215) 448 4416

Hamline Univ.
St Paul, Minnesota 55104
Psychology, Dept. of

Hampton Univ.
Hampton
Virginia 23668
Psychology, Dept. of

Hardin-Simmons
Univ.
Drawer A, HSU Station
Abilene, Texas 79698
Psychology, Dept. of

Hartford, Univ. of
Dana Hall
200 Bloomfield Ave
West Hartford
Connecticut 06117
Clinical Psychology, Dept.
of
Dept. Head: Michael D.
Kahn
Phone: (1) (203) 768 4063
Fax: (1) (203) 768 5244

Harvard Univ.
33 Kirkland St.
Cambridge
Massachusetts 02138
Psychology, Dept. of
Dept. Head: Robert
Rosenthal
Phone: (1) (617) 495
3800
Fax: (1) (617) 496 8279
Email: psychair@
harvunxw.bitnet

Hawaii, Univ. of
1776 Univ. Ave.
Honolulu, Hawaii 96822
Educational Psychology,
Dept. of
Dept. Head: Harold I.
Ayabe
Phone: (1) (808) 956
7775
Fax: (1) (808) 956 4114
Email: edpsych@
uhunix.bitnet

Hawaii, Univ. of
2430 Campus Rd
Honolulu
Hawaii 96822
Psychology, Dept. of
Dept. Head: Karl A.
Minke
Phone: (1) (808) 948
8414

Hofstra Univ.
100 Fulton Ave.
Hempstead
Long Island
New York 11550
Psychology, Dept. of
Dept. Head: H. Kassinove
Phone: (1) (516) 463
5624

Houston, Univ. of
4800 Calhoune Rd
Houston, Texas 77004
Psychology, Dept. of
Other Depts: Educational
Psychology
Dept. Head: Richard M.
Rozelle
Phone: (1) (713) 743 8500
Fax: (1) (713) 743 8588

Houston, Univ. of
Victoria
2302-C Red River
Victoria, Texas 77901
Psychology, Dept. of

Houston - Clear Lake,
Univ. of
2700 Bay Area Blvd
Houston
Texas 77058-1098
Psychology, Dept. of
Dept. Head: Dr Tulsi
Saral
Phone: (1) (713) 283 3311
Fax: (1) (713) 488 2408

Howard Payne Univ.
Brownwood, Texas 76801
Psychology, Dept. of

Howard Univ.
520 Bryant St., N. W.
Washington DC 20059
Psychology, Dept. of
Dept. Head: Leslie H.
Hicks
Phone: (1) (202) 636 6805

Hunter College
City Univ. of New York
695 Park Ave.
New York 10021
Biopsychology Doctoral
Program
Dept. Head: Dr H. P.
Zeigler
Phone: (1) (212) 772
5621
Fax: (1) (212) 772 5620

Hunter College
City Univ. of New York
695 Park Ave.
New York 10021
Psychology, Dept. of
Dept. Head: Dr Herbert
Krauss
Phone: (1) (212) 772 5550
Fax: (1) (212) 772 5620

Huron Univ.
Huron
South Dakota 57350
Psychology, Dept. of

**Illinois at Chicago,
Univ. of**
1007 W. Harrison St
Chicago
Illinois 60607-7137
Psychology, Dept. of
Dept. Head: Alexander J.
Rosen
Phone: (1) (312) 996 3036
Fax: (1) (312) 413 4122
Email: u08489@
uicvm.bitnet

**Illinois at
Urbana-Champaign,
Univ. of**
603 East Daniel St.
Champaign
Illinois 61820
Psychology, Dept. of
Dept. Head: Emanuel
Donchin
Phone: (1) (217) 333
0632
Fax: (1) (217) 244 5876
Email: psych@s.psych.
uinc.edu

**Illinois Inst. of
Technology**
IIt Center
LS252
Chicago
Illinois 60616
Psychology, Dept. of
Dept. Head: Glen O. Geist
Phone: (1) (312) 567 3500
Fax: (1) (312) 567 3493

**Illinois School of
Professional
Psychology**
1 Quincey Court Suite
220 South State St.
Chicago
Illinois 60604
Dept. Head: James D.
McHolland
Phone: (1) (312) 341 6500

Illinois State Univ.
Normal
Illinois 61761
Psychology, Dept. of
Dept. Head: Larry A.
Alferink
Phone: (1) (309) 438 8651
Fax: (1) (309) 438 5789
Email: laalferi@
ilstu.bitnet

Indiana State Univ.
Root Hall
Terre Haute
Indiana 47809
Psychology, Dept. of
Dept. Head: Virginia E.
O'Leary
Phone: (1) (812) 237 2445

Indiana Univ.
Bloomington
Indiana 47405
Psychology, Dept. of
Dept. Head: Margaret J.
Intons-Peterson
Phone: (1) (812) 855
3991
Fax: (1) (812) 855 4691
Email: intons@
iubac.bitnet

**Indiana Univ. of
Pennsylvania**
Clark Hall
Indiana
Pennsylvania 15705
Psychology, Dept. of
Dept. Head: Carl
Schneider
Phone: (1) (412) 357 4519

Iowa State Univ.
Lagomarcino Hall
Ames
Iowa 50011
Psychology, Dept. of
Dept. Head: Gary Wells
Phone: (1) (515) 294 1742

Iowa, The Univ. of
11 Seashore Hall E
Iowa City, IA 52242-1407
Psychology, Dept. of
Dept. Head: James V.
Hinrichs
Phone: (1) (319) 335 2406
Fax: (1) (319) 335 2507
Email: james-hinrichs@
uiowa.edu

Iowa, The Univ. of
338 Lindquist Ctr N
Iowa City
IA 52242-1529
Counselor Education,
Divn. of
Dept. Head: E. Richard
Dustin
Phone: (1) (319) 335 5275

Iowa, The Univ. of
361 Lindquist Ctr N
Iowa City, IA 52242-1529
Psychological &
Quantitive Foundations,
Divn. of
Dept. Head: Leonard S.
Feldt
Phone: (1) (319) 335 5577

Jackson State Univ.
1400 JR Lynch St.
Jackson
Mississippi 39217
Psychology, Dept. of
Dept. Head: Shih-sung
Wen
Phone: (1) (601) 968 2371

John Carroll Univ.
Cleveland
Ohio 44118
Psychology, Dept. of
Dept. Head: Dr Nicholas
S. DiCaprio
Phone: (1) (216) 397 4355
Email: dicaprio@
jcvaxa.bitnet

Johns Hopkins Univ.
Baltimore
Maryland 21218
Psychology, Dept. of
Dept. Head: Howard
Egeth
Phone: (1) (410) 516
6175
Fax: (1) (410) 516 4478
Email: psych@ jhuvm

Johns Hopkins Univ.
Baltimore
Maryland 21218
Cognitive Science, Dept. of
Dept. Head: Alfonso
Caramazza
Phone: (1) (410) 516
5250
Fax: (1) (410) 516 5200
Email: caram@
broca.cog.jhu.edu

Kansas State Univ.
Bluemont Hall
Manhattan
Kansas 66506
Psychology, Dept. of
Dept. Head: Frank E.
Saal
Phone: (1) (913 532
6850
Fax: (1) (913) 532 7004

Kansas, Univ. of
426 Fraser Hall
Lawrence
Kansas 66045
Psychology, Dept. of
Phone: (1) (913) 864
4131

Kent State Univ.
Kent
Ohio 44242
Psychology, Dept. of
Dept. Head: Jack Graham
Phone: (1) (216) 672 2 167
Fax: (1) (216) 672 3786

Kentucky, Univ. of
Kastle Hall
Lexington
Kentucky 40506
Psychology,
Dept. of
Dept. Head: Arthur J.
Nonneman
Phone: (1) (606) 257
5662

La Salle Univ.
20th & Olney Ave.s
Philadelphia
Pennsylvania 19141
Psychology, Dept. of
Dept. Head: David J.
Falcone
Phone: (1) (215) 951
1270
Email: falcone@
lasalle.edu

Lamar Univ.
POB 10036
Beaumont
Texas 77710
Psychology, Dept. of
Dept. Head: Ricchard G.
Marriott
Phone: (1) (409) 880
8285

Langston Univ.
Langston
Oklahoma 73050
Psychology, Dept. of
Dept. Head: Dr Albert
Appiah
Phone: (1) (405) 466
3383
Fax: (1) (405) 466 3271

Laredo State Univ.
1 West End Washington
St.
Laredo
Texas 78040-9960
Psychology, Dept. of

Lawrence Univ.
Appleton
Wisconsin 54912
Psychology, Dept. of
Dept. Head: Peter Glick
Phone: (1) (414) 832 6739
Fax: (1) (414) 832 6962
Email: glick@
lawrence.bitnet

Lee Edward Travis Inst.
for Biopsychosocial
Research
180 North Oakland Ave.
Pasadena
CA 91101
Dept. Head: Dr Warren S.
Brown
Phone: (1) (818) 584 5538
Fax: (1) (818) 584 9630

Lehigh Univ.
Bethlehem
Pennsylvania 18015
Psychology, Dept. of
Dept. Head: Dr John G.
Nyby
Phone: (1) (215) 758 3630
Email: jgn2@ lehigh.edu

Lincoln Memorial Univ.
Harrogate
Tennessee 37752
Psychology, Dept. of

Lincoln Univ.
Jefferson City
Missouri 65101
Psychology, Dept. of

Lock Haven Univ. of
Pennsylvania
Lock Haven
Pennsylvania 17745
Psychology, Dept. of
Dept. Head: Mark D.
Cloud
Phone: (1) (717) 893 2221
Fax: (1) (717) 893 2201

Long Island Univ.
C. W. Post Campus
Brookville
Long Island
New York 11548
Psychology, Dept. of
Dept. Head: Dr Sherman
Tatz
Phone: (1) (516) 299 2377

**Long Island Univ.,
Brooklyn Center**
Univ. Plaza
Brooklyn
New York 11201
Psychology, Dept. of
Dept. Head: Gary Kose
Phone: (1) (718) 403 1068

Louisiana State Univ.
Audubon Hall
Baton Rouge
Louisiana 70803
Psychology, Dept. of
Dept. Head: Irving M.
Lane
Phone: (1) (504) 388 8745

Louisville, Univ. of
Louisville
Kentucky 40292
Psychology, Dept. of
Dept. Head: James M.
Driscoll
Phone: (1) (502) 588 6775

Lowell, Univ. of
1 Univ. Ave. Lowell
Massachusetts 01854
Psychology, Dept. of

**Loyola Univ. of
Chicago**
6525 North Sheridan Rd
Chicago
Illinois 60626
Psychology, Dept. of
Dept. Head: Jill N. Reich
Phone: (1) (312) 508 3002

Maine, Univ. of
301 LIttle Hall
Orono, Maine 04469
Psychology, Dept. of
Dept. Head: Gordon E.
Kulberg
Phone: (1) (207) 581
2033
Fax: (1) (207) 581 1953
Email: kulberg@
maine

Mankato State Univ.
Mankato
Minnesota 56002-8400
Psychology, Dept. of
Dept. Head: Dr Kenneth
J. Good
Phone: (1) (507) 389
2724
Fax: (1) (507) 389 2980
Email: kjgood@ msus1

Mansfield Univ.
Mansfield
Pennsylvania 16933
Psychology, Dept. of
Dept. Head: Peter A.
Keller
Phone: (1) (717) 662
4770
Fax: (1) (717) 662 4112

Marshall Univ.
Huntington
West Virginia 25701
Psychology, Dept. of

**Maryland Baltimore
County, Univ. of**
5401 Wilkens Ave.
Baltimore
Maryland 21228
Psychology, Dept. of
Dept. Head: Leon H. Levy
Phone: (1) (410) 455
2567
Fax: (1) (410) 455 1055
Email: levy@ umbc

**Maryland System, Univ.
of**
3300 Metzerott Rd
Adelphi, Maryland 20783
Psychology, Dept. of
Dept. Head: Barry D.
Smith
Phone: (1) (301) 405 5862
Fax: (1) (301) 314 9566
Email: smith@
bss3.umd.edu

Maryland, Univ. of
College Park
Maryland 20742
Dept. Head: Irwin L.
Goldstein
Phone: (1) (301) 454 6964

**Massachusetts Inst. of
Technology**
Cambridge
Massachusetts 02139
Brain & Cognitive
Science, Dept. of
Dept. Head: Alan Hein
Phone: (1) (617) 253 0482
Fax: (1) (617) 253 9767
Email: ren@
psyche.mit.edu

Massachusetts, Univ. of
Harbor Campus Boston
Massachusetts 02125
Psychology, Dept. of
Dept. Head: James F.
Brennan
Phone: (1) (617) 929 8218

Massachusetts, Univ. of
Tobin Hall, Amherst
Massachusetts 01003
Psychology, Dept. of
Dept. Head: Charles
Clifton
Phone: (1) (413) 545 2383
Fax: (1) (413) 545 0996
Email: cec@
titan.ucc.umass.edu

McMurry Univ.
Box 86, McMurry Station
Abilene
Texas 79697
Psychology, Dept. of
Dept. Head: Dr Charles
W. Hennig
Phone: (1) (915) 691 6348

Memphis State Univ.
Memphis
Tennessee 38152
Psychology, Dept. of
Dept. Head: Dr Andrew
Meyers
Phone: (1) (901) 678
2146
Fax: (1) (901) 678 2579

Mental Health
Research Inst.
205 Zina Pitcher Place
Ann Arbour
Michigan 48109-0720
Dept. Head: Dr Bernard
Agranoff
Phone: (1) (313) 764 4130

Miami Univ.
Oxford
Ohio 45056
Psychology, Dept. of
Dept. Head: Phillip J.
Best
Phone: (1) (513) 529 2400
Fax: (1) (513) 529 2420
Email: pjbest@
miamiu.edu

Miami, Univ. of
POB 248185
Coral Gables
Florida 33124
Psychology, Dept. of
Dept. Head: A. Rodney
Wellens
Phone: (1) (305) 284 2814
Fax: (1) (305) 284 3402
Email: rwellens@ umiami

Michigan State Univ.
East Lansing
Michigan 48824
Psychology, Dept. of
Dept. Head: Gordon Wood
Phone: (1) (517) 353 9561
Fax: (1) (517) 336 2476
Email: 22497gw@
msu.bitnet

Michigan Tech. Univ.
Houghton
Michigan 49931
Psychology, Dept. of

Michigan, Univ. of
580 Union Drive
Ann Arbour
Michigan 48109-1346
Psychology, Dept. of
Dept. Head: Prof.
Patricia Gurin
Phone: (1) (313) 764 7429
Fax: (1) (313) 764 3520
Email: userk7av@
umichum

Middle Tennessee State
Univ.
Murfreesboro
Tennessee 37132
Psychology, Dept. of
Dept. Head: Larry W.
Morris
Phone: (1) (615) 898 2706

Midwestern State Univ.
3400 Taft Blvd
Wichita Falls
Texas 76308
Psychology, Dept. of
Dept. Head: Dr George M.
Diekhoff
Phone: (1) (817) 692 6611

Millersville Univ. of
Pennsylvania
Millersville, PA17551
Psychology, Dept. of

Minnesota School of
Professional
Psychology
1313 SE Fifth St.
Minneapolis
Minnesota 55414
Dept. Head: R. Paul Olson
Phone: (1) (612) 623 1811

Minnesota State Univ.
System
230 Park Office Building
555 Park St.
St Paul, Minnesota 55103
Psychology, Dept. of

Minnesota, Univ. of
Crookston
Minnesota 56716
Psychology, Dept. of

Minnesota, Univ. of
Morris
Minnesota 56267
Psychology, Dept. of
Dept. Head: Eric Klinger
Phone: (1) (612) 589 6200
Fax: (1) (612) 589 3811
Email: klinger@
umnmor.bitnet

Minnesota, Univ. of
N218 Elliott Hall
75 East River Rd
Minneapolis
Minnesota 55455
Psychology, Dept. of
Dept. Head: Thomas J.
Bouchard
Phone: (1) (612) 625 8520

Minnesota, Univ. of
Waseca, Minnesota 56093
Psychology, Dept. of

Minot State Univ.
Minot
North Dakota 58701
Psychology, Dept. of

Mississippi State Univ.
Mississippi 39762
Psychology, Dept. of
Dept. Head: Stephen B.
Klein
Phone: (1) (601) 325
3202
Fax: (1) (601) 325 3299

Mississippi, Univ. of
Lafayette Co.
Mississippi 38677
Psychology, Dept. of
Dept. Head: David S.
Hargrove
Phone: (1) (601) 232 7383
Fax: (1) (601) 232 7010

Mississippi Valley State
Univ.
Itta Bena
Mississippi 38941
Psychology, Dept. of

Mississippi, Women's
Univ.
Columbus
Mississippi 39701
Psychology, Dept. of

Missouri, Univ. of
Columbia
Missouri 65211
Psychology, Dept. of
Dept. Head: Tom Di
Lorenzo
Phone: (1) (314) 882
6860
Fax: (1) (314) 882 7710
Email: psyhigh@ umcvmb

Missouri, Univ. of
5100 Rockhill Rd
Kansas City
Missouri 64110
Psychology, Dept. of
Dept. Head: James F.
Collins
Phone: (1) (816) 235 1321

Missouri, Univ. of
Rolla
Missouri 65401
Psychology, Dept. of
Dept. Head: Ronald T.
Kellogg
Phone: (1) (314) 341
4937
Fax: (1) (314) 341 6127
Email: kellogg@
umrvmb.umr.edu.bitnet

Missouri, Univ. of
8001 Natural Bridge Rd
St Louis
Missouri 63121
Psychology, Dept. of
Dept. Head: Gary K.
Burger
Phone: (1) (314) 553
5391
Fax: (1) (314) 553 5378

Montana State Univ.
Bozeman
Montana 59717
Psychology, Dept. of
Dept. Head: Richard A.
Block
Phone: (1) (406) 994
3801
Fax: (1) (406) 994 2893
Email: upyra@
mtsunixl.bitnet

Montana, Univ. of
Missoula
Montana 59812
Psychology, Dept. of
Dept. Head: Lawrence H.
Berger
Phone: (1) (406) 243 4521

Morgan State Univ.
Hillen Rd & Coldspring
Lane
Baltimore
Maryland 21239
Psychology, Dept. of

Nebraska at Lincoln,
Univ. of
209 Burnett Hall
Lincoln
Nebraska 68583-0745
Psychology, Dept. of
Dept. Head: John J.
Berman
Phone: (1) (402) 472 3721

Nebraska, Univ. of
42nd & Dewey Ave.
Omaha
Nebraska 68105-5577
Psychology, Dept. of
Dept. Head: Timothy
Jeffrey
Phone: (1) (402) 559 5031

Nebraska at Omaha,
Univ. of
Omaha, Nebraska 68182
Psychology, Dept. of
Dept. Head: Kenneth A.
Deffenbacher
Phone: (1) (402) 554 2592

Nebraska Wesleyan
Univ.
5000 St Paul Ave.
Lincoln
Nebraska 68504-2796
Psychology, Dept. of

Nevada, Univ. of
4505 Maryland Parkway
Las Vegas
Nevada 89154
Psychology, Dept. of

Nevada, Univ. of
Reno, Nevada 89557
Psychology, Dept. of
Dept. Head: G. P.
Ginsburg
Phone: (1) (702) 784 6828
Fax: (1) (702) 784 1300
Email: gpg@
unssun.nevada.edu

New Hampshire, Univ. of
Conant Hall, Durham
New Hampshire 03824
Psychology, Dept. of
Dept. Head: Victor A.
Benassi
Phone: (1) (603) 862
2369

New Mexico Highlands Univ.
Las Vegas
New Mexico 87701
Psychology, Dept. of
Dept. Head: Carlton H.
Cann
Phone: (1) (505) 454
3343
Fax: (1) (505) 454 0026

New Mexico State Univ.
Box 3452
Las Cruces
New Mexico 88003
Psychology, Dept. of
Phone: (1) (505) 646 2502

New Mexico, Univ. of
Logan Hall
Albuquerque
New Mexico 87131-1161
Psychology, Dept. of
Dept. Head: William C.
Gordon
Phone: (1) (505) 277
4121
Fax: (1) (505) 277 1394

New Orleans, Univ. of
Lakefront
New Orleans
Louisiana 70148
Psychology, Dept. of
Dept. Head: Sarah Moody
Thomas
Phone: (1) (504) 286 6291
Fax: (1) (504) 286 6049

New School for Social Research
65 Fifth Ave.
New York 10003
Psychology, Dept. of
Dept. Head: Henri Zukier
Phone: (1) (212) 741 5727

New York, City Univ. of
535 East 80th St.
New York NY 10021
Psychology, Dept. of

New York: Brooklyn College, City Univ. of
Bedford Ave.
Brooklyn, New York
11210
Psychology, Dept. of
Dept. Head: Ching Tse Lee
Phone: (1) (718) 780 5601

New York: City College, City Univ. of
138th St. & Convent Ave.
New York 10031
Psychology, Dept. of
Dept. Head: William
Crain
Phone: (1) (212)690 5442

New York at Binghamton, State Univ. of
Binghamton
New York 13901
Psychology, Dept. of
Dept. Head: Raymond A.
Romanzyk
Phone: (1) (607) 777 2449

New York at Buffalo, State Univ. of
Park Hall, Buffalo
New York 14260
Psychology, Dept. of
Dept. Head: J. Sidney
Shrauger
Phone: (1) (716) 636 3650

New York at Stony Brook, State Univ. of
New York 11794
Psychology, Dept. of
Dept. Head: Edward S.
Katkin
Phone: (1) (516) 632 7800

New York Univ.
6 Washington Place
New York NY 10003
Psychology, Dept. of
Dept. Head: Martin L.
Hoffman
Phone: (1) (212) 998 7900
Fax: (1) (212) 995 4018

New York Univ., School of Education, Health, Nursing, & Arts Professions
239 Greene St.
New York 10003
Applied Psychological
Studies, Dept. of
Dept. Head: Cynthia
Deutsch
Phone: (1) (212) 998 5555

Noncompliance Inst. of Los Angeles
6411 W. Fifth St.
POB 48555
Los Angeles
California 90048
Dept. Head: Dr Raymond
A. Ulmer
Phone: (1) (213) 553 7387
Fax: (1) (213) 651 4102

North Carolina at Chapel Hill, Univ. of
Davie Hall 013A
Chapel Hill
North Carolina 27514
Psychology, Dept. of
Dept. Head: M. David
Galinsky
Phone: (1) (919) 962 2053

North Carolina at Greensboro, Univ. of
296 Eberhart Building
Greensboro
North Carolina 27412
Psychology, Dept. of
Dept. Head: Walter L. Salinger
Phone: (1) (919) 334 5013
Fax: (1) (919) 334 5066
Email: psychdep@ steffi.uncg.edu.internet

North Carolina State Univ.
640 Poe Hall
Box 7801, Raleigh
North Carolina 27695
Psychology, Dept. of
Dept. Head: David W. Martin
Phone: (1) (919) 515 2251
Fax: (1) (919) 515 7634
Email: martin@ poe.coe.ncsu.edu

North Carolina, Univ. of
Charlotte
North Carolina 28223
Psychology, Dept. of
Phone: (1) (704) 547 4731
Fax: (1) (704) 547 3091
Email: fpy.pwf@ unccvm

North Carolina, Univ. of
Wilmington
North Carolina 28403-3297
Psychology, Dept. of

North Dakota State Univ.
Fargo, N.Dakota 58105
Psychology, Dept. of
Dept. Head: Ruth H. Maki
Phone: (1) (701) 237 8622
Fax: (1) (701) 237 7138
Email: nuo19414@ ndsu.umi

North Dakota, Univ. of
Box 7187, Univ. Station
Grand Forks
North Dakota 58201
Psychology, Dept. of
Dept. Head: Mark Grabe
Phone: (1) (701) 777 3451
Fax: (1) (701) 777 3650
Email: grabe@ ndsuvm1

North Texas, Univ. of
Box 13587
Denton
Texas 76203
Psychology, Dept. of
Dept. Head: Russell D. Clark
Phone: (1) (817) 565 2637

Northeast Missouri State Univ.
Kirksville
Missouri 63501
Psychology, Dept. of

Northeastern State Univ.
Tahlequah
Oklahoma 74464
Psychology, Dept. of
Other Depts: Counseling Psychology
Dept. Head: Dr Bill Schiller
Phone: (1) (918) 456 5511
Fax: (1) (918) 458 2193

Northeastern Univ.
360 Huntington Ave.
Boston
Massachusetts 02115
Psychology, Dept. of
Dept. Head: Leon J. Kamin
Phone: (1) (617) 437 3076
Fax: (1) (617) 437 8714
Email: kamin@ northeastern.edu

Northern Illinois Univ.
DeKalb
Illinois 60115
Psychology, Dept. of
Dept. Head: Frederick M. Schwantes
Phone: (1) (815) 753 0372
Fax: (1) (815) 753 8088

Northern Michigan Univ.
Marquette
Michigan 49855
Psychology, Dept. of
Dept. Head: Pryse H. Duerfeldt
Phone: (1) (906) 227 2935
Fax: (1) (906) 227 2204

Northwest Missouri State Univ.
Maryville, Missouri

Northwestern State Univ.
Alva, Oklahoma 73717

Northwestern Univ.
102 Swift Hall
2029 Sheridan Rd
Evanston
Illinois 60208-2710
Psychology, Dept. of
Dept. Head: William Revelle
Phone: (1) (708) 491 5190
Fax: (1) (708) 491 7859
Email: psych@ nwu.edu

Northwestern Univ.
1890 Maple Ave.
Evanston
Illinois 60208-2710
Learning Sciences Inst.
Dept. Head: Roger C. Schank
Phone: (1) (708) 491 3500
Fax: (1) (708) 491 5258

Northwestern Univ.
Evanston
Illinois 60208-2710
Organization Behavior
Dept.
Dept. Head: Joseph S.
Moag
Phone: (1) (708) 491 3470
Fax: (1) (708) 491 8896

Norwich Univ.
Northfield, Vermont
Psychology, Dept. of

Notre Dame, Univ. of
Notre Dame
Indiana 46556
Psychology, Dept. of
Dept. Head: Naomi M.
Meara
Phone: (1) (219) 239 6659

Nova Univ.
3301 College Ave.
Fort Lauderdale
Florida 33314
Psychology, School of
Dept. Head: Frank A.
DePiano
Phone: (1) (305) 475 7550

Oakland Univ.
Rochester
Michigan 48309-4401
Psychology, Dept. of
Dept. Head: Lawrence
Lilliston
Phone: (1) (313) 370 2300
Fax: (1) (313) 370 2286
Email: lillisto@ vela.
acs.oakland.edu

Ohio Northern Univ.
Ada, Ohio 45810

Ohio State Univ.
190 North Oval Mall
Columbus, Ohio 43210
Psychology, Dept. of

Ohio Univ.
Athens
Ohio 45701
Psychology, Dept. of
Dept. Head: Gary M.
Schumacher
Phone: (1) (614) 593
1086
Email: schumach@
ouaccvmb.bitnet

Ohio Wesleyan Univ.
Delaware
Ohio 43015
Psychology, Dept. of

Oklahoma Baptist
Univ.
Shawnee
Oklahoma 74801
Psychology, Dept. of

Oklahoma City
Univ.
2501 North Blackwelder
Oklahoma City
Oklahoma 73106
Psychology, Dept. of
Dept. Head: Dr Dennis
Jowaisas
Phone: (1) (405) 521
5321
Fax: (1) (405) 521 5264

Oklahoma Panhandle
State Univ.
Goodwell
Oklahoma 73939
Psychology, Dept. of

Oklahoma State Univ.
Stillwater
Oklahoma 74078
Psychology, Dept. of
Dept. Head: Dr Vicki
Green
Phone: (1) (405) 744
7054
Fax: (1) (405) 744 7074

Oklahoma,
Univ. of
455 West Lindsey
Norman
Oklahoma 73019
Psychology, Dept. of
Dept. Head: Alan
Nicewander
Phone: (1) (405) 325
4511

Oklahoma,
Univ. of
College of
Education
820 Van Vleet Oval
Norman
Oklahoma 73019
Educational
Psychology,
Dept. of
Dept. Head: Cal D.
Stoltenberg
Phone: (1) (405) 325
5974

Oklahoma Univ. of
Science & Arts
Chickasha
Oklahoma 73018
Psychology, Dept. of

Old Dominion
Univ.
Norfolk
Virginia 23529
Psychology, Dept. of
Dept. Head: Peter
Mikulka
Phone: (1) (804) 683
4440
Fax: (1) (804) 683
5087

Oral Roberts Univ.
7777 South Lewis
Tulsa
Oklahoma 74171
Psychology, Dept. of

Oregon Health Sciences Univ.
3181 SW Sam Jackson
  Park Rd, Portland
Oregon 97201-3098
Medical Psychology, Dept. of
Dept. Head: Joseph D. Matarazzo
Phone: (1) (503) 494 8644
Fax: (1) (503) 494 5972

Oregon State Univ.
Corvallis
Oregon 97331
Psychology, Dept. of
Dept. Head: Dr Dale D. Simmons
Phone: (1) (503) 737 2311
Fax: (1) (503) 737 2434
Email: psy%ccmail@
  ucs.orst.edu

Oregon, Univ. of
Eugene
Oregon 97403
Psychology, Dept. of
Dept. Head: Steven W. Keele
Phone: (1) (503) 346 4921
Fax: (1) (503) 346 4911

Our Lady of the Lake Univ.
411 SW 24th St.
San Antonio
Texas 78207-4666
Psychology, Dept. of

Pace Univ.
Pace Plaza
New York
NY 10038
Psychology, Dept. of
Dept. Head: Dr Florence L. Denmark
Phone: (1) (212) 346 1506
Fax: (1) (212) 346 1506
Email: denmark@ pacevm

Pacific Graduate School of Psychology
935 East Meadow
Palo Alto
California 94303
Clinical Psychology, Dept. of
Dept. Head: Roger L. Greene
Phone: (1) (415) 494 7477
Fax: (1) (415) 856 6734

Pacific Lutheran Univ.
Tacoma
Washington 98447
Psychology, Dept. of
Dept. Head: R. Michael Brown
Phone: (1) (206) 535 7294

Pacific Univ.
College Way, Forest
  Grove
Oregon 97116
Psychology, Dept. of
Dept. Head: Patrick W. Conway
Phone: (1) (503) 357 6151
Fax: (1) (503) 359 2242

Pembroke State Univ.
Pembroke
North Carolina 28372

Pennsylvania State Univ.
104 Cedar Building
Univ. Park
Pennsylvania 16802
Psychology, Dept. of
Dept. Head: Joseph L. French
Phone: (1) (814) 865 1881

Pennsylvania, Univ. of
Philadelphia
Pennsylvania 19104
Psychology, Dept. of
Dept. Head: Dr John Sabini
Phone: (1) (215) 898 7300
Fax: (1) (215) 898 7301

Pepperdine Univ.
400 Corporate Pointe
Cluver Cty, Calfornia
  90230
Psychology, Dept. of
Dept. Head: Jim Hedstrom
Phone: (1) (213) 568 5606

Phillips Univ.
Enid
Oklahoma 73702
Psychology, Dept. of

Pittsburgh, Univ. of
3939 O'Hara St.
Pittsburgh
Pennsylvania
  15260-0001
Learning, Research & Development Center
Dept. Head: Lauren Resnick
Phone: (1) (412) 624 4501
Fax: (1) (412) 624 4428
Email: resnick@
  pittvms.bitnet

Pittsburgh, Univ. of
Fifth Ave. & Ruskin Ave.
Pittsburgh
Pennsylvania 15260-0001
Psychology, Dept. of
Dept. Head: Charles A. Perfetti
Phone: (1) (412) 624 4501
Fax: (1) (412) 624 4428
Email: perfetti@
  pittvms.bitnet

Polytechnic Univ.
333 Jay St.
Brooklyn, NY 11201
Psychology, Dept. of

Portland State Univ.
POB 751, Portland
Oregon 97207-0751
Psychology, Dept. of
Dept. Head: Cord B.
  Sengstake
Phone: (1) (503) 725 3923
Fax: (1) (503) 725 4882

Portland, Univ. of
5000 N. Willamette
  Blvd
Portland
Oregon 97203
Psychology, Dept. of

Princeton Univ.
Green Hall
Princeton
New Jersey 08544
Psychology, Dept. of
Dept. Head: Nancy Cantor
Phone: (1) (609) 258 4440
Fax: (1) (609) 258 1113

Puget Sound,
Univ. of
Tacoma
Washington 98416
Psychology, Dept. of
Dept. Head: Donald E.
  Pannen
Phone: (1) (206) 756 3307
Fax: (1) (206) 756 3500

Purdue Univ.
West Lafayette
Indiana 47907
Psychological Sciences,
  Dept. of
Dept. Head: Gerald E.
  Gruen
Phone: (1) (317) 494 6061
Fax: (1) (317) 496 1264

Purdue Univ. at
Indianapolis
Indiana Univ.
1125 East 38th St.
Indianapolis
Indiana 46205
Psychology, Dept. of
Dept. Head: John T.
  Hazer
Phone: (1) (317) 274 6945

Queens College
City Univ. of New York
30-65 Kissena Blvd
Flushing
New York 11367
Psychology, Dept. of
Dept. Head: Harold
  Schuckman
Phone: (1) (718) 520 7926

Research Center for
Group Dynamics
5260 Inst. for Social
  Research
426 Thompson St.
Ann Arbor
Michigan 48106-1248
Dept. Head: Prof.
  Richard E. Nisbet
Phone: (1) (313) 764 8360

Rhode Island, Univ. of
Kingston
Rhode Island 02881
Counseling Center
Dept. Head: Dr James F.
  Campbell
Phone: (1) (401) 792 2288
Fax: (1) (401) 792 5525

Rhode Island, Univ. of
Kingston
Rhode Island 02881
Psychology, Dept. of
Dept. Head: Dr Nelson
  Smith
Phone: (1) (401) 792 2193
Fax: (1) (401) 792 2892

Rice Univ.
POB 1892
Houston
Texas 77251
Psychology, Dept. of
Dept. Head: David J.
  Schneider
Phone: (1) (713) 527 4856
Fax: (1) (713) 285 5221

Richmond, Univ. of
Richmond
Virginia 23173
Psychology, Dept. of
Dept. Head: Andrew F.
  Newcomb
Phone: (1) (804) 289
  8128
Fax: (1) (804) 289 8943
Email: newcomb@ urvax

Rutgers Univ.
Psychology Building
Busch Campus
New Brunswick
New Jersey 08903
Psychology, Dept. of
Dept. Head: Charles
  Flaherty
Phone: (1) (908) 932 2556
Fax: (1) (908) 932 2263

Rutgers: The State
Univ. of New Jersey
Busch Campus
POB 819, Piscataway
New Jersey 08855
Applied Psychology, Dept.
  of
Dept. Head: Kenneth
  Schneider
Phone: (1) (201) 932 2008

Salem-Teikyo Univ.
230 West Main St.
POB 500
Salem
West Virginia 26426-0500
Psychology, Dept. of

Salisbury State Univ.
Salisbury
Maryland 21801
Psychology, Dept. of

Sam Houston State Univ.
POB 2447
Huntsville
Texas 77341
Psychology & Philosophy, Dept. of
Dept. Head: A. Jerry Bruce
Phone: (1) (409) 294 1174

San Diego State Univ.
San Diego
California 92182-0350
Psychology, Dept. of
Dept. Head: William A. Hillix
Phone: (1) (619)594 5346

Saybrook Inst.
1150 Sutter St.
San Francisco
California 94109
Phone: (1) (415) 441 5034

Scranton, Univ. of
Scranton
Pennsylvania
Psychology, Dept. of

Seattle Pacific Univ.
3307 Third Ave. West
Seattle
Washington 98119
Psychology, Dept. of
Dept. Head: Michael D. Roe
Phone: (1) (206) 281 2252
Fax: (1) (206) 281 2500

Seton Hall Univ.
South Orange
New Jersey 07079
Psychology, Dept. of
Other Depts: Counseling Psychology
Dept. Head: Sandra S. Lee
Phone: (1) (201) 761 9450
Fax: (1) (201) 761 7642

Shaw Univ.
Raleigh
North Carolina 27611
Psychology, Dept. of

Shippensburg Univ. of Pennsylvania
Shippensburg
Pennsylvania 17257
Psychology, Dept. of
Dept. Head: Dr Hugh M. Aberman
Phone: (1) (717) 532 1657
Fax: (1) (717) 532 1657

Slippery Rock Univ. of Penn.
Slippery Rock
Pennsylvania 16057
Psychology, Dept. of

South Carolina, Univ. of
Columbia
South Carolina 29208
Psychology, Dept. of
Dept. Head: Lester A. Lefton
Phone: (1) (803) 777 4137

South Dakota State Univ.
Brookings
South Dakota 57007
Psychology, Dept. of
Dept. Head: Allen R. Branum
Phone: (1) (605) 688 4322
Fax: (1) (605) 688 5822

South Dakota, Univ. of
Springfield
South Dakota 57062
Psychology, Dept. of

South Dakota, Univ. of
Vermillion
South Dakota 57069
Psychology, Dept. of

South Florida, Univ. of
4202 Fowler Ave.
Tampa, Florida 33620
Psychology, Dept. of
Dept. Head: Louis A. Penner
Phone: (1) (813) 974 2492

South, Univ. of the
Sewanee
Tennessee 37375
Psychology, Dept. of

Southeastern Massachusetts Univ.
North Dartmouth
Massachusetts 02747
Psychology, Dept. of

Southeastern State Univ.
Durant
Oklahoma 74701
Psychology, Dept. of
Dept. Head: G. Pat Powers
Phone: (1) (405) 924 0121

Southern California, Univ. of
Univ. Park SGM 501
Los Angeles
California 90089-1061
Psychology, Dept. of
Dept. Head: Joseph B. Hellige
Phone: (1) (213) 740 2203
Fax: (1) (213) 746 9082

**Southern Illinois Univ.
at Carbondale**
Room 281
Life Science Building II
Carbondale
Illinois 62901
Psychology, Dept. of
Dept. Head: James H.
McHose
Phone: (1) (618) 536 2301

**Southern Mississippi,
Univ. of**
Southern Station
Box 5025
Hattiesburg
Mississippi 39406-5025
Psychology, Dept. of
Dept. Head: John D.
Alcorn
Phone: (1) (601) 266
4177
Fax: (1) (601) 266 4175
Email: oilirwjp. king

**Southern Nazarene
Univ.**
6729 NW 39th
Expressway
Bethany
Oklahoma 73008
Psychology, Dept. of

**Southwest Missouri
State Univ.**
901 South National
Springfield
Missouri 65804
Psychology, Dept. of
Dept. Head: Dr F. R.
Maxwell
Phone: (1) (417) 836
5797
Fax: (1) (417) 836 4884

Southwest State Univ.
Marshall
Minnesota 56258
Psychology, Dept. of

**Southwest Texas State
Univ.**
Box 1002, San Marcos
Texas 78666
Psychology, Dept. of
Dept. Head: Dr Richard
L. Archer
Phone: (1) (512) 245 2526
Fax: (1) (512) 245 3847

**Southwestern State
Univ.**
Weatherford
Oklahoma 73096
Psychology, Dept. of

Southwestern Univ.
Georgetown
Texas 78626
Psychology, Dept. of
Dept. Head: Jesse E.
Purdy
Phone: (1) (512) 863 1985
Fax: (1) (512) 863 5788
Telex: 62809750

Spalding Univ.
851 South Fourth St.
Louisville
Kentucky 40203
Psychology, Dept. of
Dept. Head: Thomas G.
Titus
Phone: (1) (502) 585 9911

St Bonaventure Univ.
St Bonaventure
NY 14778
Psychology, Dept. of
Dept. Head: Harold
Geltand
Phone: (1) (716) 375 2504
Fax: (1) (716) 375 2309
Email: hgeltand@ sbu.edu

St Cloud State Univ.
St Cloud
Minnesota 56301
Psychology, Dept. of

St Edwards Univ.
3001 South Congress Ave.
Austin
Texas 78704
Psychology, Dept. of
Grand Central & Utopia
Parkways
Jamaica
New York 11439
Psychology, Dept. of
Dept. Head: Jeffrey W.
Fagen
Phone: (1) (718) 990
6368
Fax: (1) (718) 990 6705
Email: fagen@
sjuvm.bitnet

St Lawrence Univ.
Canton
NY 13617
Psychology, Dept. of
Dept. Head: Thomas F.
Cunningham
Phone: (1) (315) 379
5351
Fax: (1) (315) 379 5804

St Louis Univ.
221 North Grand Blvd
St Louis
Missouri 63103
Psychology, Dept. of
Dept. Head: James H.
Korn
Phone: (1) (314) 658
2300
Fax: (1) (314) 658 3874

St Mary's Univ.
San Antonio
Texas 78284
Psychology, Dept. of

St Thomas, Univ. of
Summit Ave.
St Paul
Minnesota 55105
Psychology, Dept. of

Stanford Univ.
Stanford
California 94305-2130
Psychology, Dept. of
Dept. Head: Prof. Mark
R. Lepper
Phone: (1) (415) 725 2405
Fax: (1) (415) 725 5699
Email: postmaster@
psych.stanford.edu

Stephen F. Austin State
Univ.
POB 13046
Nacogdoches, Texas 75962
Psychology, Dept. of
Dept. Head: Heinz A.
Gaylord
Phone: (1) (409) 568 4402
Fax: (1) (409) 568 2190

Suffolk Univ.
41 Temple St., Boston
Massachusetts 02114
Psychology, Dept. of
Dept. Head: Jack Demick
Phone: (1) (617) 573 8293
Fax: (1) (617) 573 8513
Email: j.demick@
acad.suffolk.edu

Sul Ross State Univ.
Alpine, Texas 79832
Psychology, Dept. of

Syracuse Univ.
206 Slocum Hall
Syracuse NY 13244
College for Human
Development
Other Depts: Child
Development: Drs Kathy
Lennertz & Jaipaul
Roopnarine
Dept. Head: Dr Alice
Sterling Honig
Phone: (1) (315) 443 2757
Fax: (1) (315) 443 2562
Email: ahonig@ suvm

Syracuse Univ.
430 Huntington Hall
150 Marshall St.
Syracuse
New York 13244
Psychology, Dept. of
Dept. Head: Vernon C.
Hall
Phone: (1) (315) 423
2353

Teachers College of
Columbia Univ.
525 West 120th St.
New York 10027
Clinical Psychology Dept.
Dept. Head: Barry A.
Farber
Phone: (1) (212) 678 3267
Fax: (1) (212) 678 4048

Temple Univ.
Broad St. & Montgomery
St.s
Philadelphia
Pennsylvania 19122
Psychology, Dept. of
Dept. Head: John
Lamberth
Phone: (1) (215) 787 7321

Tennessee Knoxville,
Univ. of
Knoxville
Tennessee 37996
Psychology, Dept. of
Dept. Head: Warren H.
Jones
Phone: (1) (615) 974
2531
Fax: (1) (615) 974 3330

Tennessee State
Univ.
35000 John A. Merritt Bd
Nashville
Tennessee 37209-1561
Psychology, Dept. of
Phone: (1) (615) 320 3261

Tennessee, The
Univ. of
108 Claxton Educational
Building
Knoxville
Tennessee 37996-3400
Educational &
Counseling Psychology,
Dept. of
Dept. Head: Dr R. Steve
McCallum
Phone: (1) (615) 974
5131
Fax: (1) (615) 974 8718

Tennessee, Univ. of
615 McCallie Ave.
Chattanooga
Tennessee 37403
Psychology, Dept. of
Dept. Head: Richard L.
Metzger
Phone: (1) (615) 755
4262
Fax: (1) (615) 755 5311
Email: rmetzger@ utcvm

Texas A & M Univ.
Academic Building
College Station
Texas 77843
Psychology, Dept. of
Dept. Head: Stephen
Worchel
Phone: (1) (409) 845
2581

Texas at Arlington,
Univ. of
POB 19128
Arlington
Texas 76019
Psychology, Dept. of
Dept. Head: Roger L.
Mellgren
Phone: (1) (817) 273 2281
Fax: (1) (817) 273 3511
Email: b959SS@
utarlg.uta.edu

Texas at Austin, Univ. of
Austin
Texas 78712
Psychology, Dept. of
Dept. Head: Donald J.
Foss
Phone: (1) (512) 471 5935
Email: foss@
psyvax.psy.utexas.edu

Texas Christian Univ.
2800 S. Univ. Drive
Fort Worth
Texas 76129
Psychology, Dept. of
Dept. Head: Norman Ray
Remley
Phone: (1) (817) 921 7410

Texas Southern Univ.
3100 Cleburne Ave.
Houston
Texas 77004
Psychology, Dept. of
Dept. Head: Delbert F.
Garnes
Phone: (1) (713) 527 7344
Fax: (1) (713) 527 7436

Texas Southwestern
Medical Center at
Dallas
5323 Harry Hines Blvd
Dallas
Texas 75235
Psychology, Divn. of
Dept. Head: Maurice
Korman
Phone: (1) (214) 904 2200
Fax: (1) (214) 904 2590

Texas Tech Univ.
Box 42051
Lubbock
Texas 79409-2051
Psychology, Dept. of
Dept. Head: Dr C. Steven
Richards
Phone: (1) (806) 742 3737

Texas, Univ. of Permian
Basin
Odessa
Texas 79762
Psychology, Dept. of

Texas, Univ. of
Richardson
Texas 75083-0688
Programs in Psychology
& Cognitive Science
Dept. Head: W. Jay
Dowling
Phone: (1) (214) 690 2060
Fax: (1) (214) 690 2491
Email: jdowling@
utdallas.bitnet

Texas, Univ. of, Medical
Branch
Galveston
Texas 77555-0443
Psychology Section,
Psychiatry & Beh.
Sciences Dept
Other Depts:
Neurosurgery
Dept. Head: Ernest S.
Barratt
Phone: (1) (409) 772 1439
Fax: (1) (409) 772 4288

Texas Women's Univ.
Denton
Texas 76204
Psychology, Dept. of
Dept. Head: Frank T.
Vitro
Phone: (1) (817) 898
2306
Fax: (1) (817) 898 3198

Texas-Pan American,
Univ. Of
Edinburg, Texas 78539
Psychology, Dept. of
Dept. Head: Dr Mark
Winkel
Phone: (1) (210) 381 3329

Thomas Jefferson
Univ.
11th & Walnut St.s
Philadelphia
Pennsylvania 19107
Psychology, Dept. of

Toledo, Univ. of
Toledo
Ohio 43606-3390
Psychology, Dept. of
Dept. Head: Dr Robert A.
Haaf
Phone: (1) (419) 537
2717
Fax: (1) (419) 537
2157

Towson State
Univ.
Towson
Baltimore
Maryland 21204
Psychology, Dept. of
Dept. Head: Roger W.
Fink
Phone: (1) (410) 830
2634

Trinity Univ.
715 Stadium Drive
San Antonio
Texas 78212
Psychology, Dept. of
Dept. Head: Charles K.
Prokop
Phone: (1) (512) 736
8323

Tufts Univ.
Medford
Massachusetts 02155
Child Study, Dept. of
Dept. Head: D. Wertlieb
Phone: (1) (617) 627
3355
Fax: (1) (617) 666 1008
Email: dwertlie@
pearl.tufts.edu

Tufts Univ.
Medford
Massachusetts 02155
Psychology, Dept. of
Dept. Head: Joseph F.
 DeBold
Phone: (1) (617) 627
 3523
Fax: (1) (617) 666 1008
Email: jdebold@
 pearl.tufts.edu

Tulane Univ.
2007 Stern Hall
New Orleans
Louisiana 70118
Psychology, Dept. of
Dept. Head: Barbara E.
 Moely
Phone: (1) (504) 865
 5331
Fax: (1) (504) 862 8744
Email: ps09nwf@
 tcsmusa

Tulsa, Univ. of
600 South College Ave.
Tulsa
Oklahoma 74104
Psychology, Dept. of
Dept. Head: Robert Hogan
Phone: (1) (918) 631
 2248
Fax: (1) (918) 631 2073

Uniformed Services
Univ. of the Health
Sciences
4301 Jones Bridge Rd
Bethesda
Maryland 20814
Medical Psychology, Dept.
 of
Dept. Head: Jerome E.
 Singer
Phone: (1) (301) 295 3270
Fax: (1) (301) 295 3034
Email: singer@
 usuhs.bitnet

Utah State Univ.
Logan
Utah 84322
Psychology, Dept. of
Dept. Head: Michael R.
 Bertoch
Phone: (1) (801) 750 1460

Utah, Univ. of
327 Milton Bennion
 Hall
Salt Lake City
Utah 84112
Educational Psychology,
 Dept. of
Dept. Head: William
 Jenson
Phone: (1) (801) 581
 7148
Fax: (1) (801) 581 5566

Utah, Univ. of
Salt Lake City
Utah 84112
Psychology, Dept. of
Dept. Head: Charles P.
 Shimp
Phone: (1) (801) 581 6123
Fax: (1) (801) 581 5841

Valley City State Univ.
Valley City
North Dakota 58072
Psychology, Dept. of

Vanderbilt Univ.
111 21st Ave. S.
Nashville
Tennessee 37240
Psychology, Dept. of
Dept. Head: Randolph
 Blake
Phone: (1) (615) 322 2874
Fax: (1) (615) 346 8449

Vassar College
Poughkeepsie
NY 12601
Psychology, Dept. of

Vermont, Univ. of
Burlington
Vermont 05405
Psychology, Dept. of
Dept. Head: Justin M.
 Joffe
Phone: (1) (802) 656 2670
Fax: (1) (802) 656 8783

Villanova Univ.
Villanova
Pennsylvania 19085
Psychology, Dept. of

Virginia
Commonwealth
Univ.
808 West Franklin St.
Richmond
Virginia 23284
Psychology, Dept. of
Dept. Head: Dr Steven J.
 Danish
Phone: (1) (804) 367 1179
Fax: (1) (804) 367 2237

Virginia Consortium for
Professional
Psychology
733 Hofheimer Hall
Norfolk
Virginia 23501
Dept. Head: Neill Watson
Phone: (1) (804) 446 5890

Virginia Poly. Inst. &
State Univ.
5088 Derring Hall
Blacksburg
Virginia 24061
Psychology, Dept. of
Dept. Head: Joseph H.
 Sgro
Phone: (1) (703) 231 6581

Virginia State Univ.
Petersburg
Virginia 23803
Psychology, Dept. of

Virginia Union Univ.
1500 North Lombardy St.
Richmond
Virginia 23220
Psychology, Dept. of

Virginia, Univ. of
102 Gilmer Hall
Charlottesville
Virginia 22903
Psychology, Dept. of
Dept. Head: Prof.
Richard McCarty
Phone: (1) (804) 982 4750
Fax: (1) (804) 982 4766
Email: dm3f@
virginia.edu

Wake Forest Univ.
Box 7778
Winston-Salem
North Carolina 27109
Psychology, Dept. of
Dept. Head: John E.
Williams
Phone: (1) (919) 759 5424
Fax: (1) (919) 759 4733
Email: best@
wfunet.wfu.edu

Washington & Lee Univ.
Lexington
Virginia 24450
Psychology, Dept. of
Dept. Head: David G.
Elmes
Phone: (1) (703) 463 8833
Fax: (1) (703) 463 8945
Email: elmes.dg@
p9955.wlu.edu

Washington State Univ.
Pullman
Washington 99164
Psychology, Dept. of
Dept. Head: Frances K.
McSweeney
Phone: (1) (509) 335 2631
Fax: (1) (509) 335 5043

Washington, Univ. of
Seattle
Washington 98195
Psychology, Dept. of
Dept. Head: Irwin G.
Sarason
Phone: (1) (206) 543 2640
Fax: (1) (206) 685 3157
Email: isarason@
u.washington.edu

Washington Univ.
St Louis
Missouri 63130
Psychology, Dept. of
Dept. Head: John A. Stern
Phone: (1) (314) 935 6565
Fax: (1) (314) 935 7588

Wayland Baptist Univ.
Plainview
Texas 79072
Psychology, Dept. of

Wayne State Univ.
Detroit
Michigan 48202
Psychology, Dept. of
Dept. Head: M. Marlyne
Kilbey
Phone: (1) (313) 577 2802
Fax: (1) (313) 577 7636
Email: mkilbey@
waynest1

Webster Univ.
470 East Lockwood Ave.
St Louis, Missouri 63119
Psychology, Dept. of

West Chester State Univ.
West Chester
Pennsylvania 19383
Psychology, Dept. of
Dept. Head: Edward I.
Pollak
Phone: (1) (215) 436 2945
Fax: (1) (215) 436 3150
Email: epollak@ wcu

West Texas State Univ.
West Texas Station
Canyon
Texas 79016
Psychology, Dept. of

West Virginia Univ.
Morgantown
West Virginia 26506
Psychology, Dept. of
Dept. Head: Barry
Edelstein
Phone: (1) (304) 293 2001
Fax: (1) (304) 293 6858
Email: u21B4@ wvnvm

Western Carolina Univ.
Cullowhee
North Carolina 28723
Psychology, Dept. of
Dept. Head: Bruce B
Henderson
Phone: (1) (704) 227 7361
Fax: (1) (704) 227 7388
Email: henderson@
wcuvax1.bitnet

**Western Michigan
Univ.**
Kalamazoo
Michigan 49008
Psychology, Dept. of
Dept. Head: C. Richard
Tsegaye-Spates
Phone: (1) (616) 387
4498
Fax: (1) (616) 387 3999

**Western New Mexico
Univ.**
Box 680
Silver City
New Mexico 88062
Psychology, Dept. of
Dept. Head: Laurence
Armand French
Phone: (1) (505) 538
6416
Fax: (1) (505) 538 6178

Western Washington Univ.
Bellingham
Washington 98225
Psychology, Dept. of
Dept. Head: Ronald A.
Kleinknecht
Phone: (1) (206) 676 3518
Fax: (1) (206) 647 7305
Email: knecht@ wwu.edu

Wichita State Univ.
1845 Fairmount
Wichita
Kansas 67260-0034
Psychology, Dept. of
Dept. Head: Charles
Burdsal
Phone: (1) (316) 689 3170

Widener Univ.
301 East 19th St.
Chester
Pennsylvania 19013
Graduate Clinical
Psychology, Inst. for
Dept. Head: Jules C.
Abrams
Phone: (1) (215) 499 1206

Wilberforce Univ.
Wilberforce
Ohio 45384
Psychology, Dept. of
Dept. Head: Evelyn Bland
Phone: (1) (513) 376 2911

Wilkes Univ.
Wilkes-Barre
Pennsylvania 18766
Psychology, Dept. of
Dept. Head: Carl J.
Charnetski
Phone: (1) (717) 831 4564

Willamette Univ.
900 State St.
Salem, Oregon 97301
Psychology, Dept. of

Wisconsin-Eau Claire, Univ. of
Eau Claire
Wisconsin
54702-4004
Psychology, Dept. of
Dept. Head: Dr Kenneth
A. Heilman
Phone: (1) (715) 836
5733
Fax: (1) (715) 836 2380

Wisconsin-La Cross Univ.
1725 State St.
La Crosse
Wisconsin 54601
Psychology, Dept. of

Wisconsin-Madison Univ.
432 N. Murray St.
Madison
Wisconsin 53706
Rehabilitation
Psychology, Dept. of
Dept. Head: Norman
Berven
Phone: (1) (608) 263
7917
Fax: (1) (608) 262 8108
Email: psych@
macc.wisc.edu

Wisconsin-Madison Univ.
1000 Bascom Mall - 321
Education Bldg
Madison
Wisconsin 53706
Counseling Psychology,
Dept. of
Dept. Head: Prof. Philip
A. Perrone
Phone: (1) (608) 262
0461
Fax: (1) (608) 265 3347
Email: psych@
macc.wisc.edu

Wisconsin-Madison Univ.
1025 W. Johnson St.
Madison
Wisconsin 53706
Educational Psychology,
Dept. of
Dept. Head: Ronald
Serlin
Phone: (1) (608) 262
3432
Fax: (1) (608) 262 0843
Email: psych@
macc.wisc.edu

Wisconsin-Madison Univ.
1202 W. Johnson St.
Madison
Wisconsin 53706
Psychology, Dept. of
Dept. Head: Prof. Peter D.
Spear
Phone: (1) (608) 262 1040
Fax: (1) (608) 262 4029
Email: psych@
macc.wisc.edu

Wisconsin-Madison Univ.
B6/210 Clinical Science
Ctr.
UW-Madison
Wisconsin 53706
Psychiatry, Dept. of
Phone: (1) (608) 263 6100
Fax: (1) (608) 262 0265
Email: psych@
macc.wisc.edu

Wisconsin Milwaukee, Univ. of
POB 413
Milwaukee
Wisconsin 53201
Psychology, Dept. of
Dept. Head: Harry L.
Madison
Phone: (1) (414) 229 4747

Wisconsin-Oshkosh Univ.
800 Algoma Blvd
Oshkosh
Wisconsin 54901
Psychology, Dept. of

Wisconsin-Parkside Univ.
Box 2000
900 Wood Rd
Kenosha
Wisconsin 53141-2000
Psychology, Dept. of
Dept. Head: Michael Gurtman
Phone: (1) (414) 595 2658
Fax: (1) (414) 595 2265

Wisconsin-Platteville, Univ. of
Platteville
Wisconsin 53818
Dept. Head: Dr William Miller
Phone: (1) (608) 342 1724

Wisconsin School of Professional Psychology
9120 West Hampton Ave.
Milwaukee
Wisconsin 53225
Dept. Head: Samuel H. Friedman
Phone: (1) (414) 464 9777

Wisconsin-Whitewater, Univ. of
Whitewater
Wisconsin 53190
Psychology, Dept. of
Dept. Head: Dr Douglas B. Eamon
Phone: (1) (414) 472 1026
Fax: (1) (414) 472 5716
Email: eamon@ uww.uwwvax.edu

Wittenberg Univ.
North Wittenberg Ave.
Springfield
Ohio 45501
Psychology, Dept. of
Dept. Head: Dr Jeffrey B. Brookings
Phone: (1) (513) 327 7475
Fax: (1) (513) 327 6340
Email: jbrook@ wittenbg

Wright Inst.
2728 Durant Ave.
Berkeley
California 94704
Psychology, Graduate School of
Dept. Head: Andrea Morrison
Phone: (1) (415) 841 9230

Wright State Univ.
3640 Colonel Glenn Highway
Dayton
Ohio 45435
School of Professional Psychology
Dept. Head: Ronald E. Fox
Phone: (1) (513) 873 3490

Wyoming, Univ. of
Box 3415 Univ. Station
Laramie
Wyoming 82071
Psychology, Dept. of
Dept. Head: Stephen L. Bieber
Phone: (1) (307) 766 6303

Yale Univ.
Box 11A Yale Station
New Haven
Connecticut 06520-7447
Psychology, Dept. of
Dept. Head: Judith Rodin
Phone: (1) (203) 432 4516

Yeshiva Univ.
1300 Morris Park Ave.
Bronx, New York 10461
Ferkauf Graduate School of Psychology
Dept. Head: Barbara G. Melamed
Phone: (1) (718) 430 4206
Fax: (1) (718) 430 3252

URUGUAY

Damaso Antonio Larranaga, Univ. Cat. del Uruguay
Avda 8 de Octubre 2738
16000 Montevideo
Psychology, Dept. of

República, Univ. de la
Avda 18 de Julio 1968
Montevideo
Psychology, Dept. of

UZBEKHISTAN

Nukus State Univ.
Univ. skaya ul. 1
Nukus 742012
Psychology, Dept. of

Samarkand Alisher Navoi State Univ.
Bul. M. Gorkogo 15
Samarkand
703004
Psychology, Dept. of

Tadzhik State Univ.
Pr. Lenina 17
Dushanbe
734016 Tadzhik
Psychology, Dept. of

Tashkent State Univ.
Univ. skaya ul. 95
Tashkent
700095
Psychology, Dept. of

VENEZUELA

Abierta, Univ. Nac.
Apdo 2096, Caracas 1010A
Psychology, Dept. of

Andrés Bello, Univ. Cat.
Urb. Montalbán
La Vega, Apdo 29068
Caracas 1021
Psychology, Dept. of

Carabobo, Univ. de
Avda Bolívar 125-39
Apdo Postal 129
Valencia 2001
Psychology, Dept. of

Central de Venezuela,
Univ.
Apdo 47018
Caracas 1041A
Psichología, Inst. de
Dept. Head: Euclides
  Sanchez
Phone: (58) (2) 662 39 49
Fax: (58) (2) 662 39 61

Ezequiel Zamora, Univ.
Nac. Experimental de
Los Llanos
Occidentales
Apdo Postal 19, Barinas
Psychology, Dept. of

Francisco de Miranda,
Univ. Nac.
Experimental
Calle Norte
Edif. Universitario, Coro
Estato Falcón 4101
Psychology, Dept. of

Lisandro Alvarado,
Univ.
Centro-Occidental
Apdo 400, Barquisimeto
Lara
Psychology, Dept. of

V-Z

Metropolitana, Univ.
Apdo 76819
Caracas 1070
Psychology, Dept. of
Other Depts: Centro de
  Investigación para la
  Infancia y la Familia
  (CENDIF)
Dept. Head: Angélica
  Sepúlveda de Leighton
Phone: (58) (2) 241 68 69
Fax: (58) (2) 241 68 69

Oriente, Univ. de
Edificio Rectorado
Apdo 094
Cumaná
Estado Sucre
Psychology, Dept. of

Rafael Urdaneta,
Univ.
Apdo 614
Maracaibo
Zulia

Romulo Gallegos, Univ.
Nac. Experimental de
Los Llanos Centralles
Apdo Postal 102A
San Juan de los Morros
  2301A
Estado Guarico
Psychology, Dept. of

Santa Maria, Univ. de
Avda Páez
Frente Plaza
  Madariaga
El Paraiso
Caracas
Psychology, Dept. of

Simón Bolívar,
Univ.
Apdo 89000
Prados del Este
Caracas 1081
Psychology, Dept. of
Dept. Head: Marisela
  Hernández
Phone: (58) (2) 9073715
Fax: (58) (2) 9621695

Simón Rodríguez,
Univ. Nac.
Experimental
Apdo Postal 3690
Carmelitas
Caracas 10010A
Psychology, Dept. of

Táchira, Univ.Cat.
del
Calle 14 con
  Carrera 14
Apdo 306
San Cristóbal 5001
Edo Táchira
Psychology, Dept. of

Táchira, Univ. Nac.
Experimental del
Apdo 436
Avda Univ.
Paramillo
San Cristóbal
Táchira
Psychology, Dept. of

Zulia, Univ. del
Apdo de Correos 526
Maracaibo 4011
Edo Zulia
Psychology, Dept. of

VIET NAM

Cantho, Univ. of
Cantho
Hangiang Province
Psychology, Dept. of

Ho Chi Minh City, Univ. of
227 Nguyen van Cu St.
5th District
Ho Chi Minh
Psychology, Dept. of

Hue, Univ. of
Hue
Binh Tri Thien
  Province
Psychology, Dept. of

Truong Dai Hoc Bach Khoa
Hanoi
Psychology, Dept. of

Truong Dai Hoc Tong-Ho'p
Thuong Dinh
Dong Da
Hanoi
Psychology, Dept. of

VIRGIN ISLANDS

Virgin Islands, Univ. of
#2 John Brewer's Bay
St Thomas
USUI 00802
Psychology Program
Dept. Head: Dr. Patricia
  Rhymer Todman
Phone: (1) (809) 776 9200
Fax: (1) (809) 775 4850

WESTERN SAMOA

Iunivesite Aoao o Samoa
POB 5768
Apia
Psychology, Dept. of

YEMEN

Aden, Univ. of
POB 7039
Al-Mansoora
Aden
Psychology, Dept. of

San'a Univ.
POB 1247
San'a
Psychology, Dept. of

ZAÏRE

Kisangani, Univ. de
BP 2012
Kisangani
Haut-Zaire
Psychology, Dept. of

Lubumbashi, Univ. de
BP 1825
Lubumbashi
Psychology, Dept. of

ZAMBIA

Copperbelt Univ.
POB 21692
Kitwe
Psychology, Dept. of

Zambia, Univ. of
POB 32379
Lusaka
Psychology, Dept. of
Dept. Head: Dr. Ravinder
  Kathuria
Phone: (260) (1) 228218
Fax: (260) (1) 253952
Telex: (260 (1) 44370
Email: kathuria@
  donet.org

ZIMBABWE

Gweru Provincial Hospital
P.O.Box 125
Gweru
Psychiatric Unit
Dept. Head: A. Gambiza
Phone: (263) (54) 2224

Ingutsheni Hospital
Box 8363
Belmont
Bulawayo
Clinical Psychology Dept.
Dept. Head: Odette
  Continho
Phone: (263) (9) 66463

Parirenyetwa Hospital
Box 8036
Causeway
Harare
Clinical Psychology Dept.

School Psychological Services
Box 8022
Causeway, Harare
Dept. Head: Dr Tim
  Samkange
Phone: (263) (14) 790924

St Giles Medical Rehabiliation Centre
Box A224
Avondale
Harare

Zimbabwe, Univ. of
Box MP 167
Mount Pleasant
Harare
Psychology Dept.

PSYCHOLOGY THROUGHOUT THE WORLD

In the fourth edition of the *International Directory of Psychologists* (Pawlik, 1985), entries of each country were preceded by a title page giving information on the following topics: the historical development of psychology in that country, the major scientific and professional organizations of psychology, the academic training of psychologists and important fields of research. The title pages have proved to be useful for all kinds of cooperative and exchange projects in an international perspective. Therefore, instructions for preparing similar descriptions of psychology throughout the world were forwarded in 1992 to all known national societies of psychology, irrespective of their membership in the International Union of Psychological Science. In the case of a country without a psychological society known to the Union, the material was sent to contact institutions or contact persons secured from the former Directory. Every possible attempt was made to have each and every country included in this call for participation. The time schedule given requested those participating to submit their contributions at the end of October 1992. It was pointed out that the information submitted for publication in this Directory would be printed as received.

At the time of writing (November 1992), national descriptions were received from 46 national societies of psychology. Not all societies participating were in a position to supply the information or to comply with the request to use only the English language. Nevertheless, the contributions are published almost exactly as submitted by a society. Many countries from East Europe and from the Third World are conspicuously absent. This is partially due to their transition stages. Whenever possible, a national description was constructed from information available (particularly from the former Directory).

Instructions called for the information to be organized in the eight standard sections; we have added an asterisk (*) next to each society that is a member of the International Union of Psychological Science:

1. Official English-language name (or: official name in the country's official language *plus* English language translation) of the national society of psychology (for members of the International Union of Psychological Science: of the National Member in the Union); year in which the society was founded; president and secretary-general (or recording secretary) of the national society of psychology; address, telephone number and fax number of the main office of the society; size of membership.
2. In this (optional) section, the same items of information could be provided on additional societies/associations of psychology in the country. If necessary those two (and only two) societies/associations of psychology/psychologists were selected as the most important/representative or those two that have the largest membership.
3. A brief description of the society(ies)/association(s) quoted in sections 1 and 2 with the respective membership requirements, major aims and goals, major functions(s) for the psychological community, etc.
4. A brief description of the historical development and current state of psychology (as a science and/or as a profession) in the country.
5. A brief account of major current research programs in psychology, fields of research specialization, etc.
6. A description of training facilities and requirements for psychologists in the country as well as a brief account of the legal status of professional psychology.
7. References to journals, yearbooks or monographs that provide information on the state of psychology in the country, on current professional affairs, etc.
8. Name and address of the author of this national description (optional).

Géry d'Ydewalle
Secretary-General
International Union of Psychological Science

AUSTRALIA

1. The Australian Psychological Society* Limited. Founded 1966. President 1992/1993 Dr Susan Kelly. Executive Director Dr. Adrienne Bennett. National Science Centre, 191 Royal Parade, Parkville 3052, NSW. Tel: 03 347 2611 Fax: 03 347 4841. Membership, all grades: 7,000.

2. The Society consists of two Divisions, the Division of Scientific Affairs and the Division of Professional Affairs, the latter provides for Boards covering specific areas of specialist psychological practice. At October 1992, there were Boards of Clinical, Community, Counselling, Educational and Developmental, Forensic, Clinical Neuropsychologists, Clinical and Sport Psychologists. The Society has regional Branches throughout Australia, mostly organised by States; some Branches contain local Groups.

3. The objects for which the Society was established include advancing the scientific study and the professional practice of psychology and enhancing the contribution of psychology to public welfare. The Society achieves this by encouraging the development of all facets of psychology, by promoting and improving research, and by promoting high standards of professional ethics, competence, and conduct. It disseminates psychological knowledge through meetings, lectures, conferences and publications. An Annual Conference is conducted and the XXIV International Congress of Psychology was held in Sydney, NSW in 1988. Publications include *The Australian Journal of Psychology, The Australian Psychologist*, and *The Bulletin* of *The Australian Psychological Society Limited*. Boards and Branches also issue publications.

   The Society has four grades of membership; Honorary Fellows, Fellows, members and Associate Members. There are also Foreign Affiliates, Affiliates and Student Subscribers. Associate Membership requires four years of tertiary training psychology at Institutions accredited by the Society. Membership requires (a) an additional two years post graduate qualifications or (b) an additional two years of approved supervision as a Psychologist.

4. The Australian Psychological Society Limited was formed in 1966. In 1945, however, Australian Psychologists formed the Australian Oversea Branch of The British Psychological Society, the precursor of the present Society. Under the title of Mental Philosophy the study of psychology was undertaken in the Departments of Philosophy of the six Australian Universities at various times between 1881 to 1913. Courses in Experimental Psychology began in 1913. During the 1920s trends toward independent Departments of Psychology emerged, and the first independent Department was founded at the University of Sydney in 1929. A Department was founded at the University of Western Australia in 1930. Most of the important developments occurred postwar, many of them emerging from the application of psychology to manpower planning and selection for the armed services during World War II. Before that time the application of psychology had been mainly in education. Indpendent Departments of Psychology now exist in all 18 Australian Universities and in 10 other tertiary institutions such as Colleges of Advanced Education. The major areas of psychological practice are in government; semi-government and government supported agencies. Approximately 15% of psychologists work in the private sector. The activities of the members of the APS encompass all areas of teaching, research and practice.

5. Pure and applied psychological research is carried out in all of the fields recognised in other countries, Australian psychology has achieved international recognition in perception and perpetual development, learning psycho-pathology, behavioural methods of treatment, selection and training in education and industry, educational research, acculturation and assimilation of migrants, hypnosis, achievement motivation, human factors, and social psychology of conformity. The majority of Psychologists in private practice are clinical or occupational Psychologists.

6. Training facilities are widely available in Universities and other tertiary institutions. All states require Psychologists in private practice to be registered with a State registration board, with the exception of the Australian Capital Territory, which will shortly introduce legislation. Requirements for registration are generally similar to those for Membership

of the Society but some States require higher qualifications. Where Psychologists have privilege in law, it is only in civil cases.

Approximately 60% of Psychologists in Australia belong to The Australian Psychological Society Limited. The Directory entries come from current (October, 1992) lists of Honorary Fellows, Fellows and Members, Associate members and Students.

7. Nixon, M.C. and Taft, R. (1977) *Psychology in Australia: Achievements and Prospects.* Pergamon Press Australia Pty. Ltd.

O'Neill, W.M. (1983) *One hundred years of Psychology in Australia 1881-1980. The Bulletin of The Australian Psychological Society Limited,* Volume 5, (Issue 6), pp.8-20, p.36.

Feather, N.T. (Ed.) *Survey of Australian Psychology: Trends in Research,* Sydney: George Allen and Unwin.

AUSTRIA

1. Berufsverband Österreichischer Psychologen (BÖP). Founded 1953.

3. BÖP was founded to meet the needs and interests of professional psychologists and to advance psychology as a field of science, education and practice. BÖP is the professional psychological association of Austria. Full membership is open only to persons holding a doctorate degree/diploma in psychology from an Austrian or equivalent foreign university. There exists for the members of BÖP a formalized ethical code. Since its founding BÖP has lobbied for a certification and licensing law for psychologists. Further, the association promotes the development of psychology as a profession and maintains contacts with national authorities and other important institutions.

Each year BÖP organizes several professional congresses. BÖP consists of eight regional organizations and three special sections (clinical psychology, traffic psychology, economic and organizational psychology).

4. In Austria the first university department of psychology was founded in 1890 (Graz). The first psychological institute was founded in the early twenties (University of Vienna). Since then psychology has developed from a small university subject into a medium-sized profession. This development can also be seen in the increase in the number of BÖP-members. In 1973 there were 337 members, today 827. The major fields of professional psychology are as follows: educational psychology and consultation, clinical and social psychology, research, organizational psychology, and traffic psychology.

5. Research in psychology is conducted mainly in six universities. In the period 1980-83, the major fields of academic psychological research have been: brain research, research in learning, methodology and psychometrics, research in traffic psychology, social and organizational psychology, forensic psychology, and clinical psychology.

6. In 1983 full-time university training in psychology was taken up by approximately 4000 students at four universities. Following a five-year program of study and graduate training in psychology students receive a degree of "Mag.phil." or "Mag.rer.nat.". An advanced research degree of Doctor of Philosophy (Dr.phil.) is offered to holders of a "Mag.phil." or "Mag.rer.nat.". The "Dr.phil." degree requires several additional years of study. Austria has neither a certification nor a licensing law for psychologists. The title "Psychologist" is not legally protected. Psychologists must receive their practical experience under the guidance of an experienced colleague on job or at private educational institutions. BÖP requires from its members a minimum of three years of supervised practical experience in psychology before independent practice is allowed.

7. *Psychologie in Österreich* (published quarterly by BÖP): news from the BÖP president and from sectional and regional organizations, research issues, vacancies, and notices from those seeking employment.

Pressedienst Psychologie (published yearly by BÖP). Includes annual reports of all BÖP congresses.

BELGIUM

1. Belgische Vereniging voor Psychologie/Société Belge de Psychologie*. Belgian Psychological Society (BPS). Founded: 1947. President 1990-1993: Professor Véronique De Keyser. Recording secretaries: Professor André Vandierendonck, Henri Dunantlaan 2, B-9000 Gent, Tel: (32) (0) 91 646437, and Dr Monique Radeau, Avenue Adolphe Buyl 117, B-1050 Bruxelles, Tel: (32) (0) 2 6502539. Membership: 350.
2. Belgian Federation of Psychologists (BFP-FBP). President 1989-1995: Marie-Elisabeth Houben. Permanent secretary: Louis Niveau, Kasteellaan 42, B-1652 Alsemberg. Membership 1992: 1200.
3. BPS was founded in 1947 "to bring together all those who, in Belgium, make psychology (understood as a nonphilosophical discipline) the object of their theoretical research or their practical and professional activity" (constitution). Membership is open to university-trained people working in the field of psychology (master's or doctor's degree). Persons with a degree in psychology are considered full members; others are associate members. Within the society different interest groups have been created to represent the different theoretical and applied fields within psychology: cognitive psychology and psychonomics, developmental psychology, personality and social psychology, and ergonomics. These groups have regular meetings and seminars. In addition, members are encouraged to participate and to organize inter-universitary groups sponsored by the National Fund for Scientific Research. BPS organizes an annual meeting for all members to provide the opportunity for presenting current research programs.

   BFP is the professional federation of Belgian psychologists (Dutch-speaking as well as French-speaking). It encompasses a number of specialized associations. The main purposes of the BFP are: the advancement of the profession of psychologist; the defence of the social and economic interests of their members; the exchange of information between professionals; their permanent education.
4. In almost all Belgian universities, psychology developed within programs in education and/or philosophy. Some of the founding fathers of the discipline have ahad a worldwide reputation: e.g. Delbœuf (Liège), Michotte (Leuven), Van Biervliet (Ghent), and Decroly (Brussels). In the sixties there was an accelerated growth in the number of students, which has stablized during the seventies and eighties. In the nineties the trend is again going up. Clinical psychology is most popular even while the legal position of clinical psychologists as psychotherapists is still a point of debate.
5. Research in psychology is conducted mainly in six universities: Brussels (Flemish and French), Gent, Liège, Leuven, and Louvain. It covers all the major fields of academic psychology. However, within each university, some particular research areas are more emphasized than others.
6. In general, to become a university-trained psychologist with a master's degree, it takes five years of study. Part of the last years in the curriculum is under the form of an internship in the area of preferred professional or research specialization. Until now, there is no legal licensing of psychologists. It takes an additional four to seven years to complete a doctoral dissertation.
7. *Psychologica Belgica* (published biannually by BPS: research articles, book reviews, abstracts of doctoral dissertations).

   BPS Newsletter (published bimonthly; contains news about activities of the society).

   BFP-INFO (a quarterly information bulletin for BFP-members, published separately in Dutch and in French).
8. André Vandierendonck, University of Ghent, Henri Dunantlaan 2, B-9000 Gent.

BRAZIL

1. Associação Brasileira de Psicologia* (ABP - Brazilian Psychological Association). Founded: 1945. President: Prof. F. do Piesti Seminério; Secretary-General: Diu Fanny Malin

Tchaicovsky - address: Rua de Candelária, 6-3 Andar-Centro, 20.091 Rio de Janeiro, Brazil.

2. Sociedade de Psicologia de São Paulo (SPSP - São Paulo Society of Psychology). Founded: 1945. Address: Caixa Postal 11.454, CEP 05508, São Paulo, SP, Brazil.

3. Associação Brasileira de Psicologia Aplicada (ABP) (Brazilian Association of Applied Psychology). Founded: 1949. ABP is a confederation or an association of associations, not of individual members. Its objective is the promotion of the development of psychology in a nationwide scale. It is directed by a board of directors which includes the President, the Past-President, the President-Elect, the Recording Secretary,, the Secretary of Publications and the Treasurer. The chief functions of the ABP is to assemble the several Psychology associations and to represent Brazilian Psychology at the international level by means of the IUPsyS. Any legally existent society of Psychology in the country may apply for membership. The ABP presently has six regional societies associates:

    a. The Associação Brasileira de Psicologia Aplicada (Brazilian Association of Applied Psychology), from Rio de Janeiro State;

    b. The Sociedade de Psicologia de São Paulo (São Paulo Society of Psychology), from São Paulo State;

    c. The Associação Sul Matogrossense de Psicólogos (Association of Psychologists of Mato Grosso do Sul);

    d. The Sociedade de Psicologia do Distrito Federal (Society of Psychology of Distrito Federal), from Brasilia;

    e. The Sociedade de Psicologia do Rio Grande do Sul (Society of Psychology of Rio Grande do Sul), from Rio Grande do Sul State;

    f. The Sociedade Mineira de Psicologia (Society of Psychology of Minas Gerais), from Minas Gerais State.

Other associations are being contacted in order to be associated to ABP. It is important to remark that in Brazil there is a Federal Council of Psychology (CFP), subordinated to the Secretary of Labor, whose main functions are to guide and supervise the psychologist profession in the whole country. It is also in charge of enacting a code of ethics for psychologists and to enforce it. There is a close connection between the Federal Council and ABP, as was the case in gathering data for this Directory. There are eight Regional Psychology Councils throughout the country under the supervision of CFP. Any psychologist has to enroll in one of these regional councils in order to legally exercise the profession.

4. Generally speaking, psychology in Brazil was part of philosophy even at the forties. We can cite, however, several pioneers which, influenced by European scientists, specially from France, took some steps which put our discipline in the scientific track. In normal schools (i.e., schools that prepared first grade teachers) psychology began being taught. The contribution of the French speaking psychologists: Piéron, Claparède, Binet, Simon, Piaget, Wallon, and Guillaume, were then dominant. Also Dewey and Thorndike began to influence. Around 1960 behaviorist tendencies started and are still current, although mainly at the animal study level. Psychoanalysis was, and still is, very strong in the clinical work. The first university psychology program began in 1957, while only in 1962 psychology as a profession was legally recognized. Graduate work, leading to the Master and PhD degrees began in the sixties. There are 24 different concentration areas for Master's and seven for PhD degrees. This represents an extraordinary increase in these areas and the number of students is, also showing a constant growth.

5. The most important areas of research (according to a sample, covering 1977-81, but which, we think, still indicates the present status) are, in descending order of importance: School Psychology, Exceptional Psychology, Social and Clinical Psychology. The most important psychological research center is the Institute of Psychology of the Universidade de São Paulo.

6. A full university training program takes four to five years and leads to the titles of Bacharel and Licenciado, at the end of the fourth year and psychologist at the end of the fifth year. During these years, they have to make an internship (estágio) of, at least, 500 hours. Then

they may apply at the proper Regional Council of Psychology in order to be able to render psychological services.

7. The Sociedade de Psicologia de São Paulo issues a semestral journal called *Boletim de Psicologia*. Two other important scientific journals are *Arquivos Brasileiros de Psicologie*, issued by the ISOP, which is trimestral, and *Psicologia: Ciência e Profissão*, a semestral journal issued by Conselho Federal de Psicologia.

8. Antonio P.R. Agatti, Institute of Psychology of the University of São Paulo, Caixa Postal 11.454, CEP 05508, São Paulo, SP, Brazil.

BULGARIA

1. Bulgarian Psychological Society* (BPS). Founded: 1969. President: Prof. E. Gergunov; Secretary-General: Prof. P. Stankov. Address: Ul. Kofardjev 14, Sofia 1606, Bulgaria.

3. BPS was founded in 1969 to unite all psychologists in the country for the advancement of all branches of psychology, for creating favorable conditions for scientific and applied work of its members, contributing to international exchange and safeguarding the rights and duties of its members. Members of BPS may be every person who is actively participating in the scientific and applied work in psychology as well as in teaching this subject. In every city/town in the state, having more than 10 psychologists, a branch of the BPS may be organized. Sections in different branches of psychology are formed also. Its activity embraces a national congress, conferences, seminars, round-table discussions, etc. A scientific journal *Psychologia* is published by BPS, six numbers a year.

4. In Bulgaria psychology has been taught since 1888 when the University of Sofia was founded; in 1904 a laboratory for experimental research was established at the University. During the first decades of the XXth century, psychological preparation was given as part of specialities of Pedagogy and Philosophy. A special chair of psychology was founded in 1963, but special departments for training psychologists were established in 1970.

   Most Bulgarian psychologists are engaged in teaching secondary schools where this subject is included as obligatory, in teacher training institutions and universities. Next in number are psychologists in industry, transport, medical establishments and in research institutions.

5. Research in psychology is conducted in the Universities, in the Academy of sciences and other scientific institutions. During the last decade major fields of scientific research were: educational psychology, child psychology, social, industrial, sport psychology, neuropsychology, psychology of management, of culture and creativity. Some of the problems studies are: psychology of learning and thinking, interrelations in groups, psychological foundations of labour, sport and creative activities, psychology of individuals under stress conditions, educational and vocational guidance etc.

6. Although psychology is being offered in most of the 30 institutions of higher education, only in the University of Sofia *Kliment of Ochrida* is there a department for training professional psychologists. It is done through a five year course of study following the secondary gymnasia education. There are some possibilities for further studies:

   a. One year postgraduate course of psychologists at service;

   b. Three year course of study and research for Candidate of Science (CSc) degree;

   c. Additional research and scientific publications, without time limitation, for Doctor of Science (DSc) degree.

   Every university graduate has the right to practice as a psychologist in teaching or research. There is no general regulation regulating these rights, but there are some documents for the professional status of psychologists in industry and in schools.

7. The journal *Psychologia*, published every two months by BPS; Yearbooks of Universities and scientific institutions; Abstracts of Bulgarian scientific literature - Psychology and Pedagogy, published by the Bulgarian Academy of Sciences.

8. Prof. Gencho D. Piryov, 46, Aksakov str., Sofia 1000, Bulgaria.

CANADA

1. Canadian Psychological Association/Société Canadienne de Psychologie. Founded: 1939. President: Luc Granger Ph.D., 1992-93. Chief Executive Officer: Pierre L.-J. Ritchie Ph.D., 1988-94. Address: Vincent Road, Old Chelsea, Québec J0X 1N0. Tel: (1) (819) 827 3927, Fax: (1) (819) 827 4639. Membership: 4100 (8/92).

2. The Canadian National Committee for the International Union of Psychology of Science*, established in 1987, and the Canadian Society for Brain, Behaviour and Cognitive Science, founded in 1991.

3. a. Canadian Psychological Association (CPA). The Canadian Psychological Association is the national body in Canada representing the academic, professional and scientific communities of psychologists. As stated in the preamble of the By-Laws of CPA, the mission of the Association is: "To represent the interests of, and provide leadership in, all aspects of psychology in Canada; to promote by all possible means the unity, coherence, and sense of identity among the diverse scientific and professional interests, and geographical disparities, of all psychologists in Canada; to maintain a strong and balanced commitment to psychology both as a science and as a profession; to promote by discussion and research and dissemination of information the advancement and practical applications of psychological studies in Canada; to issue such publications as may from time to time be considered necessary and feasible; to render such assistance as it can to governments and other organizations concerned with education, health, research, administration of justice, industry, and social and national problems; to promote leadership in the development of national standards, ethical principles, and such matters as may be considered necessary to advance the objectives of the Association."

Regular membership in CPA requires a minimum of a Masters degree in psychology from a recognized university. Most members hold a doctoral degree.

CPA publishes the *Canadian Journal of Psychology*, the *Canadian Journal of Behavioural Science*, and *Canadian Psychology* as well as its official newspaper *Psynopsis*, all of which appear quarterly. In addition, numerous position papers, briefs and standards are published on a periodic basis. A national convention is held in June of each year when awards for distinguished contributions are presented. Fellowship status is also accorded to members who have made a distinguished contribution to psychology as a profession and/or science.

b. The Canadian National Committee for the International Union of Psychological Science. The National Committee ensures that linkages between the Canadian psychological community, the National Research Council as the adhering member to the IUPsyS, and IUPsyS are efficiently maintained through its geographical, linguistic and gender distribution. Its primary undertaking at present is the XXVI International Congress of Scientific Psychology which will be held in Montréal, August 16-22, 1996, under the auspices of the National Research Council of Canada.

4. For most of its first half-century, the Canadian Psychological Association predominately served the academic/scientific community. With the emergence of psychology as a human-service profession, the foci and work of the Association have become more diverse and now include emphasis on professional as well as scientific issues. The organization of CPA was restructured in 1989 to enhance its ability to meet the aspirations expressed in its bylaws and to better reflect the diversity of its membership.

The work of the Association is enhanced through cooperation with several major groupings of psychologists: the Canadian Council of Psychology Departments; the Council of Provincial Associations of Psychologists; the Canadian Register of Health Service Providers in Psychology; and the Canadian Society for Brain, Behaviour and Cognitive Science.

5. Psychology is the only scientific discipline to be funded by all four federal research granting agencies: Medical Research Council, Natural Sciences and Engineering Research Council, National Health Research Development Programme, and Social Sciences and Humanities Research Council. There are active research programmes in all of the major domains of

psychology across the 60 university-based departments of psychology and in a large number of applied settings, both in the public sector (e.g. hospitals) and in the private sector (e.g. telecommunications).

6. Thirty-five Canadian universities provide graduate-level training. The Canadian Psychological Association through its Accreditation Panel also accredits doctoral-level university-based programmes and internships in professional psychology.

Psychology is a legally-established profession in all 10 provinces and the North West Territories. In each province/territory, there is a statute which establishes the legal entity which regulates the practice of psychology in that jurisdiction. In all instances, psychologists are appointed/elected by the government or their peers to oversee the administration of the regulatory process.

7. Dobson, K.S. and Dobson, D. (Eds.) *Professional Psychology in Canada*. Hogrefe-Huber (In press).

Myers, C.R. and Wright, M.J. (Eds.) *History of Academic Psychology in Canada*. Toronto: C.J. Hogrefe, 1982.

Ritchie, P.L.-J., Hogan, T.P., and Hogan, T.V. (Eds.). *Psychology in Canada: The state of the discipline*. Chelsea: Canadian Psychological Association, 1988.

Ritchie, P.L.-J. and Sabourin, M.E., "Sous un même toit: Canada's functional-structural approach to the unity of Psychology", *International Journal of Psychology* 1992, 27 (5).

CHINA

1. Chinese Psychological Society* (CPS). Founded: 1921. President 1988-93: Professor Wang Su. Vice-President 1988-93: Professor Kuang Peizi, Professor Che Wenbo, Professor Zhu Manshu. Secretary-General 1988-93: Professor Lin Zhongxian. Address: Institute of Psychology, Chinese Academy of Sciences, Beijing 100012, People's Republic of China. Tel: (86) (1) 491 9664. Membership (12/1991): 2800 (not including psychologists residing in Taiwan province, China).

2. Chinese Social Psychology Society.

3. CPS was founded in 1921. It is the professional association of Chinese psychologists, under the directorship and funded by Chinese Association of Science and Technology. The aim is to unite psychologists throughout the country to develop academic activities, promote research and exchange, in order to accelerate the development of psychological science, so as to contribute to the realization of the four modernizations of the country.

Qualifications of membership are:

a. Psychologists possessing a level equivalent to MA degree;

b. Graduate of the department of psychology or section and more than three years of professional work in psychology;

c. Non-graduate of the department of psychology but equivalent to the above level and with considerable work experience in psychology. Research seminars and inter-disciplinary workshops are organized by CPS. Two scientific journals *Acta Psychologica Sinica, Psy-chological Sciences* are published under the auspices of CPS.

4. Modern Chinese psychology can be categorized into two phases: The first 28 years (1921-49) and the next 43 years (1949-92). CPS was founded in 1921 in Nanjing. Xhang Yao-xiang was its first chairman, the society's journal was *Psychology*. After a few years activities suspended. In 1937 activities resumed with Lu Zhi-wei as chairman, the society published *Chinese Psychological Journal*. Soon the War of Resistance broke out, again suspending all activities. After the founding of the People's Republic, preparatory work for CPS began in 1950. In 1955 and 1960 the new CPS held its first and second representative assemblies with Pan Shun as the chairman. During the 10 years of "Cultural Revolution" since 1966 activities were again suspended. After 1977 teaching and research resumed. At present there are five departments and seven sections of psychology in universities. Psychology courses are required courses in normal, medical and psychical culture institutes. In 1978, university departments of psychology and the Institute of

Psychology of the Chinese Academy of Sciences began to enroll post-graduate students. In recent years international exchanges developed rapidly.

5. Research in psychology is conducted mainly in the Institute of Psychology and in universities and colleges. Research can be divided into four aspects, namely, general experimental and cognitive psychology, developmental educational and social psychology, developmental educational and social psychology, medical and physiological psychology. Besides, psychological research is also developing in the fields of sports, industrial management, legal and theoretical domain.

6. At present, full-course university training program in psychology was offered to students in 12 universities. BA or BSc degrees are given after a four year undergraduate curriculum. MA or MEd degrees are given to post-graduate students after three years of study and a thesis. Some students are working for PhD degrees.

7. *Acta Psychologica Sinica* (published quarterly in Beijing by CPS and distributed in China and abroad: theoretical articles research papers, reviews, psychology in other countries and events in psychological science).
   Psychological Sciences (published bimonthly in Shanghai and edited by CPS, distributed in China and abroad: articles on theories, general fields of psychology, reviews, information on teaching and research, also psychological events in other countries).

8. Guan Lian-rong. Institute of Psychology, Chinese Academy of Sciences, Beijing 100012, People's Republic of China.

COLOMBIA

1. Colombian National Committee of Psychology* (formed by the Colombian Academy of Psychology, the Colombian Society of Psychology, and the Foundation for the Advancement of Psychology). Founded in 1991 to represent Colombia at the International Union of Psychological Science. Address: Colombian National Committee of Psychology, Apartado 88754, Bogota, Colombia. Membership (of the three associations): 900.

2. Colombian Society of Psychology (CSP). Founded: 1978. President: Jaime Samudio (1991-93). Secretary: William Rodriguez (1991-93). Address: Colombian Society of Psychology, Apartado 53229, Bogota, Colombia.
   Foundation for the Advancement of Psychology (FAP). Founded: 1977. Manager: Elisa Dulcey (1977-); Director: Ruben Ardila (1977-); Secretary: Julio Eduardo Cruz (1986-). Address: Foundation for the Advancement of Psychology, Apartado 92621, Bogota, Colombia.

3. CSP was founded to promote psychology as a science and as a profession in Colombia. Members are people with the title of "Psychologist" obtained in Colombia or abroad. CSP organizes Congresses every two years, and symposia and other activities. It publishes a *Newsletter* twice a year.
   FAP is a scientific organization, devoted to the promotion of psychology as a science, and to encourage research in psychology. It publishes two scientific journals (*Latin American Journal of Psychology*, and *Advances in Latin American Clinical Psychology*), and also books and monographs.
   There are other psychological societies, some of them formed recently, devoted to clinical psychology, industrial/organizational, educational psychology, the experimental analysis of behavior, neuropsychology, etc. Some of them publish newsletters, scientific journals, and organize Congresses and workshops in the areas of interest.

4. In Colombia the first works in psychology were done in the 19th century, specifically by professionals of medicine, education, and philosophy. The first professional training program was founded on November 20, 1947, at the National University of Colombia, being the oldest training program - professionally oriented - of psychology in all Latin America. The number of psychologists has grown very rapidly, particularly in the 1970s and 1980s, with the founding of several Faculties of Psychology in Bogota, Medellin, Barranquilla, Cali, Manizales and Bucaramanga. At the present time the number of

professional psychologists is approximately 4,000, and the number of psychology students is 8000. The major fields are clinical, industrial, educational, basic research, and social psychology. Sport psychology, gerontological psychology, community, criminological and juridicial psychology, are more recent.

5. Research in psychology is carried out at the 16 universities with teaching programs in psychology, and also at several research institutions. Major fields of investigation are the experimental analysis of behavior, and social psychology. Also there is work in physiological psychology, perception, learning, motivation, developmental psychology, gerontopsychology, thinking and language, psychotherapy, work environments, and educational processes. Sources of funding for research exist at local and national levels.

6. Training in psychology is offered at 16 universities, and follows a similar pattern: five years of professional studies in all areas of psychology and related disciplines, a thesis, usually of an experimental nature, and supervised practice. The degree received is "Psychologist" and allows the person for working in any field of psychology. There are seven graduate programs in the following areas: clinical, child, health, industrial/organizational, educational, and community psychology. The government has formally recognized psychology as a profession, and the functions, responsibilities, and rights of psychologists have been specified (December, 1983).

7. *Revista Latinoamericana de Psicología* (Latin Americal Journal of Psychology): published three times a year since 1969 by FAP.

   Avances en Psicología Clinica Latinoamericana (Advances in Latin American Clinical Psychology): published since 1982, also by FAP.

   Revista de Psicología (Journal of Psychology): published irregularly since 1955 by the National University of Colombia.

   There are other psychology journals, newsletters, etc. published by several psychological associations and devoted to clinical psychology, experimental analysis of behavior, industrial/organizational, educational, neuropsychology, etc.

   The only book-length works about psychology as a science and as a profession in Colombia are:

   Ardila, R. (1973). *La psicologia en Colombia, desarrollo histórico* (Psychology in Colombia, historical development), Mexico: Editorial Trillas; and

   Ardila, R. (1992). *La psicologia colombiana en su contexto social e histórico* (Colombian psychology in its social and historical context), Bogota: Editorial Tercer Mundo.

8. Ruben Ardila, Department of Psychology, National University of Colombia, Bogota, Colombia.

CROATIA

1. Croatian Psychological Association, founded 1953, present President: Mišo Munivrana, MA and Secretary-General: Zeljko Jerneic MA (both for the period of 1991-93). Address: Salajeva 3, 41000 Zagreb, Croatia. Tel: (38) (41) 620 100; Fax: (39) (41) 513 834. Membership: 1130 (October, 1992).

3. Every psychologist who has finished his/her psychology studies at one of the Croatian universities (Zagreb, Split, Rijeka) or any other university whose diplomas are recognized in Croatia can become a member of the society.

   The association is mainly active through its regional branches and sections. Each member of the society is a member of at least one of the existing sections. The sections are formed of members working in the same field of applied psychology: preschool psychology, school psychology, clinical psychology, legal psychology, industrial and organizational psychology, vocational guidance.

   The main aims of the Association are:

   a. Promotion and protection of psychologists' professional interests;

   b. Organization of lectures, seminars, courses etc. in order to continually enhance expert knowledge and specialization of its members;

c. Publication of the society's newsletter *Psychological Messenger*, and a journal *Applied Psychology*.

4. The first book on psychology published in Croatian language appeared in 1877. The first book entitled *Experimental Psychology* was published in Zagreb in 1908. It is also worth mentioning that a Croat writer M. Marulic (1450-1524) was the first one to use the term "psychology" in the meaning of "the science of the soul" (Krstic, K. (1964), *Marko Marulic - The Author of the Term "Psychology"*. Acta Instituti Psychologici Universitatis Zagrabiensis, No. 36, 7-13).

Ramiro Bujas (1879-1959) who has studied psychology with Meinong at Graz, founded in 1920 Psychological laboratory as a part of the Physiological Institute at the School of Medicine in Zagreb. The independent chair of psychology, chaired by R. Bujas, was founded on the Philosophical Faculty of Zagreb in 1929. Out of it has developed the present department of psychology with its eight chairs for: general, psychology, experimental and physiological psychology, psychometrics, social psychology, developmental psychology, school psychology, clinical psychology and industrial and organizational psychology with ergonomics.

In 1932 Ramiro Bujas with his collaborators started the journal *Acta Instituti Psychologici Universitatis Zagrabiensis* in which were published mainly papers on experimental psychology, exclusively in English, French or German language. The journal is still in existence.

Croatian psychologists mainly work in various clinics and hospitals as clinical or neuropsychologists, but quite a number are already working as health psychologists on other hospital wards (paediatrics, ear, nose and throat, cardiology, oncology, physiotherapy) and in other medical institutions (institutes, rehabilitation centers etc.). Most primary and high schools now have a psychologist and so do almost all kindergartens in the Republic of Croatia. There are a few industrial psychologists, and a group working in vocational guidance and professional rehabilitation. It could be said that psychologists are now working in almost all fields of public or private human endeavor. During the recent war against Croatia the majority of them voluntarily engaged themselves as military psychologists thus helping our country to defend itself.

Quite a number of our colleagues are working in various research institutes pertaining to medicine, business, marketing, education, law etc. Most of them are members of various international psychological associations.

5. The Ministry of Science of the Republic of Croatia financially supports research projects. Some of those projects are: psychological and neurophysiological development of children; some aspects of vocational maturation of adolescents; psychosocial factors of criminal behavior and the treatment of offenders; social, personal and health facctors of quality of life; visual perception, cortical elaboration and motor effects; human performance in time-sharing tasks; functioning of brain hemispheres in information processing; the cybernetic model of personality; treatment of talented children and the follow-up of the consequences of their public identification; psychosocial climate of penal institutions; psychosocial adaptation of refugees and displaced persons; psychological basis for prediction of social behavior; shift workers features and tolerance to shift work.

The leading researchers of these projects are mostly staff-members of the department of psychology or other scientific institutions in Croatia.

6. There are three departments of psychology in the Republic of Croatia where students can get their psychology degree. The oldest and best equipped is the department of psychology in Zagreb whose staff numbers 13 professors and assistant-professors, seven assistants, eight young researchers and four technical collaborators.

Because of the long standing and permanent orientation towards experimental psychology there is a remarkable collection of old apparatus, but also some new equipment (like PCs in each laboratory).

The study of psychology lasts eight semesters (four years). The entrance requirements are: 1. high school diploma and 2. successfully passed qualifying examination. Each year we have some 350 candidates of which 45-50 are registered. The curriculum corresponds to the curricula offered by other departments of similar size in Great Britain and USA. The collaborative institutions in which (according to their own choice) psychology students have to spend at least one month are: university hospitals, schools and kindergartens and some scientific institutes.

Students finish their studies (after passing all exams) by executing an empirical study (laboratory or field study), writing it in an appropriate form and publicly presenting it to a committee of three staff members.

The department of psychology in Zagreb biannually organizes scientific (MA) and specialization postgraduate studies. The requirements are: 1. psychology diploma and 2. entrance examination. There are specialized courses for the MA in clinical, industrial and school psychology, and scientific MA degree.

The PhD degree could be obtained after the MA without any further study on the basis of a doctorial thesis. There are now 54 psychologists with a PhD degree obtained at the department of psychology in Zagreb.

The psychological profession has been legally recognized since 1953. Institutions, enterprises, schools etc. can legally employ psychologists because in most of them there is a programmed place (or places) for this profession. There is still no legally recognized private practice, although the Association is in the process of legalizing it.

7. Kolesaric, V. and Pavlina, Z. (1990). Development of Psychology at the University of Zagreb. In: *The Role of the University of Zagreb in the Development of Sciences 1669-1990*. Zagreb: University of Zagreb. (Published in Croatian language).

8. Vladimir Kolesaric, Department of Psychology, Salajeva 3, 41000 Zagreb, Croatia.

DENMARK

1. Dansk Psykologforening (The Danish Psychological Association*). Founded: 1947. President: 1988-94 J. van Petersen. Recording Secretary: Preben Føltved. Address: 4 Bjerregaards Sidevej, 2500 Valby. Tel: (45) (31) 16 33 55. Membership: (11/92) 3050 including 350 students.

3. The objects of the Danish Psychological Association are: to protect the members' financial and professional interests; to promote the general public interest in psychology as a science and the understanding of its significance to improve the conditions for psychological research and practical psychological work; to maintain the education of psychologists at a level consistent with the development of modern psychological science.

Condition for membership is a university degree in psychology from a Danish university. Psychologists with degrees in psychology from other universities may apply for membership.

4. As early as 1886 a psychological laboratory was founded at the University of Copenhagen. The founder was a student of Wundt and oriented towards experimental (perceptual) psychology. In the same period, besides this tradition, some philosophers took an interest in psychology, in experimental as well as in general psychology; an interest which has contributed to the development of psychology in Denmark. The first professorial chair in psychology was founded at the University of Copenhagen in 1919. During the first many years, only a few students graduated in psychology a year, and they were mainly oriented towards research. In 1944, an education of professional psychologists was established. From 1960, the education was built up as an indivisible study for a general psychological qualification (candidate's degree (cand.psych.)) with a duration of 5 years, the average study time however being considerably longer.

The Danish Psychological Association (DP) was founded in 1947. The number of psychologists in professional practice was rather small until the sixties, from which period there was a constant growth. The number of candidates today is approximately 3500, which means one psychologist per 1600 inhabitants. Most psychologists work in public service of one kind or another.

Distribution of members' employment categories in 1992: Teaching 144;

teaching/research 255; clinical school psychologists 350; school psychologists 55; hospital psychologists 345; social department 630; industrial and organizational psychologists 50; private practice 225; private companies 250.

5. Psychological research is mainly conducted at two universities (Copenhagen and Aarhus), two university centres (Roskilde and Aalborg), and the Royal Danish School of Educational Studies. A minor part takes place at public or semi-public research institutes.

   The major research orientations and the major fields of academic psychological research are:

   a. Research orientation: The tradition of the Copenhagen School of Phenomenology still has some influence. Besides this tradition, major influence is seen from the psychodynamic theoretical orientation; the school of critical psychology (the "Berlin School"); the Soviet cultuural-historic school; the cognitivistic orientation; neo-behaviourism and the clinical neuro-psychological orientation.

   b. The major research fields are: Working conditions; work and technology; psychodynamic oriented therapy (adults and children); neuro-psychology; clinical psychology and society; class, society and education; preventative psychology; ethnological comparative research; development of concepts; mass media and children; perception and cognition; psychology of acting; psychology of meaning; life-quality research; psychology and information-technology.

6. Psychology degrees are granted by the University of Copenhagen and the University of Aarhus. The degree is achieved after a minimum of 5 years study and emphasizes applied psychology on a scientific basis. Graduates are awarded the degree; candidatus psychologiae, abbreviated "cand.psych." The dr.phil (PhD) degree is awarded on the basis of a thesis which is the public result of independent and advanced research. The thesis is defended at a public hearing.

   There is no legal protection of the title "psychologist" in Denmark although the titles cand.psych., mag.art. and dr.phil. are protected.

7. *Dansk Psykolog Nyt* (Danish Psychology News): research and profession news.

   Nordisk Psykologi (Nordic Psychology) (published quarterly): provides the information on psychological research in Scandinavia.

   Scandinavian Journal of Psychology: empirical reports and theoretical or methodological papers within any area of psychology.

ESTONIA

1. Union of Estonian Psychologists*. Founded: 1988. President: J. Allik. Secretary: Tiia Tuulmets. Address: 778 Tiigi Street, Tartu EE2400, Estonia. Tel: (7) (1434) 30825. Fax: (7) (1434) 35440. E-mail: tiia@psych.ut.ee. Membership: (10/92) 44.

3. The Union of Estonian Psychologists is a voluntary organization for professional psychologists and it associates Estonian psychologists. Members of UEP may be persons who are practicing applied or scientific psychology and who have as a rule university qualification in psychology or a scientific degree in psychology, or who are promoting with their activity the development of Estonian psychology. The objectives of UEP are: high professsional level of Estonian psychology; advanced psychological science in Estonia and its effective application in practice; psychological welfare of Estonian people; security of Estonian psychologists; extended exchange of information and contacts between psychologists of Estonia and other countries. The tasks of UEP are: to raise the quality of education of professional psychologists in Estonia; support professional rights of psychologists in developing their professional activity; to develop professional ethics of psychologists, to help in carrying out psychological research and in applying the results in Estonia, to act as an expert in important issues of social and cultural life. UEP has the right to: open and close accounts and execute financial operations; form temporary working groups for carrying out scientific projects and finance their activity; control the justified and adequate use of psychological instruments, certify and licentiate their users;

organize scientific conferences and seminars; publish psychological and periodical publications. From the very beginning the UEP has edited a Newsletter and its own publication *Applied Psychology*. The UEP has arranged courses and conferences for members and other psychologists, supported research projects.

4. The University of Tartu was founded under the name Academia (Universitas) Dorpatensis in 1632 by the decree of the Swedish King Gustavus II Adolphus. Since psychological problems of that time played a prominent role in philosophical disputations, this year can also be regarded as the beginning of psychology in Estonia. After a considerable break, the university was reopened in 1802 and from this time psychology has been taught almost regularly as a university course. In 1886 the founder of modern psychiatry Emil Kraepelin arrived at Tartu and was appointed as head of the Department of Psychiatry. His studies on the role of caffeine on the speed of mental processes meant also the origin of experimental psychology in Tartu. The experimental spirit of psychology established by him was followed by Vladimir Chiz who received his training in the Wundt laboratory. Psychology in the independent Estonian Republic (1918-1940) did not attain any remarkable international recognition. After becoming the national university, The University of Tartu founded a chair of psychology which was occupied by Konstantin Ramul until seventies. His achievement was to keep the university course in psychology alive and to publish popular articles. The most remarkable publication in psychology of that time was *Intelligence of Estonian children* written by Juhan Tork (1940). This was methodically a whole nation study of children's mental aptitudes. The occupation of Estonia by the Soviet Union also had consequences on the situation in psychology. Thousands of Estonians were rescued by emigration, among them well-known psychologists as Endel Tulving, Theodor Annapas, Vello Sermat, Jaak Panksepp. The psychology lacked the status of an independent field of knowledge in Soviet science. In general, it was a mixture of ideological citations and Pavlov's teaching about conditional reflexes canonized by the joint sessions of Academies of Sciences. Subscriptions to all psychology journals and new books were stopped. From the late fifties the situation in Soviet psychology started to improve although ideological pressure and struggle have never stopped. At that time some of L. Vygotsky's studies were published, the first psychological journals started to appear. The number of universities and institutions that were allowed to grant scientific degrees was very limited. Personal, national or political reasons prevented several people from gaining a scientific degree. The fondness for general speculative argumentation produces the inability to discover and describe new empirical facts and regularities. Although organisationally Estonian psychology was connected with Soviet psychology, intellectually it remained relatively autonomous. The tradition of regarding experimental and empirical knowledge as the fundamental basis of psychology in general was still existing. In 1968 psychology was reestablished as the main speciality in the University of Tartu. Most currently active psychologists came to science in the seventies.

5. The most developed area of psychology in Estonia is visual perception. The long tradition of psychophysical investigations made in the University of Tartu are concerned with the perception of stochastic patterns, the perception of motion. The future perspectives are concerned with psychophysiological investigation. From other areas can be named psychoacoustics, selective attention, environmental psychology, cross-cultural and developmental psychology and psychopharmacology. The small size of Estonia makes it very appealing for population studies. Its unique cultural and historical experience makes it a proper place for testing certain psychological theories and cross-cultural studies.

6. At the present moment, the training of psychologists and educational system in the University of Tartu is not very different from other European universities. Even in a situation of almost complete isolation from the outside world during the Soviet times, Estonian psychology was able to preserve its closeness to world psychology. The active community of Estonian therapists is already integrated to the system of international cooperation and long-term training programs. All working psychologists have passed at least five years of university studies. Therapists and clinical psychologists start with

special training courses and under supervision. Most of the psychologists are employed in the public sector or in private companies. Psychologists are very much used as supervisors and consultants. Specialized commissions together with the Union of Psychologists are going to control the adequate use of psychological instruments, certify and licentiate psychologists. The aim of the UEP is to gain a Psychologists' law to protect and authorise psychologists.

FINLAND

1. Finnish Psychological Society* (FPS). Founded: 1952. President 1991: Prof. J. Hautamäki. Recording Secretary 1983- : Ms Taina Schakir. Address: Maciankatu 7B, 00170 Helsinki. Tel. and Fax: (358) (0) 633 206. Membership (9/92): 1492.
2. Finnish Psychological Association (FPA). Founded: 1957. President and Managing Director 1990: S. Saazi. Address: Rautaticläisenkatu 6, Helsinki. Tel: (358) (0) 150 2312. Fax: (358) (0) 141 716. Membership (1992): 3100.
3. FPS was founded in 1952 to "promote psychological research and publication activities, to further practical psychological work and to serve as a link between representatives of theoretical and applied psychology." Membership is open to all persons accepting the aims of the society. FPS organizes biennial congresses (recently jointly with FPA) and research seminars. FPS publishes two scientific journals, one in Finnish, the other in English.

   FPA is the professional psychological association of Finland. It consists of 17 regional associations. Persons holding a university degree (MA) in psychology are eligible for membership. FPA has a committee on professional qualification, granting the title of a licensed psychologists (LP). FPA organizes annual professional congresses, sponsors training seminars and professional development courses in various fields of applied psychology, and publishes a newsletter.
4. The first psychological laboratory was set up at the University of Turku in 1922. The first professorial chair of psychology was founded at Teachers' College (now University) of Jyväskylä in 1936. In 1957, the year FPA was founded, the number of professional psychologists was 111, 10% engaged in teaching and research, the rest almost evenly divided between the four major fields of vocational guidance, clinical psychology, child and adolescent guidance, and psychology of work. At present there are six psychologists for every 10,000 inhabitants; 90% of psychologists, with only academic teaching and research staff and those in non-psychological professions being outside. In 1992 the members of FPA were distributed among major fields as follows: 42% clinical; 18% child and adolescent guidance; 15% vocational guidance; 11% public health; 5% teaching and research; 4% primary and secondary education; 4% psychology of work.
5. Research in psychology is conducted mainly in eight universities and two research institutes. Major fields of academic psychological research are: psychology of perception and psychophysiology (attention and performance; visual perception; neural basis of sensations); cognitive psychology; developmental and educational psychology; psychology of work and traffic safety; stress; aggression. The two research institutes specialize in the psychology of work and in the psychology of health and illness. In 1992 the number of psychologists holding academic or other research positions was about 150.
6. In 1983 full-course university training in psychology was offered to 1,400 students in six universities. Upon coompleting a five-year undergraduate curriculum, the student receives an MA degree or equivalent (M.Ed., M.Psych., M.Soc.Sc.). The scientific Phil.Lic. (Lic.Psych.) and Ph.D. (D.Psych.) degrees, offered by six universities, typically require a minimum of four and six years of graduate study, respectively.

   No state licensing of professional psychologists exists in Finland. The committee on qualification of FPA grants the title of LP to holders of an MA degree who have a maximum of three years of professional experience under the supervision of a senior psychologist and have taken a sufficient number of professional development courses approved by FPA (minimum duration: 1180 h).

7. *Psykologia* (published bimonthly in Finnish by FPS: research reports and reviews, book reviews, society news).
Acta psychologica Fennica (in English; published yearly by FPS: reports on current research).
Psykologiuutiset (in Finnish; published by FPA; 16 issues a year: professional issues, calendar of professional meetings and courses).
8. J. Hautamäki, University of Helsinki.

FRANCE

1. Société Française de Psychologie* (SFP) (French Psychological Society). Founded: 1901. President (1992-95): André Bisseret. Secretary General (1992-95): Bernard Lespès. Address: 28, rue Serpente, 75006, Paris. Tel: (33) (1) 40 51 99 36. Membership (11/92): 1,230.
3. The SFP was founded in 1901 "to promote publications and to provide financial support for research". Since this time, the Society has also become a professional society open to practitioners of psychology, while maintaining its scientific orientation. The Society has revised its statutes in 1991. It now comprises three departments: one for research, one for applications, and one for affiliated associations. Furthermore, the Society subsumes eight regional branches in the country.
   New members of the Society must have at least five years of higher education in psychology and be elected by an absolute majority of voting members.
   The Society organizes an annual conference, thematic scientific meetings, and interdisciplinary symposia. The Society publishes a scientific journal *Psychologie Française* (four issues per year), as well as a newsletter *La Lettre de la SFP* (five issues per year).
4. The Society develops efforts in order to unite researchers, teachers, and practitioners in psychology. It represents the interests of the discipline at government agencies and in international organizations, including the International Union of Psychological Science, in the creation of which the Society played a leading role.
6. Four years of university studies are required for the master's degree in psychology. An additional year is required for a specialized diploma (Diplôme d'Etudes Supérieures Spécialisées, DESS, or Diplôme d'Etudes Approfondies, DEA). A total of seven years is required for the doctoral degree.
   The Society has worked actively towards legal recognition of the profession of psychologist, based on at least five years of higher education and observance of the ethical code of the Society. The law was adopted by the French Parliament in 1985.
8. Michel Denis, Université de Paris-Sud, LIMSI-CNRS, Equipe Cognition Humaine, B.P. 133, 91403 Orsay Cedex, France.

GERMANY, FEDERAL REPUBLIC OF

1. Deutsche Gesellschaft für Psychologie (German Psychological Association), (DGPs). Founded as Gesellschaft für experimentelle Psychologi (Society of Experimental Psychology, SEP) in 1904, name changed to DGfPs in 1929, and to DGPs in 1990. President 1992-94: Professor Urs Bauman; Secretary General: Professor Amélie Mummendey, Universität Münster D-4400 Münster; Tel: (49) (251) 83 4153; Fax: (49) (251) 83 8387; Membership (7/92): 1342.
2. Berufsverband Deutscher Psychologen (Professional Union of German Psychologists) (BDP). Founded: 1946; President 1990-92: Dipl.-Psych. Lothar Hellfritsch; Vice-President 1990-1992 Dipl.-Psych. Ute Stegliche, 2. Vice-President 1992: Dr Alfred Roeber; Address: Heilsbachstr. 22, D-53000 Bonn 1; Tel: (49) (228) 6410 54/55/56; Membership (9/92): 17,184.

3. DGPs was founded in order to promote scientific psychology in German speaking countries. Within DGPs 11 Fachgruppen (divisions) have been established in order to promote the development of respective sub-disciplines. In 1992 Regionalgruppe Österreich (regional group Austria) has been founded to support special national affairs of Austrian members of DGPs. Psychologists working in research and teaching, holding a doctoral degree in psychology or related fields, and having published at least two scientific papers are eligible for full membership. Associate membership is open to psychologists without a doctorate working in research. Biennial congresses of psychology are organized by DGPs, advanced research seminars and special meetings are initiated. Six scientific journals are published under the auspices of DGPs.

BDP is the professional organization of German psychologists. Membership is open only to persons holding a university degree in psychology as a profession in all fields of application. Biennial congresses of applied psychology are organized as well as training seminars and professional improvement courses are held in various fields of applied psychology.

Both of these societies are united in Förderation Deutscher Psychologen-vereinigungen* (Federation of German Psychological Societies). The chairpersonship alternates yearly between the presidents of the constituting societies; President in 1992: Dipl.-Psych. Lothar Hellfritsch.

4. The world's first psychological laboratory was founded in Germany by Wilhelm Wundt at the university of Leipzig in 1879, psychology as a science rapidly grew in Germany out of Wundt's experimental tradition, later forming special branches, e.g. Gestaltspsychologie, Berlin Topological School (Lewin), Leipzig Ganzheit School or Würzburg School. SEP was founded by G.E. Müller, H. Ebbinghaus and O. Külpe in 1904 in Giessen during the first psychological congress. In the twenties psychology as a profession was established and grew continually. Professional psychologists worked in various fields, mostly engaged in psychodiagnostics or ergonomic-related fields.

Under the influence of German nazism and World War II many achievements were lost. After World War II psychology in Germany was in a disastrous state as a scientific as well as professional discipline. It recovered in the sixties. In the seventies, the number of departments, the number of faculty members as well as the number of non-academic psychologists increased remarkably. In 1962, the Gesellschaft für Psychologie der DDR (Society of Psychology of the GDR), (GP) was founded. After the unification of Germany GP has been dissolved in November 1990.

5. Research in psychology is conducted mainly in 59 universities and about 13 research institutes (including three Max-Planck-Institutes). New fields such as psychology of knowledge, behavioral medicine, ecological psychology, psychology and language, geronto-psychology have been established. The research institutes specialize in cognition, criminology, educational psychology, human development, and sports psychology.

In 1992, the number of psychologists holding senior academic or research positions (Professor) in psychology was about 460.

6. As a rule, German students enter university after 13 years of schooling (Gymnasium, which includes some college courses). Students enrolled in psychology take a first examination (Vor-Diplom) after a two-year undergraduate program, and a second examination (Diplom-Psychologe) after at least another two years of graduate studies and completion of a thesis. Students holding the Diplom are offered in all universities an advanced research degree of Doctor of Philosophy (sometimes Doctor of Science). This requires about three years of advanced studies and the completion of a doctoral (research) thesis.

7. *Psychologische Rundschau* (published quarterly by Verlag für Psychologie Dr C.J. Hogrefe, Göttingen, as "official organ" of DGPs. Research articles, professional issues, news from DGPs, BPD and Federation, calendar of and reports about scientific meetings etc.).

Report Psychologie (published monthly by Deutscher Psychologen Verlag, Bonn, as "official organ" of BDP. Professional issues, news from BDP, calendar of and reports about scientific and professional meetings etc.).

GHANA

1. There are no societies or associations.
4. The Department of Psychology at the University of Ghana, Gegon, was established in 1967. It was the first fully-fledged Department of Psychology to be established in an Anglophone West African university. With an initial student population of only four at the time of its establishment, the Department has rapidly expanded with psychology being one of the most popular courses at the University of Ghana. The current student population is about 260 with an academic staff strength of nine. The Department has produced over 500 graduates since its establishment, including about 30 postgraduate students in the areas of clinical, developmental, industrial and organizational, and social psychology. There is a Departmental Library stocked with fairly current books and journals and some laboratory equipment (including two PCs) for practical classes. A Departmental bulletin *The Legon Bulletin of Psychology* was launched in early 1992, with the hope that it will develop into a reputable international journal.
5. Major current research programmes are on issues in social, developmental, and industrial and organizational psychology that are relevant to the needs of a developing country like Ghana. Another research area is information processing among bilinguals in developing countries. Several papers by the principal investigator in this area, Dr J.Y. Opoku, have emanated from this research and are published in several international journals or as chapters in books. A current research interest of the Department involves the attitudes of Ghanaians towards condom use as a means of prevention against the sexual transmission of HIV.

The Department offers a three-year (six-semester) Bachelors degree programme at the undergraduate level and a two-year (four-semester) Master of Philosophy (M.Phil.) programme. A one-calendar year Masters programme is also available in selected areas.

At the undergraduate level, students who intend to major in psychology are required to offer at least 12 units (four courses, each course carrying three units) in psychology during their first year. Experimental psychology, statistics, research methods in psychology, developmental psychology, and psychology of personality and abnormal behavior are core courses in year two for students majoring in psychology. Other courses offered during the undergraduate training include measurement and evaluation, social psychology, comparative and physiological psychology, applied psychology (clinical, educational, environmental, industrial and organizational, guidance and counselling, and psychometrics). In addition, all majoring students conduct and write research projects that cover a period of two semesters in the third year. Laboratory practicals constitute an essential part of experimental psychology which is taught every year over the three-year period. Students are given firm theoretical foundation in general psychology at the undergraduate level with a strong emphasis on empirical investigations of psychological problems peculiar to the Ghanaian environment.

Courses offered at the graduate level are mainly in the applied areas of psychology. The rationale behind this approach is to ensure that the graduate students we produce find it easy to obtain employment in a rather restrictive and competitive labour market. The most widely subscribed graduate courses are in the areas of clinical psychology, and industrial and organizational psychology. In these two applied areas, there are well-trained staff and facilities exist in industries, organizations, and hospitals for much-needed practical training (practicum). Students who intend to pursue graduate training in theoretical areas of psychology are normally encouraged to train outside Ghana and such students are normally absorbed back to the Department as lecturers upon successful completion of their Ph.D. programmes.

There is no Association of Psychologists in Ghana but we are working toward establishing one. Professional psychologists like clinical psychologists who work in hospitals are however, recognized as professionals by policy makers.

7. Information of the state of psychology at the University of Ghana can be found in:
   University of Ghana Annual Year Book - locally published by the University of Ghana;
   Handbook of Undergraduate and Graduate Studies - locally published by the University
   of Ghana;
   Commonwealth Universities Yearbook - this gives information on the staffing situation in
   the Department.
8. Dr J.Y. Opoku, Head of Department, Department of Psychology, University of Ghana,
   Legon, Ghana.

GREECE

1. The Hellenic Psychological Society* (HPS) was founded in 1990. The President of the
   Society is Professor Ioannis Paraskevopoulos of the University of Athens (1991-93) and
   the Secretary General is Professor Andreas Demetriou of the University of Thessaloniki
   (1991-93). The main office of the Society is at the Department of Psychology, Aristotelian
   University of Thessaloniki, Thessaloniki 540 06, Greece. Tel: (30) (31) 99 26 54; Fax: (30)
   (31) 20 61 38; Email:bczz04@grtheun1. Membership (10/92): 54 full members and 48
   associate members.
2. There is a second organization of psychologists in Greece. This is the Association of Greek
   Psychologists (AGP) which started in 1963. At present AGP involves more than 700
   members (October 1992).
3. To be eligible for full membership in the HPS one must hold a Ph.D. in psychology. A BA
   degree with major in psychology or an MA in psychology is required for admission as an
   associate member. Voting rights are given only to full members. The Society is primarily
   oriented to the dissemination and advancement of the science of psychology rather than
   to professional practice. A BA degree in psychology is required for admission in the AGP.
   This Association is professionally rather than academically oriented.
4. Psychological science is rooted in classical Greek civilization as the first theories of
   cognition and learning were advanced by Plato and Aristotle. However, despite this
   brilliant past and for historical reasons that cannot be discussed here, it is only rather
   recently that psychology started to be systematically practiced, taught, and cultivated in
   modern Greece (see Houssiadas, in press). Specifically, psychology started to be taught
   under the one scheme or the other at the University of Athens and the University of
   Thessaloniki since the late twenties. However, it was only in 1972 that the first by and
   large complete course of studies in psychology started to function at the University of
   Thessaloniki in the context of the then so called Department of Psychology and Education
   which was instituted in that year. At present there are two Departments of Psychology in
   the country which provide a four-year degree in psychology (one at the University of Crete,
   which started in 1986, and one at the Pantion University of Social Sciences in Athens,
   which started in 1991) and a third is starting this year at the Aristotelian University of
   Thessaloniki. In addition a BA degree with a major in psychology is offered by the
   Departments of Philosophy, Education, and Psychology which exist at the Universities of
   Athens, Crete, and Ioannina since 1982. Finally, the numerous Departments of Education
   which exist in most of the fourteen Greek Universities offer strong courses in several fields
   of psychology but mainly in educational and development psychology.

   At present there are only two full graduate programs in psychology leading either to
   an MA or a Ph.D. degree in psychology, one at the University of Athens and the other at
   the University of Thessaloniki. These programs started in the mid-eighties. The graduate
   program in Athens is strong in clinical and developmental psychology, although social,
   experimental, and personality psychology is well represented in the programs offered by
   both universities. A graduate program in social psychology has recently started at the
   Pantion University of Social Sciences in Athens. It needs to be stressed that at both the
   undergraduate and the graduate level psychology is cultivated as an empirical science as
   in the other European countries or in Northern America.

5. The academically oriented Greek psychologists have been very prolific in research in the recent years. Research in developmental and social processes as well as clinical research is the most productive in terms of the number of people involved and output of publications (see Markoulis and Demetriou, 1992). Special mention should be made of a rather long lasting research program in Thessaloniki which is focused on cognitive development. This program has provided the empirical basis of a theory of cognitive development. Research in moral development, the development of language, and complex cognitive processes is also strong in Thessaloniki. The Section of Psychology at the University of Athens is prolific in research on the assimilation of cultural values, socialization mechanisms, and social factors related to educational preferences and achievement. Finally, a program on the psychology of minorities and their position in society has recently started at the Pantion University of Social Sciences.

It needs to be emphasized that research in Greece is well up to the international standards. This is evidenced by the fact that Greek researchers publish their research in international journals of psychology. There are two refereed psychological journals in the country, one published by the HPS and the other by the AGP.

6. Psychology as a profession is rather well established in Greece, although the legal state of the profession is unclear. According to a law passed in 1979 but never actually put into practice, one can become a licenced psychologist if one holds a four-year degree in psychology granted either by a Greek university or by an officially recognized foreign university. A new law which will redefine the criteria for professional practice so as to be in accordance with those of the other EEC countries will be introduced in the near future. Mostly clinical but also school, educational, and work psychologists offer their services in both the private and the public sector of the society. It needs to be mentioned that the majority of professional psychologists have specialized abroad as the graduate studies in the country have only recently started.

7. Houssiandas, L. (in press). Psychology in Greece. In V.S. Sexton and J.D. Hogan (Eds.), *International psychology: Views from around the world*. Lincoln, Neb.: University of Nebraska Press.
Markoulis, D., and Demetriou, A. (1992). Academic and research psychology in Greece. In U. Gielen, L.L. Adler, and N.A. Milgram (Eds.), *Psychology in international perspective* (pp. 70-87). Amsterdam: Swets and Zeitlinger.

8. Andreas Demetriou, Department of Psychology, Aristotelian University of Thessaloniki, Thessaloniki 540 06, Greece.

HONG KONG

1. Hong Kong Psychological Society* (HKPS). Founded: 1968. President 1992/93: Dr Godfrey Harrison. General Secretary 1992/93: Ms Gillian Marcoolyn. Address: Department of Psychology, The University of Hong Kong, Hong Kong. Tel: (852) 859-2376. Fax: (852) 858-3518. Membership (July 1992): 240.

3. HKPS was founded to give Hong Kong a body: to advance the scientific study of psychology, to provide a forum for psychologists, to promote high professional and ethical standards for psychologists and to encourage the practice of psychology. Society membership is as a Fellow, Associate Fellow or Graduate Member. Membership requires a recognised honours degree with psychology as a main subject or a recognised post graduate qualification in psychology or some other qualification acceptable to Council. Affiliates of the Society are either those interested in psychology but not sufficiently qualified for membership or Overseas Affiliates who, typically, have been members, become resident overseas and wish to maintain links with the Society. The Society issues a Code of Conduct and related Guidelines for practitioners; advises Government and other agencies in Hong Kong; organises an annual conference, scientific meetings and workships as well as meetings to present psychology to young people; and publishes a quarterly *Newsletter* for members and the *Bulletin of the Hong Kong Psychological Society* which is distributed

internationally. In 1982 the Society's Division of Clinical Psychology was formed and is its largest component; similarly, the Division of Educational Psychology, formed in 1989, attracts a large proportion of the Society's members. Both Divisions work to keep members up-to-date, to develop skills and to liaise regularly with employers on opportunities for extending services and developing carrer structures.

4. The twenty-five-year-old Department of Psychology in the University of Hong Kong (HKU) is the territory's older academic department of psychology; a ten-year-old and unquestionably well established department graces the Chinese University of Hong Kong (CUHK). Psychology contributes to post-graduate studies at the Hong Kong University of Science and Technology - opened to students in October 1991. Psychologists work for various Government Departments, such as Education, Correctional Services and the Police as well as for, the newly established, autonomous Health Authority. Psychologists put their knowledge and skills to use, too, for agencies, firms and companies, in devising and implementing programmes in such fields as social welfare, rehabilitation, marketing, advertising and training. Privately, an increasing number of psychologists work with clients seeking help on emotional, educational, counselling and vocational matters.

5. Psychological research in Hong Kong has continually developed since the previous directory. Research is being undertaken in the following areas, among other projects: giftedness and creativity; dual-earning families; stress and coping - e.g. in school settings and in police work; prosocial and antisocial behaviour among adolescents and the Chinese Multiphasic Personality Inventory. Funds equivalent to over US$100000 are now available for psychological research in Hong Kong. Sources include tertiary institutions, the Universities and Polytechnics Grants Committee and bodies such as the Royal Hong Kong Jockey Club. Hong Kong, with less than seven million people, is the world's tenth greatest trading entity and has seen enormously rapid economic development. Its urbanisation and modernisation and attendant problems of change and stress have been major foci for research in academic institutions, public agencies and private enterprises.

6. Hong Kong has B.Soc.Sci. programmes in psychology at HKU and at CUHK: Ph.D. and M.Phil. research degrees and M.Soc.Sci. (Clinical Psychology) taught programmes at both universities. Additionally, HKU has a Post Graduate Certificate in Psychology and an M.Soc.Sci. (Educational Psychology) in its Psychology Department as well as an M.Ed. in the same specialism while CUHK has M.Phil. and Ph.D. programmes specifically for clinical psychology. Psychology is part of several first degree programmes in Hong Kong's three universities and two polytechnics: Business Studies, Social Work, and Speech and Hearing Sciences being examples. The Society has approved establishing a Society Register of competent psychologists and plans to introduce, during 1993, this provision for the better informing, service and protection of members of the public seeking psychological services. Legal registration of psychologists is an issue for the future. In contrast, the transfer, in mid-1997, of sovereignty from the United Kingdom to the People's Republic of China is an immediate issue for Hong Kong psychologists. With that transfer an end seems sure to any special role for the British Psychological Society (BPS), which oversaw the development of many psychology programmes but with which, since the period when the BPS was establishing its register of Chartered Psychologists, the Society no longer enjoys reciprocal membership.

7. Betson, C. and Pryde, N. (1992) *A Guide to Mental Health Services in Hong Kong*, Second edition.
   Blowers, G.H. (1987) Psychology in Hong Kong, in Blowers, G.H. and Turtle, A.M. (Eds.) *Psychology moving East*, Sydney, Westview Press/Sydney University Press.
   Clinical Division HKPS, (1991) *Directory of Clinical Psychological Services*, Hong Kong.

HUNGARY

1. Hungarian Psychological Association* (HPA). Founded: 1928. President: Dr István Czigler. Secretary-General: Dr Klára Szilágyi. Address: Erzsébet Krt 13, H-1067

Budapest, Post: 1536 Budapest Pf.: 220, Hungary. Membership: 1,400.

3. HPA was founded in 1928. Due to the war and the subsequent social changes its activities were disrupted for several years. It was reorganized as Hungarian Scientific Psychological Association in 1962, and regained its original name in 1972. The task of the Association is "the furthering the development of psychological activities in Hungary, monitoring its results and situation, increasing the professional knowledge and information of the members, formation of a democratic professional life and ethical conduct...". To pursue these aims, members of the society are active in 12 sections, one geographic branch and three committees, which embrace all important fields of psychology. The Association organizes biennial congresses of psychology, the last one in 1983, as well as numerous lectures and workshops. The Association promotes the professional protection of psychologists. In order to realize this, its Ethical Committee has elaborated a detailed Professional Code of Ethics for psychologists, which is under public evaluation and revision by the membership in.

All psychologists, persons with a university doctoral degree in psychology and colleagues with a higher education degree working in neighbouring fields are eligible for membership.

4. The first psychological laboratory was founded by Paul Ranschburg, connected to the system of special education. For many decades, psychology in Hungary has developed along the experimental lines and educational relevance established by him on the one hand, and along psychoanalytic lines initiated by Sándor Ferenczi on the other hand. These two traditions are still alive, and in the 60s they became the motor of the enormous qualitative development of psychology observed from then on. During the last two decades the number of psychologists has increased at least twenty times. Although academic psychology also has developed strongly, most of the quantitative development has meant an increasing number of psychologists in professional activities, principally in clinical psychology, followed by educational and industrial applications. Besides conventional employers - e.g. hospitals, factories - several national service chains were developed with an emphasis on practical applications of psychology, most notably Educational Guidance Centers/Ed. Guid. Cent/and Vocational Guidance Institutes/Vocat Guid Inst/.

5. Psychological research is conducted at four universities, in a large research institute of Academy, in several research establishments of a more general scope - educational, organizational, medical etc. - research institutes, and at several colleges. Psychology is involved in several colleges. Psychology is involved in several nationwide research programs of social importance, as psychology in the educational system; social adaptation disorders; ergonomics etc.

6. University training in psychology is offered at two universities for 550 students, 300 of whom are students at night classes half of them looking for a second degree. A five year study plan besides giving a sound scientific basis provides courses in all of the major applied fields, too. A Diploma of Psychologist, Dip.Psy., is given after the completion of a masters thesis at the end of the program. From 1980, three postgraduate programs were introduced in clinical, educational and industrial psychology, which after two years of training while the students also work, gives a degree of specialist psychologist, which is required for positions like head psychologist in a hospital and so on. Doctoral degree in psychology, D.Ps., are given by accredited universities with with no program, only on the basis of a dissertation and exams. Two higher academic degrees are: candidate, Cand.Psy., and doctor of psychological sciences, D.SPs.Sc., both given by the Academy of Sciences upon submission and defence of a major dissertation. Between 1977 and 1981 several degrees by the Ministries were specifically issued to regulate the employment conditions and qualifications requirement of professional psychologists.

7. *Magyar Pszichológiai Szemle* (The Journal of Hungarian Psychology) is published eight times a year in cooperation with HPA and the Committee on Psychology of the Hungarian Academy of the Sciences.
Pszicholóia (Psychology) is published four times a year as the journal of the Institute of Psychology of the Academy.

Newsletter of the HPA.
8. Cs. Pléh and J. Nagy, HPA, Hungarian Psychological Association, Erzsébet Krt 13, H-1067 Budapest Post: 1536 Budapest Pf.: 220, Hungary.

ICELAND

The Association of Icelandic Psychologists was founded in 1954. There were nine founding members. Psychology as an academic discipline was introduced in Iceland at the beginning of this century by two eminent scholars, Ágúst H. Bjarnason and Guómundur Finnbogason. Ágúst H. Bjarnason studied in Denmark and France and became professor in psychology and philosophy in the University of Iceland when it was founded in 1911 by the fusion of three schools: The Medical School, the Law School and the Theological Academy. Together, they formed the University with a Philosophical Department added. Professor Ágúst H. Bjarnason wrote a textbook of psychology (published in 1924) which was to be, for many years to come, a rich source for psychological knowledge both for students and the reading public. Guómundur Finnbogason published in 1917 a book called *Vit og strit* (Work and Reason) on the psychology of work and activity at a time when this branch of psychology was just beginning to take its first steps.

The founders of the Association were psychologists who had studied during the interwar years (in Germany and France) and during the postwar period (in Scotland, Norway and Denmark). They led the way in establishing school psychological services and in the employment of psychologists in the health system. For several years to come Icelanders had to seek abroad for university education in psychology. The next generation went mainly to Great Britain, France, the United States and also to the Scandinavian countries, and this pattern has continued to this day. However, in 1969 a new chapter was begun in the history of Icelandic psychology when the first professorship in psychology was established in the University of Iceland and Mr Sigurjón Björnsson was appointed professor. The study was organized as a three-year course ending with the BA degree. Icelandic students must still go abroad for further education but the development of the Psychological Department will in a few years lead to the establishment of a full five years course ending with the MA degree.

Membership of the Association began to grow in the latter half of the seventies when students began to return home after having finished their studies abroad. About 25% of the members are women. The members are divided among the professions in these proportions: 25% work in schools (the School psychological service), 25% work in the health service and one half of the membership is divided among several professions, mainly teaching, administration and private practice.

The Association is organized according to a regional principle, the main body of the membership being situated in the southwest (the Reykjavik City area) with a division in Akureyri, the chief town of the north. The highest authority in the Association is the Annual General Meeting which elects the president and a four member Board for the period of two years. The Board meets usually twice a month. The Board employs, as yet, no staff but the establishment of an office is being prepared. This will be in connection with our information service, already established. The Association is a member of BHM - the Central organization of the academic professions.

The Association publishes a *Newsletter* five times a year. It operates an extensive program for further education and specialization of psychologists. This program is now to be extended and planned as both theoretical and professional training.

Because of the rapid expansion of the psychological services in Iceland in the last years there is no unemployment among Icelandic psychologists.

IRELAND

1. The Psychological Society of Ireland (PSI) *Cumann Síceolaithe Éirann*. Founded: 1970.

President (1992-93): Ms Anne Halliday. Honorary Secretary (1992-93): Ms Catherine Navin. Address: Adelaide Road, Dublin 2, Ireland. Tel: (01) 783916. Membership: (10/92) 750.

3. The Psychological Society of Ireland (PSI) was founded in 1970 to "advance psychology as a pure and applied science and as a profession, more especially in Ireland". Membership is open to all who have an honours degree in psychology awarded by an Irish University or an equivalent qualification. The Society, which is governed by a Council, has established a number of specialized groups, the most active of which are the Mental Handicap Group and the Clinical Division. PSI organizes an Annual Conference at which members report on advances in psychological research and practice, an annual Society Lecture given by a distinguished Irish psychologist and many ordinary meetings of the Society. PSI's specialized groups arrange programmes to further the professional development of members and to advance the appreciation of psychology among the general public. The Society has published policy documents on the role of psychologists in the education and health services. It publishes two periodicals: *The Irish Journal of Psychology*, founded in 1971 and issued in an annual volume of four numbers; and *The Irish Psychologist*, a bulletin issued monthly since 1974.

4. The origins of psychology in Ireland can be traced back to the centuries-old tradition of philosophical studies in the centres of learning of the Early Christian Era. Internationally recognized contributors to psychological thought in the pre-scientific era range from Johannes Eriugena (Scottus) in the ninth century to George Berkeley in the eighteenth. While a Chair of Logic and Psychology was established in the Dublin College of the newly-founded National University of Ireland as early as 1909, psychology was studied then as an essentially philosophical discipline. Somewhat later, psychology came to be seen as a discipline whose practical applications justified its inclusion in programmes of teacher education. For one such course in Dublin. Ant Sr Máire published *Aigneolaíocht*, a psychology textbook in 1928. In the late forties, psychology began to emerge as an independent empirical discipline. The first Irish professional psychologists qualified in 1950 with a BEd degree from the Queen's University of Belfast. 10 years later, the first psychologists to qualify in Dublin were awarded a postgraduate DipPsych.

5. Research in psychology in the Republic of Ireland is conducted in the country's four University Colleges as well as in a number of Dublin-based specialized centres devoted to research and training in the social sciences, e.g. the Educational Research Centre. Heavy teaching loads in rapidly-growing University Departments and the absence of consistent funding have mitigated against the development of large-scale research projects. Most funded research is geared towards the improved functioning of educational and health services and of industrial organizations.

6. Full university degrees in psychology are now available at four University Colleges in the Republic of Ireland and at four University centres in Northern Ireland. In these, 496 student completed courses of either three or four years leading to a basic degree in psychology in 1991. After graduating, some students go on to take MA and PhD degrees by research. Others work for postgraduate professional degrees such as the MPsychSc degree in Clinical Psychology at University College, Dublin, the MSc in Counselling at Trinity College, Dublin or the MA in Human Resource and Occupational Psychology at University College, Cork. Some also avail themselves of the opportunities for advanced training available abroad, especially in the USA and in Britain. In the Republic of Ireland, psychologists are employed in a variety of settings. Apart from academic departments, the main employment agencies are the Department of Education, the Health Boards, voluntary organizations providing services for people with learning disabilities and the public and private sectors of industry. In general, psychology is now ell established in Ireland and continues to flourish in spite of economic difficulties. Psychologists in Ireland are not legally registered but, since 1991, PSI has operated a voluntary form of registration and has published an annual register. In 1979 the Society developed a Code of Professional Ethics to which its own members subscribe. The Code was revised and enlarged in 1991.

7. Brady, T. and McLoone, J. (1992), Ireland. In V.S. Sexton and J.D. Hogan (Eds.),

International Psychology: Views from around the World, Lincoln, NE: University of Nebraska Press.

McHugh, M. and McLoone, J. (1980). The roots that clutch: the origins and growth of PSI. *The Irish Psychologist*, 6 (10), 1-8.

McLoone, J. (1988). The development of services for people with mental handicap in Ireland: The contribution of psychologists. *Irish Journal of Psychology*, 9, 205-219.

8. James McLoone, Department of Psychology, University College, Galway, Ireland.

ISRAEL

1. Israeli Psychological Association* (IPA). Founded: 1958. President: Professor Elchanan I. Meir. Recording Secretary: D. Sylvia Silberman. Address: 74a Frishman Street, Tel Aviv 64375, Israel. Membership: approx. 2,500.

   Membership is open to Israeli citizens holding an MA degree in psychology. IPA organizes conventions, seminars, professional meetings and post graduate studies. A quarterly *Newsletter* including scientific articles and professional data is published by IPA.

3. In Israel the first department of psychology was opened at the Hebrew University in Jerusalem. Academic specialities in 1984, at five universities include: clinical psychology, educational psychology, social psychology, vocational counselling psychology, organizational psychology, rehabilitation psychology, experimental psychology, physiological psychology and cognitive psychology.

4. Research is conducted mainly at the universities, Israel Defence Forces and several public and private institutions. In 1984 the number of psychologists holding academic or other research positions was about 200.

5. In 1984 five universities in Israel offered BA studies in psychology to about 350 students per year. After completion of BA (3-4 years) students may register for MA studies at four universities with an option to continue later for Ph.D. The MA studies require two academic years plus MA thesis (most students need an additional two years for that). About 100 psychologists are registered for post-MA studies every year. After MA graduation specialization is acquired by two years of work under supervision on a full-time basis (or parallel period on a part-time basis) in clinical psychology, educational psychology, vocational and/or social psychology or rehabilitation psychology.

6. Licence for work in psychology depends on MA degree in psychology as a prerequisite and state licence examinations in the field of specialization. Only a person holding such a license is entitled to render professional psychological services, including psychotherapy (if the licence is obtained in clinical psychology). In Israel state licensing of psychologists was introduced in 1977.

ITALY

1. Società Italiana di Psicologia* (SIPs), Italian Psychological Society. Founded: 1910. President: Professor Mario Bertini. Secretary: Dr Luigi Ferdano Pierucci. Address: V. Manin n.33, I-20121 Milano, Italy. Membership: 2,600.

2. SIPs membership can include members of many smaller, more recent societies of theoretic or often professional psychology and related fields, notably: the Freudian Società Psicoanalitica Italiana; founded 1932; the Jungian and Adlerian societies founded afterwards. All these have the respective journals: *Rivista di Psicoanalisi, R. di Psicologia Analitica* and *R. di Psicologia Individuale*. In a Confederation of group treatment societies (COIRAG) is the Società di Psicoanalisi di Gruppo (SIPAG). Other associations deal with research and practice in old or new particular methods of psychology; some join only professional (AIPP), industrial psychologists, or vocational counsellors; others deal with special clinical categories. Many are members of the corresponding international

associations.
3. Changes in leaders of the original SIPs, fascism and the wars slowed development until the fifties. The renewed 1971 Statute, labels the SIPs as a scientific-professional association promoting psychology and its applications in an evolving human society. Its organs are: the General Assembly, the elected President and the Directive Council, 20 regional Sections and eight scientific-professional Divisions, internal "Services" for new members admission (see point 7), administrative and cultural affairs. Triennial Conventions are held (average attendance 1000 in the last four sessions), plus many thematic or local meetings and workshops every year. The official journal *Psicologia Italiana* is published five times yearly.
4. Italian Psychology was originated in early 1800. University labs started in Rome, 1889, Florence, 1903, and professorial chairs in 1906. This aided applications in neuropsychiatry, education, forensic and occupational psychology, that recovered slowly after the crisis of the facist period. Since the seventies new regulation, still in progress, of public health, basic and higher education, local administrative services, improve psychologists' training practice and labour market; though unluckily economic problems hinder this trend.
5. Some 40 university Institutes, quite different in size and tradition, two CNR Centres and few private teams, undertake all basic and applied research. Much of this work is poorly administered, despite the CNR and Ministry of Education efforts to organize research.
   Research subjects since 1970 show a decline of Gestalt theory while cognition and interpersonal processes improve. Psychophysiology is moving from neuroendocrinology and body potentials to brain hemisphere functions. Epistemology and historical interests are recent. In applied research, family treatment, handicaps, old age and recent views on individual and group therapy emerge.
6. University courses for "Laurea" (Dr in Psychology degree, 35% of SIPs members) started (1971) in the tradition of humanistic Faculties in Padua and Rome, this raised criticisms concerning quantity and quality, as every year some 1000 new graduates, mainly trained in theory, seek work. However, the Ministry of Education has recently agreed to increase the number of Universities conferring a psychology degree, after a five-year course with supervised training in four different branches. The other University Degree is "Specializzato" (Special, 31% of SIPs members) i.e. a Dr who attended a three-year school in special branches of psychology; since 1955 nearly 100 annually. Libero Docente (Lib.Doc.) in psychology or its branches (decreasing 5% of SIPs members), until a few years ago, was a title conferred to research fellows through national competition. Nearly 10% of Italian psychologists have also some foreign degree.
7. As well as journals quoted in points 2 and 3, the following are noteworthy:
   Archivio de Psicologia, Neurologia, Psichiatria; *Bollettino di Psicologia Applicata*; *Giornale italiano di Psicologia* (with alternate issues in English: *Italian Journal of Psych*). Are significant the more recent: *Ricerche di Psicologia, Psicoterapia e scienze umane* (publisher F. Angeli, Milano), *Storia e critica della Psicologia* (Mulino, Bologna); *Psicologia clinica* (Pensiero scientifico, Roma); *Psicologia e scuola, Età evolutiva, Psicologia contemporanea* (Giunti, Firenze). The oldest (1905) *Rivista di Psicologia* and *Rivista di Psicologia sociale*, now are issued less regularly. Among many volumes, the richest in information are: R. Canestrari & C. Cipolli *Guida a La Psicologia* (Sansoni, 1974); G. Trentini (Ed.) *La professione di Psicologo in Italia* (ISEDI, 1977); M. Cecchini and G.P. Lombardo (Eds.) *Lo psicologo* (Bulzoni, 1980). Those publishers, plus: Armando, Boringhieri, CLEUP, Giuffré, Pàtron, issue many original or translated volumes in psychology. SIPs publishes annual lists of its members.
8. L. Meschieri, L. Tev. Flaminio 22, -00196- Roma.

JAPAN

1. Japanese Psychological Association* (JPA). Founded: 1927. President 1992-: Dr Yoshinori

Matsuyama. Secretary General 1992-: Prof. Masatoshi Tomita. Address: 2-40-14-902 Hongo, Bunkyo-ku, Tokyo 113. Tel: (81) (03) 3814 3953. Membership: (including student members) (9/92) 4,900.

2. Japanese Association of Educational Psychology (JAEP). Founded: 1952. President 1989-: Dr Chitoshi Tatsuno. Secretary General 1989-: Dr Hiroshi Watanabe. Address: c/o Faculty of Education, University of Tokyo, Hongo, Bunyo-ku, Tokyo 113. Tel: (81) (03) 3818 1534 ext. 3951. Membership (9/92): 4200

    Association of Japanese Clinical Psychology (AJCP). Founded: 1982. President 1991-: Prof. Takao Marase. Secretary General 1991-: Prof. Yoshitaka Otsuka. Address: 2-40-14-402 Hongo, Bunkyo-ku, Tokyo 113. Tel: (81) (03) 3817-5851. Membership (9/92): 5,300.

3. JPA, the member society of IUPsyS, is the oldest nationwide professional association coverning every field of psychology. Each member belongs to at least one of the following five research divisions, that is:

    a. sensory, perceptual, cognitive, physiological;
    b. developmental, educational;
    c. clinical, personality, criminal, correctional;
    d. social, industrial, cultural;
    e. methodological, theoretical, historical, general.

    Qualification for membership is expertise in psychology. Graduate students of psychology-major are eligible for student membership. *JPsyA Newsletter* (semiannually in Japanese) and two official journals, *Japanese Journal of Psychology* (bimonthly in Japanese with English abstracts) and *Japanese Psychological Research* (quarterly in English) are published. There is an annual general convention. JAEP is the oldest of the specialized psychological organizations founded after World War II. It is open to those who are trained in educational psychology including graduate students and school teachers. Two periodicals are published, *Japanese Journal of Educational Psychology* (quarterly) and *Annual Report of Educational Psychology*, both in Japanese. General convention is annual. AJCP is the most recently founded. Members are principally qualified practitioners in clinical psychology but include theorists admitted with appropriate recommendation. *Journal of Japanese Clinical Psychology* (three issues a year) and *Newsletter* (semiannual) are published both in Japanese. General convention is annual.

4. Japan came to know Western psychology, as a scientific discipline in the last quarter of the 19th century. The first professorial chair was founded at University of Tokyo in 1890. The first psychological journal appeared in 1912 succeeded by a JPA journal after the inauguration of JPA in 1926. Japanese Association of Applied Psychology was organized in 1931 and Japanese Society for Animal Psychology followed in 1933. The JPA members before World War II was scarcely over 200. After the war, however, the number of psychologists increased and professional organizations ramified into many special fields. The 1990 version of *Psychological Institutions in Japan* lists 27 nationwide and nine regional psychological associations and the total estimated number of psychologists in Japan is 17000-18000. The March 1992 statistics showed that, of 4831 JPA members, 2498 (52%) are in universities and colleges, 695 (14%) are graduate students, 266 (6%) are in research institutes, 293 (6%) are in national and local governmental organizations, 223 (5%) are in hospitals and welfare institutions, 99 (2%) are in private organizations, and 104 (2%) are school psychologists, among others. JPA, in collaboration with other psychological associations in Japan, hosted the XX International Congress of Psychology in Tokyo in 1972 and the XXII International Congress of Applied Psychology in Kyoto in 1990.

5. The 1991 JPA directory lists 129 universities and colleges with which JPA members are affiliated and it also lists 28 psychological research institutes. Recent annual conventions of JPA have attendants of over 2000 with the number of papers presented being around 800. Sensory, perceptual and cognitive process as well as researches in social and cultural psychology are the major topics of interest. Developmental studies are also growing.

6. Some 20 universities offer full graduate programs for MA and Ph.D. degrees. Others offer

programs terminating in MA. To obtain a doctoral degree, a candidate has to spend at least five years in graduate residence and submit a dissertation. Ph.D. degree may be conferred on non-residents for outstanding contribution. In 1988, AJCP established Japan Association for the Certification of Clinical Psychologists (JACCP), and by the end of 1991, JACCP has issued certificates to 3486 clinical psychologists. In 1990, JPA developed another system to certify those who had taken required credits in psychology in universities or colleges and by the end of 1991, 289 certificates were issued. This JPA system was developed with a hope that in future the certificate will be a minimum basic requirement for all psychologists intending to obtain certificates in more specialized areas of psychology. Neither of the above certificates, however, has legal recognition yet.

7. Imada, H. *Psychology as a science and as a profession in Japan.* Japanese Psychological Research, 1993 (to be published).
JPA (Ed.): *Psychological Institutions in Japan*, 1990.
JPA (Ed.): *Semicentennial history of the Japanese Psychological Association, Part 1, 1980 and Part 2, 1987.* Tokyo: Kaneko-shobo Inc., (in Japanese).

8. Masatoshi Tomita: Department of Psychology, Waseda University and Hiroshi Imada: Department of Psychology, Kwansei Gakuin University.

MEXICO

1. The Sociedad Mexicana de Psicologia* (Mexican Psychological Society) was founded in 1950. The Society's President for the 1991-95 period is Juan Jose Sanchez-Sosa, Ph.D. and its Secretary General for the same term is Professor Jorge Peralta Alvarez. The Society's address is: Apartado Postal 22-211, 14000, Tlalpan, México, D.F., Mexico. Tel: (52) (5) 550-6404, 606-7720; Fax: (52) (5) 665-5228, 548-6957. The Society's membership as of October 1992 is 1,025.

3. The Society's major aims include to increase, promote and disseminate the development of scientific psychology in any of its manifestations. Membership requirements include, for voting full members, a formally awarded licensed psychologist degree in any accredited higher education institution, and the endorsement of a credentialed current full member. Affiliate (non-voting) members include those who provide a certified affidavit of completion of the licensing degree minus the corresponding thesis defense and formal awarding of the degree. Adherent (non-voting) members are psychology students who have completed at least 70% of their professional licensing training. Honorary (non-voting) members include highly distinguished non-psychologists who have made an important contribution to the development of psychology. The Society publishes the *Mexican Journal of Psychology* which, at the time of the present edition, includes eighteen issues conforming nine volumes. The Journal (*Revista Mexicana de Psicología*) publishes articles in Spanish with English abstracts, has a double-blind review editorial process and has an acceptance rate of approximately 3/10 manuscripts for publication. The Society organizes and conducts a triennial national congress where most of the highly productive and advanced research or professional psychologists show their work. It also organizes and conducts seminars, workshops, continuing education courses and specialized conferences. Since 1984 the Society has published the only formally edited and widely accepted Code of Ethics for Psychologists in Mexico and currently publishes a bi-monthly internal newsletter. Finally, the Society awards periodically the Mexican Award of Psychology, a nationwide prize in the areas of research and professional performance.

4. As a formally recognized scientific discipline, Psychology in Mexico was born in 1896 when Professor Ezequiel A. Chavez instituted psychology courses in the baccalaureate system of the University of Mexico. Originally founded in 1553, the University was renamed National Autonomous University of Mexico (UNAM) in 1910. In 1916 Professor Enrique O. Aragon founded the first fully equipped laboratory of experimental psychology at UNAM's School of Higher Studies. Outside UNAM applied psychologists' work involved mainly translating adapting and using French and US intelligence tests. Psychology was

taught at UNAM as part of philosophical studies up to 1945 when it became an independent department. Training in psychology gradually increased its professional and research format becoming a fully independent School and Faculty in 1973. Up to the decade of the fifties most professional psychologists adhered to the psychodynamic clinical models and most researchers worked in psychometric data collection of some type. The sixties saw a boom of experimentation including strong groups working within the behavioral approach. Schools of psychology, public and private, multiplied approaching ninety (30 public and 60 private) in number nationwide in 1992, 19 of them are in Mexico City.

5. Currently, research in Psychology is conducted in several universities. These include: National University (UNAM), Iberoamericana, Anahuac, de Guadalajara, Baja California, Sonora and Chihuahua and the National Polytechnic Institute among others. The main fields of research and specialization include: psychophysiology (sleep, psycho-pharmacology, inter-hemispheric correlation, biofeedback, neuropsychology); health psychology (risk factor detection, preventive psychology, epidemiology, behavioral medicine, biofeedback, health promotion); social psychology (sexual behavior, sports psychology, self esteem, social interaction, environmental psychology); cross cultural research and animal experimental models, among others. In 1991 there were approximately 870 psychologists involved in research projects.

6. Professional training involves nine to 10 semesters of formal university training exclusively in psychology. Students must then engage in supervised social service training for one semester and finally write and defend a thesis in front of an academic committee. Theses are usually expected to involve either the report of a research project or the evaluation of some type of professional intervention or service. Only universities accredited by either the National University (UNAM) or the Ministry of Education can award the corresponding diploma, which is later endorsed by the national office for the regulation of professions of the same ministry. This provides psychologists with the legal permit to offer professional services. The Mexican Civil Code states that a professional Collegium of any given discipline, composed of at least 100 licensed persons in as many states as possible, are expected to recommend post-licensure regulations. Currently the Mexican Psychological Society and the National Collegium of Psychologists of Mexico are actively collaborating in projects toward fulfilling these responsibilities. Specialities include the clinical, industrial, educational, social, experimental, psychophysiological, developmental, health and behavior analysis areas. Depending on the specific program, these specialities are sometimes built into the license degree itself or are part of post licensure graduate training. Formal speciality diplomas usually require two years of graduate supervised training. Master and doctorate degrees generally involve two and four years of post speciality training respectively.

7. The main published sources providing information on the state of psychology in Mexico include *The Mexican Journal of Psychology (Revista Mexicana de Psicología)* published by the Society; *The Journal of the Mexican Council for Teaching and Research in Psychology* (CNEIP); and the book *The Psychologist*, published by UNAM.

NETHERLANDS

1. Nederlands Instituut van Psychologen: (NIP). (Dutch Association of Psychologists). Founded: 1938. President 1990-93: Prof. P. van den Broek. Recording Secretary 1992- : Mr R.F. Baneke. Address: Osdorperbaan 27A, 1068 LD Amsterdam, P.O. Box 9221, 1006 AP Amsterdam. Tel: (020) 6109596. Membership (11/92): 6,250 (includes 500 students).

2. Stichting voor Wetenschappelijk Onderzoek in de Psychologie en de Psychonomie in Nederland, PSYCHON (The Netherlands Foundation for Psychology and Psychonomy), Laan van Nieuw Oost-Indië 131, 2593 BM Den Haag, P.O. Box 93120, 2509 AC Den Haag. Tel: (070) 344803.

3. NIP was founded in 1938 by the Dutch Society for Psychology. The event took place in the

Psychological Laboratory of Amsterdam University. Initially the new association was called Dutch Institute of Practicing Psychologists. The new association was founded primarily to serve the promotion of psychology as a field of profession. Membership is open to all university graduates and to students who passed a certain exam (candidaats or propaedeuse).

Twice a year NIP organizes a congress; one of these is organized in cooperation with SWOP and Psychonomics. On certain fields NIP-sections (clinical, developmental/children and youth, vocational guidance, educational, labor and organizational, gerontological, social etc. psychology) organize conferences on a smaller scale and on more specific topics.

The Netherlands Psychonomics Foundation was founded in 1968. Amongst its members there are some hundreds psychologists and also representatives of other disciplines. The Foundation consists of several working societies regarding different fields of psychology. They organize quite a lot of activities and the Foundation as a whole is rather successful in stimulating research with the aid of non-university financial resources.

In the near future several organizations will be brought together under the roof of SWOP, such as the Netherlands Psychonomics Foundation, the Association of Developmental Psychology, the Association of Social-psychological Researchers, the Dutch Foundation for Psychonometric and several other research societies. SWOP is already playing an important part as an intermediary institution concerning financing research between applicants on the one hand and NWO (purely scientific research) on the other.

4. Scientific psychology in the Netherlands was started with F.C. Donder's reaction-time experiments over more than a hundred years ago. The first Dutch psychological laboratory was established in 1892 by Heymans.

The number of psychologists grew rapidly from about 6000 in 1981 and over 15000 in 1992: 8000 are men and 7000 are women. Both sexes have an equally strong preference for clinical psychology (40%), but women apparently choose much more often developmental psychology (38% versus 20% at men)). Men prefer much more the other clusters, amongst them especially psychology of labor and organization. Every year almost one thousand new psychologists enter the labor market. From 1950 until 1992 the percentage of female graduates rose from 32.6 to 70. Most probably in the near future women will surpass men in the psychological occupation. There has already been an ever increasing unemployment among psychologists, which is now almost 20%. A lot of the young colleagues are trying to start a private practice in the primary health care. There is little hope for an enlargement of paid jobs. This holds also for the universities and non-university research institutes, where about one thousand psychologists are working.

5. In the Netherlands psychological research is being conducted in all the main fields of psychology. Amongst them there are of course not only traditional but also rather new fields. Anyone who has a specific interest in a certain field will be served by NIP-headquarters as well as possible.

6. In the Netherlands one can study psychology at the universities of Amsterdam (2), Leiden, Utrecht, Groningen, Nijmegen, Tilburg. From 1982 on the length of study has been reduced to five years. An initial plan for two-phase structure - theoretical until one's degree and practical/professional afterwards - has been cut. Now the Netherlands has only the first phase. At the same time several huge reorganization processes, induced by the government, are going on, which create much uncertainty for students and university people.

When one finishes university one is entitled to the title drs. which means doctorandus. After a thesis one is a doctor. University titles as well as the title of psychologist are legally protected. The title of clinical psychologist will be legally protected in the near future.

7. *De Psycholoog*, published monthly by NIP.
De hand op vandaag (on the scientific research in Dutch psychology), by P. Vroon, Basisboek, Ambo, 1982 Baarn, Holland).
Wat doet de psycholoog? by R. Roe, 1984, Van Gorcum, Assen.

8. Mr R.F. Baneke, NIP, Amsterdam.

NEW ZEALAND

1. The New Zealand Psychological Society* Inc. (NZPsS) was founded in 1967, having previously been a branch of the British Psychological Society. President (until August 1994): Dr Olive J. Webb. Executive Director (on contract): Mr Grahame G. Gillespie. National Office: 1 Edward Street, Wellington, P.O. Box 4092. Tel: (04) 8015-414. Fax: (04) 382-8763. Membership (October 1992): approx. 500.

3. Qualifications for membership of the NZPsS are a doctorate or postgraduate degree in psychology, or in education (provided there is a major psychological component plus supervision). The Society's major goals, derived from its eight constitutional Objects, are:

   a. To consolidate and extend the role of the Society as the effective voice of the psychological profession as a whole;

   b. To facilitate the role of psychology and psychologists as agents of social betterment;

   c. To enhance their effectiveness as professional psychologists;

   d. To advance the interests of psychology as a science.

4. Psychology in New Zealand developed from the British philosophical tradition brought by the early settlers in the 19th century, particularly those from Scotland. The applied tradition arrived only in the 20th century, and flourished only intermittently, except in education. Not until the 1950s did psychology begin to emerge as a modern discipline, freed from its historical ties with philosophy, with the establishment of separate university psychology departments.

   Educational psychology was the first field to which the discipline was applied, through a centralised "Psychological Service" (more recently a "Special Education Service",) providing specialist consultants to schools. Clinical psychology was not centralised, being largely in the hands of autonomous local health authorities. Mainstream hospital-based clinical psychology is dominated by applied behaviour analysis and behaviour modification procedures. Cognitive behaviourism and its clinical applications are only just beginning to have an impact.

   The remarkable growth in New Zealand industry in recent decades has led to the need for expert management and industrial psychology services, and recently course options and professional training have become available in these areas.

5. Psychological research in New Zealand is predominantly university based, with funding through a Government funded foundation and from individual universities. Doctoral programmes on predominantly British lines based on intensive study and research are the major methods for training advanced researchers. Each of the six universities has tended to develop its own specialist research traditions.

6. Registration of psychologists is the responsibility of the Psychologists' Board, established under the Psychologists Act 1981. Until now, however, registration for practice has not been compulsory, nor has the term "psychologist" been protected (though "registered psychologist" is). The Act is currently under review, largely because of:

   a. The increasing number of complaints against psychologists, which has highlighted the need to revise disciplinary procedures;

   b. The widening gulf between academic and professional practice psychologists, which has ramifications for the registration process; and

   c. The modern trend towards greater lay participation in the control of professional bodies.

7. The NZPsS publishes an academic *Journal* (twice yearly); a quarterly *Bulletin* of professional and Society information; and a monthly newsletter, *Connections*.

8. This information was compiled in the NZPsS National Office, which acknowledges the assistance of Professor George Shouksmith of Massey University, Palmerston North.

NICARAGUA

1. Asociación Nicaraguense de Psicólogos* (ANIPS): Nicaraguan Psychological Association.

Founded: 1981. President 1983-85: Lic. Silvia Narváez. Recording Secretary 1983-85: Lic. Auxiliadora Moreno. Address: CONAPRO "Héroes y Mártires, Apartado postal No. C-142.
3. ANIPS was founded in 1981 to organize Nicaraguan psychologists, to raise their scientific level and to promote their professional ethics. Membership is open to all persons holding a Bachelors (licentiate) degree in psychology whether they be Nicaraguans or foreigners residing in Nicaragua. Yearly workshops are programmed to discuss exams and solve problems faced by psychologists in their daily work. Research results are also presented in these workshops. A small bulletin is published three times a year. Lectures and seminars are sponsored to raise the scientific knowledge of its members.
4. In Nicaragua the first School of Psychology was founded in 1969 at the Universidad Nacional de Nicaragua (UNAM) and also at the Catholic University (UCA). At first, psychologists had very little opportunity and a few of them started to work in Government Institutions, others went abroad to continue post-graduate studies, and others stayed teaching at the school. Up to the revolution the professional development of the psychologists was very limited, mainly toward counselling, psychodiagnostics and personnel. Although substantial advances have not been achieved, some foundations have been established for the development of a higher scientific level through short course, exchange of experiences with psychologists of other countries in addition to scholarships for graduate studies abroad. In 1983 the membership of professional psychologists was 550 with a distribution in major fields as follows: 12% health (communitary, clinic), 15% education (special education, counselling, pre-school, adult education), 15% organizational, 10% training programs, 12% social programs, 8% private institutions; 10% political organizations, 10% academic teachers and 8% various.
5. Research in psychology has had very little development in Nicaragua due mainly to the economic underdevelopment of the country which is clearly reflected by the lack of graduate studies within the country. Presently, the permanent aggression does not allow the advancement in this area, however, some research is being conducted in several government programs such as health, education, organizational and also in the school of psychology.
6. In Nicaragua only a bachelor's degree could be obtained. Graduate studies and doctorates had to be obtained abroad. Presently, there is demand for psychologists in government and private institutions; a few of them are in the private practice. Currently there are no unemployed psychologists.

Academic studies take five years and after six months of social service and the presentation of a research paper a Diploma is graduated that permits the psychologist to work after registering it.

PANAMA

1. Asociación Panameña de Psicólogos* (Panamenian Psychologists Association). Founded: June 22, 1965. President: Psic. Saturnina Anderson; Secretary: Mercedes Ruiz. Address: Apdo. 6-7838 El Dorado, Panamá. Tel: (507) (26) 5982 (day); (507) (29) 2633 (night); Fax: (507) (25) 0221. Membership: 250.
2. Another organization is La Academia Panameña de Psicología (Panamenian Psychology Academy). Founded: 1981.
3. The Asociación Panameña de Psicólogos major goal is the realization of scientific activities and to supervise the Ethic Principles. The main objective of the Panamenian Psychology Academy is the promotion of scientific development in different areas of psychology.
4. In the country the fields and use of psychology have increased with a large number of professionals recently.
5. The Institute of Clinic Psychology and Psychotherapy was founded in 1976. The prime objective is the formation of clinical psychologists and psychotherapists, with a psychoanalytical orientation exclusively. They will publish a biannual Journal. Address: Apdo. 1977, Panamá 9A, Panamá; Tel: (36) 0466/(36) 0331; Fax: (60) 0904.

6. In Panama, two universities provide basic training facilities: Universidad de Panama and Santa Maria la Antigua with specializations in Family Guidance and Family Therapy.

PERU

1. Colegio de Psicólogos del Perú (Psychologists' College of Peru). Founded: 1980. Dean (1992-93): Ps. Héctor Sato ; General-Secretary (1992-93): Ps. Luis Zapata; Address: Camilo Carrillo 164, Jesús María, Lima, Peru; Tel: 337949; Membership (1992): 3,255.
3. The Colegio de Psicólogos is an autonomous institution of internal Public Law; it has legal existence and represents professional psychologists of the country. Its membership is absolutely indispensible for exercising the profession of psychologist in Peru. The main office of Colegio de Psicólogos is at Lima, capital of the country.

   Membership requirements: Professional degree of psychologist of Licenciatura in psychology, extended or recognized by a Peruvian university which must have in turn a Faculty or Academic Program of Psychology.

   Major aims and goals: To defend the profession of psychologist; to rule it in consonance with actual legislation, College's rules, professional ethics code, and so forth; to promote and make known to the Society the development of Psychological Science and to orientate the colleagues towards those areas in which society presents urgent needs and relevant interests.
4. Psychology as a career leading to academic and professional degrees began around 1955 in our country, at Universidad Nacional Mayor de San Marcos (Major National University of San Marcos), Lima. Some years later it also began at Pontificia Universidad Católica del Perú (Catholic University of Peru) and was progressively incorporated to the study regimes of some other universities in Peru. This year (1992), Universidad de Lima (University of Lima) received its first students for the career of psychology.
5. For some years, psychology in Peru had mainly a clinical orientation. At present, it has also developed in other areas such as the educational and/or industrial, social and communitary ones. This fact can be observed in the academic as well as the professional levels.
6. Psychologists in Peru may continue master studies, which demand two years of study plus a master thesis. This, in turn, is a condition for continuing doctoral studies which include two academic years plus a doctoral thesis.

   As regards professional training, there are several private professional associations linked either to educational psychology or to family, social, industrial, organizational, clinical and/or psychotherapeutic psychology.
7. Alarcón Reynaldo et al. *Investigación psicológica en el Perú* (Memorias del I Congreso Peruano de Psicología - Diciembre 1975). Editorial Universo S.A., Lima, 1976.
   Revista de Psicología. Facultad de Letras y Ciencias Humanas de Pontificia Universidad Católica del Perú: Sección de Psicología. Lima.
   Cuadernos de Psicología. Facultad de Ciencias Humanas de Universidad de Lima: Especialidad de Psicología. Lima.
8. Luis Ramírez Aguirre, Coordinador de Especialidad de Psicologí, Universidad de Lima, Facultad de Ciencias Humanas, Av. Javier Prado Este s/n, Monterrico, Lima, Perú. (Fax: 378066).
   David Jáuregui Camasca, Universidad de Lima, Facultad de Ciencias Humanas, Avenida Javier Prado Este s/n, Monterrico, Lima, Perú. (Fax: 378066).

PHILIPPINES

1. Psychological Association of the Philippines* (PAP). Founded: 1962. President: Dr Amaryllis Tiglao Torres; Secretary-General: Ms Flordeliza R. Punongbayan; Address: Philippines Social Science Center, Don Mariano Marcos Avenue, Diliman, Quezon City,

Philippines. Membership: 1,514.

3. PAP was founded in 1962 to advance the practice of psychology as an independent, scientifically oriented and ethically-conscious profession. Membership is open to doctoral and masteral degree holders in psychology (or with equivalent professional work experience) whose main interests are geared towards the advancement of psychology as a science and as a profession. The PAP holds an annual convention which serves as a forum for scientific papers on theoretical and methodological issues as well as trends in psychology. *The Philippine Journal of Psychology* is the official journal of the association.

4. Philosophical psychology was taught in the Philippines as early as the 17th century. In the 1920s psychology broke away from philosophy and became closely identified with education until about the 1960s. Following the return of the founding fathers of psychology from graduate training abroad, activities were aimed at establishing psychology as a distinct discipline. Departments of Psychology were set up; institutes and clinics offering psychological services were established. From the handful of schools offering degrees in psychology in the 1950s and early 1960s, there are now about 30 schools offering a bachelor's degree, 15 a masteral degree and four a doctoral degree in psychology. From the few school clinics that extended psychological services to the community, there are probably more than a hundred applied psychology groups existing in the Philippines today engaged in testing, therapy, or training. The need is now strongly felt for measures to protect and ensure the competent practice of psychology in the Philippines. It is toward this end that the Psychology Act was proposed. The Act provides for certification of psychometricians and the licensing of practicing psychologists. The main practitioners of psychology in the Philippines are the clinical psychologists and the industrial psychologists. Over the years the clinical psychologists in the Philpines have achieved greater professional identity and status. Psychotherapy used to be the domain of psychiatrists with psychologists relegated to the task of diagnostic testing. With the increase in the numbers of trained and experienced clinical psychologists and the "enlightenment" of the medical profession the clinical psychologists now has equal claim to the practice of psychotherapy. There is also a new breed of practitioners typified by the social psychologist based in government agencies and in private development groups.

5. Research activity is a major task of colleges and universities. Most programs engage in research and field applications, though the types of research work may vary. The areas of research in the 1980s are on personality variables, child development and Asian psychology; in social issues and in the dynamics of Filipino communities; and in the intricacies of the Filipino psyche. In methodology, there is the veering away from the experimental approach with more emphasis on phenomenological field approaches.

6. In the Philippines, two types of undergraduate programs are found, the BA and BS major in psychology. Following a four year under-graduate curriculum, training in psychology can be completed by two degrees: a Master of Arts or Master of Science (MA or MS) in psychology and Doctor of Philosophy (Ph.D) in psychology. The masteral program requires a minimum of 2-3 years of study, a comprehensive examination, and the completion of a research thesis. The Doctoral program also requires a written comprehensive examination and a research dissertation aside from an MA degree.

7. *Philippine Journal of Psychology*, official journal of the PAP (published yearly: research in fields related to psychology in the Philippines).
PAP Convention Proceedings, (published yearly: papers presented at each annual convention of the PAP.

8. A.M. Guerrero, Psychological Association of the Philippines, c/o Central Guidance Bureau, Ateneo de Manila University, P.O. Box 154, Manila, Philippines.

POLAND

1. Polskie Towarzystwo Psychologiczne* (PTP) (Polish Psychological Association PPA). Founded: 1948. President: Dr Malgorzata Toeplitz-Winiewska (since 1991).

Secretary-General: Mgr Krzysztof Broclawik (since 1991). Address: ul. Stawki 5-7, 00-183 Warszawa, Poland. Tel. & Fax: (48) (22) 311368. Membership (October 1992): 4500

3. PPA is the only all-Polish psychological association. PPA was founded in 1948. Persons holding a university degree Master of Psychology are eligible for membership. PPA engages in the development of psychology as a profession and organizes scientific and applied congresses (every three years). The Association arranges advanced workshops and thematic conferences and sessions (at non-regular intervals). PPA has 22 regional departments, the largest ones in Warsaw and Katowice. The organs of PPA are: *Przeglad Psychologiczny* (Psychological Review, in Polish) and *Nowiny Psychologiczne* (Psychological News, in Polish) published quarterly and monthly respectively.

4. In Poland the first chair of psychology was founded at the University in Lwow in 1901. Before the beginning of World War II research in psychology was conducted at five universities. Psychology at that time was a part of philosophy departments. The growth of psychology as an experimental science was accelerated in the 1950-60s first of all at the universities in Warsaw, Krakow and Poznan. In 1983 the distribution of PPA members among the major fields in psychology was as follows: 38% clinical psychology, 43% educational psychology, 10% research and academic teaching, 9% miscellaneous. Currently this proportion is similar with growing tendency in clinical psychology.

5. Research in psychology is conducted in: nine universities, Institute of Psychology at the Polish Academy of Sciences, several central institutes, such as Education, Defence, Health, Sports, etc. In the last decade major fields of psychological research were: developmental and educational psychology, personality and individual differences, social psychology, clinical psychology and psychotherapy, brain research and psychophysiology, organizational psychology and methodology.

6. In 1992 psychology as a major was offered in 10 universities to about 2500 students. Following a five-year training, curriculum can be completed by a university degree - Master of Psychology. In Poland there is no state licensing of psychologists.

7. The most comprehensive information regarding the members of PPA, history of PPA, legislation and standing orders of PPA, and the principles of professional ethics may be found in: *Spis Psychologow Polskich, 1992* (Directory of Polish Psychologists, 1992). Olsztyn: *Polskie Towarzystwo Psychologiczne*, 1992; available under the mailing address of the PPA.

   Przeglad Psychologiczny (Psychological Review, in Polish), published quarterly by PPA; *Polish Psychological Bulletin* (in English), published quarterly by the Committee for Psychological Sciences, Polish Academy of Sciences (CPS PAS); *Studia Psychologiczne* (Psychological Studies, in Polish), published twice a year by CPS PAS; *Psychologia Wychowawcza* (Educational Psychology, in Polish), five issues annually published by The Polish Teachers Association.

8. Professor Jan Strelau, University of Warsaw, Department of Psychology, Stawki 5-7, 00-183 Warsaw, Poland. Dr Jacek Szczechura, Institute of Aviation Medicine, Krasinskiego 54, 01-755 Warsaw, Poland.

PORTUGAL

1. Sociedade Portuguesa de Psicologia* (Portuguese Psychological Society). Founded: 1965. President of the Executive Committee: Manuel Viegas Abreu (Coimbra University), Secretary-General: Vasou Cubral (Lisbon University); President of the General Assembly and Past-President of the Executive Committee: José H. Ferreira Marques (Lisbon University). Address: Faculdade de Psicologia e de Ciências da Educaçã, Universidade de Lisboa, Alameda da Universidade, 1600 Lisboa. Tel: (351) (1) 793 4554. Fax: (351) (1) 793 3408. Membership (October 1992): 252

3. The Portuguese Psychological Society integrates individual psychologists with university formation and publishes since 1967 the *Revista Portuguesa de Psicologia* (Portuguese Psychological Review) is a scientific society aimed to promote psychological research,

scientific meetings, exchanges and publications in the field of psychology. The Society is also interested in the definition and respect of deontological standards of the professional practice.

4. The study of psychology initiated in the State Faculties of Arts. Only in the mid-70s structured courses of five years have been created in the Universities of Lisbon, Porto, Coimbra and recently in Braga, has Faculties of Psychology. The private, ISPA preceded this process. The general formation is aimed at some broad domaines of the professional practice: Clinical Psychology, Psychotherapy and Counseling, Social Psychology, Vocational and Educational Psychology.

5. Research activity is mostly developed in the department programs of the Faculties, and the post-graduate curricula, namely doctoral dissertation subjects, extends to areas such as Cognitive Psychology and Psycholinguistics, Psychophysiology, Animal behavior, Developmental Psychology, Personality Assessment, Differential Psychology of Aptitudes and Interests, Cognitive Methods of Behavior Modification, Cognitive Social Psychology, Consumer Behavior, Organisational Psychology, etc.

6. The Faculties at the post-graduate level and Societies and Associations in specific domains (Psychoanalysis, Behavior and Cognitive Therapies, Systemic Therapies, etc.) are the responsible entities for the professional practical formation of psychologists. The Deontological Code is ethical reference for the professional activity.

7. *Revista Portuguesa de Psicologia* (Portuguese Psychological Review), since 1967.
Jornal de Psicologia (Journal of Psychology), since 1983.
Análise Psicologica (Psychological Analysis), since 1976.

QATAR

Psychology in Qatar is taught at the Faculty of Education of the University of Qatar which was founded in September 1973. It is taught in the Departments of Educational Psychology and of Mental Health. No degrees are offered in psychology and all undergraduate students are required to take 12 credit hours in psychology for graduation. No psychological organizations exist in the country. Psychology as a science is still new to the country. It has not yet established itself as a profession.

Research is carried by individuals as well as by the Centre for Educational Research which is affiliated with the Faculty. A major portion of the research evolves around educational psychological subjects. Individually conducted research covers the following fields - creativity, cognitive development, attitudes and attitude change, culture change and personality.

The centre publishes individual research reports. Research is published also in the *Bulletin of the Faculty of Education* which is published bi-annually.

ROMANIA

1. Asociatia psihologilor din Romania* (APR). Psychologists Association of Romania (PAR). Founded: 1965. President 1990-94: Prof. Dr Mihai Golu; Secretary-General: Lect. Dr Ilie Puiu Vasilescu; Address: Bd. Schitu Magureanu no. 1, Bucharest 70262; Tel: (40) (0) 613 86 70; Fax: (40) (0) 312 02 09; Membership: about 500 (Jan. 1992).

2. Comisia de psihologia sportutut (The Committee for Sports Psychology, CSP). Founded: 1969. President 1990-94: Prof. Dr Mihui Eparan. Recording Secretary 1990-94: Conf. Dr Valentina Ilorghidan. Address: Str. Stefan Partuna no.170, Bucharest 76708. Tel: (40) (0) 638 53 15. Membership (1991): 20.

   Societatea romana de sugestie st hipnoza (Romanian Society of Suggestion and Hypnosis: RSSH). Founded in 1975; destroyed by the dictator in 1982; re-founded in 1990. President 1990-94: Dr Irina Holdevici. Secretary-General: Julia Gerendy. Address: Bd.

Schira Magareana no. 1, Bucharest 70262. Tel: (40) (0) 613 86 70; Fax: (40) (0) 612 02 09. Membership (1991): 30.

3. PAR was founded in 1964 to serve the promotion of psychology as a field of science. Membership is open to all persons holding a degree of graduate training in psychology, or working as specialists in adjacent fields (educational sciences, neurologists, psychiatrists, etc.). The main object of PAR is scientific exchange among all professional psychologists and research workers in psychology. Under the form of sections, the following disciplines are represented in the association: Industrial Psychology, Applied Psychology, Applied Psychology in Transports. Psychological Assistance of Disabled People, Computer Based Psychology. PAR is affiliated to IUPsyS.

The main goals and functions of RSSH are: Training of the therapists and supervision of the practitioners: Research in the field of suggestion and hypnosis; Exchange of information between psychologists; The supervision of the practitioners; Giving the license of practice in the field of relaxation and hypnosis.

The members of the RSSH are the psychologists and surgeons that were trained during special workshops and lectures in the field of relaxation and clinical and experimental hypnosis and were given the license of practice from the Society of Suggestion and Hypnosis. CSP is affiliated to PAR and European Federation of Sports Psychology. To become a member of CSP, it is necessary to work in the field of sports and to have high studies in psychology or in related area (medicine, biology, etc.).

4. In 1906 the first Romanian Chair of Psychology was founded at the University of Bucharest, including a Laboratory of Experimental Psychology. In 1921 a second Chair of Psychology was founded at the University of Cluj. Already in the early twenties psychology began to be applied, especially for the selection of the personnel, in industry, transports and the army. Psychology grew out as profession before World War II and developed after the war mostly in the sixties and early seventies. In 1977 the Romanian faculties of psychology were suppressed. The Institute of Psychology of Romanian Academy was, in the first step, joined with the Institute of Pedagogy. The Institute was suppressed by Ceausescu in 1982 and the research workers were transformed in unskilled workers. After the '89 Revolution the Faculties of Psychology from State University of Bucharest, Club-Napoca and Iassy were reborn.

5. Research in psychology is conducted mainly in three universities (Bucharest, Club-Napoca, Iassy) and in several centers of social sciences in the Institute of Psychology of Romanian Academy.

8. Ilie Puiu Vasilescu, Psychologists Association of Romania, Bd. Schitu Magureanu 1, Bucharest 70626, Romania.

SOUTH AFRICA

1. Psychological Association of South Africa* (PASA). Founded: 1982. Chairman: Prof. R.J. Prinsloo. Secretary: Dr K.F. Mauer. Address: P.O. Box 395, Pretoria 0001. Tel: (012) 26 1981. Membership: 1547.

3. PASA was founded in 1982 as a result of the amalgamation of four associations - the South African Psychological Association, the Psychological Institute of the Republic of South Africa, the Association for Clinical Psychologists and the Association for Counselling Psychologists. It consists of five Institutes (Academic and Research Psychology, Industrial Psychology, Clinical Psychology, Counselling Psychology, and Educational Psychology) and operates on a federal basis. There are six memberhsip categories each with its own requirements. Full membership is open to all persons holding a Masters degree or an equivalent qualification in an area of psychology. The major aims of the association are to promote the development of psychology as a science and a profession. PASA liaises with the Professional Board for Psychology (which controls the practice of psychology in South Africa) and organizes an annual congress as well as various meetings and seminars. The *South African Journal of Psychology* is published under its auspices.

4. Although the first professorial chair and department of psychology was founded at Stellenbosch University in 1918, the early growth of psychology was relatively slow and only by the late thirties were separate psychology departments established at most of the existing universities. Prior to this, psychology was usually taught in the Department of Philosophy. It was only after the Second World War that psychology began to develop rapidly in South Africa. In 1946 the National Institute for Personnel Research was established and although its main function is applied research, basic research is also carried out. The following year, the first association for psychologists, the South African Psychological Association was formed. The development of psychology was given a further boost in 1969 by the establishment of the Human Sciences Research Council, which not only carries out research but also provides much of the funding for research carried out at universities. Rapid growth continued in the seventies with the emphasis on clinical and industrial psychology and today psychology is one of the most popular courses at universities.

5. Research in psychology is conducted mainly in the universities and at three research organisations - the National Institute for Personnel Research (NIPR), the Human Sciences Research Council (HSRC) and the Human Resources Laboratory of the Chamber of Mines of S.A. (HRL). Research covering all the main areas of psychology is carried out with the emphasis on problem orientated research. There is also an emphasis on cross-cultural research.

6. Training in psychology is offered at 17 (of the 18) universities. Students may major in a branch of psychology in their three year Bachelors Degree, which is a general degree covering a number of subjects. This may be followed by a one year Honours degree (largely coursework) in a branch of psychology, which in turn may be followed by a Masters degree which may be either by thesis or by a combination of coursework and thesis. Psychology may be studied in a number of faculties - Arts, Science, Commerce, Education or Social Science, which means that there are many different degrees which lead to becoming a psychologist. The practice of psychology is controlled by the Professional Board for Psychology which was established in 1974 by an Act of Parliament. At present a person may register as a psychologist in one or more of five categories: Clinical, Counselling, Educational, Industrial and Research. However the system may be changed in the near future. The requirements for registration vary somewhat according to category, but essentially five years full time study of a branch of psychology (i.e. a Masters degree) plus an internship of not less than 12 months is required.

7. *South African Journal of Psychology* (published quarterly by the Bureau for Scientific Publications in collaboration with PASA: empirical, theoretical and review articles, short communication, book reviews and relevant letters. Priority is given to articles that are relevant to Africa or are cross-cultural). I. van W. Raubenheimer, Psychology in South Africa: Development trends and future perspectives. *South African Journal of Psychology*, 1981, 11, 1-5.

8. G.A. Tyson, University of the Witwatersrand, 1 Jan Smuts Avenue, Johannesburg, 2001.

SPAIN

1. Sociedad Española de Psicologia: (Spanish Psychological Association) (SPA). Founded: 1952. President (1983-): Prof. Miguel Siguán; Recording Secretary (1990-): Aurora Murga; Address: c/o Sec. Depart. Psicologia Basica, Facultad de Filosofia, Univ. Complutense de Madrid, Madrid 28040; Tel: (34)(1) 394 5275. Membership (11/92): 680.

2. Colegio Oficial de Psicólogos (Professional Union of Psychologists) (PUP). Founded: 1980. President (1990): Adolfo Hernández; Recording Secretary: Begoña Olabarria; Address: Claudio Coello 46, 2º d, Madrid 28001; Tel: (34)(1) 435 52 12; Fax: (34)(1) 577 91 72; Membership (11/92): 23000.

3. SPA was founded in 1952 to promote scientific psychology, both in its theoretical and applied dimensions. Membership is open to persons holding a university degree in

Psychology or related disciplines. SPA, structured in four national divisions (Theoretical-Experimental, Educational, Industrial and Clinical) and three regional ones (Cataluña, Valencia, Galicia), is now in the way of changing to a federal organization with regional and specialized societies as members. Annual meetings, congresses every four years, sectorial conferences are organized through SPA. One scientific journal *Revista de Psicologia General y Aplicada*, with four issues per year, is published under the auspices of SPA. There are also a number of occasional publications about annual meetings, congresses or monographic studies.

PUP is the professional psychological association of Spain. People holding a university degree in Psychology are eligible for membership. PUP engages in the development of psychology as a profession, it exerts vigilance on the accomplishment of deontological norms, and organizes professional congresses, training seminars, and professional development courses in various fields of applied psychology. Two periodical publications *Papeles del psicóloogo*, and *Guia del psicologo* are issued by the PUP. It has 14 regional delegations.

4. In Spain the first chair of experimental psychology was founded at the University of Madrid (1902), held by Dr Luis Simarro. Experimental research in psychology grew up through the groups of Barcelona (Turró, Mira-Lopez) and Madrid (Madariaga, Germain, Mallart, Rodrigo), both mainly oriented to applied research and psychotechnics. In the 1930s two Psychotechnic Institutes at Madrid and Barcelona concentrated their efforts in the development of psychology until the Spanish Civil War (1936-39). This meant a big disruption of that tradition. After the war, the tradition of scientific psychology was slowly recovered, after the foundation (1948) of a Department of Experimental Psychology at the Consejo Superior de Investigaciones Cientificas (Higher Council for Scientific Research), headed by Dr J. Germain. The leaders of the recent generations of psychologists were trained in that center (Yela, Pinillos, Siguán, Secadas). The main steps of the new developments took place as follows: SPA foundation, 1954; foundation of its journal, 1946; Professional School of Psychology (University of Madrid), 1953, and another at the University of Barcelona, 1964 - offering professional diploma in Psychology; degree in Psychology at various faculties of Philosophy, 1968; creation of Faculties of Psychology (Madrid, Barcelona, Valencia, and many others, up to 20), 1980; creation of the PUP, 1980.

5. Research in psychology is conducted mainly in the universities. In recent years, the dominant research fields have been physiological psychology of perception and sexual differentiation, learning and emotion, cognitive processes (reading, attention, verbal comprehension), social and organizational psychology, developmental psychology, history of psychology, child and adult psychopathology and methodology, mental testing and evaluation. In 1992, the number of psychologists holding academic or other research positions in psychology was about 1800.

6. Training in psychology is currently offered in 20 universities across the country, with departments organized along six main areas of knowledge: basic psychology, personality-evaluation-intervention, social, developmental-educational, psychobiology, and methodology. Psychology curricula usually consist of four/five years, for licensing, and two more years for Ph.D degree.

There are several specialized journals covering the whole psychological field, and also some specialized societies and groups of research.

7. Yeja, M., Spain, in Gilgen, A.R. & Gilgen, C.K. (1987) *International Handbook of Psychology*, New York, Greenwood Press, p. 440-460.

SWEDEN

1. The Swedish Psychological Association*. Founded: 1955. President (1992-95): Psychologist Birgit Hansson. Recording Secretary (1991): Mr Hans Persson. Address: Warfvinges väg 16, P.O. Box 30092, S-104 25 Stockholm. Tel: (46) (8) 13 02 60. Membership (12/91): 6,493.

3. The Swedish Psychological Association is the professional psychological association of Sweden. Its major aims are:
   a. to deal with professional and trade union issues for the members,
   b. to promote the scientific development of psychology and its practical applications,
   c. to increase information about psychology,
   d. to improve the development of professional training and practice of psychologists and students of psychology, and
   e. to promote cooperation with Nordic and other international organizations.

Membership is open to persons holding a professional degree in psychology, to researchers in psychology, and to students of psychology. The Association offers training seminars and courses in professional development in various fields of applied psychology.

The journal of the Swedish Psychological Association, *PsykologTidningen*, publishes articles on professional and union issues, and on the development of applied psychology.

4. Psychological research in Sweden has its domestic roots in physiology and education at the beginning of this century. In the late 1930s and early 1940s psychological research started to emerge as a domain of its own, primarily through work on test development. The first department of psychology in Sweden was created at Uppsala in 1948 by splitting the department of education into two parts. Departments of psychology came about in the same way soon after at Stockholm, Lund, and Göteborg. The latest departmental formation for psychology was done at University of Umeå in 1966. Separate departments of applied psychology were built in Uppsala, Lund, and Umeå during the 1970s.

Teaching in psychology at the undergraduate and graduate levels is offered at these five universities. An integrated training program leading up to the profession as a psychologist is also given at each of these universities. University of Linköping provides undergraduate courses in psychology at a joint department of education and psychology. The Karolinska Institute in Stockholm offers courses in psychology at the graduate level. Technical psychology is taught at the technical university in Luleå and courses in economic psychology are given at the Stockholm School of Economics.

Formerly there was only one professorship of psychology at each department. Nowadays there are several professorships at each department in specialized areas of psychology. In 1992 there are about 30 professors holding positions in psychology and various subfields of psychology at universities in Sweden.

Departments of psychology at all universities in Sweden have developed strong traditions in experimental psychology, first in perception, psychophysics, and physiological psychology, subsequently also in cognitive psychology and personality.

Over the years each department has developed its own characteristic research profile. Both departments in Lund have specialized in personality and clinical psychology. In Göteborg there are main foci on biological psychology, industrial psychology, and cognitive psychology with main emphasis on problem solving and communication. Psychological research in Stockholm is focusing on personality and social development, biological psychology, work and organizational psychology, perception and psychophysics, clinical psychology, and cognitive psychology with special emphasis on information processing and decision making. Uppsala has a long-standing tradition in perception and traffic safety with recent additions in decision making at the department of psychology. At the department of applied psychology there is a strong dominance on health psychology and clinical psychology. Umeå has ongoing projects on perception and psychotherapy.

Psychological research is also conducted at a number of agencies outside the universities, e.g. The National Defence Research Institute, The Swedish Road Research Institute, and the National Institute of Occupational Health.

Some Swedish researchers are among the leading contributors to their scientific fields. The scientific community has often recognized this fact nationally and internationally. At the national scene, the Royal Swedish Academy of Sciences included psychology as a national committee in 1985. Internationally, Swedish psychologists have being asked to serve on editorial boards of leading journals, and some have been given prestigous prizes and have been elected into influential academies and organizations. Recently, two international evaluations acknowledged that high quality research in cognitive psychology and biological psychology is being conducted in Sweden.

The number of psychologists in Sweden has been growing rapidly and is now approaching 7000. The largest fields for professional psychologists in Sweden are clinical psychology, school psychology, organizational and industrial psychology.

Since 1978 there is a state certification of psychologists in Sweden. In order to become a certified psychologist, a person has to complete a five year academic training program followed by one year as a resident. Since 1985, there is also a state certification of psychotherapists, with about 75% of these being psychologists.

6. The Swedish university training program for psychologists aims at providing a general psychological competence rather than special skills.

Special competence, e.g. as a clinical psychologist, can be acquired after the university training program has been completed.

The psychology profession has developed rapidly in Sweden. As in many other countries, early psychologists in Sweden were specialists in testing and diagnosis, whereas now the field of work is much broader with practitioners in many areas like psychotherapy, school psychology, organizational and industrial psychology.

7. *PsykologTidningen* (published every second week by the Swedish Psychological Association).
Scandinavian Journal of Psychology.

SWITZERLAND

1. Schweizerisch Gesellschaft für Psychologie/Société Suisse de Psychologie/Swiss Psychological Society*. Founded: 1943. President (1989-93): Professor F. Gaillard, Ph.D. Address: BFSH 2, CH-1015 Lausanne. Tel: (41)(21) 692 47 14. Fax: (41) (21) 692 47 04. Membership (10/92): 460.

2. Föderation der Schweizer Psychologinnen und Psychologen/Fédération Suisse des Psychologues/Federation of Swiss Psychologists. Founded: 1987. President: R. Burckhardt, Ph.D., PD. Address: Cäcilienstr. 26, Postfach, CH-3000 Bern 14. Tel: (41)(31) 46 04 69.

3. The Swiss Psychological Society is composed of collective, regular, student, corresponding and honorary members. The goal of the SPS is the promotion of psychological research in Switzerland, thereby contributing further knowledge to the science of psychology. To this end, the society places high priority on a qualitatively high, scientific education for psychologists. The scientific policy is the promotion of cooperation between the various specialized areas of psychology and applied psychology as well as the interdisciplinary cooperation with organizations with similar goals. The members of the society adhere to the "Ethic Guideline" for psychologists and thereby guarantee that the application of psychological knowledge includes respect for human values.

4. Chairs in psychology at graduate schools in Switzerland were successively established beginning at the end of the second World War. The situation in Switzerland is characterized by cultural, linguistic and political division. Thus, the Piaget School with its own ideas on psychological research and model creation is located in French-speaking Geneva, while the scientific psychological community in the German-speaking areas in the meantime was concentrated on questions taken from the area of applied psychology. Tremendous interest was generated in Switzerland in clinical and cognitive psychology predominantly in the 1970s. The gradual professionalization of psychology was completed in Switzerland in the 1960s and 1970s, primarily in the areas of applied, clinical and pedagogical psychology. During the 1970s, various groups of non-MD psychological therapists were formed, the great majority of whom were drawn from the ranks of psychologists.

5. Scientific psychology and research in Switzerland is concentrated in seven Psychological Institutes located at seven University Graduate Schools. In addition, both of the Swiss

Federal Institutes of Technology as well as the Swiss University of Commerce all maintain a department of psychology. The main research fields of interest in the most recent past cover the whole spectrum of modern scientific psychology. Even areas which previously held only marginal research interest, such as ecological psychology, have been worked on lately. In Geneva, the emphasis is on the relationship between the genetic epistemology of Piaget and pedagogical development psychology. Three institutes are doing research in clinical psychology. Zurich, Lausanne and Neuchâtel all have extensive facilities in their institutes for Applied Psychology. Special emphasis on research into the principles of work and organisation psychology is being given by the chair at the Swiss Federal Institute of Technology in Zurich which is dealing with the alternations and modifications necessitated by technological progress in the modern world of work.

6. Graduate courses with a major in psychology require a minimum of eight semesters for completion at all seven universities in Switzerland. In 1992, there were more than 2000 students registered at the various institutions. This four-year program of study culminates with a "Lizenziat" (Master's) degree and the title of Master in Philosophy/Master in Psychology. Such a course would in turn lead to a Ph.D Program with various course and time requirements and which bestows the title of Dr.phil/Dr.psych. A major in psychology would include practical competence with regard to professional psychological practice as well as systematic study of the prevalent standards of scientific psychological research.

The legal regulation of the professional activities of psychologists in Switzerland is in the hands of the individual cantons. Only one canton provides for this kind of regulation. Several cantons have, however, provided for the regulation of the activities of non-MD therapeutic practitioners in that a scientific education in psychology at a recognized psychological institution as well as a minimum of three years of psychotherapeutic qualification at a recognized institution are required. Several other cantons are in the process of esstablishing similar regulations.

7. The society edits the *Schweizerische Zeitschrift für Psychologie/Revue Suisse de Psychologie/Swiss Journal of Psychology*, which includes articles of actual scientific research, and the *Swiss Monographs in Psychologie*, which reflects the state of the art in psychological science in Switzerland through international and Swiss contributions (Hogrefe & Huber, Publishers, Lewiston, N.-Y, Bern, CH).

TUNISIA

1. Société Tunisienne de Psychologie (Tunisian Society of Psychology); Founded: 1962; President: Dr Chafik Ghorbel; Address: University of Tunis 1, 94 Boulevard 9 Avril, 1007 Tunis, Tunisia; Tel: (216)(1) 260 950/260 858; Fax: (216) (1) 567 551; Membership (1991): approx. 200.

2. The Tunisian Society of Psychology is the only existing association in Tunisia. There are only two Departments of Psychology in the country: one department in the "Faculté des Sciences Humaines et Sociales" of Tunis, and another department in a national research center "Centre d'Etudes et de Recherches Economiques et Sociales", also in Tunis.

3. In order to become member of the Tunisian Society of Psychology, a master degree in psychology is required. The major goals of the Society are: To diffuse the psychological knowledge in the large Tunisian Society; to inform the authorities and social agents about abilities and competences of psychology and psychologists; to contribute in improving the scientific backgrounds of the psychologists (through meetings, congresses, conferences, etc.); and to defend and protect the professional interests of Tunisian psychologists.

4. Scientific psychology is a rather new discipline in the country; only since the early eighties is it taught as an academic discipline. There are now good academic programs but its teaching faces many material problems (lack of laboratory equipment, books, and meetings; difficulties to attend international meetings).

To obtain a status of psychologist, four years of a master program and two years for the practical program are required.

5. Major current research programs: Educational psychology (scholar and acadamic program evaluations; test standardisations, studies on academic failure, school adaptation, etc), Developmental psychology (theory and measurement of intelligence), Social psychology (social representations, attribution theory, locus of control, social perception, work psychology, violence, war trauma in children, women development), and Clinical psychology.

6. To practice psychology, a postmaster practical diploma ("diplôme d'études spécialisées en psychologie appliquée", involving six years of university studies) is required. Since August 1992, the Tunisian psychological profession is regulated and protected by a legal status.

8. Dr Chafik Ghorbel, Faculté des Sciences Humaines et Sociales, Université des Lettres, Arts et Sciences Humaines, 94 Boulevard 9 Avril 1938, Tunis, Tunisia.

TURKEY

1. The Turkish Psychological Association* was founded in 1956. Currently (1992-94) the President is Çigdem Kagitçibasi, and the Secretary-General is Emre Konuk. Address: Inönü Cad. Isik Apt. 48/1, Gümüssuyu-Taksim 80090, Istanbul; Tel: (90)(1) 244 9339; Fax: (90)(1) 243 4472. Membership (September 1992): about 500.

2. Psychologists Association is the other national organization of psychologists in Turkey. It was founded in 1976. Its current (1992) President is Nesrin Sahin and Secretary-General is Zeynep Ekmekçioglu. Address: Bilkent University, Psychological Counselling and Research Center Block 20, no. 5-6-; Tel: (90)(4) 266 4040/1785. Membership (1992): about 800.

3. The Turkish Psychological Association is the oldest national society of psychology in Turkey. It is based in Istanbul. It aims to promote psychology both as a science and as a profession and conducts conferences symposia and on the job training seminars for this purpose. A related aim of the association is contributing to a better recognition of psychology in the country and to greater relevance of psychology for human welfare and societal development in general. The minimum requirement for membership in the TPA is a university degree in psychology. Associate (non-voting) membership can be offered to graduates of related disciplines such as guidance and counselling. (Historically psychiatrists can also be members, but this membership category is negligible in number). The TPA prints a newsletter and has just started a biannual Bulletin. Psychologists' Association is based in Ankara. It also has a branch in Izmir. PA shares the same aims with TPA. Membership is open only to psychologists with at least a university degree. The PA publishes *The Journal of Psychology* since 1977 (comes out twice a year). The PA also conducts the biennial national psychology conventions in collaboration with major university psychology departments. The first convention was held in 1981. Many psychologists in Turkey are members of both associations. The PA was established as a reaction to the rather dormant state of TPA over years. However, with the recent resurgence of TPA, the two associations are presently running parallel courses of activity.

4. 1915 marks the beginning of psychology as a science when a German professor was invited to teach at Istanbul University. In that year also, the Binet-Simon Test of intelligence was translated into Turkish, a year before its American adaptation in 1916. Again at that time a first psychology textbook was published, and psychology courses were introduced into teacher training institutes. During the tumultuous years during the First World War, the collapse of the Ottoman Empire, the rise of the Turkish Republic, and the Second World War, psychology remained a rather obscure academic discipline. The field has developed slowly, though rather steadily over the years, first under European influence but especially after the 1960s with a dominant American orientation. Independent psychology departments offer undergraduate and some graduate degrees in only six universities. Psychology courses are also widely taught in medical schools, schools of education, management, social work, nursing, dentistry and journalism. The scientific and

professional recognition of psychology is growing in the general public though slowly.

5. Psychological research has greatly increased in number in the last two decades. It is carried out mainly in universities. Research is being done in all fields of psychology, spanning the whole spectrum of methods and content, from laboratory research conducted with computer technology on the brain to longitudinal intervention studies of early enrichment for socio-economically deprived children. Most research is conducted in social psychology, followed by clinical and developmental psychology; testing and educational psychology. Substantial research projects span more than one field and often involve an applied emphasis. For example, recent research includes studies to design simple screening-detection instruments for developmental delay among socio-economically deprived children; to establish norms for psychosocial development; to formulate environmental indicators of healthy development at young ages; to design educational TV programs for young children (the Turkish Sesame Street) and to assess its effects on children's cognitive development; to utilize and test the effectiveness of group facilitation techniques in community-based women's empowerment and mother-child education programs. Still most research is of small scale and is not of an applied nature. A promising new trend in research and theorizing is cultural/cross-cultural orientation. It is beginning to sensitize psychologists to the possible cultural bias of imported theory and to the need to test it and to develop theory anew.

6. In Turkey university entrance is subject to a nation-wide competitive examination system. Placement in a department is based on a combination of the score obtained on this examination and the student's choice. Psychology departments are among the most preferred in the social sciences. Four years of undergraduate training is presently the minimum requirement for becoming a psychologist. However, there is an effort to increase this minimum requirement for independent applied work. Most psychologists (about 70% of the total) hold only an undergraduate degree. Graduate programs are offered at both masters and doctoral levels though the numbers of students accepted are very limited, especially at the doctoral level. In general the academic programs at both the undergraduate and graduate levels are designed after those commonly seen in American universities. Practical training and internship are required for graduate programs in clinical psychology. A proposal for a law for the profession of psychology has been submitted to the National Assembly and is currently being processed, however, it is facing the resistance of some competing professional groups such as psychiatrists. The law sets the requirement of a masters degree for independent applied work of (clinical) psychologists, which is now not the case, for a psychiatrist's supervision is required.

7. Acar, G. and Sahin, D. (1990) Psychology in Turkey *Psychology and Developing Societies*, 2, 241-256.

Basaran, F. and Sahin, N. (1990) "Turkey". In Shouksmith, G. and Shouksmith, E.A. (eds.) *Psychology in Asia and Pacific*. UNESCO RUSHSAP Series, Bangkok.

Kagiçibasi, Ç. (1993) Psychology in Turkey. *Psychology and Developing Societies*, in press.

8. Çigdem Kagitçibasi, Bogaziçi University, 80815 Bebek, Istanbul, Turkey.

UGANDA

1. The Uganda National Psychological Association (UNPA). This is the only national psychological society, founded in August 1992 and has 50 members. President: Mr Peter Baguma, Senior Lecturer, Department of Psychology, Makerere University, P.O. Box 7062, Kampala, Uganda. Fax: (256) (41) 530412; Tel: (256) (41) 545040. Secretary: Mr Otim Tom, Academic Registrar's office, Makere University, P.O. Box 7062, Kampala, Uganda. Tel: (256) (41) 545040. Tenure of office is one year renewable. Address: The President, Uganda National Psychological Association, c/o office 5, Department of Psychology, Makere University, P.O. Box 7062, Kampala, Uganda. Tel: (256) (41) 545040; Fax: (256) (41) 530412.

2. Makere University Psychological Association is a smaller organisation mainly including

staff and students of Makere and has a membership of 100. (For address see above).

3. UNPA membership is open to all people with basic qualifications in psychology and related fields but after scrutiny by the governing council which is advised by the qualifications board.

   Aims, goals and functions: UNPA oversees all matters relating to psychology in Uganda and to those of practising and teaching psychology, promotes the diffusion of knowledge both pure and applied, efficiency, and usefulness of members by promoting high standards of professional education, knowledge and application. UNPA creates awareness of the use of psychology in a better exploitation of human resources through gatherings e.g. conferences, workshops, use of print media and research.

4. A fully fledged Department of Psychology started in 1975 when the Educational Psychology Department merged with the unit of social psychology that was in the Sociology Department. This was the first Department of Psychology in East and Central Africa. Presently the Department is housed in the School of Education for administrative purposes.

   Psychology is a young discipline in Uganda so has not had much impact yet. Very few Ugandans hold advanced degrees in psychology or are involved in active research or consultancies. The few psychologists are mainly teaching psychology at the National University or teacher training colleges.

5. The major fields of research are health psychology, industrial, organisational, educational, child development and environmental psychology.

6. Training in psychology which is mainly for undergraduates involves a lot of theory and less practicals. Psychological laboratories are unknown. Equipment and other facilities are very limited. For employment purposes one needs to have taken a 3.1.1 or 3.2.2 psychology course. Psychology enjoys no legal status in Uganda and employment opportunities are similar to those of other social scientists in general.

7. The work of Ugandan psychologists is found in the following Journals: *East African Journal of Education, Journal of Cross-cultural Psychology, Human Relations, British Journal of Social Psychology, Makerere Medical Journal* and *Journal of Psychology in Africa*.

8. Peter Baguma, Senior Lecturer, Department of Psychology, Makerere University, P.O. Box 7062, Kampala, Uganda.

UNITED KINGDOM OF GREAT BRITAIN AND NORTHERN IRELAND

1. The Royal Society* (the United Kingdom national academy for all sciences) founded in 1660, is the National Member of the IUPsyS. Foreign Secretary (1992): Dr A. McLaren; Executive Secretary: Dr P.T. Warren. Address: 6 Carlton House Terrace, London, SW17 5AG. Tel: (71) 839 5561; Fax: (71) 930 2170.

2. The British Psychological Society (BPS). Founded in 1901, incorporated under the Companies Act 1941 and subsequently incorporated by Royal Charter in 1965. President (1992-93): Professor E. Miller; Honorary General Secretary (1992-92): Dr J. Groeger; Address: St Andrews House, 48 Princess Road East, Leicester LE1 7DR; Tel: (533) 549568; Fax: (533) 470787; Membership (1992): 15,400.

   The Experimental Psychology Society (EPS). Founded in 1946; President (1992): Professor P.M.A. Rabitt; Honorary Secretary (1992): Professor A.W. Young; Address: Department of Psychology, University of Durham, Science Laboratories, South Road, Durham DH1 3LE; Membership (1992): 480.

3. The principal aim of the British Psychological Society is to promote the advancement of the scientific study of psychology and its applications and to maintain high standards of professional education and conduct. The Society is the only national organisation of psychologists within the United Kingdom to which all psychology graduates can belong, there being no comparable organisation within the United Kingdom representing all

aspects of psychology and all sub-specialisms within psychology.

As a learned society, it publishes eight scientific journals of international repute and in conjunction with the University of London maintains what is believed to be the world's second largest collection of psychology periodicals.

It sponsors many conferences and scientific meetings each year. In recent years the Society has become a publisher of books and reviews within the field of psychology. It has 10 Sections which focus on scientific areas within the discipline. The sub-specialisms within applied professional psychology are served by five Divisions concerned with clinical, educational, occupational, and with criminological and legal psychology, and by five Special Groups. The Society has regional Branches in Scotland, Wales and Northern Ireland and two Branches within England.

As a learned society and as a professional body the Society is frequently invited to advise Government and other official bodies on matters that concern psychology and psychologists. Government Departments look to the Society for advice on the recognition of professional qualifications in psychology. Through its Training Committees, the Society reviews and accredits professional training courses offered by universities and other institutions in clinical, educational and occupational psychology. In addition over 250 university first degree courses are accredited by the Society as providing qualifications that confer eligibility for Graduate Membership and the Graduate Basis for Registration as a Chartered Psychologist. Under the Royal Charter the Society maintains the national Register of Chartered Psychologists, a code of conduct and disciplinary provisions.

The Experimental Psychology Society is for the furtherance of scientific enquiry within the field of psychology and cognate subjects. It holds periodical meetings at which papers are read and educational material made available as a consequence of psychological research, including the publication of the *Quarterly Journal of Experimental Psychology* Section A: Human Experimental Psychology, and Section B: Comparative and Physiological Psychology.

The EPS does not engage in any activity intended to affect the professional status of its members or of psychologists generally.

4. From its inception in the last century, psychology is now taught in over one hundred universities in the UK and the following professional fields of psychology are well established: clinical psychology, educational psychology, occupational psychology, legal and criminological psychology and counselling psychology.

5. Psychological research in the United Kingdom covers the whole spectrum of the discipline and is carried out in over a hundred departments of psychology in universities and other institutions of higher education, in about 10 specialised research units and within industry and departments of Government.

5. In the United Kingdom at present psychology is not a statutory registered profession, however, registration with the BPS as a Chartered Psychologist is often a necessary requirement for appointment to posts in professional applied psychology. For most teaching or research posts in universities and other institutions of higher education, a doctorate degree will often be needed. The BPS publishes a *Compendium of Postgraduate Studies in Psychology in the United Kingdom and Ireland* which gives details of all postgraduate training courses and doctoral research training opportunities in universities throughout the United Kingdom. The names and specialist areas of scholoarship and research of all staff are given in this book.

7. *The Psychologist*, the Bulletin of the BPS (published monthly; articles of general interest to psychologists, Society news, calendar of professional/scientific meetings professional issues). Annual reports of the British Psychological Society. Newsheets of the Experimental Psychology Society.

8. This information has been prepared by Dr C.V. Newman, Executive Secretary, The British Psychological Society, St Andrews House, 48 Princess Road East, Leicester LE1 7DR.

UNITED STATES OF AMERICA

1. US National Committee for the International Union of Psychological Science (USNC/IUPsyS) effectuates the membership of the National Academy of Sciences, USA. Founded: 1985. Chairman (1993): Willard Hartup, Ed.D; Vice-Chair (1993): Bruce Overmier, Ph.D.; Senior Staff Officer: Beverly Huey, Ph.D.; Address: 2101 Constitution Avenue, HA156, NW Washington, DC 20418; Tel: (202) 334-3027; Fax: (202) 334-3829; Membership (12/92): 9 voting members, 5 ex-officio members.

2. American Psychological Association (APA). Founded: 1892; President (1992): Jack Wiggins, Ph.D.; President (1993): Frank Farley, Ph.D.; Recording Secretary (1992-93): Patrick DeLeon, Ph.D.; Executive Officer (1988-99): Ray Fowler, Ph.D.; Address: 750 First Street, NE, Washington, D.C. 20002-4242; Tel: (202) 336-5500; Membership (11/92): 114000.

    American Psychological Society (APS). Founded: 1988; President (1991-93): Gordon Bower, Ph.D.; Recording Secretary (1991-93): Michela Gallagher, Ph.D.; Treasurer (1991-93): Milton Hakel, Ph.D.; Executive Officer: Alan Kraut, Ph.D.; Address: 1010 Vermont Avenue, Suite 1100, NW, Washington, D.C. 200005-4907; Tel: (202) 783-2077; Membership (11/92): 15000.

    APA and APS are the largest of the US psychological organizations which also include the Psychonomic Society, the Society for Research in Child Development, and many others.

3. The National Academy of Sciences, USA* is the US national member, and the USNC/IUPsyS provides for US participation in the activities of the Union. National membership was transferred from the APA to the National Academy of Sciences (NAS) in 1985. The USNC/IUPsyS is charged with informing the President and members of the National Academy of Sciences and American psychologists of all IUPsyS recommendations, nominating representatives to meetings sponsored by the Union, planning and sponsoring scientific meetings in the United States relevant to the work of the IUPsyS, and taking action directed toward the benefit and advancement of the science of psychology in the United States and throughout the world. Regular voting members are nominated by the representative national scientific societies and the committee, and are appointed by the NAS President to serve for six years.

    APA, the nation's largest psychology organization, works to advance psychology as a science, a profession, and as a means of promoting human welfare. APA's programs aim at disseminating psychological knowledge, promoting research, improving research methods and conditions, and developing the qualifications and competence of psychologists through standards of education, ethical conduct, and professional practice. The sole requirement of full membership is a doctoral degree in psychology from a regionally accredited institution.

    APS is a national organization devoted to scientific psychology whose mission is to promote, protect, and advance the interests of scientifically oriented psychology in research and application, and in the improvement of human welfare. The impetus for creating APS came from the recognition that the needs and interests of scientific and academic psychologists were distinct from those members of the professional community primarily engaged in clinical practice, and there was a strong need for a society that would advance the interests of the discipline in ways that specialized organizations were not intended to do. Requirements of membership are a doctoral degree or evidence of sustained and significant contributions to scientific psychology.

4. When APA was established in July 1892, the profession it sought to advance was almost as new. National membership that month was less than three dozen, a number that multiplied rapidly over the next 100 years as Americans coped with the increasing complexity of modern life. Current APA membership is 114000 psychologists (MA/MS, Psy.D., and Ph.D. level) in the United States. As of 1989, of APA's full members (Ph.D. or Psy.D.), approximately 31% are educators, researchers, or administrators within universities, colleges, and schools. Another 57% provide or administer human services in (1) independent practice (32%), (2) in hospitals and clinics (18%), or (3) in other human

service settings (7%). Approximately 5% work in business, industry, or government.

5. Research conducted in psychology in the United States is very broad and covers many speciality areas, but is limited in integration. No one descriptor or phrase can accurately describe the research being conducted in all of these areas. Indeed, there are some 65 different focal psychological science research societies in the United States. Undergraduates (BA/BS) degrees in psychology are awarded by over 2000 colleges and universities, over 600 of which offer advanced degrees in psychology. Research programs exist in almost all fields of psychology. Although most research programs are university-based, many are private, performing research under contract to industry or government. Several government research institutes also employ psychologists.

6. All fifty states of the United States, the District of Columbia, and Puerto Rico have laws regulating the practice of psychology. These laws generally provide that individuals wishing to offer psychological services to the public for a fee must meet certain educational standards and pass an examination. As the minimum requirement for licensing or certification, most states require a doctoral (Ph.D. or Psy.D.) degree "in a field of study primarily psychological in nature" plus two years of supervised experience. Typically a psychologist trained to the doctoral level has completed at least two extensive research projects (master's thesis and doctoral dissertation) and a wide variety of courses in the basic science of human behavior, statistics, and research methodology. Individual states ordinarily require that applicants have obtained their doctoral degree from a psychology program accredited by the APA or from a program in an institution that is itself accredited by one of the regional accreditation councils for schools and colleges. Certificates and licenses issued under state statute do not refer to any speciality within the profession of psychology. However, the APA "Ethical Principles" require that psychologists limit their practice to those areas in which they have developed professional competence through training and experience. Many states require that psychologists wishing to maintain their licensure or certification follow courses of continuing education. Unless otherwise qualified, psychologists do not engage in the practice of medicine.

7. Of the hundreds of US psychological journals, space permits listing only three for illustrative purposes: *Psychological Bulletin*, *Psychological Review*, and *Psychological Science*.

8. Beverly M. Huey, Ph.D., 2101 Constitution Avenue, HA156D, NW, Washington, D.C. 20418.

URUGUAY

1. Sociedad de Psicologia del Uruguay: (Psychological Association of Uruguay). S.P.U. Miembro de la IUPsyS. Fundada en 1953. Presidente (1992-94): Elida J. Tuana; Secretaria (1992-94): Aurora Isasmendi de Pin; Tesorera (1992-94): Ruth Rodino de Pérez Diaz; Adress: colonia 1342 Esc. 3, C.P. 11100; Tel: 803066; Fax: 921980 (Ipsa); Miembros (9/93): 98 titulares, 245 adherentes.

2. Coordinadora de Psicólogos del Uruguay (Psychologist Coordinator of Uruguay). C.P.U. Fundada en 1987. Secretario General (1991-93): Psic. Humberto Giachello; Adress: Yi 1445 apto. 7, C.P. 11100 Montevideo, Uruguay; Tel: 598-2-90 20 19; Fax: 598 2 90 20 19.

3. S.P.U. fue fundada en 1953 con la "finalidad de propender al desarrollo de la Psicologia como ciencia y como profesión". Se establecieron dos tipos de miembros: adherentes, los que tuvieran interés en la Psicologia y titulares los que además de ser graduados pudieran demostrar competencia mediante publicaciones, intervención en congresos, jornadas, etc., con trabajos originales. Para promover la Psicologia como ciencia se organizaron cursos, conferencias, jornadas anuales de presentació y discusión de trabajos de investigación y teoria, contratación de Psicólogos o investigadores extrajeros y coorganización de Congresos Internacionales (SIP, ALAR). Se formaron grupos de investigación. La defensa profesional se llevó a cabo con la finalidad de obtener el reconocimiento legal de la

profesión, la delimitación del campo laboral, el establecimiento de los estandares éticos, la apertura de nuevos campos de trabajo y la creación de una Facultad de Psicologia.

La Coordinadora de Psicólogos del Uruguay (CPU), es la asociación profesional que nuclea a los Psicólogos egresados de la Universidad de la República. Sus objetivos son: (a) Promover, delimitar y defender el rol del Psicólogo y su inserción social, garantizando su independencia profesional; (b) Procurar la aprobación de leyes y reglamentaciones necesarias para la legalización del carácter profesional del Psicólogo; (c) Crear espacios de producción, intercambio y discusión cientifica de las diferentes lineas teóricas de la Psicologia en el Uruguay, tendiendo a la amplicación y el perfeccionamiento de la formación técnica y cultural de sus afiliados.

4. En Uruguay, a nivel oficial, la Psicologia nació en los institutos de formación docente. 1925: Primera Cátedra de Psicologia en los Institutos Normales de Montevideo; 1933: Creación del Laboratorio de Psicopedagogia en los IINN; 1944: Contratación de profesores extrajeros por la Universidad de la República y los Consejos de Educación; 1950: Cursos de Psicologia Aplicados a la Infancia en el Hospital Pedro Visca; más tarde pasaron a integrar la Escuela de Colaboradores de Médico que otorgó el titulo de Técnico en Psicologia Infantil; 1952: Cursos de Psicólogos Escolares en el Laboratorio de Psicopedagogia; 1956: Licenciatura de Psicologia en la Facultad de Humanidades y Ciencias. Fue clausurada en 1973; 1975: Creación de la Escuela Universitaria de Psicologia; 1986: Creación del Instituto de Psicologia de la Universidad de la República (IPUR) asimilado a la Facultad. 1992: Bestiones de egrasados y docentes del IPUR para la creación de la Facultad de Psicologia. Como profesión fue ganando espacios gracias a los trabajos de las sociedades y en la actualidad es importante la Psicologia Social, Laboral, Educacional, la inserción de los Psicólogos en los equipos de salud, psicoterapia de distintas orientaciones, con formación especifica una vez obtenido el titulo de Psicólogo.

5. La investigación en Psicologia fue conducida principalmente por el Laboratorio de Psicopedagogia, que se dedicó 35 años a la misma. Se publicó en los Bolentines del Laboratorio de Psicopedagogia desde 1943 a 1961. También el Departamento de Orientación de UTU realizó investigación como actividad paralela. Importante impulso le dieron las Jornadas Universitarias de Psicologia, organizada por Sociedad de Psicologia del Uruguay desde 1960 y que continúan. Se publicaron los trabajos de la Primeras, Cuartas, Quintas, Décimas, Trece, Catorce y Quinceavas. En la actualidad, en el IPUR las actividades y proyectos de investigación muestran el particular tránsito del desarrollo cientifico de la Psicologia en los distintos momentos históricos. Predomina la investigación educacional y cognitiva y la investigación social.

6. La formación del Psicólogo se realiza en 5 ciclos que obedecen a una lógica curricular de cursos con contenidos programáticos donde se pretende dar cabida a todas las orientaciones teóricas y teórico-técnicas que producen el discurso cientifico en la Psicologia. Por otra parte el plan de estudios se sustenta en una lógica basada en núcleos de problematicidad que transversalizan la estructura curricular y permiten pensar los contenidos de los cursos en función de ejes temáticos.

Las orientaciones que se privilegian son: social y comunitaria, laboral, educacional, introducción a las técnicas psicoterapéuticas y de diagnóstico.

La estructura académica se apoya en unidades de coordinación por áreas, con cuatro grandes lineas de investigación y formación especifica; coordinadora de áreas y departamentos, coordinadora de grado, coordinadora de servicios y coordinadora de unidades asesoras. Estas coordinadoras incluyen la participación de los tres órdenes en la planificación de sus acciones especificas y promueven una modificación de la estructura de "cátedra" sustituyéndola por una múltiple inserción del docente en diferentes funciones y niveles de formación.

Con la creación del IPUR se concentró la formación universitaria en una sola carrera con lo que se unificaron los titulos. Desde 1984 además del IPUR existe una Universidad Católica que otorga diplomas en Psicologia. Existe un anteproyecto de ley de reglamentación del ejercicio profesional de la Psicologia, presentado por la Coordinadora de Psicólogos del Uruguay y que está a estudio en el Parlamento.

7. *Revista de la Sociedad de Psicologia del Uruguay*, Año 111, Números 5 y 6 - 1991.
(Bic) *Revista de la Coordinadora de Psicólogos del Uruguay*, Año 1, Número 1, 1989.
8. Elida J. Tuana, Estero Bellaco 2712 CP 11600.

VENEZUELA

1. Federación de Psicólogos de Venezuela* (FPV) (Federation of Psychologists of Venezuela). Founded: 1957. President: Dia. Carlota Léon de Moros; Secretary-General: Dia. Belty Contreras. Address: Apartado 47563, Caracas 1041, Venezuela.

3. In 1978, having the Venezuelan Parliament approved the "Law for the Practice of Psychology", it became obligatory for all practicing psychologists to be registered at the FPV. Only those psychologists graduated from one of the three Venezuelan universities that have School of Psychology can be members of FPV. Psychologists graduated in other countries have to revalidate in a Venezuelan university first. FPV has sponsored several Scientific Societies of Psychology, among them the societies of School Psychology, Community Psychology, Learning Psychology, Social Psychology, Road Psychology, Industrial Psychology, Clinical Psychology, Humanistic Psychology, Aeronautical Psychology, Adler Psychology and Rorschach Psychology.

4. FPV was founded in 1957 with the name of "Asociación Venezolana de Psicólogos" with a group of only 20 Venezuelan professionals graduated abroad, and it was only in 1960 that a first group of psychologists were graduated from a Venezuelan university. In 1978 the Venezuelan Parliament approved the "Law for the Practice of Psychology". With that Law our association became the present FPV, being benefited by that Law with all the privileges and protections that the Venezuelan Nation grants us. According to that Law, each year we must organize a National Assembly of Psychologists. Also a regional "Colegio de Psicólogos" is constituted in each State where there are a minimum of 10 psychologists. Also, in 1981 the INPREPSI was created, which is the Institute for Social Security of the psychologists. Once a month we try to publish an informative bulletin of all our activities for all our members, through one of the most important newspapers of our country. In 1984 the number of licensed psychologists in Venezuela are almost 4000 (70% of them are women). About half of that number has already registered at the FPV, as required by Law. From that total of almost 4000, one third works in the country's public administration, especially in the Ministries of Education, Health and Justice. 10 percent of all are engaged in teaching of psychology at different levels. The area which shows greater growth in School Psychology (schools and special schools)). As some additional and interesting information, in the last 10 years our guild of psychologists has promoted the idea that psychologists should also aim at the top posts of our society and government. So we have recently had in our country the first psychologists in positions such as ministers, parliamentarians, aldermen, directors of government agencies and rectors and vice-rectors of some universities.

5. Research in psychology is conducted mainly in five universities, three hospitals and two research institutes. Major fields of academic research are: Experimental Analysis of Behavior, Social Psychology, Experimental Psychology and Learning Psychology.

6. At the present time there are three universities in Venezuela that offer programs of psychology: Universidad Central de Venezuela (Caracas) since 1956, Universidad Católica Andrés Bello (Caracas) since 1957 and Universidad Rafael Urdaneta (Maracaibo) since 1979. These programs require five years of study. Postgraduate courses in psychology are offered in the three already mentioned universities, and also in Universidad Simón Bolívar (Caracas) and Universidad del Zulia (Maracaibo), as well as in the Hospital Militar (Caracas), Hospital Psiquiátrico (Caracas) and Clínica El Peñón (Caracas). Research in psychology is conducted mainly in Instituto de Psicología de la UCV (Caracas) and in Laboratorio de Psicología de la Universidad de los Andes (Mérida). The postgraduate studies offered are mainly: Social Psychology, Organizational Psychology, Group Dynamics, Learning Psychology, Clinical Psychology and Experimental Analysis of

Behavior. Usually these postgraduate programs require three years of study.

7. *Directorio de la Federación de Psicólogos de Venequela* (published in 1977, 1980, and 1985: History of our guild, the Law, regulations, ethical code).
Revista del INPREPSI (published biannually: information about the guild of psychologists, scientific articles).
Boletín informativo Mensual de la FPV (published monthly in one of the most important newspapers of Caracas - when enough financial resources: news from the guild of psychologists, scientific events).

ZIMBABWE

1. Zimbabwe Psychological Association* (ZPA). Founded: 1971. President (1992-93): Mr Emmanuel Chidamahiya. Recording Secretary (1992-93): Mr Avron D. Moss. Address: P.O. Box 8346, Causeway, Harare. Tel: 303211 Ext. 454. Membership (10/92): 45.

3. ZPA was founded in 1971 in order to encourage the advancement of psychology as a pure and applied science, to promote and maintain at a high level the standards and professional status of psychologists, to determine the qualifications of psychologists for professional purposes, and to advise legislative and statutory bodies in matters relating to the profession. Full membership is open to registered psychologists or to persons eligible for such registration, but associate, student and subscribing memberships are allowed.

The Association provides a forum for discussion of professional matters through regular seminars or meetings and via its newsletter *Feedback*. A sub-committee of the Association advises the Health Professions Council on professional training and registration and on other legal matters such as professional conduct and the use of psychological tests by non-psychologists.

4. In Zimbabwe the first professional chair of psychology was established in the Faculty of Social Studies at the University of Zimbabwe in 1973. Psychology is also taught as a subject in teacher training colleges, the School of Social Work and in institutes for industrial psychology.

The practice of psychology in Zimbabwe is controlled by the Psychological Practices Act and all psychologists practising psychology professionally must register with the Health Professions Council. In September 1992 there were 64 registered psychologists resident in Zimbabwe.

5. Research in psychology is conducted mainly at the University. Recent major fields of academic psychological research are: AIDS and human sexuality, health psychology, and occupational psychology relevant to local issues. Some research is also carried out by government departments, notably in health and education.

6. Full-course university training in psychology is offered to students at the University. Following a three year undergraduate curriculum leading to a BSc Honours degree in psychology, graduate training can be completed at the Masters level - in pure research the M.Phil is awarded and for taught courses with a dissertation, the MSc is awarded. An advanced research degree, the PhD, requires a minimum of three years of study and the completion of an advanced research thesis.

For professional registration, psychologists must have an Honours degree in psychology on the British Commonwealth Universities pattern, and a postgraduate degree or diploma in psychology, or three years professional training under a registered psychologist. Although registration is not required for research or teaching of psychology, all other areas do require such registration.

Many psychologists in Zimbabwe received their training and various degrees outside the country. A BA Honours is normally the equivalent of the BSc Honours and the MA, MEd or MPsych equate with the MSc. Some extra qualifications are in other disciplines such as education (STD, UED, DipEd), nursing (SRN, RMN) or social work (DipSocWork).

7. *Feedback* (published bi-annually by ZPA: research reviews, association news, calender of professional events, professional issues).

150.25/IUP
overnight.

The IUPsyS Directory:
Major Research Institutes and Departments of Psychology

ADDITIONAL INFORMATION FOR
INCLUSION IN THE DIRECTORY:

If your Institute or Department is not in the Directory or the entry is incorrect, please type or print the details on this form, and return it to: The IUPsyS Directory, c/o Lawrence Erlbaum Associates Ltd., 27 Church Road, Hove, East Sussex, BN3 2FA, UK. Alternatively, please fax the form to: (44) (273) 205612.

NAME AND ADDRESS OF INSTITUTE:

. . . .
. . . .
. . . .
. . . .
. . . .
. . . .

NAME OF HEAD OF DEPARTMENT:

. . . .

DEPARTMENT TELEPHONE NUMBER:

. . . .
(AREA CODE)   (NUMBER)

DEPARTMENT FACSIMILE (FAX) NUMBER:

. . . .
(AREA CODE)   (NUMBER)

DEPARTMENT TELEX NUMBER

. . . .
(AREA CODE)   (NUMBER)

DEPARTMENT E-MAIL NUMBER

. . . .

Please indicate whether this is a NEW ❏ or REVISED ❏ entry.